"Harry Lee Poe has produced an in-depth sequel to his earlier book *Becoming C. S. Lewis*. This second volume offers detailed information about Lewis's early adulthood and examines all the people, ideas, and experiences that influenced his pilgrimage from sharp-tongued atheist to golden-tongued apologist for Christian faith."

David C. Downing, Codirector, Marion E. Wade Center, Wheaton, Illinois

"While not all pictures are worth a thousand words, *The Making of C. S. Lewis* paints an image that is clearly worth every bit of its 120,000 words. Taking the reader from just before Lewis's first published book and stopping five years prior to his Narnia debut, Poe masterfully unfolds details that even those familiar with Lewis might not know. This is especially true with the relatively recent discovery of *The Norse Spirit in English Literature*. Anyone wanting to understand why Lewis is so widely respected needs to read this book."

William O'Flaherty, author, *The Misquotable C. S. Lewis*; Host, *All About Jack* podcast

"Hal Poe's *The Making of C. S. Lewis* is the much anticipated second installment of Poe's comprehensive biography of the foremost Christian apologist of the twentieth century. Much as he did in *Becoming C. S. Lewis*, Poe draws on multiple primary and secondary sources in order to offer an articulate and informed reading of Lewis's life from 1918 to 1945. Of particular significance is Poe's exploration of how Lewis's conversion impacted his writings after 1933 through World War II."

Don King, author, *C. S. Lewis, Poet*; *Plain to the Inward Eye*; and *The Collected Poems of C. S. Lewis*

"Harry Lee Poe has a remarkable ability to highlight and explore central moments of Lewis's life in a highly readable way. Not only does his narrative retain an absorbing continuity of unfolding events, but he also shows the significance of the role that Lewis's friends and family members, including his adoptive mother, played in shaping the journey of his life. J. R. R. Tolkien once remarked to an Oxford student that they would never get to the bottom of their tutor C. S. Lewis, but *The Making of C. S. Lewis* succeeds in doing so. It is refreshingly accessible as well as deeply knowledgeable, covering all aspects of the complex Lewis, whose learning, storytelling for adults and children, wisdom, and humor are known throughout the world."

Colin Duriez, author, *C. S. Lewis: A Biography of Friendship* and *Tolkien and C. S. Lewis: The Gift of Friendship*

THE MAKING OF
C. S. LEWIS

Also by Harry Lee Poe

Becoming C. S. Lewis: A Biography of Young Jack Lewis (1898–1918)

THE MAKING OF
C. S. LEWIS

From Atheist to Apologist
(1918–1945)

HARRY LEE POE

WHEATON, ILLINOIS

The Making of C. S. Lewis: From Atheist to Apologist (1918–1945)

Copyright © 2021 by Harry Lee Poe

Published by Crossway
            1300 Crescent Street
            Wheaton, Illinois 60187

Extracts from the following reprinted by permission: *The Abolition of Man* © copyright CS Lewis Pte Ltd 1943, 1946, 1978. *The Allegory of Love* © copyright CS Lewis Pte Ltd 1936. *All My Road Before Me* © copyright CS Lewis Pte Ltd 1991. *Beyond Personality* © copyright CS Lewis Pte Ltd 1947. *Broadcast Talks* © copyright CS Lewis Pte Ltd 1942. *The Collected Letters of CS Lewis*, vol. 1 © copyright CS Lewis Pte Ltd 2000. *The Collected Letters of CS Lewis*, vol. 2 © copyright CS Lewis Pte Ltd 2004. *The Collected Letters of CS Lewis*, vol. 3 © copyright CS Lewis Pte Ltd 2007. *Dymer* © copyright CS Lewis Pte Ltd 1926. *The Great Divorce,* © copyright CS Lewis Pte Ltd 1946. *Memoirs of the Lewis Family 1850–1930* © copyright Estate of Albert Lewis. *Mere Christianity* © copyright CS Lewis Pte Ltd 1942, 1943, 1944, 1952. *Miracles* © copyright CS Lewis Pte Ltd 1947, 1960. *Norse Spirit in English Literature* © copyright CS Lewis Pte Ltd. *Of This and Other Worlds* © copyright CS Lewis Pte Ltd 1982. *An Open Letter to Dr Tillyard* © copyright CS Lewis Pte Ltd. *Out of the Silent Planet* © copyright CS Lewis Pte Ltd 1938. *Perelandra* © copyright CS Lewis Pte Ltd 1944. *The Pilgrim's Regress* © copyright CS Lewis Pte Ltd 1933. *The Problem of Pain* © copyright CS Lewis Pte Ltd 1940. *The Screwtape Letters* © copyright CS Lewis Pte Ltd 1942. *Surprised by Joy* © copyright CS Lewis Pte Ltd 1955. *That Hideous Strength* © copyright CS Lewis Pte Ltd 1945. *The Weight of Glory* © copyright CS Lewis Pte Ltd 1949.

Cover design: Jordan Singer

Cover image: Photo of C. S. Lewis used by permission of the Marion E. Wade Center, Wheaton College, Wheaton, IL / William Morris Textile design, Bridgeman Images

First printing 2021

Printed in the United States of America

Scripture quotations are from the ESV® Bible (The Holy Bible, English Standard Version®), copyright © 2001 by Crossway, a publishing ministry of Good News Publishers. Used by permission. All rights reserved.

Hardcover ISBN: 978-1-4335-6783-4
ePub ISBN: 978-1-4335-6786-5
PDF ISBN: 978-1-4335-6784-1
Mobipocket ISBN: 978-1-4335-6785-8

Library of Congress Cataloging-in-Publication Data

Names: Poe, Harry Lee, 1950– author.
Title: The making of C.S. Lewis : from atheist to apologist (1918–1945) / Harry Lee Poe.
Description: Wheaton, Illinois : Crossway, [2021] | Includes bibliographical references and index.
Identifiers: LCCN 2020041654 (print) | LCCN 2020041655 (ebook) | ISBN 9781433567834 (hardcover) | ISBN 9781433567841 (pdf) | ISBN 9781433567858 (mobi) | ISBN 9781433567865 (epub)
Subjects: LCSH: Lewis, C. S. (Clive Staples), 1898–1963—Religion. | Authors, English—20th century—Biography.
Classification: LCC PR6023.E926 Z8394 2021 (print) | LCC PR6023.E926 (ebook) | DDC 823/.912—dc23
LC record available at https://lccn.loc.gov/2020041654
LC ebook record available at https://lccn.loc.gov/2020041655

Crossway is a publishing ministry of Good News Publishers.

LB   32   31   30   29   28   27   26   25   24   23   22   21
15   14   13   12   11   10   9   8   7   6   5   4   3   2   1

To
Mary Brandon Poe Hays

Contents

Acknowledgments

This is the fourth book about C. S. Lewis I had not planned to write. When I completed *Becoming C. S. Lewis*, I felt there was much more to say. The book ended with the end of World War I. Lewis had become a man, but he had not yet become a Christian. *Becoming C. S. Lewis* focused on how his teenage years prepared the way for the conversion of Lewis and for the academic and popular writing he would do the rest of his life. It seemed a shame not to continue the story. When I proposed a volume to tell of how Lewis went from being an atheist at the end of World War I to being the most prominent Christian apologist in the world at the end of World War II, Crossway agreed to this second volume if I would also write a third that would take Lewis to the end of his life.

I am grateful to my acquisitions editor at Crossway, Samuel James, for his interest in this project and the support that he and his colleagues have offered. Thom Notaro has given careful editorial attention to making this a better book. Jill Carter has handled an array of administrative tasks throughout the publishing process with efficiency and good cheer. Claire Cook has been an invaluable contact in Crossway's design department, which has beautifully packaged the book. Darcy Ryan and the marketing team have been so creative and shown such initiative in making people aware of the book. I am so grateful for these and all the other people at Crossway who did so much to make this book possible.

Several excellent biographies of Lewis have been written. A biographer must make choices about what material to include and what to lay aside. To that extent, a biography is not simply a chronicle of what someone has done but a story of the significant moments in that person's life. To tell this story, a biographer must choose the most significant episodes in a life. In sifting all the days of the life of C. S. Lewis, I have had the benefit of several important primary sources that have been published, in addition to the unpublished holdings at the Marion E. Wade Center of Wheaton College and the Bodleian Library of Oxford University. The primary sources are *The Collected Letters of C. S. Lewis*, edited by Walter Hooper in three volumes, and *All My Road before Me: The Diary of C. S. Lewis, 1922–1927*, also edited by Hooper. It would have taken years to write this volume had Hooper not done the tedious and meticulous work of editing the letters and diary of C. S. Lewis. Scholars and lovers of Lewis can now examine those letters at their leisure in their own studies without facing the enormous expense of traveling to the research libraries and special collections that hold those letters. Walter Hooper has done an enormous service to generations that will come after him.

Other helpful primary sources are *The Letters of J. R. R. Tolkien*, edited by Humphrey Carpenter, and *To Michal from Serge: Letters from Charles Williams to His Wife, Florence, 1939–1945*, edited by Roma A. King Jr. In addition to *Surprised by Joy*, Lewis's own memoir of his conversion, the most important secondary sources are the collections of memoirs written by those who knew Lewis:

Como, James T., ed. *Remembering C. S. Lewis: Recollection of Those Who Knew Him.* 3rd ed. San Francisco: Ignatius, 2005; originally published as *C. S. Lewis at the Breakfast Table.*

Gibb, Jocelyn, ed. *Light on C. S. Lewis.* London: Bles, 1965.

Graham, David. *We Remember C. S. Lewis: Essays and Memoirs*. Nashville: Broadman & Holman, 2001.

Keefe, Carolyn. C. S. *Lewis: Speaker and Teacher*. Grand Rapids, MI: Zondervan, 1971.

Poe, Harry Lee, and Rebecca Whitten Poe, eds. *C. S. Lewis Remembered: Collected Reflections of Students, Friends and Colleagues*. Grand Rapids, MI: Zondervan, 2006.

In addition to presenting papers at conferences and writing articles for magazines and journals, I have had a number of invitations over the years to speak and write about Lewis. These lectures have all informed this biography and helped to shape my thinking about Lewis. David Dockery and Greg Thornbury invited me to contribute a chapter titled "The Influence of C. S. Lewis" for an edited volume, *Shaping a Christian Worldview* (2002), in which I first explored the relationships between *A Preface to Paradise Lost, The Screwtape Letters, Perelandra*, and *The Great Divorce*. In 2006, I gave the keynote address for the Christianity in the Academy Conference, in Memphis, on C. S. Lewis's understanding of a classical education. I was invited to contribute an article "C. S. Lewis and the Ladies" in a special 2007 issue of *Christian Scholars Review*, which explored Lewis and gender. I am grateful to W. E. "Nick" Knickerbocker and his wife, Sandra H. Knickerbocker, who established the C. S. Lewis and His Friends lectureship, and to the Memphis Theological Seminary, which invited me to give the inaugural lectures in 2008. These lectures allowed me to explore the way Lewis used various literary forms in different apologetic ways. I took advantage of another invitation to give a lecture at Williams College in 2009 on Lewis's understanding of imagination, which I further developed for the Inklings Week in Oxford in 2013 and published in the *Sewanee Theological Review*. Dick Staub invited me to present "The Inklings and Friendship" for the Kindlings Fest on Orcas Island in 2010. In 2015, I gave two lectures for the Humanitas Forum that explored Lewis's conversion, titled "From Ardent Atheist to Mere Christian," and his treatment of hardship in "Pain, Evil, and Suffering." For the Inklings Week in Oxford in 2019, I delivered a lecture titled "'Friendship Must Be about Something': The Case of C. S. Lewis." One way or another, all of these invitations have found their way into this biography.

Even with the enormous amount of material that Hooper has edited, much remains unpublished at the Wade Center of Wheaton College and in the Bodleian Library. I am indebted to the center and its staff for their great kindness, generosity of spirit, encouragement, and helpfulness during several trips for extended periods of research into the primary documents related to Lewis during his middle years. Marjorie Lamp Mead has always been gracious to me and all those who come to use the resources of the Wade. Laura Schmidt and Elaine Hooker went out of their way to find things I did not know existed. David and Crystal Downing arrived at the Wade Center as the new codirectors while I was finishing my research on the first volume of this biography. Since then they have extended to me the warmest of possible welcomes, including the opportunity to talk with them on a podcast about this research. I am delighted that they will be leading this important research library into the future. Finally, I am grateful for the Clyde S. Kilby Research Grant for 2020 from the Wade Center, which has aided me in writing this book.

I also appreciate the help and courtesy given me by Rachel Churchill of the C. S. Lewis Company in securing permission to quote Lewis. The C. S. Lewis Company has safeguarded the work of Lewis, preserving his legacy for future generations, for which many are grateful.

I have had the pleasure of dialogue with many colleagues over the years with whom I have shared an interest in Lewis. Insights often come in undocumented conversations long forgotten. I am particularly indebted to Don King, Colin Duriez, Rebecca Hays, Walter Hooper, Paul Fiddes, William O'Flaherty, Dennis Beets, Barry Anderson, Malissa and Russ Kilpatrick, Stan Shelley, Nigel

Goodwin, Joseph Pearce, Jerry Root, Holly Ordway, and James Como. Gregory Poore, my former student research assistant, brought a number of memoirs to my attention when I edited *C. S. Lewis Remembered*, which have contributed significantly to this volume. For a number of years, I have taught a course on C. S. Lewis at Union University. My students have sparked my imagination with their questions, and I have found that new insights often come in the process of answering questions on my feet before the students. Connections are made that would otherwise have gone unnoticed. I have long believed that some of the best scholarship emerges from the classroom experience. I am grateful to those students over the years who have been my dialogue partners: Kelly Barron, Chelsea Blakley, Sarah Bradley, Valerie Burnett, Laura Bush, William Cherry, David Clark, Adam Craig, Ian Crawford, Ben Dockery, Jon Dockery, Jessica Farneth, Alyce George, Luke Hall, Meah Hearington, Graham Hillard, Jennifer Johnson, Jonathan Wade Jones, Stephanie King, Kelly Krebs, Jin Langford, Adam Lickey, Seth Massa, Kevin Minister, Brian Mooney, Katie Murphy, Eric Murrell, Chelsea Mytyk, David Patterson, Gregory Picard, Jennifer Powers, Kyle Riddle, Katie Sorrell, Greg Talley, Kerstin Ure, Travis Wales, Josh Wamble, and Brian Wells.

Also Naomi Addison, Benjamin Bailey, Erin Brassert, Robert Brown, Abigail Carpenter, Tiffany Collins, Katherine Conkling, Beth Cossiboom, Dustin Curtis, April Daigle, Jesse Daigle, Ashley Donahue, Amber Garrett, Matthew Gentry, Bevin Gracy, Jacob Hall, Lindsey Hall, Andrew Helms, Ryan Hill, David Kartzinel, Cody King, Daniel Lindley, Brett Logan, Devin Maddox, Christina Manchester, Danielle Montgomery, Lori Morris, Amanda Norris, Brent Parrish, Zachery Pendergrass, Amanda Pennington, Bess Perrier, Christopher Peterson, Austin Ward, and William Williams.

Also Joshua Abbotoy, Jordan Baker, Brad Boswell, Michael Brown, Patrick Brown, Amanda Bush, Joshua Cantrell, Bradley Carter, Kyle Clark, Elizabeth Davis, Sallie Duell, Caleb Dunlap,

Megan Evans, Tiffany Fredericks, Dena Fritts, Jeffrey Harper, Mary Holliday, Chad Keathley, Christopher Lee, Christopher Malloy, Jewell Marshall, Renae Matz, Patricia McGarrah, Timothy O'Day, Mary Olson, Matthew Pinckard, Raina Schults, Shane Shaddix, William Sipes, Lauren Smothers, Chase Steinmann, Rachel Ware, Ben Watson, Brittany White, Cameron White, Matthew White, David Wickiser, Leah Wilkerson, and Jessica Yates.

Also Virginia Allen, Emily Anderson, Elizabeth Blevins, Hannah Brantley, Stephen Capps, Amanda Chambers, David Conway, Katherine Crutcher, Taylor Dartt, Dwight Davis, Erika Dean, Abigail Ebensberger, Rebecca Edgren, Daniel Garrett, Christopher Gibbons, Laura Grossberndt, Abigail Harris, Grant Kelley, Rebeckah King, Lauren Lester, Karl Magnuson, Ryan Mantooth, Kayla McCanless, Kelsey Meadows, Mary Beth Moore, Jesse Myers, Stephanie Netland, Abigail Nolen, Amanda Parrish, Cameron Puckett, Katherine Pullen, Liana Saffel, William Seaton, Spencer Smith, Victoria Stargel, Anika Strand, Beth Watson, Tucker Watson, Elissa Weber, and Whitney Williams.

Also Amanda Bennett, Amiee Brassert, Chelsea Coudriet, Scott Cravey, Caleb Creel, Nick Dean, Kyle Dwyer, Melissa Fields, Tracy Frisbee, Justin Goodson, Stacey Hanburry, Rachel Harkins, Micah Hayes, Autumn Hitt, Blake Hooten, John Keller, Molly King, Phillip Kurtzwell, Danny Linton, Haaken Magnuson, Thani Magnuson, Betsy Marsch, Renee Marshall, Kylie McDonald, Joseph McFatridge, Kiley Morin, Janie Owen, Lucas Peiser, Dylan Pelley, Peter Riggs, Grant Riley, Katie Ritchie, Wil Sloan, Tyler Stephens, Andrew Stricklin, Rusty Tuders, Caleb Valentine, Olivia Wallace, Abby Winters, Gracie Wise, Lydia Wright, and Stephen Wunrow.

Also Stephen Ballard, Virginia Bantz, Joshua Burton, Miracle Burton, Drake Denning, Ashley Ellis, Evan Estes, Lizi Frasier, Asa Gee, Jared Harrison, Hunter Hawes, Jacob Hayes, Lisa Herod, Brady Heyen, Joshua Johnston, Adam Lang, Kelsie Leaf, Cherish Lo, Eric Massey, Laura McCuin, Chris Mimms, John Monroe, Evan Nichols, Andrew Parks, Sarah Paschall, Grace Pepper,

Robbie Pierson, Laura Reiswig, Amanda Rohde, Jordan Sellers, Rachel Sette, Trevor Sewell, Caleb Shaw, Bailey Shearon, Logan Smith, Jalen Sowell, Elizabeth Tomyn, Rian Trotter, Jessica Vinyard, Will Walker, William Watson, Laina Willoughby, Abigail Wills, Christian Winter, and Rachel Wukasch.

Also J. P. Bardon, Chandler Bell, Holden Bennett, Emma Bilbrey, Jay Bishop, Deloma Bowling, Hannah Brandt, Andrew Campbell, Cayley Cantwell, Brittany Carroll, Jacob Carroll, Brady Cook, Jordan Daughrity, Joseph Delaney, Heather Dockery, Caleb Dunbar, Rebecca Duttweiler, Charlie Ellis, Mary Mattison Evans, Brandon Harper, Anna Harris, Joel Holland, Trenton Holloway, Ellen Howard, Hannah Johnson, Karis Lancaster, Jake Leach, Josh Leamon, James Martin, Shauna McCauley, Ben Melton, Yoo Jin Moon, Stephanie Olford, Avery Parks, Briley Ray, Blake Reeves, Russell Richardson, Samuel Riebel, Becca Robertson, Nicole Snover, David Taylor, Cooper Thompson, Adam Tomes, Anderson Underwood, Jessica Vaughn, and Anna White.

And finally, Alexander Bitterling, Riley Boggs, Lauren Butler, Nathan Chester, Jacob Collins, Jonathan Cooper, Madde Ely, Holly Gilbert, Jesse Greer, Nehemiah Guinn, Christopher Hearn, Rachel Hickle, Cameron Johnson, Ethan Judge, Rebekah Lisle, Robert Martin, Gabrielle Massman, Amelia Moore, Melanie Nassif, Ashley Rimmer, Kellen Robbins, Madison Rowland, Ashleigh Slusmeyer, Callie Teague, Chloe Thomas, Zach Tyler, Camille Wehrman, and Savannah Wright.

I could not undertake projects of this sort without the support of Union University: particularly our president, Samuel W. ("Dub") Oliver; the provost, John Netland; and the dean of the school of theology and missions, Ray Van Neste. My wife, Mary Anne Poe, has long supported my interest in Lewis and has been a great encouragement in the writing of this book. Finally, to the many participants in the retreats sponsored by the Inklings Fellowship over the past twenty years, I am grateful for your support and interest in the life and work of C. S. Lewis.

1

Return to Oxford

1918–1922

C. S. Lewis spent the better part of 1918 convalescing from shrapnel wounds from which he would never fully recover. Two pieces of shrapnel remained in his chest.[1] The pain in Jack's shoulder would plague him for years after the war, as would the headaches and nightmares.[2] His wound may have inspired the shoulder wound of Frodo Baggins when J. R. R. Tolkien wrote *The Lord of the Rings*. Of greater concern than his wounds in the months after his evacuation from France, however, was his desire to have Mrs. Janie Moore near him whenever the army moved him from one place to another.

A Concealed Relationship

Lewis had been wounded in battle near Riez du Vinage on April 15, 1918. The Liverpool Merchants Mobil Hospital at Étaples cared for him initially. Then he was transported back to England and the Endsleigh Palace Hospital, in London, from which he telegrammed his father, Albert Lewis, of his move on May 25.

In anticipation of his move to London, Lewis wrote to his friend Arthur Greeves that he hoped Arthur could come see him at the London hospital because it would also give him a chance to meet Mrs. Moore.[3] Regardless of where the army would move Jack in the ensuing months, Mrs. Moore found lodgings nearby. Greeves, to whom Lewis had confided his inmost thoughts and feelings since they became friends in 1914, enjoyed the confidence of Jack Lewis concerning his relationship with Mrs. Moore. He would help Jack conceal the nature of that relationship from his father for years.

To Albert, Jack wrote that Mrs. Moore had been in London to visit her sister and had called on him. He claimed that they had seen a good bit of each other because it seemed to offer her some comfort to visit an old friend of her son from Officer Training Corps days in Oxford.[4] Her son, Edward ("Paddy"), had been reported missing and assumed dead on March 24, 1918.[5] On June 24, the army transferred Jack from the hospital in London to a convalescing hospital in Bristol, where Mrs. Moore made her home with her daughter, Maureen. Jack wrote to his father that it was awful bad luck, because he had hoped to be sent to a hospital in Belfast, but at least he would have the consolation of the company of Mrs. Moore.[6] As was often the case, Albert Lewis appears to have suggested that he could use one of his political contacts to get Jack transferred to Belfast. In reply to his father's proposal, Jack wrote frantically that it was best for his situation to go unnoticed. Since his original plan for convalescence would be up on August 4, he would more likely be sent back to the front instead of being transferred to Belfast. If he were quiet, the army would not notice him. Nonetheless, he suggested that his father visit him in Bristol, where he could meet Mrs. Moore.[7]

The extent to which Albert avoided traveling, almost never going with Flora and the boys for their annual summer holiday by the sea, is illustrated by the description of his holiday in August 1918. He told Warnie (Jack's brother, Warren) that he had spent it at home dividing his time between the little end room, Warnie's room, and the garden. Albert reflected that the enormous worry involved in planning a trip would prevent him from ever taking one. He allowed that he might enjoy a trip, but the irksomeness of preparing for it was too much to manage.[8] When Albert rationalized his failure to cross the Irish Sea and visit Jack in the hospital, he told Warnie it was because of the pressing demands of work and that he might lose his job if he took a holiday. Despite his rationalizations, Albert worried about what Jack would think of him for not visiting, which resulted in Albert's bouts of depression and sleepless nights.[9] He also had a dread of German submarines plying the Irish Sea, which he had constantly impressed upon Jack when he was living with William T. Kirkpatrick. This fear was not without basis. People actually did lose their lives making the passage, as the passengers on the *Lusitania* had discovered.

On October 4, the army transferred Lewis to the Perham Downs Camp, at Ludgershall in Hampshire. Mrs. Moore rented a cottage near the camp, where she kept rabbits and pigs. Jack begged Arthur Greeves not to tell Albert of this move, lest his father attempt once again to have him transferred to Belfast.[10] In the end, Jack could not hide, so he assured his father that the transfer to a command depot as a convalescing officer was a normal thing in the army, but that under no circumstance should Albert try to intervene. Jack explained that the easiest way to obtain a discharge would be from his present posting.

The week of the Armistice in November, Jack's entire unit was moved to Eastbourne, in Sussex.[11] Mrs. Moore and Maureen followed him straight away, and Jack told Arthur that he spent most of his time with them.[12] Jack advised his father that he had suggested that Mrs. Moore come to Eastbourne and rent rooms near his camp until he went on Christmas leave.[13] This bit of information, however, was slipped into a long letter that focused attention on his publishing prospects and on the best way to get a discharge from the army, with the war over. The army settled the problem by discharging Jack from the hospital on Christmas Eve and demobilizing him. He arrived in Belfast on December 27, so one might assume that he spent Christmas with Janie and Maureen Moore before going home unannounced. Had he informed his father that his demobilization had come through on Christmas Eve, Albert would have expected him home immediately.[14]

On November 10, Jack had written his father to tell him that he had taken the flu vaccination and that Albert should be inoculated as well. It was a mild inoculation that Jack thought worthwhile if it could save a person's life. The war ended the next day, but death was still in the air. That winter alone, twenty million people would die worldwide during the influenza pandemic.[15] Among its victims was Harry Wakelyn Smith, the teacher known as Smugy, who had been Jack's one bright spot at Malvern.[16]

Not until September had Mrs. Moore received confirmation that her son, Paddy, had been killed in action the previous spring. Despite his reservations about Mrs. Moore, Albert wrote her a letter of condolence upon hearing the tragic news. Her letter of acknowledgment to Albert on October 1, 1918, was signed "Jennie K. Moore" rather than "Janie." She remarked that of the circle of five friends of which Jack and Paddy were a part in Officer Training Corps, only Jack had survived the war. She also confided to Albert that Paddy had asked Jack to look after her if her son did not return from the war.[17]

On Jack's birthday two weeks after the Armistice, Warnie wrote to his father admitting how he had worried about Jack during the war. He would wake up in the middle of the night wondering if Jack were still alive. For Warnie, Jack's safety was always "the great thing."[18] He added the news that it just might be possible for him to arrange for leave to be home by Christmas, but that his father should not get his hopes too high.[19] Warnie did manage leave for Christmas, so he was at home when a taxi pulled up to the front of Leeborough House just before lunch on December 27 and Jack emerged. The family was together again, and they celebrated with champagne at dinner that night, the first time Warnie had ever seen it in their house.[20] Jack spent several weeks with his father before returning to Oxford in mid-January of 1919 to resumes his studies.

Publishing a Book

When he first went to the hospital in London, Lewis decided it was time to try to publish his poetry. From his hospital bed he wrote to ask Arthur Greeves to send the notebook of poetry in his care.[21] By the time Jack was transferred to Bristol, he had nearly completed revising his poetry, which he then had typed. By July, he informed Arthur that he would soon be ready to send his manuscript around to the publishers.[22] By August 7, 1918, his book of poetry had been rejected by Macmillan, and he next sent it to Heinemann.[23] On September 3, William Heinemann wrote to Jack to say that his firm would publish the book.[24]

Perhaps surprisingly, Jack first wrote to his father several days before sending Arthur the news that Heinemann had accepted his manuscript, originally titled "Spirits in Prison: a cycle of lyrical poems by Clive Staples."[25] Despite the personal difficulties that continued to grow between father and son, Jack wanted to make his father proud of him and to win his approval. From his father, young C. S. Lewis had learned the love of books, and now his own book was to be published. Albert wrote to Warnie with the news, having assumed that Jack would not. The proud father celebrated Jack's achievement in glowing terms—to publish a first book, and not just a book, but a book of poetry![26]

Though excited by the news of his son's impending fame as a writer, Albert suggested that the title was wrong, since Robert Hitchens had written a novel by the same title.[27] Jack also had to explain why he intended to publish under a pseudonym. He confessed that he did not want the other officers to know that he was a poet, lest they ridicule him.[28] Despite his pride in Jack's achievement, Albert expressed his concern confidentially to Warnie that it might be a mistake for Jack to publish his poetry before he was twenty years old.[29]

Waiting in a convalescent hospital with little to do, Jack grew impatient for word from his publisher about the status of his book and for the page proofs for him to correct. Between William Heinemann going on vacation and Jack moving to a new post, the normal long delay grew longer. By October, he had hit upon the final title for his book and the final pseudonym. It would be "Spirits in Bondage," by Clive Hamilton, using his first name and his mother's maiden name.[30] In late October, Jack secured permission to go to London to visit his publisher, where he was given the hope that John Galsworthy would publish one or more of his poems in a new magazine, *Reveille*.[31] The poem "Death in Battle" appeared in the February 1919 issue, the magazine's third and last.[32] Albert told Warnie that the poem was the best one in the issue, which included the poetry of Hilaire Belloc and Siegfried Sassoon.[33]

Upon reading Jack's poetry in manuscript form, Albert Lewis appears to have thought that it might be taken as blasphemous. Jack assured his father that he was not being blasphemous against "the God you or I worship."[34] He was simply being "honest." Honesty was an interesting virtue for him to raise at this point, because his letter was suggesting that he was a Christian when he was not and vehemently knew he was not. He compounded the deception by telling his father that he would be reading the lesson in chapel that week as well as saying grace before a meal in the college hall.[35]

By the end of March, the much-anticipated publication of *Spirits in Bondage* finally arrived. The *Times Literary Supplement* for March 27, 1919, published what Lewis considered a "very insolent" review, but he feared even more how his father would regard the review.[36] On a happier note, *The Bookman* of June 1919 gave him a flattering review full of praise.[37] Oxford had what Lewis called an "extreme literary set" at Balliol and Exeter who controlled the *Oxford Poetry* book issued each year, in which

J. R. R. Tolkien had published "Goblin Feet," and which Dorothy L. Sayers had coedited for several years. Word had gotten back to Lewis that he was being noticed. The pleasure of being noticed was tempered, however, by the pity that he had been noticed by people who wrote the new free verse.[38]

Albert told Warnie that though the reviews were not enthusiastic, they were "decent, sober praise, all things considered." Nonetheless, he feared that Jack was disappointed in spite of his father's efforts to help him feel satisfied.[39] On the other hand, Jack told Warnie that he feared their father would be disappointed by the reviews.[40] To add insult to injury over the tepid reviews, the publisher mistakenly attributed *Spirits in Bondage* to George S. Lewis instead of Clive Hamilton in the catalog. So much for pseudonyms.[41]

Back in Oxford

By mid-January 1919, Lewis was back in Oxford at University College for the beginning of Hilary term. In *Surprised by Joy*, Lewis named the chapter that dealt with his postwar return to Oxford "The New Look." Warnie and Albert had taken note of Jack's new look at the time, but Warnie referred to it as the "New Thought." He joked that Jack might not want to take part in paying for a memorial to Smugy at Malvern, not only because he hated Malvern but also because he might view memorials to the honored dead "as an exploded superstition ranking with witchcraft and the Divine right of Kings!"[42]

Though Jack had been accepted into University College with a scholarship, he had not passed the Oxford entrance exam, known as Responsions, before the war. For all his brilliance in some areas, Lewis had little hope of passing Responsions because of the math section. He flunked it in 1917, but after the war, ex-servicemen were exempted from Responsions.[43] Lewis could go to Oxford after all. He wrote to Arthur Greeves with news of his new academic life and gave an overview of his daily routine. His scout (a college servant) woke him at seven thirty each morning. He bathed, attended chapel, and then went to breakfast in the great hall. After breakfast, he attended lectures or worked on his weekly assignment from his tutors, either in the college library or in one of the lectures halls, both of which were heated. At one o'clock he rode his bicycle to Janie Moore's rented house at 28 Warneford Road, where he had lunch. He spent the afternoon working on his tutorial paper until tea, then studied more until dinner. After dinner, he might resume study or have a relaxing evening talking with Mrs. Moore or playing bridge before riding his bicycle back to the college at eleven. Back in his room, he made a fire and did a bit more work before going to sleep at midnight.[44] This kind of schedule with so much time each day spent with Mrs. Moore necessarily meant that Jack would not "see very many people."[45]

At this point, Arthur Greeves was the only person in Jack's world who knew that he and Janie Moore had an arrangement. As far as Albert Lewis was concerned, Mrs. Moore lived far away in Bristol and Jack was safely ensconced in Oxford. Jack made the point in a letter to Arthur that he must not let Albert know about his domestic situation with Mrs. Moore.[46] At the end of Hilary term in 1919, Jack wrote to his father that he could not come home during the short Easter vacation because his tutor told him he needed to stay for another week, and then he had promised to go to Bristol to help Mrs. Moore with moving. He said that she could not find anywhere else to go in Bristol or London. The housing shortage after the war would have been a problem known to many. Jack told his father that he had even suggested that she try to find a place in Oxford.[47] By this time, however, Janie had been living in Oxford for two months, and Jack would be staying with her over his vacation, far from his father's prying eyes.

Jack continued his neglect of Warnie, who wrote to him regularly with no reply. In exasperation, Warnie complained to his father of Jack's failure to inform his own brother that he would be home in Belfast in April 1919, when Warnie probably could have arranged for leave to be together again.[48] Jack's inconsiderate attitude toward his father and brother continued when he promised to send Albert a telegram indicating safe arrival back in Oxford after his April 1919 visit. Not only did he not send the promised telegram, but when Albert telegrammed to find out if Jack was all right, he failed to reply.[49] When Jack did finally write to Warnie, he evaded any specific information on his plans to visit Little Lea, the alternate name for Leeborough House. Warnie feared that Jack spent all his time working and was neglecting any personal time for relaxation, though Warnie had never thought Jack was given to overwork any more than Warnie was.[50]

When he did write to his father, Jack discussed the strategy he would pursue to secure an Oxford fellowship once he completed his studies. His tutor, Arthur Poynton, had advised him to undergo Classical Honour Moderations, a public examination in Greek and Latin midway through the second year of study. It was not necessary to take Mods, as they were called, in order to become a philosopher, but it would establish his credentials in the academic world of Oxford tradition. Lewis explained to his father, "People might feel that they could never be quite sure of you unless they knew what you had done in Mods."[51] The pursuit of philosophy fell under the program of study at Oxford known as *Literae Humaniores*, which involved philosophy and ancient history.

Oxford, a formidable institution with, in many ways, its own culture, prides itself in the articulate command of the English language, so much so that it has its own accent and dialect. Many a young person goes up to Oxford with a provincial or urban accent, only to go down three years later with the refined and slightly snobbish Oxonian accent. In this odd world of meticulously spoken English that abhors the common slang of the broad culture, the Oxonians use their own slang and institutionalized corruption of English pronunciation for almost everything imaginable. Thus, one does not speak of Classical Honour Moderations but of Mods. One does not speak of *Literae Humaniores* but of Greats.

It is the town where Mary Magdalen Church is pronounced as it would be anywhere else in the English-speaking world, but where Magdalen College a few blocks away is pronounced "Mawdlin." Jack Lewis, with his prominent Irish brogue, was learning the dialect and the slang well.

The system of education employed by Oxford and Cambridge, known as Oxbridge, does not involve a series of courses on various subjects with major and minor areas, nor is there a core curriculum that everyone takes. Instead, a pupil meets with a faculty member, known as a tutor, once a week. The tutor "recommends" several books for the pupil to read in preparing an essay to be read at the ensuing tutorial. During that meeting, the pupil reads the essay, and the tutor interrupts to ask questions and offer a critique. Lectures do not play the primary role in the Oxbridge system that they play in the American system. Nonetheless, the fellows of Oxford offer lectures on subjects of interest, or not, within their respective schools. Lectures are optional, though a good tutor advises pupils on lectures they ought to attend. The whole system aims at preparing pupils for the single examination at the end of their three years that will determine their fate. In the case of Greats, however, Lewis could expect a fourth year. He complained to Greeves that he had to read all of Homer, Virgil, Demosthenes, Cicero, and also do logic.[52] He did not mention that he had already read most of the texts with W. T. Kirkpatrick, so that much of his university work was review.

Jack informed his father that the lectures given by Gilbert Murray were the best he attended. Lewis already knew Murray by reputation before going up to Oxford. Jack had read Murray's treatment of *The Bacchae* of Euripides when Jack was living with Kirkpatrick in Great Bookham. Jack had recommended Murray's translations to Greeves, even while confessing that he had no fondness for Euripides himself.[53] Murray held the Regius Chair of Greek at Oxford in the fading twilight of an age when some still recalled how the command of Greek was the apex of intellectual and academic achievement.[54] Jack Lewis, newly arrived at University College in 1917, had been impressed that his new friend Butler actually knew both Murray and W. B. Yeats![55]

Arthur Poynton had been Lewis's tutor when he first went up to Oxford in 1917. During the war, he also filled the post of bursar, the business manager of an Oxford college. He would go on to serve a brief term of two years as master of University College.[56] Lewis thought that Poynton was "an exceptionally good tutor," which was high praise indeed, since he had only W. T. Kirkpatrick with whom to compare him. In fact, Lewis thought that Poynton was the equal of Kirk.[57] Lewis took tea with Poynton, his wife, and a small company of undergraduates soon after his arrival. In the social setting, the esteemed tutor turned out to be an amusing and skilled teller of tales.[58]

In addition to his academic pursuit, Jack Lewis began to show signs of his growing ability to enjoy contact with other people, an ability he lacked prior to his time with the officers and men in the trenches of France. Early in his first term, Jack was elected to the Martlets, one of innumerable clubs and societies of Oxford that come in and out of existence. According to legend, the Martlets were over three hundred years old. In fact, they dated to 1892.[59] In Oxford, however, the pursuit of truth and knowledge is exceeded only by the perpetuation of legend and the propagation of gossip. Nonetheless, the minutes of the meetings of the Martlets are kept in the Bodleian Library, a point of pride for Lewis, who was elected the secretary and charged with keeping the minutes. The Martlets provided Lewis with a social outlet, but they also were a context to exercise his mind and develop powers of discussion and critique, for the Martlets were a literary society in which the members wrote and presented papers on a wide variety of subjects. The group was limited to only twelve undergraduate members, so it also provided an air of exclusivity for Lewis. For his first paper, Lewis chose to write on William Morris, whose writing he had devoured since Great Bookham days.[60] In his early days back at

Oxford, his fellow Martlets included John Robert Edwards, Rodney Marshall Pasley, Edward Fairchild Watling, Basil Platel Wyllie, Cyril Hughes Hartmann, Alfred Kenneth Hamilton Jenkin, and Donald Frederick Wilkinson.[61]

In addition to the twelve undergraduates, the Martlets also had members who were fellows. The Reverend Alexander Carlyle, chaplain of University College, was a political philosopher, church historian, and social reformer.[62]

Oxford Friendships

One of Jack's first acquaintances in college was his fellow Martlet Rodney Pasley, who also wrote poetry. At first, Jack was suspicious of him because he thought that Pasley might be a modernist. Jack may also have been slightly jealous at the prospect that Pasley might publish a book of poetry. He informed Arthur Greeves that a man named Mais was reportedly helping Pasley publish his book of poems.[63] As it turned out, Pasley was the old-fashioned type of poet that Jack favored, and they soon became friends. Jack not only approved of Pasley's poetry but envied him for some of it.[64]

Once the weather turned warm in Oxford, Jack renewed one of the greatest pleasures of his life. He went swimming. As its ancient name suggests, the city of Oxford began at the ox ford on the river Thames many miles above London. To complicate matters as only Oxford can, as it flows past Oxford, the Thames becomes the Isis River, only to become the Thames again below Oxford. The small Cherwell River flows into the Isis in Oxford at Christ Church Meadow. This was the river on which Toad, Mole, Ratty, and Badger lived in Kenneth Grahame's *The Wind and the Willows*. Christ Church Meadow is where Alice followed a white rabbit down a hole into Wonderland. Up the Cherwell at the lower corner of University Parks, the river makes a large *S* bend, and here the men of Oxford went swimming in the nude. Known as Parson's Pleasure, the favored swimming hole was visited by Lewis most mornings before breakfast.[65]

Sons and Fathers

Relations between Jack Lewis and his father had gone steadily downhill since Albert sent his son to Wynyard School in 1908. Jack had learned the art of deceiving his father in his mid-teens, but by 1919 he had ventured on an elaborate double life. In *Surprised by Joy*, Lewis publicly acknowledged that the art of concealment from his father had grown into a habit.[66] He complained to his brother, Warnie, that their father had grown unbearable with his continual fussing, sulking, and demanding to know all about his son's life.[67] Albert Lewis had grown older, but whether he had actually become more unbearable in his manner is open to conjecture. At this point in his life, Jack had much more to conceal than cigarettes. Any question about almost anything of his life in Oxford would require another lie, and the effort to lie requires a great deal of emotional energy for most people. Any routine, normal, polite inquiries that a father who was paying the bills might make of a beloved son might feel like badgering and a vile intrusion on privacy to someone who had something enormous to hide.

One of the reasons that C. S. Lewis could speak so authoritatively and insightfully about the dynamics of temptation and personal sin in *The Screwtape Letters* and *The Great Divorce* is his own considerable experience with them. In 1955, when he looked back on this period and relations with his father between his school days and his father's death in 1929, C. S. Lewis said that his behavior lay "heavy on [his] conscience."[68] One of the ironies of human nature is that when we sin against another person, we tend to blame the other person for our sin, thereby adding contempt and loathing for the other person to the injury we have already inflicted. So it was with Jack Lewis and his father. By concealing his secret life from Albert, Jack grew increasingly sensitive to any overtures by his father to share his life. The teenage boy's irritation with parental supervision could not make the adjustment to the normal interest a parent would show in an older son's life at the university.

By 1919, however, a new cause for contempt of Albert had arisen. Arthur reported to Jack the growing rumor that Mr. Lewis was drinking alone! Arthur had heard his parents speaking in hushed whispers about Jack's father. Then, one day when he dropped by the Lewis home, Arthur found Albert alone in his study apparently drunk to the point that he could not speak. Jack could now take the moral high ground and look down on his father's "solitary tippling" with disgust.[69]

While Jack was growing increasingly irritated by his father, both Albert and Warnie grew increasingly disturbed by Jack's relationship with Mrs. Moore, based on what little they knew, which was not very much. Albert wrote to Warnie at his army posting that the Mrs. Moore business was a mystery to him. By now, the father knew that his son was providing Mrs. Moore with money, as evidenced by his canceled checks made over to her. On May 10, 1919, Warnie wrote to his father that he hoped the mystery was a product of their imaginations, though he thought it a freakish situation. On May 20, Albert wrote to Warnie that Mrs. Moore's husband was reputed to be a scoundrel, and he might be the sort who would attempt to blackmail Jack. On the other hand, Albert acknowledged that all his concern might simply be the result of a mind made overly suspicious by years as a police court lawyer. On June 3, Warnie replied with expressed relief at the news that Mrs. Moore was still married, which meant that Jack could not be contemplating matrimony. Furthermore, Jack was too poor to be blackmailed successfully. What concerned them most, however, was the report that Jack wrote daily to Janie Moore whenever he was in Belfast, though both Albert and Warnie had seen a dramatic decline in letters from Jack to them.[70] Jack and Janie exchanged letters through the help of Arthur Greeves, who served as their go-between. Though Jack thought he had cleverly deceived his father, Albert knew all about it.[71] Jack had a new primary relationship, and it was not centered in Belfast.

Only Arthur continued to have Jack's total confidence. He knew all about Mrs. Moore. He visited Jack in Oxford the last week of June 1919. By this time, Mrs. Moore had moved again into "Invermore," which Jack described as a "jolly little house" without a bathroom.[72] Arthur stayed at the Mitre Hotel on the High Street, which would become a favorite watering hole and dining spot for Lewis and his friends until World War II. Arthur would have met Mrs. Moore for the first time on this visit, though they had been in correspondence for some time.[73] Arthur would assist Jack in his deception of Albert regarding his relationship with Mrs. Moore until Albert's death. It was probably during this visit that Jack and Arthur began using "Minto" as an affectionate nickname for Janie.[74] She also had a visit during this period from her brother Dr. Robert Askins. Rob Askins had what Jack called "a very bad state of nerves."[75] He arrived in Oxford in a suicidal state and kept Janie up all night talking. This episode was probably the first hint Jack had that the Askins family might have a tendency to mental distress.

C. S. Lewis had a lifelong habit of constructing nicknames. Some of these reflected his affection, others his contempt. He had numerous nicknames for his brother and father, which developed as life circumstances changed. His nicknames for them depended on his mood and the states of their relationships at the time. Now and then his letters addressed his brother as A.P.B., which stood for Archpiggiebotham, a reference to the way their nurse had threatened to spank their piggiebottoms when they were little. Jack was S.P.B., which stood for Smallpiggiebotham.[76]

When the long summer vacation of 1919 came, Albert Lewis expected his son to return home to Belfast as he had done since he first went away to Wynyard School, but Jack had other ideas. He told his father that the Trinity term did not actually end in late June as published but continued unofficially for two or three weeks into July. Furthermore, he claimed that Poynton had told him he should stay in Oxford after the term ended in order to do more work. Jack reasoned that life would be so pleasant at home in Little Lea that he could not possibly get any real work done with so many happy distractions. He told Warnie a slightly different story. He said that Oxford had four terms a year, which Warnie took to mean that they squeezed a short term "somewhere in the middle of the summer."[77] As an alternative, Jack proposed that Albert and Warnie venture to Oxford, where they could stay at the Mitre and go punting. The wily Jack would have known that Albert, who hated to travel on vacation, would never leave the comfort of Little Lea for the uncertainty of the food and beds at the Mitre.[78]

Warnie wanted to coordinate his leave during the summer of 1919 with the Oxford long vacation, but Jack would not tell him the dates, much to Warnie's frustration.[79] Albert advised Warnie not to hope for too much, because Jack had not been so scrupulous in his visits home since he first met Mrs. Moore.[80] As they tried to make plans for a summer 1919 reunion, Albert complained to Warnie that with Jack, it was always Mrs. Moore first. When Jack had six weeks leave, he spent five with Janie Moore. Not even Arthur Greeves provided an attraction, whose company must "pall" in comparison with Janie's.[81]

The trip to Belfast and home could not be avoided entirely, however, though Jack delayed it as long as possible. In the end, he conspired with Warnie to spend a few days together in Oxford and London before visiting Kirkpatrick in Great Bookham, and only then traveling on to Ireland. It can be assumed that Warnie, while in Oxford, did not cross paths with Mrs. Moore, who remained safely away in her lodgings during Jack's pretense of receiving and entertaining Warnie at his rooms in University College. Warnie arrived on July 23, and on July 26 the brothers sailed for Ireland, where they remained with their father until August 22.[82]

This summer visit home to Little Lea would prove to have disastrous consequences for the relationship between Albert and Jack Lewis. Albert discovered that Jack had lied to him about the state of his finances. Jack was overdrawn by £12.9.6d at Cox and

Company bank.[83] Albert had found the letter from the bank lying on a table in the little end room where the boys played as children.[84] When he confronted Jack with the evidence, a horrendous argument ensued in which Jack laid bare all of his father's failings since Jack's childhood. All of the resentment, bitterness, contempt, and disrespect that Jack had accumulated since his mother's death came pouring out in a hot, insulting assault on his father. Albert wrote in his diary that the episode left him "miserable and heart sore."[85] That his son had no respect for him hurt, but the loss of his son's love proved unbearable. Having been caught red-handed in a lie, Jack Lewis did the only thing any reasonable reprobate would do. He lashed out at the one who found him out. It was churlish behavior in a decorated war hero, but the memory of it would haunt him till his dying day and would provide him with keen insight into the human condition that would serve him well in later life. What upset Warnie most was that it made it impossible for him "to touch" his father for the money to spend a week at Malleranny![86]

After this disastrous confrontation at Little Lea in the summer of 1919, Warren and his father had little to say about Jack in their correspondence for several years. The vacation visits in summer and at Christmas continued as before, and when Warren was assigned to a post in Aldershot, he regularly made weekend visits to Oxford several hours away. Nonetheless, things had changed. Curiously enough, during the early 1920s, Albert and Warnie stopped referring to Jack as "It" and reverted in their letters to speaking of the youngest Lewis man as Jacks, the little boy of fond memory.

When Jack returned to Oxford at the end of August, he found that Janie Moore had moved from Warneford Road to 76 Windmill Road in Headington, where she took a flat in the home of Mr. and Mrs. Albert Morris.[87] In the small flat, Jack slept on the sofa.[88] Instead of feeling remorse after his verbal attack on his father, Jack began referring to him contemptuously in letters to Arthur as "his

Jack and Albert Lewis in Little Lea garden, July 1919. Used by permission of the Marion E. Wade Center, Wheaton College, Wheaton, IL.

Excellenz," which not only suggested that Albert had an inflated view of his own importance but also mocked his Irish accent as a mark of ignorance.[89] Only two letters survive from Jack to his father in the period between summer vacation and Christmas vacation in 1919. Perhaps he did not write more. The two are both short, and the second, written in October, expressed the view that he would blame himself more if he had not spoken so frankly to his father in August. He was not in an apologetic mood. He had written to Arthur to the effect that he would not apologize until his father apologized first.[90] Mr. Lewis did not stand alone in experiencing his son's neglect. Arthur received only two letters from Jack between September and the following February. Jack made his excuses, but he had other fish to fry and had begun to collect a new set of friends in Oxford.

A New Best Friend

During the fall of 1919, Rodney Pasley, of the Martlets, introduced Jack to Leo Baker, an undergraduate at Wadham College
reading modern history. Pasley knew of Baker through a friend
who had been hospitalized with Baker as they both nursed their
war wounds. Baker won the Distinguished Flying Cross for his
service in the Royal Air Force during the war, but suffered severe wounds in August 1918. Like Lewis, Baker had gone up to
Oxford in 1917 and to war from there. Pasley told Baker about
Lewis and their common interest in poetry, and introductions soon
followed.[91] Baker soon became Jack's walking companion on his
afternoon romps about Oxfordshire. The men were the same age,
just twenty-one, shared a love of poetry, enjoyed long walks, suffered war injuries, and were "intellectuals." Beyond those things
in common, however, their interests diverged. Baker had an interest in contemporary events, politics, social causes, and marriage.
Jack did not.[92]

Baker saw Jack as a man driven by ambition and the determi-
nation to win the highest marks in the examinations at the end
of their Oxford careers. At this time, Lewis reflected his training
with Kirkpatrick in terms of attacking any discussion of religion
that even hinted at the assumption that God might exist. At the
same time, Baker had a strong interest in mysticism. Despite their
differences over the supernatural, the friendship grew and Baker
became Lewis's closest Oxford friend for a while. He even gained
an invitation to visit his "family" at their home in Headington.
Baker's assessment of Mrs. Moore in 1919 is most important for
understanding a relationship that always remained a mystery to
Warnie Lewis. Baker knew her soon after Jack had first met her.
Baker said that she had an exuberant, cheerful, sunny disposition.[93] He would have many opportunities to get to know her, for
Baker dined at the Headington home often.

On their afternoon walks, Jack and Leo Baker talked about
poetry. They hated the modern free verse poets and all they had

done to poetry. Both of the young poets insisted on rhythm and rhyme as the mainstay of poetry. They wanted to defend and advance traditional poetic forms. They both wondered about the process of creating poetry and how "the muse" operated. They discussed how inspiration arises and the part played by the will in constructing verse. At this point in Jack's life, his greatest ambition was not to have a distinguished career as a professor of philosophy at Oxford but to be recognized as a great poet, like his heroes from the past: Homer, Spenser, Milton. He was not a humble young poet.[94]

Baker described his friend as secretive and private, not given to socializing.[95] It was Pasley who first told Baker that Lewis seemed to live in secrecy and took no part in the life of the college. Jack had been noticed slipping in and out of college, but no one knew if he might be a messenger or a tutor of some obscure subject.[96] Through Baker, however, Lewis would come to know several other people interested in poetry. Baker's best friends in Wadham College were W. E. Beckett and Owen Barfield. Through Barfield, Lewis also met A. C. Harwood and W. O. Field.[97] In time, Barfield would become Lewis's closest friend in many ways. This informal little group of friends regularly met in each other's rooms to talk about anything and everything except "revolution and sex."[98]

Lewis had an impressive conversational style even in his early twenties. He did not ask questions; he gave answers. He practiced the logical rhetorical style he had learned from Kirkpatrick as he made declarations and explanations. He punctuated the steady flow of his monologue with a steady stream of quotations, illustrating the power of his memory. His words seemed rehearsed because of a clarity of expression often absent from oral discourse, yet Baker felt sure that Lewis had not prepared his remarks before they got together.[99] Though not humorless, the young Jack Lewis was not "a laughing man," Baker noted. Instead, he appeared to have his share of troubles that he bore stoically.[100]

Another Move

Jack spent what must have been an extraordinarily awkward Christmas vacation with his father in Belfast. In the new year of 1920, Janie Moore changed residences again, moving from 76 Windmill Road in Headington to a flat at 58 Windmill Road in a house owned by Mr. and Mrs. John Jeffrey.[101] Relations with the landlady, who was a butcher, deteriorated rapidly, arguments ensued that almost became violent, and the little family withdrew to find happier lodgings in late March. They could find nowhere to live immediately, so they dispersed their belongings around Headington and Oxford where they could. Then they took a holiday during the Easter vacation to the north coast of Somerset on the Bristol Channel at the village of Old Cleve.[102] Upon their return, they took rooms with Mrs. Marshall at Courtfield Cottage, 131 Osler Road in Headington.[103]

While all the distress of a disagreeable landlady oppressed the small household and kept everyone in a bad state, Jack had to study for and take his Classical Honour Moderations examinations. He told Arthur that Mods lasted for eight days, and that they began with the renewal of a health problem he had in the past, a swollen gland in his throat.[104] Jack's frequent childhood illnesses would continue into his young adulthood as he regularly had bouts of ill health. The severity of the breach between Jack and his father managed to subside with the news that Jack had earned a first in Mods. In reporting this news, however, Jack also lied about his vacation to Old Cleve, telling his father that he was traveling with an old friend and was paying back an engagement.[105]

The countryside around Old Cleve, with its view of Wales across the water, and the books he was reading renewed in Jack a sense of the "well at the end of the world" and the spiritual journey that had so caught his imagination in the stories that had delighted him when he lived with W. T. Kirkpatrick.[106] Though a staunch and emphatic atheist, Jack continued to find himself engaged in fascinating conversations with his friends about death, ghosts, life after death, heaven, and hell. These subjects would not go away. Leo Baker thought himself a spiritualist or clairvoyant and claimed to have had many experiences with ghosts and out-of-body experiences.[107] Baker could frighten Jack, who began to wonder, perhaps facetiously, if Baker were mad.[108] Whatever his quirks, they did not prevent Baker from being "the best person" in every way that Jack had met in Oxford, and he was terribly distressed that Baker planned to leave Oxford at the end of Trinity term in 1920.[109] Leo's war wounds continued to plague him, and Oxford proved too great a physical challenge.

Jack's friendship with Arthur Greeves continued, but their correspondence diminished considerably. Arthur entertained the idea of going to Oxford, an idea that Jack encouraged, but nothing came of it, and Arthur eventually entered the Slade art school in London.[110] While advising Arthur on how to study for the entrance exams, however, Jack casually mentioned that the simple routine of work had done wonders for his brain, so much so that he even understood Henri Bergson, a French philosopher whom Jack had been reading.[111] Bergson had suggested to Jack the necessity of the existence of the universe in contrast to Schopenhauer's idea that the universe might just as easily "not have existed."[112] Jack now accepted the universe as the whole, without skeptical reserve. It was the great fact—neither to be blamed or praised. Without blame or praise, however, Jack would come to be reminded of thoughts he had just before leaving Kirkpatrick: such a universe would have neither good nor evil—just what is. Lewis was on the slippery slope toward faith.[113]

With the end of Hilary term at the Easter vacation, Jack had fulfilled the residency requirement for undergraduates and left his room at University College to live with Janie Moore and Maureen in Headington. With Mods behind him, he entered into the study of Greats with a fury at the beginning of Trinity term after Easter. He had two tutors in his classical studies: George Hope Stevenson in ancient history and Edgar Frederick Carritt in Greek philosophy.[114]

The Guild

During Hilary term of 1920, the small circle of friends that Jack had accumulated around Leo Baker and poetry had coalesced to the point that he called them "The Guild."[115] This group of literary friends proposed to publish an anthology of their collective poetry, in many ways as a challenge to the new trend in poetry that T. S. Eliot had set in motion.[116] The collection would be called "The Way's the Way." The odd title is a quotation from Bunyan's *The Pilgrim's Progress* that laments how hard the path of life might be but concludes that the way is the way.[117] With his knowledge of Scripture, Jack probably knew that Bunyan's passage alluded to the words of Jesus at the Last Supper, where he claimed to be the only way to God (John 14:6). Perhaps surprisingly, the contributors, in addition to Pasley, Baker, and Jack, included two women: Carola Oman, the daughter of the historian Sir Charles Oman, and Margaret Gidding, a friend of Pasley.[118]

Blackwell's, the famous bookstore in Oxford, which for several years had been publishing the annual editions of Oxford poetry to which J. R. R. Tolkien and Dorothy L. Sayers had contributed, planned to publish the volume. By August 1920, when back in Old Cleve for the long vacation, Jack wrote to Leo Baker that he would have abandoned the anthology altogether except that Pasley had his heart set on it. Blackwell no longer seemed as excited by the project.[119] By September, however, Basil Blackwell had suggested that the anthology still might see the light of day if the contributors could contribute some of their own money to underwrite its publication. Jack did not think much of that idea.[120] Blackwell's reluctance finally led Pasley to the view, endorsed by Jack, that if Blackwell would not publish their poetry, they should give up the project. Jack wrote to Leo on December 22 of the final fate of the anthology. Blackwell had refused to publish without a subvention from the contributors.[121]

At this point in his university studies, Jack had no time for writing poetry. He had to write a philosophy paper and a history paper each week for his tutors, and as a member of the Martlets, he had to write papers for that society on a regular basis. He had no time or energy left for his poetry, and he wondered to Baker if the guild could long hold together. Since Baker left Oxford without taking a degree, Jack did not have another close acquaintance to stimulate and encourage his thought. He had good intentions of looking up Baker's friend Owen Barfield, but had not found the time.[122] Grudgingly and somewhat coincidentally, he mentioned to Baker in passing that he had made a slight adjustment to his philosophy. In addition to matter, the existence of some sort of "God," certainly not a personal being, is the least objectionable theory to account for the universe. Lewis had no alternative theory to offer and could live with an idea of God just so long as the idea had no concrete or specific claims, since no one could possibly know the real God.[123] His atheism had lost its vibrancy, but not its bite. He deplored a worldview that saw heaven above, hell below, and a merely six-thousand-year-old universe. He preferred his own data, even if it led to destruction.[124]

Jack's birthday in 1920 brought with it a singular triumph. The Martlets elected him their president, and he presided over a trip to Cambridge to meet with the society of the same name at "the other place." He presented a paper "Narrative Poetry" at the meeting in Cambridge and gave his father a full account of the trip shortly after his return to Oxford. He liked Cambridge but recognized that it had a different character from Oxford. He had prepared himself to be disappointed in the legendary King's College Chapel but found it beautiful beyond belief. Though he thought Oxford more magnificent, he thought Cambridge more intriguing. The dons, however, seemed inferior to Oxford dons, and Jack thought one was "hardly a gentleman."[125] As for his future, Jack informed his father that he intended to compete for the Vice Chancellor's Essay Prize the following April. The subject of the essay was "Optimism," a true challenge for a young man who paraded his pessimism.[126]

Jack's contempt for the English people as a class continued to be almost as intense as his contempt for Americans. He delighted in telling his father that when "old Carlyle" presented a paper at the Martlets, he prefaced his presentation by saying that he had meant to publish the paper, but it was so unsatisfactory that he had sent it to an American magazine instead. Jack endorsed this attitude with the rejoinder "That's the proper spirit!"[127]

By March 1921, Jack finally looked up Owen Barfield.[128] Pasley and Baker had both taken a path that would make them less available as literary friends: they had both become engaged to be married. Jack thought that marriage ruined many friendships, and it had no appeal to him at all, possibly because of his own domestic relations, which did not involve marriage. When he wrote to Warnie of Pasley's engagement, he condemned engagement as "that fatal tomb of all lively and interesting men."[129] Barfield would become increasingly important as his closest friends drifted away. Jack liked some of Barfield's poetry, but thought that Barfield did not have the vision to carry off the kind of poetry that Jack relished.[130] Nonetheless, Jack appreciated what Barfield was trying to do. At that time, Barfield lived with Cecil Harwood at Bee Cottage, in the village of Beckley, near Headington. In March 1921, however, Jack had a closer friend than Owen Barfield.

Hobnobbing with the New Set

Warnie set sail on RMS *Appam* on March 9, 1921, for an overseas posting in Sierra Leone, the white man's graveyard.[131] After neglecting Warnie for quite some time, Jack began writing a collection of long serial letters to him, almost like installments in a diary. Because of this fortunate change of heart and fraternal rapprochement, we know a great deal more about Jack in 1921 than we could have gleaned from his letters to his father. We know that he became friends with A. K. Hamilton Jenkin and with William Force Stead.

Jenkin went up to Oxford in 1921 as an undergraduate at University College, where he belonged to the Martlets along with Jack. How soon their friendship grew, we do not know, but Jack described him to Warnie in a letter dated March 1, 1921. Jenkin was two years younger than Jack and had not gone to war. Jack mentioned him because Jenkin had shown Jack two books about Cornwall. One involved a tour of Cornwall in the seventeenth century, and the other involved a smuggler who found himself imprisoned in France and bound for the guillotine.[132] The connection with his brother was Warnie's growing interest in French history during the age of Louis XIV. Jenkin would spend the rest of his life devoted to his beloved Cornwall, and Warnie would publish a half dozen books on the age of Louis XIV. The few lines in Jack's letter happily presaged the lives of two men Jack loved. Jenkin also wrote poetry, but Jack lamented that it was sad poetry and usually about Cornwall.[133]

Through the agency of one of Jack's lesser poetry friends, he gained an invitation to visit one of his heroes, the poet William Butler Yeats, who had recently moved to Oxford. Jack told Warnie that his friend William Force Stead wrote poetry just like he did, only it was like all the bad parts of his poetry. Jack continued to have a wicked sense of humor. Stead was an American who served as a Church of England curate in a nearby parish. From Jack's description to Warnie, Stead had married an unpleasant American woman named Frances Goldsborough, who happened to be the sister of the wife of Dr. John Askins, one of Janie Moore's brothers.[134]

Despite Stead's bad poetry and lackluster wife, his acquaintance with Yeats made his friendship one worth cultivating. On March 14, 1921, Stead took Jack along for an evening at Yeats's house, in Oxford. What followed gave Jack all the material he needed for a thorough roasting of the most absurd quack. Yeats surrounded himself with subservient souls who sat in a circle of hard, antique chairs. The room was draped in orange flame curtains and was illuminated by candles. The effect of Yeats's speech approximated a sé-ance, punctuated as it was by theosophy, magic, the Kabbalah, and Yeats's magisterial manner.[135] Jack thought it was all too ridiculous.

Spring was in full bloom by mid-March, and Jack grew less diligent in his studies, taking to the open road on his bicycle to ride about Oxfordshire in search of pretty little stone villages with pleasant churches and pubs. He liked a low-raftered bar with a stuffed fox in a glass case and good draft cider on offer.[136] As often as not, he chose cider over beer.

A week after his evening with Stead at Yeats's salon, the great man asked Stead to bring Jack back again. This time the circle included only Yeats, Stead, and Jack. They talked about "books and things." Jack told Warnie that on this second visit, Yeats "was almost quite sane."[137] Nonetheless, the experience had satisfied Jack's need to draw near to the literary greats.

Some months later, Jack wrote a long letter to Arthur in which he described the Yeats salon against the background of their interests. The staircase in Yeats's house in Broad Street was lined with framed William Blake illustrations to *Paradise Lost* and the book of Job. The candles in his sitting room included two six-foot candlesticks of the sort associated with a Church of England altar. After describing to Arthur the kinds of fantastical, magical dialogue that went on between Yeats and his disciples, Jack remarked that what he and Arthur had always liked as fantasy was actually accepted as real by people all over Europe.[138]

Perhaps the most important feature of this letter with respect to Arthur, however, is that it demonstrates how seldom Jack and Arthur wrote to each other as young adults and how superficially the letters dealt with their lives, compared with how they had bared their souls to each other in their youth. At this point, Arthur had been a student at the Slade School of Art for some time, but Jack seems to know nothing of Arthur's experiences. Jack did mention the visit of his cousins Kelsie and Mary to Oxford, and how they bored him to death. In spite of all the kindness they had shown him his entire life, he lamented that seeing them out of their setting left him impressed by their provincialism, Ulster bigotry, and sleek unreality. Jack was losing his Irishness and becoming critical of the world he had always defended against the horrid English. To illustrate just how far he had come, in a letter to Warnie, he described the two of them as "we English"![139] Another way of putting it is that he had grown embarrassed by his background.

Rethinking Life and Death

A few days after Jack's visit with Yeats, W. T. Kirkpatrick died at home on March 22, 1921. Albert received the news first and sent Jack a telegram.[140] To his credit, Jack recognized that he owed Kirk for his scholarship to Oxford. Beyond that, he realized just how much Kirk had shaped his intellect and possibly tamed his sense of humor.[141]

While so much had been happening, Jack had finished his essay titled "Optimism," which had to be both literary and philosophical, but which he feared was too literary for the philosophers and too philosophical for the English faculty.[142] He advised his father not to expect a prize. He also confessed that his war wound continued to bother him, and that it appeared to have bestowed on him the gift of rheumatism.[143] These maladies would plague him the rest of his life, though few would know it.

In the aftermath of Kirkpatrick's death without benefit of a funeral and all of Albert's distress over Kirk's disbelief, Jack came to have some odd reflections on life and death—at least odd for an atheist. He knew it would have been wrong to pronounce over his lifeless body words of a religious nature Kirk had not believed. On the other hand, Kirk was so stamped on Jack's mind and present to his thought that Kirk's own idea of annihilation seemed unthinkable. In war, Jack had witnessed death often, and he always found it extraordinary and incredible. A living person is so different from a dead body that Jack found it hard to believe that "something has turned into nothing." He confessed that he reached this idea not by reason but by "feeling." He wondered if "feelings" were not "what we call our beliefs."[144]

Jack did not visit his father during the Easter vacation of 1921. Albert rationalized the neglect to Warren by explaining that Jack had only a ten-day break, and it would have been an expensive trip for such a short stay. Somehow this explanation ignores the fact that he had been making such trips since his days at Wynyard. Albert also mentioned that Jack's old war wound had continued to give him trouble, manifesting itself as rheumatism. Albert believed, however, that Jack's pain was due to stress over his academic aspirations.[145]

Leo Baker returned to Oxford for Trinity term following the Easter vacation. Jack mused that Warnie and Leo, two people he loved, could not possibly have understood each other. He thought that Baker always spoke in metaphors but did not realize they were metaphors. He observed that Baker's "poems are like rooms full of exotic and insolent ornaments, but with nowhere to sit down."[146] Baker's return would play an unheralded but vital role in the direction of Lewis's thinking about the possibility of the existence of God because of the exotic subjects he would raise in casual conversation.

One of the frequent visitors to the Moore-Lewis household in Headington was the Reverend Dr. Frederick Walker Macran, known affectionately as Cranny. He was an old friend of Janie Moore and her brother John Askins. Born in Ireland and educated at Trinity College in Dublin, Cranny served parishes in county Down before relocating to the small parish of Childrey, near Oxford, in 1905. A proud atheist who could not afford to give up his living, Cranny rationalized that we do not worship the man Jesus. Rather, we worship the Christ that was in Jesus. Jack thought this side step was a too-clever manipulation of language.[147] He enjoyed the cynical company of Cranny and their shared atheism, yet, oddly enough, so many of their conversations would revolve around the question of God and life after death.

Looking back on his conversations with Cranny more than thirty years later, Lewis explained that Cranny had wanted immortality, or at least he had wanted whatever he called "himself" to survive death. Yet he wanted it without any of the trappings of God or goodness. He did not seek reunion with lost loved ones or release from wrong deeds. He just wanted to continue to exist. Lewis claimed that the very idea of immortality grew disgusting to him as a result of conversations with Cranny.[148]

A Surprising Prize

Much to the surprise of Jack, the eternal pessimist, he won the Vice Chancellor's Prize for his English essay "Optimism." As a devoted pessimist, he had not been optimistic of his chances for success. In a letter to Warnie during this period, Jack had commented on a horrible young woman he had encountered at a tea given by the Carlyles. Her greatest offense was her optimism. He and Pasley attempted to instill a little pessimism in her but failed utterly.[149] To his greater surprise upon his triumph within the university, the big, beefy louts in the college were both polite to him and congratulatory. Basil Blackwell talked about publication, but Jack had grown cautious about publishing too early for fear of outgrowing his earlier views. He had already come to regret publishing *Spirits in Bondage* while so young. As it is, no copy of this winning essay on optimism survives.[150]

Jack sent a telegram to his father on May 24, 1921, with news that he had won the Vice Chancellor's Prize. Albert saved the telegram along with the news clipping about the award from the *Times*.[151] Albert expressed great pride when he wrote to Warnie of the news, for while Oxford offered many scholarships, it had only one Vice-Chancellor's Prize! The pride was shadowed with sadness, however, for Albert feared that Jack would not come home that summer without Warnie there to attract him.[152] To Arthur,

Jack disclosed that the prize included a cash award of twenty pounds, but he did not want his father to know about the money. He realized that the biggest benefit of the prize involved the attention it would draw to him, which might help him secure a job when he finished his degree. He thought it marked him out from the crowd.[153]

Having won the prize, Jack was required to read a selection from his essay before the assembled congregation of the university in the ceremony of Encaenia at the end of the academic year, when honorary degrees were conferred and honors awarded. An honorary degree went to Georges Clemenceau, wartime prime minister of France. Jack had two minutes in which to impress his audience, but he had difficulty finding a short passage that made sense! He met with two surprises from the ceremony. First, he was delighted to learn that he understood the oration in Latin given by the professor of poetry, Jack's first experience with spoken Latin oratory. Second, he was shocked by the appearance of the other prize winners, "a collection of scrubby, beetle-like, bespectacled oddities," only one of whom looked to be a gentleman.[154] Jack was still a snob.

Though we have no extant copy of "Optimism," Jack explained to Warnie the principal challenge he faced in writing the essay: Is optimism possible without God? To heighten the challenge, Jack had the experience of being a pessimist in the absence of belief in God. He wanted to avoid a direct denial of the existence of God on the off chance that one of the judges for the prize might be a Christian. He chose a path used by Kirk to argue that grounds for optimism do not depend on whether God exists.[155]

Several of Jack's long letters to Warnie went astray in early summer, and one from Warnie to Jack went to Liverpool, so Jack held off writing again until he had a clear address. He told Warnie that it all reminded him of what Leo Baker had said about God and prayer. It was like corresponding with someone who never answers one's letters, leaving a fellow with the view that either the party does not exist or that you have the wrong address.[156]

Years would pass before Jack would write essays and books about prayer. In the meantime, he did wonder about the divine address.

Leo had sent Jack a copy of *The Gospel of Buddha*, which prompted some remarks that simply could not coexist with Jack's old materialism.[157] Jack was surprised to learn that Buddhism denies the existence of "the Self." He could not accept the idea of a "bundle of thoughts" instead of someone who actually does the thinking. He decided that Buddhism was inferior to Christianity. Though he sometimes felt that a complete denial of everything was his only refuge, in his healthier moments he hoped for something better. He might yearn for the complete loss of individuality and identity with Nirvana, but he really preferred something of more positive joy.[158]

The kinds of discussion he once had with Greeves about the nature of beauty he now carried on with Baker. He wondered if beauty necessarily involves a joy remembered. He thought that beauty must involve an invitation to "come into me" and not merely an opportunity for reflection. He was coming to believe that beauty has an objective reality apart from the personal opinion of the viewer, but how could it? It certainly could not in a materialistic universe. To heighten the matter, he linked beauty with the concept of right and wrong, which also seemed to have an objective reality.[159] With these two streams of thought, we see the path opening toward Jack's apologetic work twenty years later, when he wrote *The Abolition of Man* and "Right and Wrong as a Clue to the Meaning of the Universe," later incorporated as the opening section of *Mere Christianity*.

Once they settled into their larger house in Headington, Janie Moore and Jack kept open house. They offered Pasley a place to stay for his *viva* (an oral examination). By this time, Pasley had taken up spiritualism, to Jack's surprise. Pasley had gone from believing that immortality had no charm at the end of Hilary term, to believing that life had no meaning without immortality by the end of Trinity term. Jack was merely amused by this shift.[160]

Keeping Albert at Bay

By mid-summer, Albert Lewis was threatening a vacation excursion to England with a stop in Oxford. Jack informed his father that he had now moved out of college and was sharing a room with a man who was overwhelmed by his workload. Out of consideration for his roommate, they would not be able to spend any time at Jack's lodgings. Instead of a rendezvous in Oxford, Jack suggested that they meet in Westmoreland or North Wales! The object was to stay well away from Oxford.[161]

Contrary to all of his life's experience, Albert exerted himself beyond all imagining and took a vacation to England in July 1921, thus fulfilling his threat and igniting Jack into action. Pasley answered the call and became Jack's "overworked roommate" in a quickly decorated room to give the impression of studiousness. In the end, the grand masquerade was not necessary, because the vacationing party from Belfast stopped in Oxford only long enough to eat lunch at the Clarendon Hotel and pick up Jack for a week-long journey with them across southwest England. The party included Albert's in-laws, Augustus and Anne Hamilton. Augustus drove his car for the expedition, which left Oxford on July 24. Jack wrote a long, humorous account of the journey in a letter to Warnie, devoting most of his attention to their father's outrageous remarks and violations of logic.[162]

As it turned out, Jack did return to Belfast suddenly and "unheralded" at the end of the summer and stayed with his father for several weeks. The awkwardness of the preceding year was mollified and Albert thought the talk was "distinctly good."[163] By the end of August, however, Jack had a case of neuralgia, which he attributed to getting water in his ear, though friends told him that was impossible.[164] By November, he had also had a bout of the flu.[165] December 1921 found Jack in the hands of the doctor in Oxford, while Albert made excuses for his son's inability to attend a dance in Belfast. According to Albert, Jack had never fully recovered from his war wounds.[166] Jack's wounds would continue to plague him, and they may have played a part in the inspiration of Frodo's wound that would never heal.

Only three letters from Lewis exist for the period between August 1921 and May 1922. It is possible that letters were lost, though that seems unlikely given the habits of Albert, Warnie, and Arthur, who saved everything. Perhaps Jack had other fish to fry, and he certainly treated his examinations as if everything depended on them. In the meantime, Warnie received a six-month leave following the end of his service in Sierra Leone. He arrived home in Belfast on April 7, 1922. Finally, at the end of May, Jack broke his silence with a letter to his father about his strategy for a career. It would involve Albert.

As Jack prepared for his final exams, he broached the subject of his future to Albert. Instead of putting his name with an employment agency, Jack was advised by one of his tutors to stay on one more year in Oxford and do a second degree. His degree in classics and philosophy held great prestige, but no one knew what kind of market he would find for such a degree in the new educational world developing after the war. If Jack were to add a degree in English literature, one of the up-and-coming new fields, the combination with Greats would seem highly desirable. Because of reforms to the curriculum, Jack realized that he already knew more about the subject than some would know at the end of their degree, so it would be an easy course of study compared with what he had already done. He believed that his college would continue his scholarship for another year, but he needed Albert's continued support to make up the difference for an unanticipated year. He assured Albert that he could get some sort of job, but because of his failure at playing sports when he was in school, he probably could not get a job as a schoolmaster. The point he wanted to drive home to Albert was that the dons at University College did not want him to leave Oxford. They thought he could obtain a position, but he had to play the game. Lewis took his examinations for Greats between June 8 and 14.[167]

In the course of the summer, Jack sought several positions at Oxford, including a fellowship at Magdalen College. Under the circumstances, he told his father it would be best to stay on the scene and not come home to Belfast during the summer vacation. He had to make the sacrifice for his future. Jack was not only forgoing the pleasure of his father's company; he was also giving up a chance to spend time with Warnie. Arthur Greeves had been to Oxford for a visit, and Jack mentioned to his father that he had seen a good bit of Arthur. Given the earlier story about sharing a room with a hardworking student, it would not do to give Albert the impression that Arthur had stayed with him and Mrs. Moore! In a rare moment of candor, however, Jack confessed to his father that he once had qualms about introducing Arthur to Oxford friends. Greeves lacked the social skills that abounded in Jack's new circle of literary friends. They were all great conversationalists, and Arthur was not, though Jack thought he had greatly improved.[168] A subsequent letter to Arthur following his visit suggests that he was deeply immersed in the household and with all the comings and goings of the wide circle of friends and relations associated with his Headington family. The reason Jack had managed to see a good bit of Arthur was that Arthur had stayed with him.[169]

Jack underwent the oral exam known as *viva* for his degree on July 28. On August 4 he learned that he had earned a first, the English equivalent of *summa cum laude* (with highest praise). On August 1, 1922, Jack, Janie Moore, and Maureen moved into Hillsboro House at 14 Western Road (now Holyoake Road) in Headington, where they would reside for a decade before buying the Kilns. It was a busy time, a time of great transitions. For one who began to realize that he would probably never hold a philosophy post at Oxford, Jack took his situation philosophically. He reasoned to his father that English might be his "real line" after all. It had always been his great love until his hero worship of W. T. Kirkpatrick turned him toward philosophy. In many ways, the failure to secure a fellowship in philosophy simply allowed him to return to himself. The only real loser was Albert, to whom Jack did not manage to write again until October, and who would bear the brunt of the additional expense of another year at Oxford.[170]

2

From Philosophy to Literature

1922-1925

On April 1, 1922, Jack Lewis began keeping a diary with rather detailed accounts of what he did and how he felt about all aspects of his life until March 2, 1927. For the inquisitive biographer, this diary provides insight into Lewis during a critical time of his life that we would not otherwise have, because during this same period, he wrote comparatively few letters, and these provided maddeningly slight information about his life. As we have seen, Jack completed his first Oxford degree in July 1922, but his personal life grew increasingly complicated even as he realized that his best chances for a teaching post at Oxford would come in English literature. Yet the diary must be read with caution. Normally, when someone writes a diary, it is intended for his or her eyes alone. This diary, however, was written at the encouragement of Janie Moore, and Jack regularly read it to her, so it is an account of his life in a tone intended to meet her approval.[1] Jack also allowed Warnie to read it along the way when he visited Oxford.[2]

Throughout his diary, Lewis referred to Janie simply by the letter *D* without explanation. From childhood, Lewis had given every one of his acquaintance a nickname of either affection or ridicule. We may assume that *D* stood for something, but we are left to speculate. In fact, the *D* in the published diary is actually a rendering of the Greek letter delta. Lewis chose this cryptic Greek letter to represent Janie Moore. A romantic interpretation might lead one to think of the beautiful Diana, except that Diana was a Roman goddess. A more likely possibility is that Janie represented Demeter, the great mother goddess. Alister McGrath has drawn attention to Lewis's poem "Reason," which may have been written about this time, in which Lewis contrasts Athena, allegorical figure for cold reason, with Demeter, who provides an allegorical representation of warm imagination. McGrath pondered whether Lewis saw in Janie Moore the fusing of these two elements, but the poem seems to have more to do with the internal struggle within Lewis himself between his rational and imaginative sides, which did not want to cooperate. Besides, Janie Moore does not seem to have embodied either reason or imagination, as will become evident. She would have embodied, however, the motherhood of Demeter.[3] Jack and Janie referred to her husband, Courtney Edward Moore, as the Beast, and Jack regularly remarked on the precarious state of their affairs if the Beast failed to deposit money into her bank account on a regular basis.[4]

After several years of moving from house to house, the Lewis-Moore household finally settled down at Hillsboro House after one last stint in a loaner cottage, Red Gables, on the Headington Road. Red Gables was owned by Lady Gonner, whose daughter Sheila attended Headington School with Mrs. Moore's daughter, Maureen.[5] Throughout the period leading up to the examinations for his degree, while finances seemed a constant concern, Jack regularly complained of a variety of ailments, including sore throat, colds, neuralgia, toothache, severe headaches, and pain from his old war wound.[6] In May 1922, he had complained of shooting pains from his war injury.[7] These would recur. Just as frequently, Mrs. Moore complained of her own set of ailments, including chronic indigestion, neuralgia, headaches, constant colds, a sore back, and varicose veins.[8] As the 1920s wore on, Janie also showed a tendency to fall and hurt herself. Jack's references to her ailments always come with expressions of deep sympathy and concern.

The Headington Routine

A certain amount of routine filled the days. Lewis submitted poems to the London-based magazine *Mercury*, which were rejected. He blamed the modern style of poetry that had come to fill its pages. He went for long walks, especially across Shotover Hill, the prominent landmark that abutted the brickyard he would buy a decade later to make his home. He loved Shotover so much that he explored renting a new estate home a developer had built at its foot, but Lewis was too late.[9] While he had hated tea with Mrs. Kirkpatrick and her friends in Great Bookham, he normally sat by Janie Moore's side when she entertained all and sundry for tea. Her brother John Askins had moved to the neighborhood from Bristol and often came to tea with or without his wife and daughter, as did their atheist clerical friend, Cranny. Mrs. Moore made numerous other friends quickly, and Jack's routine now included entertaining the steady stream of visitors. Jack also cycled everywhere when on business and tied to a schedule. He alternated between cycling and walking on his long jaunts with Baker or Jenkin across the length and breadth of Oxfordshire.

With Dr. Askins, whom Jack normally referred to as the Doc, and Cranny, Jack often discussed theology, even though none of them were believers. Somehow in the course of their theological ramblings, Cranny got the idea that the Doc should pursue ordination, which Cranny began to pursue for him, much to the amusement of the Doc and Jack. Cranny believed in natural selection, which in great measure accounted for his loss of faith, yet he managed to believe that the process had stopped when evolution arrived at humans. Observing the irrationality of this view, Jack noted facetiously in his diary that he wondered if mastodons had held the same view.[10] This notion of the current state of affairs as the final culmination of all things would be a critical cog in Lewis's conversion to faith in Christ. Owen Barfield would refer to this view as "chronological snobbery." The Doc's conversations often turned to spiritualism, ghosts, and the possibility of life after death. Mrs. Moore could not keep from "skeptical interruptions" on these occasions.[11] She abhorred religion in all its forms. Jack had the same sort of conversations on a more heightened intellectual plane with Baker and Barfield. Though Baker had an affinity for spiritualism, Jack and Barfield remained avowed materialists who disdained any thought of immortality, even though they felt quite miserable about it. Jack called their worry about the possibility of immortality their Victorian disease.[12]

By now, Jack had turned from writing individual poems to taming the vision he had nurtured since his years at Great Bookham for an extended piece that he named "Dymer." From its earlier prose form, he had now settled on an extended book-length poem. He worked on it when he could spare the time from his domestic routine and scholastic obligations. Even though he had read most of the books required in the English syllabus, he still had to work through the material now from an academic perspective and not simply as pleasure reading. He needed time, but it was in short supply. He also tried to keep up with his friends. Leo Baker had a role in a play put on by a professional company, and Owen Barfield also had a part that involved dancing.[13] After the success of this play, Baker and Barfield decided they might try for careers on the stage.[14] In the meantime, Barfield got a job as subeditor at the *Beacon*, a literary magazine where Jack said he would have the unpleasant job of turning down his friends' poetry.[15] Instead, Barfield accepted Jack's poem "Joy," which first expresses in print the experience that drove his conversion and illuminated his awareness of the existence of spiritual reality alongside the physical world.[16] In 1922, he was also attempting to write his own version of the Psyche myth without success.[17] He would not succeed until he had the help of Joy Davidman Gresham some thirty years later.

Maureen Moore turned sixteen in 1922. She attended Headington School for Girls, where she gave her attention to music. Miss Brayne taught Maureen the violin and often came to tea. Miss Baker, another of Maureen's teachers, often came to tea as well. Jack had little positive to say about Maureen during her teenage years. He deplored the way she tended to shirk her share of the work, from his perspective, which left so much on Mrs. Moore but more on Jack. He commented if she stayed in bed on Sunday until lunch.[18] He derided her "outbreak of feminism" with her complaint that men have it easier than women.[19] For her part, Mrs. Moore cooked and did sewing to earn a little money. She also made jam perpetually. Of the making of jam there was no end, much to the disgust of Jack, who ironically was the prime beneficiary at tea. He never complained about washing dishes, building coal fires in the fireplaces and then clearing away the ashes, tending to the garden, and a dozen other household chores, but he abominated picking gooseberries and currants, and any other task for which he might be conscripted in the making of jam.

During the summer of 1922, Jack's pleasure reading had turned to psychology and psychological interpretations of sexuality. He read Freud's *Introductory Letters* and went away wondering if all human love was a perversion rather than a simple appetite.[20] The question was not a mere academic musing. He had been concerned with the issue of love for many years, and it would drive his first great book, *The Allegory of Love*. The problem of love was one of those annoying pointers to a transcendent reality beyond the physical world, and Jack needed to resolve it before he could be completely at peace in a brute universe. If any quality existed apart from sheer matter, then the universe he had constructed with the aid of W. T. Kirkpatrick would collapse, and he would have to start all over again. Meanwhile, his psychological reading had seeped into his writing of "Dymer." While Baker and Barfield loved the installments they read and lavished Jack with praise, Jenkin complained that it was a "psychological soliloquy."[21]

Even as he enjoyed the progress he was making with "Dymer," his hymn to materialism and self-obsession, an odd thing happened—something that had not happened in years. It was in the midst of the long week in which he wrote his examinations for his degree. Having slept late on Sunday morning, he cycled into Oxford to University College, where he left his bicycle to walk through Christ Church Meadow and across the river to the top of the hill in Hinksey. There he sat down in the woods surrounded by ferns when it happened. Jack was surprised by Joy. He had not had the experience in years, but there it was, "a whiff of the real joy." He immediately went back into Oxford to the Oxford Union, where he checked out William James's *Varieties of Religious Experience*, which reassured him that the experience was all in his head.[22] Months, later, however, the memory of the real Joy lingered, and he remarked on it in November when he went back to these woods with Jenkin.[23] Just as there would be many ways into Narnia, with the same way rarely working more than once, Jack Lewis continued to find that the real Joy came upon him unexpectedly but could not be retrieved from the same situation.

By the time Jack finished his exams, the wolf was at the door. He and Mrs. Moore regularly ended each day by discussing "ways and means."[24] They had run out of money without prospects of any new source of revenue. The week after exams, Jack woke up deeply depressed and collapsed into a torrent of tears without apparent explanation.[25] Even while anticipating doing another year at Oxford, he was desperately looking for a job. Edgar Frederick Carritt, Jack's tutor in philosophy, had suggested that Jack might try for the subdean position at Wadham College, which Baker had already mentioned. The position would involve enforcement of rules and discipline, maintaining order, and general administration. Jack told Carritt that he did not think he would be very good at "ticking people off," to which Carritt replied that he thought Jack would be very good at ticking people off.[26] Time would prove Carritt right. Other similar situations came and went without success, until Jack began selling his books to have money for them to live on.[27] He realized that his adolescent "possessive love of books" and their beautiful covers had passed.

Any consideration of the relationship between Jack and Mrs. Moore needs to include an examination of their respective views on marriage. She, trapped in a loveless marriage to a brute and separated for years, had a positive view of marriage. When Jack expounded on how marriage always ruins friendships, Mrs. Moore countered that the problem usually lay with the single person rather than with the one who had married.[28] Baker joined Jack in his contempt for matrimony, but Janie took Baker aside and, in the course of a long conversation, discussed the possibility of Jack getting married.[29] Later, Jack and Baker discussed the idea of group marriage as a possible alternative to monogamy, which Jack thought would be a great improvement over prostitution and a thousand times better than an affair of the heart, but Baker remained unconvinced.[30]

Mrs. Moore talked easily and freely with anyone who crossed the threshold of their house, and many came. Hardly a day passed when they did not have company for tea. Jack's friends were always welcomed and encouraged by her. She also extended the offer of a bed for the night to any of Jack's friends who needed a place to stay. This number included Baker and Barfield, as well as Arthur for the occasional extended visit. Jack and Janie Moore often talked late at night, and she helped him think through his other relationships. She thought it odd that he liked Baker more than Barfield and Harwood. He decided that it was because Baker liked him more than the others did. He also considered Baker his equal, while he viewed Barfield as towering above him in every way he thought important.[31] This view of Barfield probably played no small part in his influence on Lewis when Barfield's views on materialism changed a few years later.

The Doc continued to drop by for tea and could always be counted on to provide some entertaining topic of conversation, such as "his philosophy of the primal One and its objectification" or his exploration fifteen hundred miles up the Amazon.[32] Jack liked the Doc, for even though he expounded ideas that Jack thought utter rubbish, the Doc could always laugh at himself in the midst of it all. He could also be counted on to bring the conversation around to some aspect of the spiritual/mystical/religious/occult eventually, which made for even more fun if someone like Baker was present as his foil.[33]

Anyone who knows anything about C. S. Lewis has heard that he never read the newspapers. He said that if anything important happened, someone would be sure to tell him. This kind of sensational, self-deprecating remark is always sure to have its effect on the audience, but of course, it was not true. It was a typical Lewis gag. It would be more accurate to say that sometimes Lewis read the paper and sometimes he did not. It all depended upon his time of life. He enjoyed reading the *Sunday Times*. It was a good alternative to church when he did not attend.[34]

Perhaps through Janie Moore's influence, Jack began to tire of Baker. Jack noted that Baker was good at serious conversation and at uproarious humor, two things that Jack had always loved. On the other hand, Janie helped Jack see that Baker was no good at chatting, something Jack had always hated but Mrs. Moore's specialty.[35] To make matters worse, Baker barely managed to take his degree once the grades were posted, for he only managed a third, a gentleman's C. He was not Jack's equal, and Jack was still a snob.

Company and Companions

In August 1922, when the little trio moved into Hillsboro House initially for just one month rent free, they sublet the house at 28

Warneford Road to Jack's recently married friend Rodney Pasley. They also took in a boarder to help with expenses. She was Andrée Cahen, from Paris, a young but formidable woman who spoke English fluently enough to impress Jack, but whose striking beauty did nothing to mask the initial effect of being "unlovable."[36] By and by, however, Jack warmed to her. Shortly before moving to Hillsboro House, they had also acquired a maid named Dorothy, whom Jack regarded as a "dead beat."[37] By August, she would be joined by her sister Ivy.[38] The household had also hosted Miss Wiblin, Maureen's music teacher, who regularly appeared for tea and supper in addition to lessons, and who persuaded Jack to tutor her in Latin. She passed from the formal to the familiar when Jack bestowed on her the nickname "Smudge."[39]

For someone who did not like games and complained not only of team sports but also of the sort of games played by the gentry to amuse themselves in Ireland, Jack took up games rather enthusiastically once he was under the same roof as Janie Moore, who appears to have enjoyed parlor games. They played a prodigious amount of bridge in the evenings, but also croquet in the afternoons. He even played ping-pong and badminton, but he drew the line at tennis, which he always managed to avoid. There always seemed to be a crowd of people around who needed entertaining with games.

Janie's hospitality went beyond her near relations, Jack's friends, and acquaintances of their acquaintances. She also extended herself to every hard-luck story in the neighborhood, and she seemed to always know everything going on in Headington. The case of Maisie Hawes illustrates the compassionate turn of Janie Moore and the ensuing unintended consequences. Maisie was badly treated at home, suffering both emotional and physical abuse from her parents, Commander and Mrs. Hawes. Maisie related tales of being forced to do all the work at home and to discontinue her schooling. Finally, Mrs. Hawes told her and the other children that Maisie was not her child but the illegitimate child of her sister. This information only added to her abuse by other children.[40] Jack thought Maisie was honest, cheerful, intelligent, and talented as a dancer, while having only a slight "vulgar accent," so he decided to consult Owen Barfield about how she could advance her dancing career, since Barfield was a keen dancer himself. While this drama unfolded, Smudge seemed to be moving toward a nervous breakdown, often sinking into hysterics and fits of nerves while somehow present at Hillsboro House almost every day.

Maisie spent more and more time at Hillsboro House and regularly danced for the assembled crowd after supper. Jack, who could not resist calling people by other names than those given at birth, including himself, took to calling Mrs. Hawes "the Bitch."[41] Jack then took the matter to his friend Baker, who had moved back to London to live with his three aunts upon finishing his degree. There he planned to pursue a career on the stage. Baker's "sensible aunt," who ran a club for young girls on the stage, took an interest in Maisie's situation.[42] Next, Mrs. Moore consulted a solicitor to determine if Maisie, who was nineteen, could leave home without her parents' permission. Learning that Maisie was free to leave, Jack wrote to Baker to solicit his help and that of his sensible aunt in finding a place for Maisie in London.[43] Meanwhile, Smudge grew ever more hysterical and somehow managed to be sleeping at Hillsboro House.[44] After a fierce altercation between Maisie and Commander Hawes with Jack present, Maisie fled her home under cover of darkness for refuge at Hillsboro House, and Mrs. Moore, Jack, and Andrée concocted a plan to spirit Maisie away to London, where Baker and his sensible aunt could help her find a place dancing.[45] After much surreptitious traveling by Maisie back and forth between London and Oxford, where she stayed at the Warneford Road house that the Pasleys had sublet, Ivy had a heart attack. By this time Jack had bestowed on Maisie her new name— "Moppie."[46] Meanwhile, Smudge flitted about saying she really should go home to her own house, until Mrs. Moore insisted that she stay, much to the consternation of Jack, who had finally grown tired of Smudge's constant presence.[47] Finally, Moppie found a position in Cardiff, and Jack was sure that Mrs. Moore's kindness had not been misplaced.[48]

Which leads to the punch line. From Baker, Jack learned that Moppie had not been entirely truthful with them.[49] Nonetheless, Janie signed as guarantor of Moppie's contract, obliging Janie to pay fifty pounds if Moppie broke the contract.[50] In the end, Jack and Janie went to considerable expense to help Moppie relocate, with the understanding that they would be repaid a little each week. Time went by without any money forthcoming, and the philanthropic pair realized that Moppie was not quite as honest as they had originally thought.[51] One night sitting up late talking, Lewis and Mrs. Moore discussed the large number of people who had failed them or even become their enemies. Jack reflected that with few exceptions, he "loathed the female sex."[52] This sentiment would find expression in some of his fiction.

With the coming of October, Jack began his tutorials in English with Frank Percy Wilson of Exeter College and Edith Elizabeth Wardale of St Hugh's Hall, one of the few women's colleges at Oxford. Jack viewed Wilson as young and fat with an impressive face, while Miss Wardale was old and pallid with a monstrous lower lip that hung low to expose her irregular gum.[53] With Miss Wardale's help, however, he finally realized his dream that began at Great Bookham of learning Anglo-Saxon.[54] Jack's diary reflects the usual activity at the start of Michaelmas term in Oxford: buying an undergraduate gown (though one wonders what happened to the one he already had), finding lectures of interest, and meeting tutors. One passing remark deserves notice. A large group of undergraduates had assembled in a lecture hall in the Examination Schools building, only to be told they were in the wrong lecture hall. Though they had come early, they arrived in the correct hall late. Jack noted that this situation fulfilled the scripture that the first should be last.[55] This kind of offhand humor demonstrates an important matter in the case of young atheist Lewis. He had a thorough knowledge of the Bible while not believing a word of it. This storehouse of knowledge, however, helps us understand one of the reasons Lewis could acquire the role of Christian apologist so soon after his conversion, but other reasons shall become apparent. That first lecture he attended also reinforces the idea, already advanced, that Lewis could earn his English degree in one year because he had already mastered the material through his pleasure reading at Great Bookham. His remark about the lecture was that Henry Cecil Kennedy Wyld, whom Jack would nickname "the Cad," went on for an hour without saying anything that he had not known for five years.[56]

Though Jack Lewis was still growing out of his earlier arrogance in 1922, he had also become his own severest critic. While writing one of his first essays in the English School, he observed that his prose style was "abominable" and he doubted that he would ever improve it.[57] Time would prove him wrong in this matter, as in others.

His new studies in English literature gave Lewis the opportunity for many conversations with friends about things that had interested him for years. He had long loved the stories of chivalry and the knight in service to a great lady, a dangerous quest in which the hero risked all for the great prize at the end of the world. In a conversation with his friend Jenkin, Jack argued that the chivalric ideal, regardless of the extent to which it might ever have been realized, had been a great advance in civilization. Everything that Jack attributed to the "Knightly standard," however, Jenkin argued had come as the result of Christianity. So many of his conversations kept turning to Christianity in the end.[58] On another occasion, Lewis found Jenkin in a deep depression the morning after a conversation with a Christian about death and the possibility of life after death. They then rode their bicycles out to the Church of St Margaret in Binsey, an establishment that dated from 730, and there they commiserated that they had both lately suffered from a fear of death.[59] Back in Jenkin's rooms at tea they continued to wonder if it was better to think about death or not. Jack resolved that one should continue to think about it until one no longer cared.[60]

At the end of October, Jack's aunt Lily Hamilton Suffern, his mother's eldest sister, moved to nearby Forest Hill, where her cottage had a view of Shotover Hill, a place Jack loved more and more. He noted in his diary that within three days of her arrival, she had "snubbed a bookseller in Oxford, written to the local paper, crossed swords with the Vicar's wife, and started a quarrel with her landlord."[61] She was a brilliant, difficult woman who began writing a tract on women's suffrage that somehow had grown to include "the significance of heroism and maternal instinct, the nature of matter, the primal One, the value of Christianity, and the purpose of existence."[62] Her idiosyncratic philosophy managed to synthesize Schopenhauer, theosophy, Bergson, and Plotinus. Jack liked her very much and visited her often. On the other hand, she could exasperate her nephew, who noted in his diary that what he could not "stand about her is that she knows everything: the Holy Ghost discusses all his plans with her and she was on the committee that arranged creation."[63]

Regardless of the topic of conversation, every time Jack spoke with the Doc, the subject seemed to end in an exploration of some deep dimension of the spiritual, and usually death. On Armistice Night in 1922, while Jack walked with the Doc back to his home after tea, the Doc said that if you really thought about all the horrors of life, "you couldn't endure this world for an hour."[64] A few nights later, Jack and Mrs. Moore ended the evening with a gloomy discussion of "death and chance and permanent danger."[65]

A few days before his birthday, Jack walked over Shotover Hill thinking about how he could write his own version of the Psyche myth. By this time, he had named Psyche's older sister Caspian, a name he would save till he could use it in his Narnia stories. It was a gray day, and he chanced upon a path he had never taken that led into a glen with large trees that reminded him of Ireland. And then it happened. He had the feeling again. It was a "very good touch of the right feeling."[66] He had experienced joy again, but at this time in his life, he sought to give this experience of longing a psychological explanation of wish fulfillment. He had now absorbed Freud and his company deeply into his understanding of the world. His aunt Lily offered him an explanation of his "complexes" through the lens of his ongoing poetic masterpiece, "Dymer."[67]

Several times during the fall of 1922, Jack and Maureen had gone to concerts in Oxford. They had attended orchestral performances as well as opera. In early December they attended an afternoon concert in the Sheldonian Theatre, where the orchestra played a number of selections, including some pieces from Handel's *Messiah*. Lewis was surprised that the *Messiah* had given him such pleasure, since he had turned against Handel during his "Wagner craze."[68] The concert ended with the audience joining in the singing of Christmas carols, but what Lewis liked most was the view he had from the top box window where they sat, which gave him an afternoon perspective on the "Bridge of Sighs" framed by the Clarendon Building and Bodleian Library.[69]

Even at the end of the term, Lewis stayed busy attending the lectures that George Stuart Gordon gave on Shakespeare, attending the Martlets, visiting his friends, preparing for his tutorials with Wilson and Wardale, and reading voluminously. The continuing drama of his domestic situation came on top of all his academic responsibilities.

The drama that came with his adopted family never let up. He attended Maureen's confirmation at Christ Church Cathedral on Thursday, December 14, with the bishop presiding. Lewis felt suffocated and nervous. Afterward, he had a long discussion with the Doc during which they agreed that the whole ceremony was a "farce." They then proceeded to discuss epiphenomenalism and parallelism before drifting into psychology and Jack's difficulty in being "self conscious in solitude."[70] When they did not talk about psychology or death, however, Jack liked to hear the Doc repeat his stories of adventure up the Amazon. The Doc had actually been to the world's end when he sailed the Straits of Magellan.[71] He had lived out the romantic ideal that Jack had loved in the stories of Spenser, Mallory, Morris, and MacDonald.

The drama of the Moore-Askins family only reminded Lewis of the drama of his own family. December meant the annual trip home to Little Lea and his father for Christmas. He left Oxford on December 23 to spend the morning with Leo Baker in London before meeting Warnie at Euston Station in the late afternoon. Baker told Jack that Owen Barfield was engaged to a woman who was about thirteen years his senior. Baker was acting at the Old Vic Theatre and making a go of it. Throughout the day, Jack was worried about the recurring pain of his old war wound, which he would long bear silently. He had noted the pain from time to time, but it had hurt more than usual during this week as he anticipated his journey to Belfast.[72] In addition to the pain under his arm, he suffered a perpetual headache during his visit. It was a miserable time as he reacted to every utterance and mannerism of his father, attempted to dodge invitations from family and friends, and sought to avoid the obligatory church services. In that mood, 1922 came to an end. The Christmas vacation, however, had not ended. Jack spent a fortnight with his father after Christmas before return- ing to Oxford on January 12. During this time, his greatest en- ergy was devoted to preventing his father from knowing that Mrs. Moore was writing to him via the good services of Arthur Greeves's mother, who was not very clever at maintaining a subterfuge. The night before leaving Little Lea, however, Lewis took up his volume of George MacDonald's *Phantastes*, which he had read many times and which, he noted, filled for him the place of a devotional book.[73]

Upon arriving in Oxford, Lewis found that 1923 had not gotten off to a very good start. It would get worse. Moppie had written to suggest that she would stay with Mrs. Moore and Jack for six months while traveling into London three days a week for dancing lessons—all at their expense! Mrs. Moore and Jack labored over a reply that would meet the situation, making clear that they were poor. At this point, we begin to see a parting in the ways of personality between Jack and Janie Moore. Though she was enthusiastic about getting involved in Moppie's life, she soon tired of it all. Jack, on the other hand, held out hope in spite of their experience.[74]

Far worse than Moppie, however, were the growing signs of a change in the Doc. Conversation between him and Jack ceased to be interesting. Mrs. Moore and Jack heard him swearing to himself in the bathroom, which Jack thought a bad sign in a man like Dr. Askins. He also seemed to dwell on theosophical philosophy. While the Doc deteriorated, they still had Cranny on their hands regularly at tea. One of their conversations bears noting, because it contains the core of a question that perplexed Lewis and would make its way, in slightly refined form, into *Mere Christianity*. Cranny asked what they should make of Christ apart from the question of his divinity. Was he a teacher or a fanatic?[75] Here we have the kind of actual question in life that prompted Lewis's threefold option: devil, madman, or God.

The year also began with Jack observing that he had no more friends at the university. Every one of his close friends had "gone down." Late in the month, Barfield burst upon the household for a quick visit. He was in town giving dancing lessons. The *Beacon*, the little literary magazine where he worked, was going under even as he faced the prospect of marriage. His conversation with Jack revolved around the tug within him as to whether materialism was the real answer to reality. He was back and forth on the matter at this point, but the struggle had begun for him, and Jack would follow.[76]

An Enthusiastic Sensible Man

The few people that Jack still knew in Oxford did not interest him, but then the Hilary term began. George Gordon held a discussion class that Jack attended, and there he met Nevill Coghill, who read a paper that earned Jack's approval. In his diary, Jack noted that Coghill "seems an enthusiastic sensible man, without nonsense, and a gentleman, much more attractive than the majority."[77] He liked Coghill from the start and was "pleasantly surprised" when Coghill arrived at tea with Miss Wardale two days later. They had what Lewis had come to value highly—a good long conversation. They agreed on many matters. Coghill was also Irish and had served in the war. He had even been seized by a mob during the Irish uprising and had been threatened with hanging or shooting. Two things came out, however, that set them apart. Coghill was not a materialist, and he was a Christian. Lewis thought that Coghill's mind was inferior to Barfield's and Beckett's, but he had a high regard for him nonetheless.[78] He would become a good friend in the years to come. Far sooner, he became a member of the Martlets with the responsibility for taking minutes of the discussion. On occasion, the minutes were recorded in Chaucerian verse![79]

Looking back on his first meeting with Coghill, Lewis recalled that their friendship occurred immediately, for Coghill was a man after his own heart.[80] Coghill threatened Lewis in a new way he had not expected. Jack had taken on what he called his "New Look" since going up to Oxford. He had no time for the old romance, the dreams of the end of the world, anything supernatural, or even his old pessimism. He was a thoroughly modern man. Coghill, on the other hand, had something old-fashioned about him. Remembering Coghill from some thirty years later, Lewis thought of him as the sort of fellow who would fight a duel. His old-fashioned sense of chivalry, honor, courage, freedom, and gentility all conspired to make Coghill a thoroughly admirable character. It made Jack wonder if the modern world had actually lost something along the way that Coghill, with all his Christianity and supernaturalism, had retained.[81]

Coghill belonged to one of those Anglo-Irish aristocratic families, complete with estate and baronetcy. As a younger son, he would not inherit title or estate, but he did inherit the frame of mind. His uncle, for whom he was named, had been killed in the Zulu War in South Africa and became a bit of a national hero for his part in upholding the empire. His father, Sir Patrick Coghill, had studied painting in Paris and became an accomplished landscape artist. Coghill's mother was the younger sister of Edith Somerville, who, with their cousin Violet Martin, wrote a number of successful stories and novels under the pen name of Somerville and Ross.[82] Perhaps the most long-lasting of these was *Some Experiences of an Irish R. M.*, which was adapted and produced as a series by the BBC, starring Peter Bowles (1983–1985). In future years, Coghill would develop a love of theater that seems consistent with his family's artistic and romantic nature. Within ten days of their first meeting, Jack had spent a good deal of time with Coghill and had learned that he agreed with his view "that women were bores until they were forty."[83] What Lewis did not then know, nor perhaps Coghill, was that Coghill would live quietly as a homosexual the rest of his life after first marrying, fathering a child, and obtaining a divorce.[84]

On Saint Valentine's evening in 1923, Lewis took part in an important conversation following his paper on Spenser at a meeting of the Martlets. The conversation is important because he recorded it nearly verbatim in his diary, something he rarely did. In the discussion, Lewis expounded his view of art, which he would expound for the rest of his life. In brief form, he made clear his opposition to the trend of all the arts following World War I, a trend that focused on art as the expression of the artist. Lewis insisted that such an understanding of art would not do because art is "a social thing." He insisted that art has always involved communication and not merely expression. Thus he identified himself with a critical tradition that he probably never realized he had joined. Edgar Allan Poe had argued that the purpose of art is to create an effect in its audience. Lewis insisted that art aims at creating "the right emotion in the audience."[85] True art, therefore, depends not simply on the artist intending that it be art but on it actually succeeding at some level to be art. It requires intention on the part of the artist to have some impact on the audience: sorrow, mirth, terror, excitement, longing. Lewis's insistence that art involves communication also meant that art involves meaning. He returned to this idea in his inaugural lecture at Cambridge in 1954, when he accepted the chair of Medieval and Renaissance Literature. For the time being, however, Lewis had to abandon reflection and analysis due to the domestic travails of his household. Janie Moore's brother Dr. John Askins, whom Lewis adored, was swiftly going mad.

The Doc's Descent into Madness

On Wednesday, February 21, 1923, the Doc turned up at the house in an agitated state. Jack and Mrs. Moore were engaged in high-level negotiations with the landlord, and the Doc left. Mrs. Moore told Jack that she thought her brother was close to a breakdown.[86] On Friday, he returned and began raving that he was filled with "horrible blasphemous and obscene thoughts."[87] He calmed down, but then he had two more episodes of raving about going to hell and being doomed to insanity and death. He was sure his misery stemmed from his case of venereal disease during college days. Dr. Hitchens, the local general practitioner, was summoned, and Dr. Robert Askins, the brother of Janie and the Doc, also arrived. Rob Askins insisted that the Doc was suffering from neurasthenia, the condition known colloquially at the time as "shell-shock," or what is now called post-traumatic stress disorder. The Doc responded to this opinion by rolling on the floor, screaming, and contorting his face with shrieks that he was damned forever and ever. They chloroformed the Doc and tried to keep him sedated in the evenings with narcotics while deciding what to do with him. For the next three weeks, Lewis would spend much of his time trying to restrain the Doc, who had surprising strength.[88]

The efforts of the family focused on having the Doc admitted to the Pensions Hospital for military veterans who suffered from neurasthenia. Maureen went to stay with Lady Gonner, their neighbor and friend. The Doc and his wife, Mary, came to live with Mrs. Moore, who had the responsibility of caring for them both. Rob Askins went back to Bristol, much to the irritation of Jack.

The Doc's growing madness had an unnerving effect on Jack, who sat with him and held his hand for hours on end. He had never seen madness before, and he feared that it could happen to him as well. For four days, Jack got little sleep, and he feared sleeping, lest he have nightmares himself. Only after four days did Jack find time in the midst of the turmoil to shave.[89] When he had time to think again, he found himself highly resentful of Rob Askins and Mary Askins. Rob simply left. Mary expected to be waited on: prepare her bath, fix her cocoa, bring her biscuits in bed. Jack could not abide her selfish, rude, ungrateful gluttony.[90] We may see echoes of her in *The Great Divorce*.

The days took on a sullen sameness as Jack and Janie struggled to keep the Doc under control until something could be done. The Doc continued episodically with screams and horrible contortions while raving hysterically about going to hell. Between attacks, he could behave somewhat lucidly, but without the old ability to carry on a conversation. Nights may have been worse. They tried to sedate him, but his constitution resisted the effect of the drugs for an hour or more after they gave his dose, which he usually resisted. Jack and Mrs. Moore got little sleep. The Doc and Mary slept late each morning after his nocturnal attacks, while Jack and Janie had to get on with their daily responsibilities.

In this climate, Jack could not do his preparation for his tutorials with Wilson and Wardale. They were sympathetic, but they reminded him that "this waste of time" was a serious matter for him.[91] He missed the better part of three weeks in an eight-week term when he was trying to do a three-year degree in nine months! Throughout this three-week ordeal, he managed to get to Gordon's discussion class and to his tutorials, even though unprepared. Jenkin regularly came out to see him and take him out for a long bicycle ride around the county, but they never discussed anything of importance on these jaunts.

Rob Askins returned from Bristol on March 1, 1923, and stayed till March 5, during which time he arranged for Dr. Goode from the Pensions Hospital to exam the Doc for eligibility to be admitted there. What terrified the family concerned the actual cause of the Doc's condition. If the examiner determined that he suffered from effects of syphilis, then he would not only be ineligible for care at the military hospital; he might also lose part of his pension.[92] Goode came to Headington to examine the Doc. Mrs. Moore listened at the door as Goode examined him with just Dr. Askins present. Jack could not stand the suspense and went upstairs to smoke for what was the "windiest" time he had endured, except when he was under fire during the war.[93]

In the end, Dr. Goode concluded that the Doc was not insane or suffering from the aftereffects of syphilis. He had neurasthenia as a result of his war experiences; therefore, he was entitled to a place in the Pensions Hospital at Henley.[94] With this matter settled, Rob went back to Bristol and left the Doc with Mrs. Moore and Jack to handle. The Doc grew more agitated and violent with each passing day until he was finally admitted on March 12. In the end, however, the Doc was moved to Richmond.[95] This aspect of the ordeal was over. When Mary finally left on March 14, she gave Jack a wool waistcoat to express her appreciation. He noted that even though she was an American, she was not stingy.[96]

The whole terrifying experience of being so close to the Doc as he descended into insanity had a sobering effect on Jack. He thought that the Doc's interest in spiritualism and his "undigested psychoanalysis" had caused his unraveling, and Jack intended to avoid such things in the future.[97] Years later, C. S. Lewis recalled that the combination of his belief that the Doc's insanity was a result of his preoccupation with spiritual matters and Cranny's relentless effort to find some evidence that he might survive death created in Lewis a complete aversion to the whole idea of life continuing after physical death. In addition to these experiences, Jack's enamoredness with psychology had convinced him that the idea of anything beyond the whole of the universe constituted nothing but fantasy or "wishful thinking." He classified his experiences of Joy as similar flights of imagination that somehow must be only sex substitutes.[98]

After three weeks in Dante's inferno with the Doc, the household slid into a state of depression as Jack and Mrs. Moore contemplated their finances in relation to their desire to find a better housing situation. These concerns only led to a deeper state of anxiety over Jack's employment prospects once he finished his English degree. He wanted to stay in Oxford, but no positions seemed to be opening for him. Carritt and Stevenson advised him to think about finding something at one of the minor universities. (Other than Oxford and Cambridge, all other universities were minor universities.) They assured him that freelance work as a private tutor was a thing of the past. Mrs. Moore told him that wherever he went, she and Maureen would have to stay in Oxford for Maureen's music instruction.[99] After weeks of silence without writing to his father while distracted by the Doc's descent into madness, Jack finally wrote to lie that he had been down with the flu.[100]

Warnie returned to Oxford for a five-day visit on March 29. Jack had looked forward to the visit, but in the aftermath of the ordeal with the Doc, he found Warnie's cynicism unconducive to a jolly time. Then it occurred to him that he could borrow money from Warnie, who had a good income. Alas, Warnie spent his money faster than it came in, so he could not help Jack in his plan to change residences, a scheme always on the minds of Jack and Mrs. Moore. Those familiar with C. S. Lewis may think of the Eagle and Child as his favorite pub. It was where he went with his literary friends on Tuesday mornings for many years, but it would not have been his favorite pub. When Warnie came to town, they first tried the Roebuck and later chose the Mitre, which would be a favorite for decades.[101]

No sooner had Warnie left than news came from Rob Askins that the Doc had died of heart failure—a rather imprecise condition of which everyone dies—on Friday, April 6, 1923.[102] The family held the funeral in the coastal town of Clevedon, near Bristol. Cranny shared the responsibility for saying the funeral with Mrs. Moore's third brother, the Reverend William Askins, known as Willie, a clergyman from Cavan, in Ulster. Jack and Cranny had more talk of immortality and the unlikeliness of the proposition. The whole experience left Jack depressed, anxious, lazy, and irritable so that he stopped writing in his diary for a week. Just when things looked the darkest, news came that he and Mrs. Moore could rent Hillsboro House on a more or less permanent basis, which lifted their spirits tremendously. Janie's brother Willie loaned her thirty pounds to pay the furniture movers.[103] Then, at Janie's insistence, Jack once again resumed keeping his diary.[104]

Before moving into Hillsboro House, Janie required a complete redecoration. They put up new wallpaper, and what they did not paper, they painted. They rented a stove for the kitchen. With the flurry of activity, Jack did not keep his diary for three weeks, resuming on May 21. He had also neglected writing letters. When he finally wrote to Arthur Greeves, Jack urged him never to get a neurosis like the Doc. Jack reasoned that both he and Arthur were susceptible to neurosis since they had both been afraid of their fathers as children. The Doc's consulting physician, who was both a psychoanalyst and a neurological specialist, appears to have advised Jack to avoid introspection, brooding, spiritualism, and anything eccentric. In addition, Jack thought they should work hard, get plenty of fresh air, and have a cheerful disposition (this from Jack, the pessimist). Jack cautioned Arthur that they held their mental health by a thread![105]

Examinations and Beyond

Jack had lost much time and energy with the Doc's breakdown and death. He had only a short time left before his examinations for his English degree, and then he would have to find a position. He had dreams of obtaining a fellowship that had just come open at Exeter College.[106] In a letter to his father in May, Jack expressed his disappointment upon hearing a rumor that the fellowship at Exeter College was not really an opening at all, since the college had always intended to fill the position with one of their own. He was learning the way of the world. He acknowledged to his father what he had already noted before, that his success in the English School resulted primarily from already knowing all the material from his youthful years of pleasure reading.[107]

As it turned out, the Exeter fellowship went not to the young Exeter man, as gossip had foretold, but to a most deserving Balliol man. While not restoring his faith in humanity, the facts made Jack feel better about losing to a man of merit. Looking forward, he explained to his father in a 1923 letter that he felt sure he would be qualified for a schoolmaster position somewhere. Then he broached the idea that he could even stay in Oxford and do a research degree like the BLitt or the DPhil without actually asking his father to foot the bill. Finally, he requested that his father send him some ready money to cover his current expenses.[108]

In May and June as he prepared for his examinations, Jack somehow found time to go cycling around the county with Jenkin and to talk with him about the kinds of things Jack liked to discuss. They had the idea of writing a horror story about a scientist who discovers how to keep the brain and nerve endings of a corpse alive after a person dies.[109] This idea would eventually find its way into print when Lewis wrote *That Hideous Strength* at the end of World War II. Besides Jenkin, Nevill Coghill was the friend he spent most time with in the final weeks of his undergraduate days. He wrote in his diary that he liked and admired Coghill but that, for some reason, he tended to misrepresent him in writing about him, a habit he strove to overcome. He pondered why this should be so.[110] Perhaps it was because this man, whom he admired and with whom he found no real fault, was a Christian.

On June 14, 1923, Lewis began his examinations for his degree. Known as Schools, the examinations involved a series of essays and continued from Thursday through the following Tuesday with a break on Sunday. On the last day, Coghill informed Jack that one of their number, Strick by name, had a nervous breakdown in the middle of Schools.[111] After the exams, Jack slipped into a mild depression for a few days and managed to pull himself out of it only by a fit of anger over his poverty after Mrs. Moore fell and hurt her elbow while housecleaning. In response, he threw himself into the redecorating by laying linoleum tile.[112] Next, he undertook to refinish the floors![113] Then, after many games of croquet with Maureen Moore and many afternoon excursions, Jack came upon a hedge of wild roses while exploring a new path in the country. In a moment, he had a renewal of that experience of Joy that had captured him since childhood: "This, in the cool of the evening, together with some curious illusion of being on the slope of a much bigger hill than I really was, and the wind in the hedge, gave me intense pleasure with a lot of vague reminiscences."[114] The feeling did not linger. He was soon back in the world in which he needed to find a place. It was a world of stress in which Mrs. Moore added a new tendency to fall and Jack had more-frequent headaches.

Most of Jack's closest friends had gone down from Oxford the previous year, none of them having secured academic appointments. Cecil Harwood came for a visit for the weekend of July 7 full of excitement about his new discovery, Rudolf Steiner, who Harwood claimed had "made the burden roll from his back."[115] Steiner had abandoned theosophy (divine wisdom) to create anthroposophy (human wisdom) a decade earlier. Owen Barfield had also joined in devotion to Steiner, whom Lewis viewed with some contempt. All that Lewis could make out at the time was that Steiner promoted some sort of panpsychist spiritualism, which Lewis regarded as little more than an imaginative anthropomorphic projection on nature. This new venture for Harwood and Barfield would have enormous repercussions for Lewis over the next seven years, but one would never suspect it from this first encounter. In the course of the weekend, a rare conversation about politics arose when Jack's American friend, Stead, arrived for tea with tales of his trip to Italy. He praised the new spirit abroad in Italy under the leadership of Mussolini. Everyone regarded the fascist movement favorably except Harwood, who said that it was only a more successful version of the Ku Klux Klan.[116] Lewis would come to change his mind about the Italian leader and his movement, but that change, along with others, lay in his future.

A few days after Harwood left, Arthur Greeves arrived for a fortnight at Hillsboro House. During the first week of his visit, Jack learned that he had earned a first in English, a distinction he shared with only one other person that year—Nevill Coghill.[117] Jack and Arthur reminisced about the things that thrilled them as teenagers, but they had both changed. Jack was annoyed that Arthur had fallen in with a crowd that extolled the virtues of being oneself, which to Arthur meant that he should do whatever he felt like doing. Arthur insisted that it was wrong to suppress one's inclinations, to which Jack tried in vain to distinguish between self-control and repression. The worst offense came when Arthur came into the dining room at midday and propped his bare feet on the table.[118] The episode is important for the development of Jack's views, because Arthur sought to be a "natural" man while also insisting on being kind to people. Jack insisted that kindness does not happen in the natural state of people, except by accident. Kindness is alien to the concept of natural selection. Yet Arthur was kind. Could something else be going on besides nature? This is the kind of thought that would begin to plague Lewis.

Making Ends Meet

Albert Lewis had funded an extra year at Oxford so that Jack would be a more marketable candidate for a teaching post there. Having completed his second degree without the offer of a fellowship at a college, however, Jack had to find a way to survive with Janie Moore in their poverty. To earn some money, he spent twelve hours a day grading English essays for the English certificate offered by the board of education. In a letter to his friend Jenkin, he posed the situation of reading one illiterate essay after another on the same subject, "The Conquest of the Air," and having to read about Montgolfier balloons and the possibility of a helicopter. He wondered what a helicopter might be.[119] Further income came from renting out a room.

Maurice Delanges came from Valenciennes in France.[120] He spoke good English, but Jack did not like him. He combined Jack's lifelong prejudice against the French with rude manners and money. Jack referred to him as nouveau riche and called him the Blackguard.[121] Jack also mentioned to Jenkin that the Blackguard had some mixture of black blood, so some level of racial prejudice typical of a great colonial power at the time probably operated.[122] In his diary, Jack described the ordeal of enduring the Blackguard's table manners as he reached in front of others to grab food, and the trials of restraining him from pulling Maureen's hair and pressing his hands against her while they were eating. He also recorded a series of unendurable conversational exchanges.[123] The Blackguard ruined Jack's happy homelife. Jack hated being poor, and the Blackguard's stay was only a reminder of the fact. He remained at Hillsboro from July 30 until September 10, 1923, a period of misery for the little household during which not even a visit from Warnie made things better.[124] The one bright spot was that their maid, Dorothy, with whom they had been dissatisfied for some time, was replaced by Ada, "an enormous girl of fifteen" who worked hard and spoke only when spoken to.[125] By the following January, however, Ada would prove as mortal as Dorothy.

The other major changes to the household included the addition of the puppy, Pat, and the demise of the old cat, Tibbie.[126]

Without a real job, Jack worked as much as he could on his grand poem, "Dymer," which he hoped would establish his reputation as a major poet. He had been sending portions to his most valued literary friends for their comments and advice, and Janie Moore was particularly encouraging of his literary ambitions. In September, he also made a renewed effort at a treatment of the story of Psyche and Cupid. He had tried it as a ballad and in couplet form, but nothing quite worked. He would struggle with the problem for years until he worked it out in prose form as *Till We Have Faces*.[127]

At the end of September, Jack went for his dreaded but obligatory three-week visit with his father in Ireland. He did not keep his diary during this period, probably because the visit filled him with too much anxiety and distress. Nor did he keep his diary on several other occasions in 1923, always periods of great distress. Two important things happened, however, that relieved the pressures of life. First, his father offered to continue supporting him until he found a permanent position.[128] Second, Jack had a new experience of Joy while walking along the Castlereagh hills.[129] His rational self had decided that he wanted no more of the supernatural after witnessing the Doc's slide into insanity, but his spiritual self longed for the renewal of the inexplicable experience.

In November, perhaps to demonstrate to his father that he was doing all he could to earn a little money on his own, Jack wrote to Albert to say that the new master of University College, Sir Michael Sadler, had sent a book review written by Jack to six different editors in an effort to help him earn a little side income, though it came to nothing. He also let Albert know that he had undertaken the coaching of a private pupil in writing essays.[130]

Jack did not keep his diary after October 21, 1923, until January 1, 1924. It is unfortunate in one respect. A note in his diary gives a general picture of what had transpired during the interval, the most interesting matter involving Owen Barfield's abandonment of materialism as he embraced anthroposophy. Barfield and Lewis had several long discussions about the change, but we do not have the substantive details.[131] We do know that their prolonged dialogue would eventually play a role in Lewis's abandonment of materialism.

Matter, Morality, Money, and Moore

The most important matter at this stage in their relationship, however, involved a view of history. Like all good modernists since the Enlightenment, Lewis held the view that new ideas were good and old ideas were bad. Perhaps more charitably, he believed that old ideas had been superseded by superior ones. This kind of thinking is a by-product of modern technology, in which new machines and labor-saving devices are better than old ones. Thus, Lewis had a prejudice against the validity of old beliefs from an earlier time simply because they were old. Ideas about the spiritual world and biblical faith came under this category. In conversation with Barfield, Lewis abandoned this view, which Barfield called "chronological snobbery."[132] Jack came to recognize the distinction between an idea or belief being out of fashion and being untrue. He was slowly realizing that the "spirit of the age" was merely the latest fad and not grounds for belief or disbelief. This shift freed him from the emotional constraint against accepting the possibility of old ideas like spiritual reality in addition to physical reality.

With the beginning of 1924, Jack explored the possibility of pursuing the DPhil degree with a thesis on the ethics of Henry More (1614–1687). He eventually decided against it, but the exercise demonstrated Lewis's concern for the problem of right and wrong. It would prove an impossible or impassable obstacle to his comfortable materialism. After reading Bertrand Russell's "Worship of a Free Man," Jack concluded that Russell did not grasp the real problem of ethics and morality: "that our ideals are after all a natural product, facts with a relation to all other facts, and cannot survive the condemnation of the fact as a whole. The Promethean attitude would be tenable only if we were really members of some other whole outside the real whole: wh. we're not."[133] Here in brief form, we have the argument Lewis would advance for the existence of God in "Right and Wrong as a Clue to the Meaning of the Universe," later published as the opening section of *Mere Christianity*. He did not believe it yet, but he had worked it out. A brute, material universe has no values, no ethics, no morality. It only has facts. How then do we account for ethics and morality? The term "Promethean attitude" would refer to the mythological figure Prometheus, who gave to humans the gift of fire, for which he was severely punished by the other gods. It seemed to Lewis that ethics and morality must come from outside the material world of chance, cause, and effect. Lewis thought this answer could not be true because, to his materialist mind, nothing existed apart from the chain of causality in matter. It was a nagging problem.

When Jack learned of a fellowship that had opened at St John's College, he began work on a thesis to present to that college in support of his application. He intended to refute the idea of ethics coming from outside the material world in an essay titled "The Promethean Fallacy of Ethics."[134] He managed to complete his application just before contracting chicken pox on January 28, having caught it from Maureen, who had been sick for the previous two weeks.[135] He did not keep his diary during his illness, but he did grow a beard. Once recovered, he shaved the beard but kept the moustache for a while.[136] Just before he came down with chicken pox, Jack had learned that Nevill Coghill had been offered a fellowship at Exeter College. Jack, however, did not have such good news with his application to St John's. After a long silence between Oxford and Belfast, he wrote to Albert with all his news, and to ask for money. His scholarship had come to an end, so Jack needed not only what his father had been sending him for four years but more, in order to make up the portion that the scholarship no longer provided. It was a humiliating situation to ask for money from a generous father for whom Jack felt such contempt.[137] On the happy side, a new cat named Biddy Anne had decided to live at Hillsboro.[138]

Until 1924, Janie Moore had exuded hospitality. She served tea to one and all. She always had room for one more overnight guest. She could always add water to the soup. Then Pasley and his wife invited themselves for the weekend. Mrs. Moore insisted on doing all the cooking, the washing up, and every other task at hand. Jack tried several times to intervene before she finally burst out in exasperation, "Do you want me to die?" The work excused her from sitting with the Pasleys, who proved to be a laborious couple to entertain. She decided that she was getting too old to slave over "two young slips who thought such a lot of themselves."[139] Young Lewis felt real anguish over watching Mrs. Moore work like a servant because he was born into a family with servants. Cooking, washing, making beds, and all the other family tasks that went on in houses all over England and Ireland were for servants, from the perspective of Jack Lewis. His parents had intended him to live as a gentleman and not to do menial labor. He learned the lesson well, and this outlook made ordinary life without money a terribly depressing ordeal. In the end, his father agreed to send him more, increasing his allowance from sixty-seven to eighty-five pounds per term. Albert also suggested that Jack could save money if he spent more time at home with him—the ultimate horror.[140]

At a dinner given by Carritt, his old philosophy tutor, Jack learned of a fellowship in philosophy coming vacant at Trinity College with a handsome salary of five hundred pounds per year.[141] A fellowship at All Souls College also came open. While Mrs. Moore encouraged him to apply for the fellowships, she discouraged him from pursuing the DPhil, which she regarded as a waste of time. Jack complied in all regards and so informed his father.[142]

The Hand of God

In early March 1924, Jack had been reading G. K. Chesterton's biography of Francis of Assisi and mused over whether Christianity had made any immediate difference in the lives of the masses. The next day when he left the library at University College at four o'clock, he found himself suddenly enraptured again by the experience of Joy. The stone seemed softer, the birds sang, the air felt cold and rare. Oxford looked better than it had ever looked before.[143] Then he went on with his business.

It was an ordinary week in the ordinary life of Jack Lewis, but looking back from the perspective of middle age, C. S. Lewis would describe the events of five days between March 4 and 8 in 1924 as involving three of the most critical moments in his capitulation to the God who was not supposed to exist. On March 4, Lewis decided to read the *Hippolytus*, by Euripides, as part of a spontaneous decision to practice his Greek. On March 6, he had his renewed experience of Joy. On March 8, he took Samuel Alexander's *Space, Time, and Deity* from the Oxford Union library and read it in the garden of Wadham College. Mixed between these events, he reread his paper on the Promethean fallacy, and he read Chesterton. When he wrote *Surprised by Joy*, Lewis placed these events in the final grand move leading up to his conversion, which still lay years in the future. He placed these events after his long debates with Owen Barfield, which he dubbed "The Great War." In fact, the debates with Barfield would come several years later.

How could Lewis have been so confused about the timing of these things? I do not believe that Lewis was confused at all. As we learned in *Becoming C. S. Lewis*, Lewis did not concern himself with dates and the chronology of events. He focused on the logical relationship between events. Though he had these experiences in 1924, they would not take effect until after the conversations with Barfield catalyzed them, at which point they became the final pieces, stored up for when they would be needed. This is not a very Greek way of thinking, but it is the essence of the Hebrew mind and the way of the Bible. As we shall see, it is also the way Lewis usually wrote.

One other point should be made about "The Great War" between Lewis and Barfield. It is ill-defined. It had several aspects, and we know for certain only that it took place over several years, perhaps as many as seven or eight. We have few letters or documents from this prolonged conversation, and few of these are dated.[144] Much of the conversation took place in face-to-face dialogue in London, in Oxford, or on walking holidays. The disagreements between the two men involved a number of things: the nature of imagination and how mythology works, the anthroposophical notion of the "spiritual science" that demonstrates the evolution of consciousness from physical to immortal, and a variety of other related issues arising from anthroposophy. The two things that "The Great War" did not involve were the two matters that helped Lewis change his mind about God: his chronological snobbery, which Barfield had helped him sort earlier, and the idea that abstract thought produced valid values. While "The Great War" went on for years, the aspects of the argument that contributed to Lewis's conversion were settled by 1926.

Lewis would view these random events later as the very hand of God interfering with his complacent life. First, he read Euripides again after many years. All of the "world's end" imagery that he had rejected with his new look came rushing back, and he liked it in spite of himself.[145] He wanted the longing for he knew not what to return again, the same experience he had enjoyed during his Great Bookham rambles. Then the experience of Joy came the next day like the answer to the heart's deepest prayer.

Second, he picked up Samuel Alexander's book *Space, Time, and Deity*, derived from his Gifford Lectures of 1915. Lewis was struck by Alexander's explanation of the relationship between enjoyment and contemplation.[146] Enjoyment involves an actual experience, while contemplation involves thinking about the experience. Lewis reasoned, based on this distinction, that enjoyment and contemplation are incompatible. In other words, we cannot experience love and think about experiencing love simultaneously. We must attend to one or the other, and they are not the same thing. The two may alternate back and forth rapidly, but they are distinct activities. With this insight, Lewis realized that all of his efforts to discover Joy through introspection were merely contemplation. Contemplation never leads to the actual experience. The contexts in which he had experienced Joy were not the cause or the thing itself; they only survived in memory as reminders of enjoyment. The experiences actually pointed elsewhere.[147] But that could not be, because for the materialist Jack Lewis in March 1924, there was nowhere else to point. What he had figured out did not yet make sense, even though these were the final pieces of the puzzle. What he yet needed were the first pieces.

Jack broke off his friendship with Leo Baker soon after the death of the Doc. Baker had sent no letter of condolence, and Jack had been troubled for some time by what he regarded as Baker's egoism and his thinly veiled contempt for Mrs. Moore and everyone else he met at Jack's house.[148] A letter from Baker did not arrive until the end of April, when he offered the explanation that some misunderstanding had occurred between them, for he claimed to have written to Mrs. Moore when the Doc died. Jack did not believe him but accepted the explanation while also laying before Baker all his failings with the hope that they might take up their old friendship again.[149] The breach would not be mended until ten years later, after Jack's conversion. It is entirely possible that Mrs. Moore misled Jack about not receiving a letter from Leo Baker, whom she did not like.

By the middle of March, Jack learned of an All Soul's fellowship, but it provided only two hundred pounds a year, and the successful candidate would have to sleep in college.[150] Between March 26 and April 26, Jack and Mrs. Moore took Maureen on a holiday to Clevedon, in Somerset, on the coast near Bristol. While they were there, they had an overnight visit from Janie's brother

Willie and his wife, and a week's visit from Warnie Lewis. Jack spent much of his free time working on "Dymer" with mixed success. He alternated between reading Nietzsche's *Beyond Good and Evil* and longing for a retreat into his "romantic Avalon-Hesperides-Western business."[151] In fact, Jack had a dream in which he and Warnie came upon the end of the world. The vision presages the apocalyptic passages in *The Magician's Nephew* and *The Last Battle*, with a moon blotted out from the sky and ruins strewn everywhere.[152] At the end of their vacation, Maureen and Mrs. Moore returned to Oxford by train while Jack rode in the sidecar of Warnie's motorcycle. The combination of the speed, the sunlight, and the anticipation of going home suddenly evoked in Jack a renewed experience of Joy![153] At the beginning of June, he almost had the experience again while sitting in his favorite fir grove after hiking through bracken on his way to Horsepath.[154]

Over the last few days of April, back in Headington and now ensconced in the attic as his new study, Jack completed his first full draft of "Dymer." Unfortunately, it brought him no real satisfaction. Something was wrong. It had no unity. He would have to rewrite large sections before it could please him.[155] He also continued working on his paper titled "Hegemony of Moral Values," which he hoped to send for publication in *Mind*.[156] The problem of morality and ethics vexed Jack throughout this period of his life, and his paper provided him with an opportunity to work it out. During the middle of May, he was reading Locke, and Bosanquet's *Suggestions in Ethics*.[157] Throughout this year, he continued his participation in the Martlets and the Philosophical Society, where he regularly presented papers.

As unexpected as his experiences of Joy, on May 5, 1924, Jack had the best news he had yet received regarding his professional career. Edgar Frederick Carritt would spend the next academic year in the United States and University College needed someone to take Carritt's pupils. The master of University offered the temporary post to Jack. He even assured Jack that if he received the offer of a fellowship from Trinity College, the university would release him from any obligation.[158] For the modest salary of two hundred pounds, Lewis would also lecture twice a week during the eight-week Michaelmas term. Finally, he had the beginnings of some financial security.

Jack spent the weekend of June 21–24 in London where he visited Cecil Harwood. The weekend was packed with significant but not ultimate experiences. Discovering that Jack had never seen the Elgin Marbles, Harwood hustled him off to the British Museum to complete his classical education.[159] Then he took Jack to see the Old Vic's production of *As You Like It*, in which Leo Baker appeared. Harwood and Jack thought it was a dreadful production, but after the play, Harwood took Jack backstage to see Baker. Jack agreed to go because he thought his first meeting with Baker after their rift would go best with a third party present. They all decided to meet the next day for lunch in Kew Gardens, where Baker announced he was engaged to be married.[160]

Next, Harwood entreated Jack to attend a meeting of the Anthroposophical Society with him and Barfield. At the meeting, Lewis also met again Daphne Olivier, whom Harwood would marry the following year. Barfield and Harwood had embraced Rudolf Steiner's anthroposophy and taken wives some fifteen years their senior at the same time. Afterward, when Jack expressed his objections to George Adams von Kauffman, who had been the speaker for the evening, Barfield and Harwood accused him of disliking Kauffman because he was a rival![161] On Monday at lunch, Barfield and Harwood renewed their attack on Jack for his skepticism of anthroposophy, but the day ended well enough. They attended a performance of *The Valkyrie*, which renewed Jack's boyhood enthusiasm for Wagner. He thought "it was like revisiting one's native town."[162]

The next renewal of boyhood days came soon after when Warnie took Jack on a motorcycle tour back to St Albans and Watford over the weekend of July 3. At one point they ate their lunch on a railroad bridge where they used to go as boys in their Wynyard days. They talked of bygone times. Fifteen years after the horrors of Wynyard and thirty years before he would write of those days as the most miserable of his life, Lewis reflected on how happy he was to be safe from being a boy at school.[163] He mused that he and Warnie had completely won, and his insane headmaster had completely lost.[164]

Once August arrived, Jack learned a form of busyness he had not known. He had agreed to grade higher certificate papers, and he also had to prepare for his first tutorials in philosophy and write two sets of lectures: "The Good: Its Position among the Values" and "Moral Good: Its Position among the Values." The problem of ethics and morality continued to haunt him. He could find no satisfactory way to explain moral values in a closed physical universe, and he had turned over every materialist stone in his search to confirm the security of his position. With all that he had to do, his diary suffered.

Lewis stopped keeping his diary for six months between August 1924 and February 1925. When he resumed, he observed that his lectures had not been an overwhelming success. In Hilary term, only two people attended, and one of these was an old clergyman.[165] It was an inauspicious beginning for the man who would become the greatest lecturer at Oxford, filling the vast rooms in the Examinations Schools building with standing-room-only crowds. Those days, however, lay in the future. His life had settled into a routine of tutorials, lectures, meetings of the Philosophical Society and the Martlets, and domestic duties punctuated, when possible, with efforts at revising "Dymer." At the beginning of March, he once again set aside his diary for another six months until August. During this period, however, he received even better news than the previous year. Magdalen College offered him a fellowship in English with a salary of five hundred pounds a year.

3

From Undergraduate to Fellow

1925-1927

Having failed at a series of fellowship openings at various colleges for which Jack had high hopes, he wrote in one of his now rare letters to his father that a fellowship in English had been announced at Magdalen College, but he had no hope of getting it since senior fellows, including Frank Percy Wilson, his old tutor, had all applied.[1] It had taken remarkable skill for Jack Lewis to win a prize for his essay on optimism, a subject about which he had little experience, and his old pessimism came rushing back. Nonetheless, his pessimism failed him this time, and Magdalen offered him the fellowship. The *Times* of London published the announcement on May 22, 1925.[2]

A Fellow of Magdalen College

A week after sending his father a telegram to give him the news of his election as a fellow at Magdalen, Jack wrote to Albert a long letter expressing in tender terms his gratitude for all the support his father had given him over the previous six years. Then he gave the details of all that had transpired to bring about his election. As it turned out, Wilson had never intended to apply for the position, but his chief rival was Jack's good friend Nevill Coghill. Both of Jack's English tutors, whom he had counted on to write letters of recommendation, had already promised to support Coghill because they thought Jack was committed to a philosophy position. Then, crediting his stars rather than God, Jack explained that Coghill was offered a fellowship at Exeter College, where he was an undergraduate. That stroke of good fortune left the field wide open for Jack as the leading contender.

What followed was a series of comic-opera interviews, including a dinner at Magdalen to which Jack wore white tie at the advice of A. S. L. Farquharson, one of Jack's former philosophy tutors, only to find that everyone else was dressed in black tie. Casual conversation ensued between Jack and his only remaining serious rival, another man from Belfast, and then an awkward chance meeting on the street with Sir Thomas Herbert Warren, the president of Magdalen. Finally, Jack received a note asking him to meet with Warren the following morning on important business. When Jack arrived, he was kept waiting for half an hour. In the end, the important business was to clarify that Magdalen intended to vote on Jack as the candidate, but they wanted to be sure he understood the terms before the vote. They wanted someone who could take a few philosophy pupils as well as English pupils, thus justifying Jack's double qualification with the time and expense it had involved. The next day, the faculty elected Jack at a salary of five hundred pounds per year plus rooms in college, a pension, and a dining allowance. The election was for five years, but if he did well, he could expect it to become permanent. To prevent him from lapsing into optimism upon his good fortune, a cat bit him on his way home.[3]

Jack continued his sideline as an examiner for the board of education, but he was promoted to the position of awarder as well as examiner. This new function involved overseeing the examination results and rendering a verdict on each candidate. This phase of the operation took place at Queen's College, Cambridge, where he met with his counterparts from nine o'clock in the morning until seven in the evening until the work was done. In a telling remark reflecting all that had gone into his education and preparation for life, he said that his counterpart from Cambridge had "no breeding."[4]

In accepting the English fellowship, Jack knew he had burned his bridges for philosophy. He had taken one career path and not another. His own English tutors had assumed that he was all for philosophy and had only done a second degree in English to fill out his résumé while he waited for a philosophy position to open. Jack saw it differently, and he appears to have left philosophy with a sense of relief. He told his father that he did not think he had "the brain and nerves for philosophy."[5] Philosophy would have meant a life of constantly questioning what everyone else takes for granted. Some people might like such a bleak and skeptical life, but he did not think he could face a life like that for the next fifty years. Nonetheless, he did not regret his courtship with philosophy, even if there was no marriage. He told Albert,

> It will be a comfort to me all my life to know that the scientist and the materialist have not the last word: that Darwin and [Herbert] Spencer undermining ancestral beliefs stand themselves on a foundation of sand; of gigantic assumptions and irreconcilable contradictions an inch below the surface.[6]

These are the words of a man on the slippery slope toward theism. If a love of Kirkpatrick's approach to logic and philosophy had given Jack rational grounds to support his atheism, it had also provided him with the analytical tools to question his own atheism. These tools had already led him out of a strict materialism, and in the end they would lead him to the borders of faith. Once he became a Christian, Lewis used these tools in constructing his approach to apologetics. At the beginning of his academic career

C. S. Lewis at Stonehenge, April 8, 1925. Used by permission of the Marion E. Wade Center, Wheaton College, Wheaton, IL.

as a literary scholar, however, it is enough to know that he had recognized the unwarranted assumptions and flurry of contradictions of naturalism and materialism.

With the prospect of full employment in an excellent academic post on the horizon, Jack and Janie went off on a month-long holiday in August 1925 with Maureen to Cloud Farm on Exmoor, in Devon. Jack made his daily jaunts across miles and miles of countryside in rain, wind, fog, and blazing sun, all to his delight. One notable feature about the vacation after almost a year of silence in his diary is the daily commentary on Janie Moore's health. She was now fifty-three years old and declining rapidly. She had almost daily complaints, and her physical ailments inevitably found expression in her mood and temperament. Her temper did not escape Jack's notice. When Maureen and Jack commented on the packing for their extended vacation, Janie grew so angry that the other two quickly dropped the subject.[7] For some time, she had complained of toothache, and she began the vacation with a new set of false teeth, a mortifying badge of old age.[8] Throughout the month she felt a little sick, or felt her lumbago, or had a chill on the kidneys, or had a bout of rheumatism—all of which resulted in bad nights, which resulted in bad following days. At the end of this vacation, Jack stopped keeping his diary for eight months and did not resume until April 27, 1926.

Establishing Himself in Magdalen

The first big surprise Jack had upon his election to a fellowship was that he had to furnish his three rooms at Magdalen. These rooms consisted of one large sitting room where he might meet his pupils and entertain guests, a smaller study, and a bedroom. It all cost him ninety pounds to furnish his rooms—almost 20 percent of his annual income. His rooms were in New Building, dating from the 1730s, a neoclassical building of warm-colored stone. His windows overlooked the deer park where Magdalen College has maintained its own herd of reindeer for centuries. He thought that living in the bishop's palace at Wells could not have been better, and Jack was a great admirer of the bishop's palace at Wells. The venerable beauty of the Magdalen buildings, all medieval except New Building, surrounded by majestic woodlands and flowering gardens, created the kind of atmosphere that Jack regarded as beyond expectation and hope. As for his colleagues, Jack found that the other dons treated him well and that a more casual atmosphere prevailed at Magdalen than at University College, even though Magdalen was the grander and richer of the two.[9] The prince of Wales had belonged to Magdalen a decade earlier, thus reinforcing its status in the empire and on the world stage.

Jack encouraged Jenkin to visit him in November 1925, though he could not invite him to Hillsboro, because Mrs. Moore was

Magdalen College tower, 1920s

suffering from varicose veins. His rooms in college, however, had plenty of room, if Jenkin could come for a Monday and Tuesday. Jack could not invite him for a weekend, because Jack was expected at Hillsboro then.[10] During term, he slept in his college rooms during the week and stayed at Hillsboro on the weekends. Out of term, he slept at Hillsboro but went into Magdalen each morning to work.

The friends that Jack had made during his undergraduate days had scattered, and it seemed to him that it was more difficult to make friends after the undergraduate days. To Jenkin, he confided that he realized his closest friends all met different needs. From Barfield he received wisdom and a "richness of spirit." From Jenkin he found a closer and more intimate connection with feelings and the gusto of life. Harwood provided "humours" and their appreciation. He lamented that his time for making good friends seemed to have passed.[11] He discovered that he had many professional colleagues in his new college and the university English faculty, but few of these showed any promise of becoming true friends. He often dined with colleagues and joined them for tea or sat up at night talking, but he did not find the promise of friendship. Even as he found it harder to acquire new friends, Jack's old friends were succumbing one by one to the chains of matrimony. A. K. Hamilton Jenkin added his name to the list of Jack's friends who were following the marriage path. Jack wrote to Jenkin a note of congratulations in which he described the change in his frame of mind about marriage that coincided with a toothache. When his tooth hurt, he thought people who married betrayed a weakness of character, but once the tooth was out, he felt that he could actually approve of the match.[12]

Because he would have to spend his time working on a new set of lectures, Jack warned Albert that he could come home for only one week at Christmas, though he promised to try to come for a visit at Easter as well.[13] Jack, always conscious of his social class, was surprised to enjoy a literary conversation on his way back to Oxford after Christmas with a man whom he did not consider "educated" but who had read Pepys, Boswell, Macauley, Trollope, Thackeray, Ruskin, Morris, and others. He expected a good literary conversation at home or at Magdalen, but to have such a conversation in a third-class rail car simply thrilled him. He mentioned this conversation in a letter to his father on January 5, 1926. He then went on to comment on the vast flooding across Warwick and Oxford and the beauty of the effect. Some of his earlier adolescent callousness showed through his comments as he remarked that he could not save anyone's life or fortune by not enjoying the beauty of the flooding.[14]

During January 1926, Jack had a case of German measles. He thought it was a very pleasant illness after the first twenty-four hours. He was too ill to get up, and work was impossible, but he felt well enough to read! He reread his favorite Jane Austen novels and brushed up his Italian by reading *Orlando innamorato*, by Matteo Maria Boiardo, a long, fairy-tale poem full of dragons and damsels in distress. The worst part of measles was going back to work and regaining one's legs. Soon after his illness, Jack had to deliver his first lecture of the term. Following his disappointing experience as a lecturer the previous year, he asked for the smallest lecture room. On the appointed day, however, an overflow crowd of undergraduates showed up, and the crowd had to go across the street to another building owned by the college, where Jack held forth.[15]

Probably the most important feature of his lectures and tutorials, however, involved his changing thoughts about spiritual reality. He had the problem of making things clear to his philosophy pupils. He thought it awkward to talk about the "Absolute" or "Nobody-knows-what" or a "superhuman mind" to undergraduates having a hard enough time understanding philosophy. In the end, he started using the well-worn word *God*.[16] Of course, he meant the god of the philosophers and not the God of popular religion, but it constituted a seismic shift in his practice.

"Dymer"

On February 3, Jack sent Nevill Coghill several cantos of his monumental poem, "Dymer." They had discussed Jack's poem at length the night before, and Coghill appears to have asked Jack to let him read what he had written. In his accompanying note, Jack stressed that the poem was confidential. He did not want all of Oxford to know that he was writing poetry.[17] Coghill replied the next day with praise for Jack's work. Nonetheless, Coghill offered helpful criticism designed to improve the work. Jack betrayed no feelings of defensiveness in the face of criticism. Instead, he expressed deep appreciation for comments that indicated problems with the writing along with what Jack might do to improve the work. In Coghill, Jack had found a friend with whom he could talk about his work and who could offer helpful criticism that he valued. Arthur Greeves had never been able to fill this place. Jack particularly liked the fact that Coghill recognized the spiritual experiences in "Dymer."[18] Coghill went one step further than encouraging Lewis. He sent the manuscript to his friend Guy Pocock, an editor at the publishing house of J. M. Dent, who accepted it.[19] Jack's second book of poetry had found a publisher.

Lewis had wrestled with the story of Dymer and how best to tell it since his days with W. T. Kirkpatrick in Great Bookham. After several false starts, he settled on the present form, a long narrative poem consisting of nine cantos in rhyme royal. It is 104 pages long in the first London edition. In canto 1, the young student named Dymer escapes from the "Platonic and totalitarian" city.[20] He escapes to nature where he rids himself of the entanglement of clothes. In canto 2, he stumbles upon a castle, where he discovers beauty and dresses himself in fine clothes, all of which arouses his desire. He then meets a girl who satisfies his sexual desires. In canto 3, Dymer leaves the castle to enjoy the morning after his encounter with the girl, but when he seeks to return to her, he only finds a hag who blocks the entrance to the castle. When reason fails to move her, Dymer hurls himself against the hag but is struck senseless in the effort. He stumbles away broken and crushed. Canto 4 finds Dymer wandering in a storm when he meets a man whose hands and feet have been cut off. The man explains that Dymer's flight from the city prompted a general revolt and a devastating battle in which atrocities were committed in Dymer's name. The man dies cursing Dymer for causing the horror.

In canto 5, Dymer runs away but is beset by nightmares and guilt. In his loneliness and misery, he contemplates death, but the beauty of the dawn and the singing of a bird encourage him. In canto 6, he meets a magician, whom Lewis based on his encounter with Yeats in Oxford. The magician invites Dymer to drink from his cup of dreams, the only way to recover his beloved. Dymer had thought his only path back to the girl lay through repentance, but he succumbs to the magician's entreaties. In canto 7, the magician's dreams grow wilder and wilder until he descends into madness. Dymer wakes from his dream after having met the girl he desired, but he realizes that the dream of the girl was of his own making, so that he only loved his own desire. At the end of this canto, the magician shoots Dymer, who flees with a terrible wound. In canto 8, Dymer finally sees what he believes to be his beloved while experiencing the deep pain of his wound. The phantom he sees, however, is actually only his desire for desire. He grieves for his lost love and the absence of true affection before struggling to a bell tower in a graveyard to rest. In canto 9, Dymer enters a ruined landscape where he meets the monster that is the offspring of his tryst with the girl. Dymer confronts the monster, which kills him. With the death of Dymer, however, the landscape transforms into a garden and the monster transfigures into a glorious, heavenly being.

It is a story of despair, lacking all hope, in which each one strives for himself and his own glory.[21] Ironically, it is not the kind of plot that Lewis liked. Lewis loved the story of the journey to the end of the world in which the pilgrim returns a changed person. As it happens, Lewis would bury the Dymer story with Dymer himself. All of Lewis's future stories would have the plot he loved.

Though Jack had spent his adolescence discussing literature with Arthur Greeves, he realized that Arthur could never be the literary friend that Coghill was becoming. The last of Jack's letters that we have from 1926 was to Greeves. Somehow, they had been out of touch, and Jack had no idea where Arthur was until he wrote to Jack. Arthur had decided to write a play and wrote to ask if Jack thought he could introduce incest into the play in order to heighten the feeling already established by other tragic situations. Jack patiently explained why adding something for no reason other than "more so" was never a good idea with drama and had ruined much of Elizabethan drama. Arthur never wrote his play.[22]

Albert and Jack entertained the idea with Warnie of a visit to England after Jack and Warnie visited Little Lea during the long summer vacation. The logistics of such a visit would be much easier for Jack to execute now that he had his own rooms in college (and his father need never know about Hillsboro house).[23] The importance of this correspondence, however, lies not in summer plans but in the fact that Jack made reference to "floating islands" in an offhand comment. The idea of floating islands would finally take shape almost twenty years later when he wrote *Perelandra*. In the end, Albert could not be lured out of Belfast, so Jack and Warnie returned to Little Lea for a visit of a little over a week from September 11 through 20. During this visit, J. M. Dent released Jack's second book, his long poem on which he had worked for many years. *Dymer* was published on September 18, 1926, under the pseudonym that Jack had used for *Spirits in Bondage*, Clive Hamilton.[24]

Differences with the Anthroposophists

The publication of *Dymer* came at a significant moment in Jack's life, as he reached a milestone in sorting out all the questions he had about life. Once Cecil Harwood and Owen Barfield had become disciples of Rudolf Steiner and his highly stylized vision of spiritual reality, they seemed determined that Jack should join them. By this stage in his journey, Jack admitted to Harwood in a letter that he had accepted the idea that there was more to life than the physical and that an experience with the nonphysical was possible. He reacted, however, against the various attempts by Harwood and Barfield to explain ultimate spiritual reality in a highly rationalistic system, such as those expressed by Steiner, Emanuel Swedenborg, and the Platonists. Jack did not like the idea of trying to express the inexpressible and preferred to simply feel it in his bones. His anthroposophist friends, on the other hand, tended to dismiss Jack's spiritual, noncognitive experience that he called Joy.[25]

For a number of years, Jack had dismissed his experiences of Joy as fantasy, but Alexander's distinction in *Space, Time, and Deity* between having an experience (enjoyment) and thinking about or imagining an experience (contemplation) had convinced him that his experiences were real and that they referred to something that caused them to happen. He had even begun to tell his students about Alexander's ideas.[26] On May 3, 1926, Lewis even had the chance to hear Alexander when Frank Hardie took him to a meeting of the Philosophical Society where Alexander spoke.[27] Until he came to appreciate Alexander's point, Lewis dismissed his Joy experiences as typical adolescent sex fantasies in which all the "northernness" was merely a form of psychological wishful thinking in symbolic form. He called these experiences "Christina Dreams."[28]

Christina Pontifex, a character in Samuel Butler's Victorian novel *The Way of All Flesh*, inhabited a fantasy world of daydreams as she imagined all sorts of wonderful things about herself.[29] Jack had been preoccupied with understanding the nature of Christina dreams for years within the general Freudian climate of the time.[30] After reading Alexander, he began to suspect that his experiences were not fantasies involving contemplation but actually the enjoyment of something objective. The experiences pointed to something real, but he did not yet know what. By 1926, Jack had "learned his lesson" and now wanted to encourage the Christina dreams.[31] The whole business, however, left him perplexed about the imagination and how it works. He would remain perplexed as he wrestled with the problem of imagination for years to come with his dialogue/disputation partners, from Owen Barfield to J. R. R. Tolkien to Dorothy L. Sayers.

He also had finally concluded that all those values he had been affirming for years must have some source outside the whole of nature. Lord Bertrand Russell's view that all values are self-authenticating simply would not do. Such a perspective allows only for personal opinion and temporary group consensus, but not objective values. This view would mean that no real values exist at all. By 1926, C. S. Lewis believed that some sort of mind exists outside or alongside or other than the whole of nature, and this mind provides the basis for objective values that humans share.

Many years later, when he delivered a series of lectures at the University of Durham published as *The Abolition of Man*, Lewis would call the sum of universal values known in all cultures "the Tao." It would probably be too much to say that he was a "practicing theist" at this point, as George Sayer declared, but he was definitely on that trajectory.[32] Ironically, by the time *Dymer* was in print, it no longer reflected Jack's view of reality.

Lewis had come to the point he describes in the fourth chapter of the first section of *Mere Christianity*:

> I am not yet within a hundred miles of the God of Christian theology. All I have got to is a Something which is directing the universe, and which appears in me as a law urging me to do right and making me feel responsible and uncomfortable when I do wrong. I think we have to assume it is more like mind than it is like anything else we know—because after all the only other thing we know is matter and you can hardly imagine a bit of matter giving instructions.[33]

In fact, *Mere Christianity* is not the theoretical but well-reasoned bit of semi-philosophical apologetics that many people take it to be. In the radio talks that became *Mere Christianity*, Lewis simply shares his own testimony of the steps by which he moved from being a materialist to being a Christian.

A Busy Fellow

Once Lewis settled into his new post at Magdalen, he established a routine that would carry him. When he lived at Gastons with W. T. Kirkpatrick, he recognized that he did best when he had a regular daily routine. A routine provided him with a discipline that enabled him to function and be productive. During the three eight-week terms of the Oxford academic year when Jack stayed at his rooms in college, he ate breakfast with the other Magdalen fellows. He met his pupils and attended to his tutoring responsibilities beginning at nine o'clock and continuing until one, when he ate lunch in the hall or went home to Hillsboro to eat with Mrs. Moore. He spent the afternoon at Hillsboro and usually took a long walk. At five he resumed seeing his pupils until a quarter past seven, when he went to dinner in the hall. After dinner, he would usually join the other fellows in the Senior Common Room for coffee, conversation, smoking, and port. He then went back to his rooms to work on his own interests.[34]

He soon found, however, that he had lost most of his personal time when he would normally have written poetry, corresponded with friends, worked on papers to present at the various groups to which he belonged, and read. He had joined so many groups that most of his evenings were filled. On Monday nights, he met with the Mermaids. On Wednesday nights, he invited pupils to his rooms to read Anglo-Saxon. Two other groups met every other week: the Kolbítar, or Kolbiters, met every other Tuesday, and his philosophical group met for dinner every other Thursday.[35] He appears to have modified his involvement in the Martlets, which had been such an important association for him since the beginning of his undergraduate days.

The Mermaids proved to be Jack's least favorite group. They met to read Elizabethan drama. Lewis agreed to join the group in June 1926, but by early 1927 he had come to regret the decision. He found that the participants lacked the depth for such an undertaking. He complained that the majority were vulgar, strident young men who guffawed at the racy bits like schoolboys. He lamented that in leaving Greats for English, he had exchanged the company of "the men of taste and wit and humanity for a mere collection of barbarians."[36] He could not easily drop the group, however, since they made him their president. It would take some time to extricate himself and free up the evening.

The Wednesday evening gatherings to read Anglo-Saxon came to be known as "Beer and Beowulf." Lewis invented mnemonic devices to help his pupils learn the twists and turns of Old English. Aiding their valiant attempts to read *Beowulf* as originally written,

Lewis provided beer to stimulate courage and assuage failure.[37] The two student groups suggest the degree to which Lewis took his teaching responsibilities seriously and sought to stimulate and invigorate his pupils.

The philosophical dinners developed through Lewis's growing friendship with another young don, William Francis Ross Hardie, known as Frank, who spent a year as fellow at Magdalen before taking a philosophy post at Corpus Christi College in 1926. He remained there for the rest of his career and was elected president in 1950.[38] Hardie was a few years younger than Lewis, but they spent a good deal of time together during their first years as fellows. In his diary, Lewis noted that Hardie was "near enough to my own helplessness to be able to give me some vague lights."[39] They often met in each other's rooms to talk, dined together, and even went to see the moving pictures. Hardie provided Lewis with a companion from Greats with whom he could have intelligent conversation when the literary group failed him.

Of all the groups with whom Lewis met during his early years as a fellow, the Kolbítar was by far the most important in terms of his development and later life. Soon after joining the group, Lewis wrote to Greeves with the news:

> We have a little Icelandic Club in Oxford called the 'Kólbitar': which means (literally) 'coal-biters', i.e. an Icelandic word for old cronies who sit round the fire so close that they look as if they were biting coals. We have so far read the Younger Edda and the Volsung Saga: next term we shall read the Laxdale Saga. *You* will be able to imagine what a delight this is to me, and how, even in turning over the pages of my Icelandic Dictionary, the mere name of god or giant catching my eye will sometimes throw me back fifteen years into a wild dream of northern skies and Valkyrie music: only they are now even more beautiful seen thro' a haze of memory—you know that awfully *poignant* effect there is about impression *recovered* from ones past.[40]

High Street, Oxford, 1920s

While Lewis was engaged in a philosophical exploration of the basis and validity of values leading to his conclusion that something like "mind" alongside the universe was responsible for values, he had stumbled once again into the land of Norse mythology that entranced him as a teenager. The old stories still affected him in a powerful way and revived the memories of the earlier effect.

John Ronald Reuel Tolkien, the new professor of Anglo-Saxon at Oxford who was known to his friends as Ronald, had started the Kolbítar shortly after his arrival in Oxford. Tolkien was named to his professorship in 1925. He and Lewis first met at an English faculty meeting and tea. Tolkien had tried to persuade the faculty to revise the syllabus so that a degree in English focused on the development of the language rather than on the literature. In his diary, Lewis noted, "He is a smooth, pale, fluent little chap—can't read Spenser because of the forms—thinks language is the real thing in the school—thinks all literature is written for the amusement of *men* between thirty and forty. . . . No harm in

108

him: only needs a smack or so."[41] Tolkien had proven to be an acquired taste for Lewis, who said that his background in Ulster had made him suspicious of Catholics, and his literary colleagues in the English faculty had warned him against philologists. Tolkien was a Catholic philologist. But he was a Catholic philologist who shared his love for northernness and its mythology. Lewis had also made peace with the fact that no one person could satisfy all the expectations of friendship for him. He would have many friends, each with his own small area of common interest with Jack. He could not expect everyone he liked to like everything he liked. Tolkien was not suited to philosophy, or even literature, for that matter. He never cared for modern writing after Chaucer in the fourteenth century. In truth, he never cared for English literature after 1066, because it had been ruined by the French invaders. But he could share a love for Norse mythology with Lewis just when Lewis needed it.

Lewis had long regarded the Christian Gospels as myths of the kind produced by all ancient cultures. He paid them no more attention than any other myths except, perhaps, to hold them in lower regard. In this context, his colleague Thomas Dewar Weldon stopped by his rooms on the evening of April 27, 1926, to talk and drink whiskey until after midnight. Weldon was one of many colleagues who never rose to the level of friend and whom Lewis dreaded. Lewis mentioned Weldon many times in his diary during his early years at Magdalen College, but never with pleasure. His diary says that they had talked about the historicity of the Gospels.[42] His recollection of the event thirty years later was remarkably vivid, in keeping with the impact of the shock. Though Weldon was the "hardest boiled of all atheists" Lewis ever knew, including Kirkpatrick, he observed that the evidence for the historicity of the Gospels was remarkably strong: "Rum thing," he went on. "All that stuff of Frazer's about the Dying God. Rum thing. It almost looks as if it had really happened once."[43] It was a horrifying thought to Lewis.

Lewis had long taken delight in Norse mythology. It touched him at a deep emotional level. In his dispute with Barfield, he allowed that mythology was meaningful but not that it was true. This sort of distinction formed a critical element in the newly developing linguistic analysis of Ludwig Wittgenstein, who would come to dominate British philosophy in the years ahead. Rather than take the old positivist view that only objects that can be known through the senses can be said to exist objectively, Wittgenstein shifted to a more condescending position. Religious language and all language dealing with nonempirical values has meaning to the users, but it has no objective meaning. Religious language may have great coping value, but it has no basis in fact. Now Weldon was suggesting that a myth might have a basis in fact. All the while, Jack's new friendship with Tolkien was slowly developing over their common interest in Norse mythology. With all his modernity meeting one reasonable challenge after another, Jack noted on May 26, even while enjoying a field of buttercups and daisies hedged with hawthorn, that "all my ideas are in a crumbling state at present."[44]

Life in Hillsboro

Though Jack now had a regular income, he and Mrs. Moore never turned down an opportunity to bring a little extra cash into the house. They now had Dorothea "Dotty" Vaughan as a boarder while she attended Headington School alongside Maureen. Having two girls in the house tended to multiply the drama, and Jack grew ever more conscious of his annoyance with Maureen's "patient, endlessly repeated prim nagging."[45] In fact, Maureen was no longer a mere girl. She turned twenty in 1926, and she reeled under her mother's authority and struck back with vigor. The rows became more frequent and more intense. Argument and strife had become so common that Jack commented in his diary on May 11 that he knew little peaceful homelife.[46]

Jack described several of the arguments that arose in Hillsboro between mother and daughter. On one occasion, Maureen offered to wash the dishes for Jack. She went about the task her own way, but it was contrary to the way that Mrs. Moore wanted it done, so a "violent altercation" ensued. Maureen insisted that she should be judged by the outcome, but Mrs. Moore insisted that her servants had to learn her ways and so must Maureen. By implication, Jack was one of the servants, since he normally did the dishes.[47] The fight subsided for a while, but once they had all gathered in the dining room, it all began again. In what Jack regarded as "her usual tactless way," Maureen complained of her mother's imprudence, and Mrs. Moore flashed into a rage.[48] Her fury grew so strong that Jack attempted to say something on Maureen's behalf—something he never did—which only made matters worse. Mrs. Moore then resorted to the injured-martyr strategy and declared that she would continue to do her duty no matter what Maureen and Jack said. This line of self-sacrifice would eventually find its way into *The Screwtape Letters*. The evening ended when Mrs. Moore declared that she had a headache.[49]

During one of Warnie's brief visits, Mrs. Moore commented to Jack that Dotty was practicing on Warnie. With all her other faults, Dotty was free of flirting, or so Jack had thought.[50] Her other faults included the new habit of inviting her friends from school to go punting and asking Mrs. Moore to prepare them a picnic basket for lunch.[51] Jack believed that taking in Dotty had proven to be yet another of their many mistakes. By assuming joint responsibility for "their mistakes," Jack made excuses for Janie Moore. She, in fact, had made all the decisions and all the mistakes. Yet, in the midst of all of this strife and drama at home, Jack had another "whiff" of "the real joy" on the morning of June 4, 1926, with wood pigeons calling, a heavy dew upon the landscape, and a transparent, luminous mist all around.[52]

With the end of term and a move back to Hillsboro from the quiet of his college rooms, Jack discovered that the constant flurry of activity at home made it almost impossible to write. He had taught himself to work under those conditions before he obtained his fellowship, but now he had to learn all over again. Between Janie Moore's constant cleaning and jam making, Maureen's piano playing, and interruptions for Jack to do chores that needed attention immediately, he had trouble maintaining a flow of thought.[53] The problem of working at home would constrict Lewis for the next twenty-five years. He had long since noted that Mrs. Moore seemed to pile on the domestic drudgery to take his mind off the work he wanted to do and could do. It was maddening.[54]

A year later, Jack described to Warnie the kind of episodes in which Mrs. Moore snared him. "Minto," Jack's nickname for her in his correspondence with Warnie and Arthur, had befriended a Mrs. Struder, the widow of an Oxford professor, who had a fragile hold on sanity. One day, Minto announced to Jack that Mrs. Struder had attempted suicide three times that day, and that her friend Mrs. Wilbraham and she were on their way to the Warneford Asylum to consult a doctor and secure a nurse. The announcement was a directive for Jack to join them, because Minto was doing poorly. They returned from the asylum with Nurse Jones but without a plan, since Struder had not asked for their help or requested a nurse. To complicate matters, they only suspected Struder had attempted suicide three times that day because a neighborhood child had said so. Mrs. Wilbraham, who never tired of doing good, announced that she would conceal herself in Mrs. Struder's garden all night while Nurse Jones stayed across the street in the bungalow of a complete stranger. Wilbraham then hinted broadly that if her nephew were there, *he* would stay with her in the garden. Jack finally agreed to spend the night in the garden.

Jack nonetheless pointed out that Mrs. Struder might be alarmed to find two shadowy figures in her garden in the middle of the night. Mrs. Wilbraham suggested that they put their stockings on the outside of their boots to muffle their footsteps. A neighbor opened a window to inquire what was going on. As this whole exchange took place on the street a few doors down from

Struder, a small crowd of neighborly ladies assembled in hopes of not missing out on the excitement. Jack suggested that they keep watch on the street rather than in the garden. While he insisted on the importance of not letting anyone know about their concern for Mrs. Struder, Wilbraham gave a full account to each new onlooker.

Jack then went home with Minto to be fortified with tea and to gather supplies of biscuits, pipe tobacco, apples, a waterproof sheet, two rugs, two cushions, and his great coat. A neighbor brought them some sandwiches and three thermos bottles. Mrs. Wilbraham immediately set about eating the sandwiches, but Jack insisted that she stop since they would be more needed later. He then established the right to seek the call of nature in private, during which time he could light his pipe without the fear of waking Mrs. Struder with the sound of his match. Once midnight had come and gone, a fine rain began to fall. Wilbraham grew surprised by the rain, more surprised when the temperature fell, and most surprised that she felt sleepy.

In his misery, Jack thrust his hands into his great coat pockets only to meet mothballs placed there by Minto. Then when he took out an apple to eat, he found that it tasted of mothballs. Quickly tiring of Wilbraham's constant monologue, Jack suggested a game of animal, vegetable, mineral. This was life at Hillsboro—a never-ending adventure as Minto encumbered Jack with her acts of mercy.[55]

June found Lewis immersed in the drudgery of correcting the proofs to *Dymer*.[56] Instead of a complete set for the entire book, for some reason the publisher sent the proofs in batches. With the proofs coming at the end of term before the long summer vacation, Lewis appeared ready for some comic diversion from this last menial task that all authors hate. To pass the time, he concocted a plan to parody and ridicule T. S. Eliot, whom Lewis blamed for the collapse of poetry in the West. He contrived to write a number of poems in the style of Eliot, which he would then send to Eliot's journal, *The Criterion*, with hopes that Eliot would be fooled and publish them as serious poetry.

He then enlisted into this conspiracy his friends Hardie, Coghill, and Henry Yorke. Yorke proposed the opening line, "My soul is a windowless façade," which Lewis suggested could rhyme with de Sade.[57] Coghill suggested that if they succeeded and exposed their jest, Eliot might still say that the poems had been written in all seriousness and that afterward the authors merely pretended that they were parodies. Finally, the conspirators created the brother and sister Rollo and Bridget Considine as the authors of the poems. Bridget would write to Eliot from Vienna, where Hardie had a friend who could post the letter and poems. Lewis stoked the fire by sitting next to Archibald Campbell, an avid admirer of Eliot, at the annual Greats dinner and plying him with conversation about the Considines and their poetry.[58] In the end, nothing came of the venture except the pleasure of attempting it.

The diversion probably helped Lewis maintain some balance while he struggled with what he now believed about God, the universe, and everything. In late May 1926 he had read G. K. Chesterton's *The Lunatic at Large*.[59] By the middle of June he was reading Chesterton's *Eugenics and Other Evils*.[60] Then he started rereading George MacDonald's *Lilith*.[61] During this period, Lewis began attending college chapel services, where he read the lesson.[62] He was not regular in attendance, but going at all represented a marked change in behavior. This was also the point at which he had begun self-consciously to shift his philosophical perspective from a realist concerned with the observable physical world to an idealist aware of a nonphysical realm.[63] In *Surprised by Joy*, Lewis remarked of this time in his life:

> Realism had been abandoned; the New Look was somewhat damaged; and chronological snobbery was seriously shaken. All over the board my pieces were in the most disadvantageous

positions. Soon I could no longer cherish even the illusion that the initiative lay with me. My Adversary began to make his final moves.[64]

Added to this cumulative effect, Jack reread Morris's *The Well at the World's End* and discovered that it still had an enormous evocative power over him: "The old spell still worked."[65] He called it humiliating. He was bothered by how easily the romances of his youth came flooding back to him.[66] In the preface to the third edition of *The Pilgrim's Regress*, Lewis described the progress of his intellectual journey as "from 'popular realism' to Philosophical Idealism; from Idealism to Pantheism; from Pantheism to Theism; and from Theism to Christianity."[67]

Midway through July 1926, Jack once again stopped keeping his diary. He did not resume it again until January 1927. This time he only kept up the practice through February and then ended it for good. His last entry relates the way Mrs. Moore grew tired and bothered by her many efforts to be involved in the lives of other people who turned out to be disasters. The house had become a constant bedlam of Dickensian characters, seemingly bent on the disruption of Jack's life. It grew increasingly apparent that Mrs. Moore's temperament inclined her to "fly into a flaming temper" when she encountered the least resistance to her regime, resistance that usually came from Maureen.[68] His diary would end with the cry "Oh curse it all! Is there never to be any peace or comfort?"[69]

The Problem of Imagination

On January 18, 1927, Lewis remarked in his diary that he had been thinking about imagination and intellect. He found himself trying to sort out Barfield's anthroposophy, the psychoanalysis of the Oxford "New Look," orthodox idealism as understood by the philosophy faculty at Oxford in the 1920s, and Kirkpatrick's rationalism. He could only say, "Lord what a mess!"[70] He wanted to work on his new poem "King of Drum," but the problem of imagination would not leave him. A few days later, Lewis noted in his diary that he planned "to work up the whole doctrine of Imagination in Coleridge," and that he found Wordsworth reassuring when it came to imagination. Along these lines, he poured over Coleridge's *Biographia Literaria*, which drew a distinction between imagination and fancy.[71] This discussion by Coleridge has dominated the discussion of imagination for two hundred years. Lewis wanted to sort out what is real about imagination without the bogeys, Karmas, gurus, and "damned psychism" that he presumably found from Barfield and his anthroposophy.[72] The next weekend, Owen Barfield and his wife arrived in Oxford to spend the weekend. While Maud Barfield bared her heart to Mrs. Moore about how she "hates, hates, hates" anthroposophy and thought that Owen should have told her about his beliefs before their marriage, Lewis and Barfield probably began the next phase of their "Great War," which focused on imagination.[73]

With Barfield living in London and the friends seeing each other only once or twice a year, their extended exchange of ideas took place primarily through letters. Unfortunately, Lewis often failed to date his letters. Walter Hooper has grouped these letters as an addendum to volume 3 of *The Collected Letters of C. S. Lewis*, and he has divided them into two parts: "Series I" deals with the differences between Lewis and Barfield over imagination, and "Series II" deals primarily with Lewis's objections to anthroposophy. By correlating the content of the letters with Lewis's diary entries from 1927, it is possible to date the beginning of the correspondence to 1927. The first major face-to-face exchange probably occurred during a walking tour over Easter break from April 19 through April 24. Barfield planned the walk and stacked the deck by adding Cecil Harwood and Walter Ogilvie "Wof" Field, another anthroposophist, who became a teacher with Harwood at the Rudolf Steiner School.[74] Three on one did not bother Lewis at all, and the annual walking tour would become a highlight of Lewis's year until World War II ended such pleasures. On this first trip, they walked from Goring, near London, to Shepton Mallet, near Wells. Lewis bragged in a letter to Warnie that he had almost walked across the whole of England from east to west.[75]

The great point of contention between Lewis and Barfield concerned the nature of the imagination and its relationship to knowledge. Barfield asserted that the imagination deals with truth, while Lewis insisted that the imagination concerns neither truth nor falsehood. In many ways, the letters reflect the enormous gulf between the two friends. Lewis wrote about how his imagination worked, beginning with images in his mind. In the "Great War" letters he began by talking about imagination in terms of images, as Aristotle had done.[76] The Greek word that Aristotle used for imagination is *phantasia*, from which we get the modern word "fantasy." Thus, Lewis held to the view that the imagination does not provide a way of knowing truth. Barfield countered that he did not think in that way at all. For Lewis, truth concerned the outer world of phenomenal experience, to which we have access through our senses. The external is true while the internal is opinion or fantasy. Truth and falsehood do not apply to all entities but apply only to certain ones. For instance, Lewis did not believe that truth applies to emotions or passions. For Barfield, truth is "reality itself taking the form of human consciousness."[77] As in other matters, Lewis would change his mind about the nature of imagination over the years, but Barfield would not.

This discussion played out in the context of anthroposophy and Barfield's BLitt thesis, which would be published in 1928 as *Poetic Diction*. Thus, Lewis often speaks of the "poetic imagination," particularly under the influence of passing inspiration. Essentially, Barfield took the view that the poet grasps the totality of reality through the imagination. This idea fit with Steiner's teachings about how human consciousness can grasp the eternal. Lewis countered that if poetic imagination does contain truth at the moment of inspiration, once the moment passes, the remnants of that vision must be tested in the light of day.[78]

While the discussion continued along the pleasant consideration of whether poetry contains truth, the real issue for Lewis lay in another area. He had come to accept the idea of a cosmic intelligence, but he also believed that an impassable barrier separated human consciousness from communication with that Absolute or Ultimate Mind. Since his early teenage years, Lewis had dismissed any truth claims for the Bible, along with any truth claims for the Norse or Greek mythologies. They were all works of human imagination. They did not deal with truth, only feelings. Lewis was on the verge of changing his mind again, but not as a result of Barfield's arguments, which were rather thin. Lewis changed his own mind under the relentless process of reason and by honestly facing matters before him. The discussion had raised the possibility that imagination might be the bridge between two worlds.

In many ways the discussions with Barfield proved maddening for Lewis. While Lewis's formal training in logic, reason, and philosophy had gone on for a decade, Barfield had no training in logic at all.[79] He was purely a literary man, which made it extremely difficult for Lewis to counter his arguments. Barfield simply failed to respond to Lewis's critique. Lewis had to remind Barfield along the way of how logic works and the difference between a judgment and the science of logic.[80] Then he had to clarify for Barfield the difference between universals, universal propositions, certainty, and probability.[81] For his part, Barfield stressed that he was not so interested in making a logical argument as in giving Lewis a sense of the "general mood and quality" of his thinking![82] At one point in the exchange, Lewis went so far as to remind Barfield of his tendency to fall for one grand scheme after another over a period of years, or what we in the twenty-first century would call conspiracy theories. Anthroposophy, with its teachings on the evolution of consciousness into the cosmic mind, was just another grand theory that required no logical proof.[83]

Lewis assured Barfield that he did not think poetry, as the product of imagination, was false. When Lewis spoke of the poetic imagination as fantasy, he did not mean falsehood. Fantasy is simply not real. It is neither true nor false.[84] Lewis argued that there are other values beside truth, and beauty is the value that applies to poetry.[85] He thought that the value of poetry might relate more to moral value than to truth.[86] Nonetheless, he came to accept the idea that imagination involves more than the image-making capacity of fantasy and that it involves the concept of meaning.[87] Lewis explained that imagination could tell "what it would 'mean' *if* there were a god," but it cannot tell that there *is* a god.[88]

In Lewis's eighth letter to Barfield in the "Great War," he did not give the date, but he provided the address from which he wrote. He was at home in Ireland at Little Lea. The letter would seem to have been written around the end of December 1927 or the early part of January 1928, when Lewis made his annual Christmas visit to his father. By this point, the friends had settled on the question of knowledge itself. Lewis insisted that having an idea about something does not make it so in fact. In this discussion, Lewis kept himself almost exclusively to logical examples rather than to examples in life. Were he to have given examples from life, he might have mentioned Aristotle, who had the idea of the whole of reality: a universe without beginning, eternal in duration, characterized by absolute time, with the Earth at its center, containing heavenly bodies of perfect smoothness in round circumference, and on and on. Aristotle's idea governed the scientific world until the seventeenth century and then began to erode as it became obvious to experimental science that nothing he imagined was true. Lewis, however, put the argument in logical form: "To wonder is to have hypotheses. To have hypotheses is to imagine. But to know is to have one assertion, and one or more rejected hypotheses."[89]

In the end, this phase of the discussion simply stalled. Neither man moved in any significant way, and in the last letter that Lewis wrote to Barfield on the subject of imagination and knowledge, he pointed out the ultimate impasse. Lewis believed in the existence of the individual thinking person. Barfield did not. Barfield believed that everyone is part of a collective cosmic consciousness into which humanity is evolving. Thus, to imagine something is to share in the universal imagination that knows the truth. While the physical body known as Owen Barfield might exist, the self-conscious person inhabiting that body was part of a great whole. Lewis thought that if Barfield's idea were true, then he might as well cut his throat.[90]

The "Great War" then shifted to Lewis's concerns about anthroposophy and his desire for Barfield to give it up. The last phase of the "Great War" resulted in several more letters and a few lengthier essays, most of which have never been published.[91] After Lewis's conversion to Christianity, he simply lost interest in the anthroposophy discussion. He realized that he and his friend occupied two different worlds now, and neither was inclined to change. Among the features of anthroposophy, Steiner proposed not one devil but two: Lucifer and Ahriman. Neither is such a bad fellow, since they both provide humans with gifts that advance their evolution to the heavenly realm. Humans must learn to balance their gifts.[92] Anthroposophy included a complicated multitude of heavenly hosts, but Lewis explained to Daphne Harwood that it lacked the one feature he required: "God the Father Almighty."[93]

Whereas Lewis had changed his mind about a number of matters along his way to faith, Barfield found a belief system that fitted his outlook. In later years, Barfield pointed out with some pride or irony that he believed in evolution but had never changed his mind, while Lewis did not believe in evolution (the way Barfield did) and changed his mind about a number of things.[94] Barfield would never again be a dialogue partner with Lewis about spiritual matters. Their friendship would involve good company and literary conversation, but they parted ways spiritually over Steiner's anthroposophy.[95]

4

From Idealist to Christian

1927–1931

Around the onset of the "Great War" between Lewis and Barfield, the health of Albert Lewis had begun a precipitous decline. Before their "Great War" ended, Albert Lewis would die.

Albert's Failing Health

After the most pleasant Christmas with his boys in years at the end of 1926, Albert entered 1927 with what sounded to Jack like a severe case of gout.[1] Jack thought it was time for Albert to find a new and effective doctor instead of feeling bound by loyalty to his longtime physician. Since Warnie sailed for Shanghai and a new posting in the Far East on April 11, 1927, Jack faced a new prospect—the care of his father as his health grew worse.[2]

Warnie had suggested, and Jack adopted a plan, to bring Albert to England for a rest at a health spa and then on to Oxford. In proposing the plan to his father, Jack offered himself for the whole of September and early October, which is remarkably generous, considering how he had done all to avoid long visits with his

Jack with Maureen and Janie Moore (and their dog, Baron Papworth) at a Cornwall tea shop, 1927. Used by permission of the Marion E. Wade Center, Wheaton College, Wheaton, IL.

father for a decade. In the end, Albert could not be coaxed away from Little Lea, but he did agree to change doctors. He went to his nephew, Dr. Joseph Lewis, son of Albert's older brother and one of Jack's few childhood playmates, known to the family as Joey.[3] Jack had confidence in his cousin's medical ability, but he disapproved of the way he had shirked his duty and avoided the war. Before going to Belfast in lieu of Albert's visit to England, Jack spent his usual August holiday with Minto, Maureen, and their dog, Baron Papworth, in the southwest of England on the coast of Cornwall, where he relished the body surfing.[4]

At Little Lea, Jack found that his cousin was giving Albert injections twice a week of a serum composed of throat swabbings, urine, and excrement. With such care, one could hardly wonder why Albert continued to decline.[5] The necessity for continuing his injections provided Albert with his first ironclad excuse for not going to England. The second excuse came in the form of a visit from his bother Richard's daughter, Eileen, who was visiting other relatives. Albert explained to Jack that he would have to invite her to dinner.[6] Jack wrote to Warnie that their father suffered a great deal while they were together, and he was frustrated that Joey had not given him a diet that might help.[7] Jack also noted an increase in the coarseness of the stories he told, and then provided Warnie with a few examples. Otherwise, Albert continued to interfere and supervise Jack's life as always, constantly misunderstanding situations and taking offense, as had been his father's pattern for years while ever on the lookout for hidden meanings.

After his Easter visit to Belfast in 1928, Jack wrote to Warnie that their father's health seemed tolerable, but that his eccentricities, which had often been a cause for joking behind his back for years, were now a permanent feature of his behavior.[8] Jack returned to Belfast again in mid-August through mid-September, but he made no mention of this visit in a letter to Warnie, the normal means by which posterity knows about his visits. Albert had always encouraged Jack's literary aspirations, and Jack made the effort to keep his father informed about his scholarly activity, if not his personal life. He had decided it was time to write an academic book. At first, he told his father that he was thinking about something on Erasmus, but then he realized that he would have to go back farther than Erasmus to understand Erasmus. Then he thought he might write something on the medieval allegorical courtly love poem *The Romance of the Rose*. Finally, he decided he would write on the entirety of medieval allegorical courtly love poetry.[9] By the first week of November 1928, Jack could report to his father that he had completed the first chapter of the book that would become *The Allegory of Love* and that it was at the typist.[10]

Albert had shown a great interest in the election of a new president for Magdalen College following the retirement of Sir Thomas Herbert Warren. To gratify his father, Jack wrote a brief letter explaining the politics by which George Gordon was elected the new president. To Owen Barfield, however, he confided that the charm of Magdalen had worn thin, and he now knew it to be a "cesspool, a stinking puddle," inhabited by false, hypocritical, evil-mouthed traitors. He now saw his colleagues as things in men's shapes climbing over one another and biting one another in the back: ignorant of all things except their own subjects and often even of those: caring for nothing less than for learning: cunning, desperately ambitious, false friends, nodders in corners, tippers of the wink: setters of traps and solicitors of confidence: vain as women: self-important; fie upon them—excepting always the aged who have lived down to us from a purer epoch.[11]

Lewis would never enjoy his colleagues at Magdalen. When he left in 1955 to go to Magdalene College, Cambridge, he warned Emrys Jones, a former pupil who succeeded him at Magdalen, to beware of the Senior Common Room.[12]

At Christmas in 1928, Jack spent three weeks with his father while Warnie was still far away in China. Other than writing to Warnie that it had been a good visit, Jack made none of his usual extensive commentary on the ridiculousness of his father.[13] As a side note, we may observe that in this letter, Jack commented on a declaration he had made to Warnie and insisted that it was original with him: "To have no philosophy is to *have* a bad philosophy."[14] C. S. Lewis would repeat this declaration ten years later in his sermon "Learning in Wartime," delivered at the beginning of World War II.[15]

Jack and Albert both had flu in the winter and spring of 1929. In a rare letter to his father in May, Jack described his annual walking tour with the anthroposophists through Salisbury to Lyme Regis and gave him the good news that he had completed the second chapter of his book on medieval love poetry.[16] Perhaps most interesting, Jack mentioned that he attended evensong at Salisbury Cathedral while walking with Barfield and Harwood. Evensong had not been his habit, but strange things were happening to Lewis.

Jack wrote to his father in June to make plans for his annual summer visit to Little Lea. Normally he went in September, but in 1929 he told his father that he planned to come in mid-August for three or four weeks. He also planned to bring his dog, but he was not supposed to have a dog as a fellow living in college, so he explained that he was keeping a dog for a friend who was away in Switzerland. His father advised him against taking on the care of the dogs of friends, so Jack backed away from that plan. Albert also told his son that he had not been well.[17] Jack told his father that he had been reading Andrew Lang's *Myth, Ritual and Religion* (1887).[18] After rejecting strict materialism, Lewis was now determined to make sense of the relationship between mythology and what people called God.

Albert Lewis was not merely unwell. His brother Richard Lewis commented on how unwell he looked the first week of July. He had severe pains during the night of July 20. He consulted his doctors, who advised an x-ray.[19] Jack wrote to Warnie that the x-rays were inconclusive. Albert might have cancer, but Joey did not think so. The doctors decided that a light diet would be a good alternative to an operation. Though Albert began to experience convulsions and shivering, the doctors did not think these symptoms serious, and they prescribed bed rest. After his temperature rose to 103, the doctors decided he should have surgery.[20] Jack took mild comfort in the fact that his father's exchanges with the doctors were as ludicrous as the lifetime of maddening conversations he had with his father.[21] The doctors urged Albert to abstain from his routine of whiskey, but that was out of the question. By this point in his life, it would be fair to say that he had a drinking problem. Jack mentioned to Warnie that his father kept two bottles in his wardrobe.[22]

When the light diet failed to produce any favorable result except that Jack could finally eat a light meal at Little Lea, the doctors admitted Albert to a nursing home in the second week of September. There he underwent surgery, which revealed colon cancer. The doctors assured Jack that his father was in no immediate danger and would live for some time, so he returned to Oxford on September 22 to prepare for Michaelmas term. On September 24 he received word that his father had taken a turn for the worse.

He died on September 25, 1929, before Jack could see him again. The funeral took place on September 27 at St Mark's, Dundela, where Jack's grandfather had been rector and where Jack had been baptized and confirmed. Albert was buried next to his wife, Flora, in the city cemetery. Jack sent a cable to Warnie with the news.[23]

Life after Albert Lewis

In his biography of Lewis, A. N. Wilson declared that Jack's conversion to theism "coincided more or less directly with the death of his father."[24] Wilson seems to suggest that the turn to faith in God had something to do with the death of Albert. Unfortunately, Wilson's biography makes many such suggestions. The chronology of events, however, does not necessarily imply a causal relationship between them. The Latin phrase *post hoc ergo propter hoc* (after that, therefore because of that) describes a logical fallacy to be avoided in reference to the life of C. S. Lewis: concluding that an event happening after another event is *caused by* the earlier event. Lewis was not a sentimentalist. He had once had reasons for not believing in God, but these reasons had slowly fallen away as he went through the mental exercise of examining those reasons. He had traveled some of the journey with Barfield, during which time he had acquired a somewhat pantheist notion of the ultimate as a reasonable solution. As he argued against Barfield's anthroposophy, however, he found that he had eliminated pantheism as an option.

As strained as relations between father and son tended to be for the last fourteen years of his life, Albert Lewis continued to play an important part in Jack's life that might be overlooked. The greatest encouragement of Jack's literary life had always come from his father, beginning when Jack was a little boy. Albert Lewis funded Jack's thirst for books and appears to have always been a dialogue partner about what Jack was reading until the end. Albert Lewis also supported his son's plan to do a second degree, in English literature, which created an additional burden on his limited finances. He supported his son's choice of a career that would never make him a prosperous, much less a wealthy, man, when social advancement had always been the aspiration of the Lewis and Hamilton families. What is more, Albert also expressed pride in Jack's academic and literary achievements. He was enormously proud of his son's two books of poetry, even if he had reservations about the sentiments that Jack expressed. He might have insisted that his son follow him in a law career, as Owen Barfield's father did, but Albert Lewis always wanted his son to be happy in his work. While Jack Lewis constantly withheld from his father the fact of his double life in maintaining a home with Janie Moore and Maureen, he also told his father all the details about prospective employment, publishing opportunities, relations with colleagues, academic politics, and how his literary life was developing. In the end, Albert Lewis had the greatest role in the making of C. S. Lewis as a literary man.

With the death of Albert Lewis, however, the Lewis brothers finally had to tend to business on their own. They had little experience with money except in spending what Albert gave them. Jack, through his efforts to maintain a home in Headington, had learned that money does not go very far. Warnie had learned the same lesson through his efforts to live the life of a gentleman on a low-ranking officer's pay. With Warnie in China, it fell to Jack to begin settling his father's estate. He wrote to Warnie with the initial decisions he had made. He negotiated the assumption of the titular head of his father's law office by a solicitor named Hayes. Albert Lewis's clerk, J. W. A. Condlin, would actually do the work for his remaining clients, but the office needed to operate under the name of a qualified solicitor. Jack also set in motion an effort to sell the law practice as a going concern, by which the brothers would receive a set amount each year for a set period of years. Finally, Jack had to make decisions about Leeborough House, or "Little Lea." He retained Mary Cullen—always "the Witch of Endor" to the Lewis men—as the housekeeper, but he dismissed the gardener and the housemaid. He impressed upon the Witch of Endor that Leeborough was no longer a rich house. He placed all the silver in the vault at the bank, retaining only enough for the brothers to use at Christmas, when Warnie returned from China. He would make no effort to sell the house until after Warnie's visit, when he could share the decision about what to keep and what to sell of the furniture and personal effects.[25]

As it happened, Warnie could not return from China until Easter, so Jack and Minto went to Belfast at the end of term in December 1929 to perform the initial sorting of all that filled Little Lea. Scrupulous in not offending the local sensibilities by staying at Little Lea together, Jack and Minto stayed with Arthur Greeves across the street.[26] Jack wrote to Warnie just before Christmas to explain how he had arranged matters. He had put all the books that he thought they would want in the study. He collected all the Boxonian materials from their childhood and placed these in the study. He collected all the family's papers, letters, and diaries and placed these in the study. He saved all the family photos and pictures except for photos of a few cousins and unknown people and put these in the study. He brought all the valuable books and first editions back to Oxford. The "dud" books he left on the floor for the local librarian to examine. He kept Warnie's civilian clothes and his father's clothes that might fit them. His mother's clothes, with which his father had never parted, he thought might be given to female relatives. All the other clothes he delegated to the Witch of Endor to use or disperse. All of Warnie's souvenirs were taken to the study. Minto and the Witch of Endor agreed that the china was not very good and not worth keeping. He sold the piano for eighteen pounds to the man who valued the estate for death duties. He opened a bank account for the estate to handle all proceeds. He sold his mother's stamp collection for four pounds. He also set aside a number of pieces of furniture, all relegated to the study.[27]

Warnie arrived from Shanghai on April 16, 1930, after a journey of fifty-five days. He had been away in the Far East for three years and five days. He spent a night with Jack in Oxford before joining Minto and Maureen on holiday in Southbourne for a few days before traveling on to Belfast on April 23. The brothers spent only one day at home, where they buried their childhood toys in the garden. They then returned to Oxford, where Warnie stayed until he was posted to his new assignment as assistant to the officer in charge of supplies at Bulford, Wiltshire.[28] Warnie had dreams of re-creating their little end room at Little Lea as a museum, but Jack thought a museum would be more like a mausoleum. Warnie was yearning for the time when he and Jack had been close, but Jack insisted that an attempt to imitate the little end room would be like embalming a corpse that was not dead. Jack acknowledged the rift that had come between them over Malvern and added, "We have both changed since the real old days, but, on the whole, we have changed in the same direction."[29] Jack and Minto invited Warnie to become part of their household in Headington with the hope of one day finding a larger house for them all to enjoy.

Mythology and the Knowledge of God

The friendship between Lewis and J. R. R. Tolkien grew slowly but steadily after the founding of the Kolbítar. The group also functioned under the name of the Icelandic Society, and it formed a regular part of Lewis's life. In a letter to Greeves a month after Albert's death in which Jack complained of having "too many irons in the fire," he related how Tolkien had come by his rooms at Magdalen and had stayed until two thirty in the morning talking of the gods and giants of Norse mythology.[30] Later that week, Lewis met with Tolkien and the Kolbítar group until midnight. He clearly enjoyed his heavy schedule of self-inflicted commitments, but he acknowledged that it was hard on him and especially bad for him spiritually.[31] That he was concerned about anything being bad for him spiritually indicates just how far his mind had begun to grasp the implications of spiritual reality.

A few months later, in February 1930, Lewis again mentioned a Kolbítar meeting and Tolkien. He described something that Tolkien was writing that included metrical romances and maps, the mountains of Dread, of Nargothrond, the city of the Orcs! Lewis assured Arthur that part of Tolkien was what they were. He loved northernness![32] Sometime in November 1929, Tolkien had showed Lewis something he had been writing. It was *The Lay of Leithian*, a poem about Tinúviel, which he had begun writing in 1925. Lewis read it with delight and wrote to Tolkien with his initial criticism on December 7, 1929.[33] The two matters that had thrilled him most were "the sense of reality in the background and the mythical value." Then Lewis gave his definition of myth: "the essence of a myth being that it should have no taint of allegory to the maker and yet should suggest incipient allegories to the reader."[34] Lewis would draw out this distinction between myth and allegory in *The Allegory of Love*, which would not be published until 1936, but upon which he was hard at work. Lewis was in the midst of a shift from viewing myths as only symbolic representations of ideas or the made-up projections of daydreams conjured from the imagination to a view that myths actually conveyed something real. Barfield, so enmeshed in his anthroposophical system, could not help Lewis move to this view, but Tolkien could.

Lewis appears to have been the first person that Tolkien allowed to enter the world of Middle-earth, which he had been creating since his convalescence in 1917 following a case of trench fever contracted in October 1916. The first tale he wrote of his lifelong work, *The Silmarillion*, was "The Fall of Gondolin."[35] This act of showing Lewis his private world of elves and orcs demonstrates a profound level of trust and confidence that had grown up between the two men, because this kind of writing would not have done Tolkien's professional reputation any good at Oxford in 1929, when Tolkien was engaged in the politics of revising the English syllabus. From hours and hours of long conversations about Norse mythology deep into the night over a period of several years,

Tolkien appears to have recognized in Lewis someone who would value what he had done and was doing. Tolkien's trust and confidence were well placed, for Lewis undertook to provide Tolkien with a detailed critique, along with extensive recommendations for changes and improvements. The critique ran to fourteen pages in Lewis's fine hand. Not content with a straightforward criticism, Lewis produced a parody of an academic commentary on the text as though it were of ancient origin and had undergone numerous emendations and alterations over the centuries. Thus, he critiqued not the writing of Tolkien but the obvious flaws of those who had altered the text over the years.[36] Tolkien adopted most of Lewis's suggestions, but he struggled with his writing. Having begun this long poem in 1925, he abandoned it in September 1931, an auspicious month, as we shall see.

Tolkien, in fact, always struggled with his writing. His son Christopher spent most of his adult life editing his father's uncompleted manuscripts. The collection runs to over a dozen volumes covering the history of Middle-earth. Tolkien's reputation stands on the two works he did complete, *The Hobbit* and *The Lord of the Rings*, both of which were distractions from his main project, *The Silmarillion*. That great project, over fifty years in the making, remained unfinished when Tolkien died in 1973. Christopher Tolkien published his edited version of *The Silmarillion* in 1977. That Tolkien ever finished *The Hobbit* and *The Lord of the Rings* we may credit to C. S. Lewis, as Tolkien did. Lewis provided encouragement but also a disciplined structure through which Tolkien could bring his work to a conclusion. The structure involved regular meetings with Lewis at which times Tolkien had to have something to read, just like a tutorial. This kind of relationship appears to have developed out of Lewis's reading of *The Lay of Leithian*, and it appears to have grown during 1930.

Early that year, the Tolkiens bought the house next door to their residence at 22 Northmoor Road and moved into 20 Northmoor. The new house had belonged to Basil Blackwell, the noted proprietor of Blackwell's Bookshop. Sometime during this period of an intensifying interest in Norse mythology and Tolkien's imaginary world, Lewis began meeting with Tolkien on Monday mornings, normally at the Eastgate Hotel, to talk and share a pint of beer.[37] Lewis was working on the book that would establish his academic reputation as a major scholar of medieval literature, *The Allegory of Love*. He had finished the second chapter in December 1929.[38] Tolkien continued to struggle with *The Lay of Leithian*. From letters to Arthur Greeves, we have an idea of how Lewis might have expounded his literary ideas to Tolkien.

During this period, Lewis was also engaged in the last stage of his "Great War" with Owen Barfield, which focused primarily on Lewis's objections to anthroposophy. Lewis's arguments appear to have inadvertently led him to belief in a single, personal God—an *I* rather than an *It*. He seems to have worked through the process between the time he began reading *The Lay of Leithian* and early February 1930. Sometime in the fall, he had begun the practice of meditation as a spiritual (not Christian) discipline.[39] He had also developed a friendship with one of his former pupils, Alan Richards Griffiths, a once-avowed materialist who was on the same spiritual pilgrimage as Lewis. Griffiths had become one of Lewis's walking and talking companions.[40] His other new walking and talking companion was an eighty-year-old retired country parson named Foord-Kelcey, who shared none of his literary interests, but who had "such tenderness of heart that one never feels bleak."[41] They walked together every Monday.[42] In addition, Jack resumed his regular correspondence with Arthur in a way he had not done since his Great Bookham days.

After his visit to Little Lea in December 1929 following his father's death, he wrote to Greeves about reading John Bunyan's conversion account, *Grace Abounding*. He was struck by Bunyan's uncertainties, doubts, and fears even after his conversion, when he "felt himself united to Christ." Lewis wanted to know what Greeves thought of the darker side of religion they found in the old books that had once seemed like mere devil worship to him. Then he added, "Now that I have found, and am still finding more and more, the element of truth in the old beliefs, I feel I cannot dismiss even their dreadful side so cavalierly."[43] On Christmas Eve, he wrote to Greeves that he was indexing Bunyan!

One of the glib arguments against the existence of God that some materialists raise is the vastness of the universe. Contemplating the vastness of time and the universe while at the same time enjoying the coziness and homeliness of County Antrim, Lewis remembered something Greeves had mentioned when Jack was with him earlier in the month: "the 'broad-mindedness' of the infinite" (by which Greeves, but not yet Lewis, meant God). Jack reflected that the human mind could never be contented with a small universe. He confessed to Arthur, "You can't have elbow room for things like men except in endless time and space and staggering multiplicity."[44]

By January, Lewis was reading Jacob Boehme's *The Signature of All Things* (1912), in which he found Boehme's description of the "mystery of creation" and the making of all things. Lewis felt that Boehme "was talking about something tremendously real." He said the whole experience of reading the passage had an enormous impact on him. It was tantalizing, moving, exciting, mysterious, distressing, and even horrifying. It shook him up more than anything else he had read since he first read George MacDonald's *Phantastes*.[45]

Lewis had been changing his mind about God, but he had not yet changed his mind about everything related to Christianity. He wondered, in a letter to Arthur in early January 1930, if the saintly pleasure of sharing in the judgment of the damned was not contrary to the spirit of Christ. Then he recalled that the privilege had been promised by Christ to his disciples. He concluded, for the time being, that "in spite of all my recent changes of view, I am still inclined to think that you can only get what *you* call 'Christ' out of the Gospels by picking & choosing, & slurring over a good deal."[46] Lewis assured Arthur on January 26 that he had not yet come to religion, but he was enjoying his attempt at religion. He was reading MacDonald again, and he mused, "One finds oneself on the main road with all humanity, and can compare notes with an endless succession of previous travelers."[47]

By January 30, Jack could assure Arthur that he was getting along "very, very well" spiritually. He had come to experience the grace of God. For the previous ten days he had felt the support of God in dealing with his sex drive and his anger. In his youth, he and Arthur had referred to sex as *It*; by this time, he spoke of God as *It*. Over the previous ten days he had "the most delicious moments of *It*."[48] He told Arthur that "the sweetness was so great, & seemed so to affect the whole body as well as the mind, that it gave me pause—it was so very like sex."[49] In that moment, Lewis realized that Freud had gotten everything backward. Belief in God is not sublimated sex. Citing Plato's idea that the material world is an inferior copy of the spiritual world, he reasoned that the powerful experience of sex must be an inferior copy of something in the spiritual world. Sex is the sublimated experience of knowing *It*.[50]

Lewis wrote a brief, urgent letter to Owen Barfield in early February pleading with him to come to see him on the following Saturday, February 8. He wrote: "Terrible things are happening to me. The 'Spirit' or 'Real I' is showing an alarming tendency to become much more personal and is taking the offensive, and behaving just like God. You'd better come on Monday at the latest or I may have entered a monastery."[51] In his letter to Arthur on Monday, February 10, Lewis remarked that Barfield had come to tea on Saturday and that they had a splendid talk. As for the outcome of this phase of his spiritual journey, he remarked that Griffiths had also spent the night with him before Barfield's visit. He said that Griffiths had been "all mucked up with naturalism, D. H. Lawrence, and so on, but has come right and is I do believe really one of 'us' now."[52] Lewis had come to believe in God along with his oldest friend, Arthur Greeves.

In *Surprised by Joy*, Lewis explained that during Trinity term of 1929, he had come to believe in God. Trinity term follows Easter, when Lewis made his annual walking tour.[53] His memory, however, seems to have failed him at this point, as it did when he misremembered when he first discovered George MacDonald at a railroad book stall. As Alister McGrath has pointed out, Lewis's letters indicate that his conversion to theism came the following year.[54] The final moment came while riding on the top of a bus up Headington Hill on his way back to Hillsboro from Oxford. He simply made up his mind without fanfare or emotion and chose to believe that God exists. All the many pieces of philosophy, science, theology, ethics, metaphysics, and logic that had been dancing around in his brain for some fifteen years finally fell into place. He was no longer an idealist or a pantheist. For better or worse, God made the most sense, so that is where Lewis landed and planted his feet most reluctantly. Though he felt he had a choice, he also felt that God was the only choice that made any sense.

In March, Lewis wrote to his old college friend A. K. Hamilton Jenkin, with whom he had hoped to coordinate a visit. It had been several years since they had been together, and Jenkin had since married. Lewis gave Jenkin a bit of the news of Oxford and then mentioned his own news. He now had a religious outlook. He made it clear that he was not "precisely Christian," but that he might become a Christian before he finished his journey. He explained that he had once wondered if he would adopt Christianity, but now he wondered if Christianity would adopt him, because he now knew that there was "another Party in the affair."[55]

Lewis appears to have taken the reality of God to heart. He accepted the implications of God as one would gravity. It cannot be avoided and neither can God. Having devoted years to the study of ethics and morality, the problem of "the good," and the failure of character, Lewis took great comfort in God who seemed to be doing something about Jack's many flaws. He confided to Arthur in a letter on June 1, 1930, that he was receptive to God, but that he had "fallen" twice, just as he was about to drift off to sleep and was patting himself on the back for doing such a good job of resisting temptation. He noted that "the enemy" had been forced by God to resort to "*stratagems*" in dealing with him.[56] With this remark, we have a glimpse of Lewis's growing awareness of the nature of temptation and its subtlety that would form the basis for *The Screwtape Letters* a decade later. Then he described how he had been listening to the old gramophone records that had produced such vague longings and desire when he was younger, and still did. It occurred to him that "the enemy" would take advantage of these feelings to persuade him later that *he* had the way to fulfill those longings. At that point, Lewis immediately sent the longings deeper until his mind turned to the one who is the end of all longing and desire.[57] To cap things off, he had been reading *The Practice of the Presence of God*, a devotional classic from the seventeenth century.[58] Before long, Lewis would confront himself with just how hard it would be for him to lead the spiritual life. He told Arthur that "it is so fatally easy to confuse an aesthetic appreciation of the spiritual life with the life itself."[59]

By July, Lewis had returned to William Morris and a book by him that Jack had not read, *Love Is Enough*. From his new theistic perspective, Lewis lamented that Morris had the power to describe the beauty of the world, the vague longings that it arouses, its failure to satisfy those longings, and the sense of time and change that make the world heartbreakingly beautiful precisely because it will be lost, but without ever explaining why. Morris seemed to have no "inkling" of why the world should have such an effect on people. He did not seem to know what reality lay behind the world to which the world's beauty pointed. Then Lewis read *Love Is Enough*. Finally, Morris laid bare the eternal values, and "*holiness*" shone through the romanticism of Morris. Jack told Arthur that he had been a "dry prig" with *Dymer*, but he was ready to return to what he had once not understood. He now had the key. He observed "that the road is always turning round and going back to places we seemed to have left—but they are different (yet in a way the same) when you come to them again."[60] This insight would transform the fiction writing of Lewis and, by his influence, Tolkien, as we shall soon see.

At the end of July, Nevill Coghill introduced Jack to his friend Hugo Dyson, who had been an undergraduate with Coghill at Exeter College. Dyson taught English at the University of Reading. Lewis liked him immediately. He invited Dyson and Coghill to dinner at Magdalen, and they did not leave until three in the morning. Like Coghill, Dyson was a Christian. Lewis recognized him at once as a man who loved truth. No dilettante, Dyson expressed critical and literary judgments that emerged from his faith informed by sound philosophy.[61] These two friends would continue to play an important role in the growth of C. S. Lewis.

The Kilns

Jack had lived with Janie and Maureen Moore at Hillsboro House in Headington, just off the High Street, for a number of years, during which time they had longed for a larger house they could own. The death of Albert Lewis finally made the purchase of a house possible. Janie and Jack had invited Warnie to cast his lot with them and make his home in Headington when he retired from the army. Disarmament had been a theme of the great powers in the 1920s, and Warnie had wondered if he would have a place in the army. If he could hold on just a few more years, he could retire before he was forty years old with a pension. He longed to renew the closeness he had experienced with his brother when they were young, but Jack impressed upon him that life would be different because it would be a life shared with others. Warnie agreed to these terms. Whether he understood is another matter.

On Sunday, July 6, 1930, Jack and Warnie went to see a house situated on eight acres at the foot of Shotover Hill on the eastern edge of Headington. The property had been the site of a brickyard. Two large kilns for firing the bricks still stood on the grounds, as well as a few large sheds. From the two ruined brick kilns, the house took its name: the Kilns. The house was a modest story and a half. It faced away from the road toward Shotover Hill. Between the house and the hill lay a small pond against the edge of which, just as the path turns to climb the hill through the trees, a circular brick seat had been constructed into the hill. The brothers were enchanted. For a number of years, Jack had loved Shotover Hill and made his way there regularly for his long afternoon walks. He mentioned it forty-four times in his diary between 1922 and 1927. It is of the same style of architecture as Little Lea, though not on so grand a scale. Under the eaves in the half story, it even had a little end room, which Jack would claim as his bedroom. They bought the house and grounds for thirty-three hundred pounds.[62]

The finances were complicated. Little Lea would not finally sell until January 1931, when the brothers realized twenty-three hundred pounds for their father's house.[63] Mrs. Moore had a small legacy from the estate of her brother Dr. John Askins. The trustees of the estate allowed her fifteen hundred pounds.[64] Warnie put up the initial deposit of three hundred pounds and secured a mortgage of five hundred pounds. Jack secured a mortgage of a thousand pounds.[65] The property was bought in Mrs. Moore's name, which left Jack and Warnie without any legal right to the property in spite of their investment. For their security, Mrs. Moore wrote a will that gave the brother's the dower right to live in the Kilns as long as they lived, at which point the property would pass to her daughter, Maureen.[66]

Warnie drove to Headington on October 10, 1930, to help with the move from Hillsboro to the Kilns. He found everything at both Hillsboro and the Kilns in a state of "complete chaos."[67] The initial move took place on Friday, but settling and unpacking and arranging would continue for days. By Sunday, Mrs. Moore was entertaining a Mrs. Armitage and her daughters for tea while Jack was recruited to take Mrs. Armitage punting on the pond, where her dress was ruined when she sat on the slime-covered seat. After tea, Jack and Warnie went walking through the new neighborhood and past Holy Trinity Church, where they resolved to attend.[68] They would attend services at this church regularly for the rest of their lives, and in the churchyard they lie buried.

Warnie and Minto appear to have gotten off to a bad start from the first weekend in the Kilns. Warnie planned to leave for his post on Monday morning before the sun rose, and he gave specific instructions that no one get up to see him off. When he crept downstairs, he found that Minto had gotten up before him to make him some tea.[69] Minto's effort at self-sacrifice only annoyed Warnie. C. S. Lewis would have a lot to say about self-sacrifice as a vice over the next few years. The following weekend, when he returned to the Kilns, Warnie experienced a repeat of the early morning routine, much to his embarrassment. The night before, Warnie had a sample of Mrs. Moore's temper when she thought the brothers had arrived late for supper, but Warnie was certain that they had arrived before supper was ever served by Mrs. Moore.[70] Warnie would grow to dislike her immensely as they both grew older.

Jack settled into life at the Kilns. The small estate provided him with a connectedness to England that he had not theretofore known. The Kilns lay at the outskirts of civilization. Woods and wildlife now stood at his door. He had to give up his walking for a time because of all the domestic work that occupied his time: chopping firewood, clearing the paths, feeding birds, and "messing about" in the old punt on their pond.[71] As the winter wore on, Jack and Warnie began planting trees for what Warnie called the Kilns Afforestation Scheme.[72] Until life with Mrs. Moore, Jack had never known any form of manual work, whether inside or outside a house. Little Lea had servants to do the work. As for his faith in God, he told Greeves that the trouble was his *lack* of faith. He had no rational ground for abandoning his newly acquired belief in God. Arguments had convinced him, possibly because the arguments had come from within him rather than assaulting him from

The Kilns property from Shotover Hill, ca. 1930. Used by permission of the Marion E. Wade Center, Wheaton College, Wheaton, IL.

without. His problem was that he had no feelings about God. He prayed, but he found himself still mired in his old skeptical habits, the spirit of the age, and the cares of the day. He did not *think* God was not there and listening, but he often *felt* that way. Rational Lewis wanted the feelings.[73]

By the end of 1930, the effects of the Great Depression were beginning to be felt. No one had made a good offer on Little Lea. The few investments that Albert Lewis had made were not providing his sons with much income. Jack's friend Owen Barfield had also come to face the results of his father's straightened conditions. Like Albert, Barfield's father had supported his son's lifestyle for many years as he sought to pursue a literary career without success. Barfield failed to acquire an academic appointment like Jack. He had also failed as a poet and writer. Like Greeves, he had spent a good deal of time writing a novel that was never published. The senior Barfield could no longer afford to support his son in the face of dwindling prospects. In the end, Barfield went to work in his father's law office.[74] With a regular job, the casual trips up to

Oxford ended. Lewis and Barfield would see each other only a few times a year in the future. Following the "Great War" and Lewis's conversion to theism, the discussion of theology and philosophy ceased.[75] Their friendship continued, and the annual walking tours remained a hallmark of the year until the beginning of World War II, but from henceforth, the two men traveled different spiritual paths. Their friendship, however, was far from over. Even as their "Great War" came to an abrupt end, they embarked on a campaign to read Dante, which they did together with great pleasure.

The Influence of New Friends

After his surrender to theism, Lewis found himself firmly on the same path with Nevill Coghill, Hugo Dyson, and Ronald Tolkien. All four had academic vocations and similar literary interests. They were all good company. All except Lewis had been at Exeter College in their undergraduate days. Lewis, Tolkien, and Coghill had been meeting for several years to read Old Icelandic with the Kolbítar group.

Jack was also growing closer to Warnie again after a general separation of sixteen years. From January 1 through 4, 1931, Jack and Warnie took a walking tour from Chepstow to Gloucester and on past Monmouth and Tintern Abbey for fifty-four miles.[76] Jack had developed his love of walking after he and Warnie had grown distant, so it was a pleasure that Warnie had not enjoyed— a pleasure that Jack feared he might not share. Fortunately, Warnie loved the experience, perhaps even more than Jack did.[77] More important than love of walking, however, Warnie and Jack attended church together twice on their trip. Warnie disclosed that he had come to believe that the religious view of things was true after all. He had not wanted God to exist any more than Jack had, but he feared that God must exist.[78] On May 9, 1931, Warnie would begin to say his prayers again for the first time in years upon coming to the conviction of the truth of Christianity. It seemed to him that the existence of the universe and the origin of life could not be explained by the materialists. He had come full circle from indifference to skepticism to atheism to agnosticism to Christianity.[79] While Warnie was going through this revolution, Jack was devouring the novels of George MacDonald, which Greeves had passed on to him. He faulted MacDonald for subordinating the plot to doctrine, but he loved the doctrine.[80] He was caught.

Lewis discovered that his lifelong love of astronomy and science fiction had left him. He suspected that philosophy and theology had "taken the shine out of" his interest in the physical universe. He hoped it was only a temporary matter. In fact, he told Arthur that, on further reflection, he had not lost interest at all. Instead, he had an intense interest for brief periods that he could not sustain. It was an unsettling situation that he did not recommend.[81] In such a state, there was nothing for him to do but grow a beard.[82] By the end of the year, however, he would have passed through that confused state, and all the wonder and lure of astronomy and science would come rushing back, along with a renewed love of science fiction. First, he had to finish understanding what kind of universe existed that he loved so.

Lewis began to read in a new way. Until this point in his life, he thought of the novel as a "*dangerous* form" of literature.[83] He thought the novel divided readers into the low-brow type and the high-brow type. The low-brow simply have a "narrative lust" to get to the ending and find out what happens.[84] If the best-loved characters marry, regardless of whatever misery may enshroud the rest of the characters, then it is a happy ending. If the main characters do not marry, no matter how happy the state of all the other characters, then it is an unhappy ending. In reading Tolstoy's *War and Peace*, however, he discovered a new kind of writing in which it is possible to remain detached from the main characters. He insisted to Greeves that it was not a blank indifference but almost like "a submission to the will of God."[85] He would continue to think about low-brow and high-brow approaches to reading until he put it all down on paper in *An Experiment in Criticism*, published in 1961, two years before he died. To think in terms of submission to the will of God, however, meant that he did not have much time left as a mere theist.

Jack had learned the virtues of honest toil at the Kilns, but he also discovered that the Kilns had great pleasures. Once term was ended, he had troves of time to spend lolling in a deck chair, reading, punting, and swimming in his pond. The pond did, and still does, look profoundly dirty, but Jack assured Arthur that he emerged perfectly clean after swimming. Arthur visited Jack for the first time at the Kilns at the end of May 1931, and Warnie was able to join them for a weekend leave. In August, Jack and Warnie returned to Ireland for the first of many visits after they no longer had a home in Belfast. On the visit, Jack's love of science having revived, he had a long argument with his uncle Gussie Hamilton about the metaphysical implications of Einstein's theory and the nature of the atom. Warnie, who despised philosophy in any form, managed to change the subject by interjecting, "How are things at the yard, Gussie?"[86]

Warnie returned to his post after touring many of their favorite places in Ulster, but he left Jack in Ireland where he spent a week with Greeves at his family's house across from Little Lea. Arthur sent him back to Oxford with volumes of Thomas Hooker and Jeremy Taylor, two of the great theologians of the seventeenth century. Jack was reading Hooker in September 1931.[87]

On a Saturday night, September 19, Lewis invited Hugo Dyson and Ronald Tolkien to join him for dinner at Magdalen College.[88] Michaelmas term would not begin for a few more weeks, so their dinner conversation would not be overwhelmed by the noise of scores of undergraduates in the hall. Dinner at Magdalen was a grand affair with multiple courses. It was not a rushed meal and could easily last until almost nine o'clock, when the fellows retired to the Senior Common Room to smoke, have their coffee, and perhaps drink port wine. It was a memorable evening full of the kind of talk that Jack enjoyed: metaphor and myth, which had been

Addison's Walk, Magdalen College

the focus of much of his disagreement with Barfield. The three men began strolling along Addison's Walk, a wooded path about a mile in circumference within the grounds of Magdalen College that circles a meadow and is bounded by small waterways, like an island. In the warm mid-September night, a sudden wind came up and scattered the newly fallen leaves, producing a sound like falling rain. It was one of those magical moments in nature that Lewis loved. The men then retreated to Lewis's rooms to continue their conversation, which turned to Christianity.[89]

On October 1, Jack wrote to Arthur with the news that he had passed "from believing in God to definitely believing in Christ."[90] Arthur would have to wait for more than two weeks, however, to learn the story of what had happened in that long night of talking.

Almost a month after the evening with Tolkien and Dyson, in one of his again frequent letters to Arthur, Lewis explained what had happened to him in the course of that late-night conversation. For the previous year since his acceptance of the reality of God, Lewis had been struggling to understand what Christianity *means*. Once you believe in God, then believing that God might take on flesh is not a problem. Lewis's problem was not believing that it could happen but understanding why God would become man and what difference it would make. He struggled to understand what it means that Jesus died to save the world. Lewis did not see how the death of someone two thousand years ago could have anything to do with him. He had no problem with the necessity of some kind of miraculous salvation, because he had a strong awareness of the flawed nature of people, especially himself, that leads them into degradation incompatible with God. Jesus might help as an example, but Lewis knew that the Gospels and the epistles of Paul describe something quite different from a simple example. Something very mysterious was going on with such phrases as "propitiation," "sacrifice," and "the blood of the Lamb."[91]

In their conversation about myth, Lewis realized that he did not mind the idea of sacrifice when he found it in pagan myths. He gave the example of Odin in *The Hávamál*, which he had quoted on the page facing the title page of *Dymer*: "Nine nights I hung upon the Tree, wounded with the spear, as an offering to Odin, myself sacrificed to myself."[92] In fact, when he found the case of a god sacrificing himself to himself, he liked it very much and thought it mysteriously moving. He also was powerfully moved by the myths of a dying and rising god that he found in so many cultures; such as the story of Balder in Norse mythology, Adonis in Greek mythology, and Bacchus in Roman mythology. To these he might have added Baal of the Canaanites and Osiris of the Egyptians. He realized that he liked these stories anywhere he found them, except in the Gospels.[93] He could enjoy the myths and revel in the feelings they gave him without having to ascribe any particular objective meaning to them. As he had been taught in school, the old myths were just made-up stories. On this account, he had decided that the story of Jesus dying for the world and rising from the dead was just another myth.

In an earlier conversation, T. D. Weldon had made the offhand remark that the Gospels appeared to be based in fact.[94] The remark had stuck in Lewis's mind, coming as it did from a virulent atheist. The conversation had taken place in 1926. Yet, in *Surprised by Joy*, Lewis mentioned it in relation to his move to theism in 1930. Its full impact, however, did not hit him until late September 1931 in his discussion with Tolkien and Dyson about the story of Jesus as a myth like all the others. It struck him as like the other myths, but somehow different. All the others had taken place "once upon a time," but the story of Jesus unfolded in Palestine shortly after its incorporation into the Roman Empire. Jesus was born the year that a decree went out from Caesar Augustus that the entire Roman world should be taxed, the same year that Quirinius became governor of Syria and Herod was king of Judea. Jesus did not die outside space and time, as things happen in all the other myths; he died on Golgotha Hill outside Jerusalem when Pontius Pilate was governor of Judea and Herod Antipas was tetrarch. Lewis decided that the story of Jesus was the myth that really happened.[95]

In the late-night conversation that continued between Lewis and Dyson until four in the morning, even after Tolkien went home at three, all the streams of thought and confusion that had been weighing on him for several years sorted themselves out. Imagination, rationality, truth, meaning, feelings, myth, and sensory knowledge all fell into place. He saw them all clearly in beautiful relationship. They were not enemies. The story of Jesus is a myth in the sense that it works on people the same way the other myths do, but more was going on. Lewis decided that the pagan myths from all over the world, which continued to tell the story of a dying and rising god, involved god expressing himself through the minds of the pagan poets, speaking to their imaginations, within the context of their setting. With Jesus, however, God expressed himself in the flesh and dwelt among us. The pagan myths contain snatches or faint glimpses of God, but in Jesus, God showed himself without blinders. Thus, the gospel story does not give us a description of God. Instead, God chose to appear to our sensory faculties. Thus, the revelation of God in Jesus is the true myth. In this sense, Lewis saw a distinction between theology (what people think about God) and revelation (what God himself makes known). Theology, or the doctrines of the church, are merely translations of the truth that is the revelation from God. Theology attempts to explain and discuss Jesus in terms of contemporary concepts and ideas, but the actual incarnation of God in the flesh, the death of Jesus for our sins, and the resurrection of Jesus from the dead are the real truth.

Lewis took away from the late-night talk a conviction that he could not simply dismiss the account of Jesus as a made-up story, a mere product of human imagination. He had argued against Barfield's notion that *all* imagination is true. What he had not considered is that *some* imagination may be true. He had rejected Barfield's idea of a universal corporate imagination, but once he believed in God, he had available to him the possibility that God might use imagination as the faculty for receiving knowledge of him. Lewis knew that as an honest scholar and a man of integrity, he must treat the story of Jesus fairly and not dismiss it outright. During this period, he had begun to read Paul's epistle to the Romans, chapter 6 of which deals with the thorny problem of how the death of Jesus two thousand years ago might work on someone living in the twentieth century.[96] Death was the answer. Lewis had been reading about death in the novels of George MacDonald for months.[97] He saw it again in *Hamlet*.[98] Sin must be destroyed in those for whom sin is part of their life, indistinguishable from who they are. Paul explained to the Romans, who did not seem to understand it, that on the cross, Jesus bids the world die with and in him. The invitation is to share his death and to share his resurrection.

Lewis mulled these matters over in his mind from the evening of September 19 until Monday, September 28, 1931. The day had started poorly with the usual conflict between Maureen and Mrs. Moore over whether they should cancel their plans to visit the zoo at Whipsnade due to the fog. Warnie recorded the skirmish in his diary. He made a strategic withdrawal from the breakfast table until matters sorted themselves out. The new plan called for him and Jack to travel to the zoo on his motorcycle while the rest of the group took the car. Jack and Warnie had loved zoos since their mother took them to the zoo in Regent's Park on their way to France in 1907. The fog soon dissipated, and Jack and Warnie stopped for bottles of beer when Warnie filled the gas tank. The brothers arrived shortly before one o'clock, but the others did not finally arrive until almost two thirty. After a substantial lunch of sandwiches, they all began their tour of the zoo, except for Jack, who had to remain outside with Tykes, the new dog that Minto insisted on bringing with them. Warnie spent an hour seeing the limited number of animals in the zoo, and then he relieved Jack of dog duty. A week later, on Monday, October 5, Jack and Warnie returned to the zoo by themselves so that they could actually enjoy it. Jack particularly loved the bears. He wanted to have a bear of his own at the Kilns and name it Bultitude.[99] He made Bultitude the bear a key figure in *That Hideous Strength*, the last of his three science-fiction novels.

On the way to the zoo for the first visit, as Lewis's October 1 letter to Arthur Greeves implies, something important happened. In *Surprised by Joy*, Lewis remarked that the end of his conversion to faith in Christ came gently: "I was driven to Whipsnade zoo one sunny morning. When we set out I did not believe that Jesus Christ is the Son of God, and when we reached the zoo I did."[100] He said that he had not been thinking about it. Nor had it been an emotional experience. It was more like lying motionless in bed and gradually being aware that you are awake. Two days later, Warnie left England bound for China and his last tour of duty before retirement the next year.[101]

We know what was going on in the head of C. S. Lewis related to his conversion because he explained it all in his letter to Greeves of October 18, 1931. In many ways, the letter is a repudiation of all he had written in his letter to Arthur from Gastons on October 18, 1916, in which he expounded his theory of the story of Jesus as mere myth. The immediate impact of his conversion, however, is seen in his letter of October 1, in which he acknowledged and apologized for his intellectual and social priggery, his affectation, his posturing, his showing off in all of his early letters, and his complete self-absorption. Looking at his old letters after his conversion made him feel humiliated. On the positive side, his earlier behavior provided him with a keen insight to the human condition that would aid him when he wrote *The Screwtape Letters* and *The Great Divorce*.

5

From Poet to Scholar

1931–1939

While C. S. Lewis had taken the journey from idealism to pantheism to theism to Christianity, carried on his "Great War" with Owen Barfield, reconnected with his love of Norse mythology through his Kolbítar friends, reestablished his closeness and correspondence with Arthur Greeves, buried his father, bought the Kilns, and revived his childhood relationship with his brother, something else had happened that played a role in his development which has often been overlooked. Lewis was writing a book. He kept his father informed of his progress as he finished the first chapter and then the second. By the time of his conversion, he was working on the third chapter.

The Only Book C. S. Lewis Ever Wrote

The book was *The Allegory of Love*. In many ways, it is the only book Lewis ever wrote. All the other books flow from it like a stream. In it can be found the synthesis of all the ideas that had been swirling in his head for years. At first, he thought he would write a book about *The Romance of the Rose*, one of the foremost medieval allegorical courtly love poems. Then he was taken by a grander vision that placed this poem in its context from the development of allegory in first-century Rome to the development of courtly love in the eleventh century and to the beginnings of love as a basis for marriage at the end of the medieval period. In order to attempt this monumental task, he first had to master Christian theology from the time of Augustine through Thomas Aquinas and the Scholastics until the eve of the Reformation. Otherwise, he could not possibly understand what the poetry of the Middle Ages meant.

The central device of *The Romance of the Rose* is the walled garden. It represents great longing and desire. In this case, the desire is for the love of a woman. Lewis often spoke of the walled garden when discussing the most elusive of longings and desires. Within the walled garden at the end of the world lies the great prize for which the valiant will risk any danger and sacrifice all. Lewis would place the walled garden at the end of *The Magician's Nephew*, where it guards the tree of life. He would place the journey to the end of the world at the end of *The Voyage of the Dawn Treader*, where Reepicheep, the embodiment of the courtly love tradition, goes on alone, like Galahad, in order to reach the only thing worth having. Lewis was working on the third chapter of *The Allegory of Love*, entitled "*The Romance of the Rose*," after the death of his father.

Essentially, Lewis was writing a scholarly book about the stories from the Middle Ages that had affected him so powerfully as a teenager. These stories were all variations of the same story. The ones he loved the most were about the journey to the end of the world for the one great thing worth giving up all else to acquire, and then returning as a changed person. This was the story that William Morris and George MacDonald had imitated and Jack had tried but failed to imitate in *Dymer*. Even as Jack argued with Barfield over metaphor, myth, and imagination, he studied what the great authors of the classical and medieval worlds had said about these things. He realized that his questions were not

new and that he had dialogue partners who had been dead for
centuries.

When he finally finished the book and published it in 1936,
Lewis dedicated it to Owen Barfield, calling him the "wisest
and best of my unofficial teachers."[1] The dedication frustrated
Barfield, who did not think he had managed to teach Lewis much
at all.[2] Barfield particularly criticized Lewis for rejecting his idea of
"Historicism." By this term Barfield did not mean history or histo-
riography. He meant that people were getting better and better as
they evolved into the divine spirit, which Barfield also called the
evolution of consciousness.[3] It should also be noted that Barfield
viewed the evolution of consciousness not as happening only
in individuals but as a corporate experience in which all minds
are joined by common imagination.[4] Barfield never succeeded in
teaching Lewis to believe as he believed, but he did succeed in
teaching that imagination and history matter.

Lewis had better instruction on the meaning of history from
reading G. K. Chesterton's *The Everlasting Man*.[5] In *The Allegory
of Love*, Lewis demonstrated a profound sense of history, as well
as an understanding of the development and decline of culture. He
traced the career of allegory from its beginnings in the first century
through the decline of the Roman Empire, and then its place in
the medieval world from the time of Augustine in the fifth century until its fading away with the passing of the medieval world
in the sixteenth century. During that period, customs changed.
Technology changed. Government changed. Religion changed.
Art changed. Philosophy changed. The one constant was human
nature, which has not changed. No, Lewis did not accept Barfield's
thin view of historicism, but he knew that history was important
and that sometimes the past has more to say about the present
than the present does. Thus, Barfield had taught him to shed his
chronological snobbery.

Unfortunately for the twenty-first-century reader, we must now
discuss allegory, which has grown alien to our culture but for over

a thousand years was how Western culture thought. In modern terms, we might think of the way a culture thinks as the difference between an Apple operating system for a computer and a Microsoft operating system. The systems "think" and "process information" differently. We have a few vestiges of allegory in American culture, the most prominent of which stands in New York harbor. The Statue of Liberty personifies that most cherished value of our culture as a woman. She stands strong and fierce with upheld arm holding the torch of liberty as a beacon. Allegory involves expressing an intangible value, quality, idea, or emotion such as liberty as a physical, visible thing. The personification of such an intangible matter was a favorite device of the allegorists. When the apostle Paul wrote the first book of the New Testament, his letter to the Galatians, he chose to explain the concepts of slavery and freedom through *allēgoroumena* (allegory). He said that Hagar, the bondwoman by whom Abraham had his son Ishmael, is an allegorical figure for slavery and the old covenant. Sarah, the wife of Abraham and a free woman by whom Abraham had his son Isaac, is an allegorical figure for freedom and the new covenant (Gal. 4:22–31).

In discussing the relationship between allegory and the immaterial world (for emotions and values are not material things), Lewis remarked, "If our passions, being immaterial, can be copied by material inventions [e.g., the Statue of Liberty], then it is possible that our material world in its turn is the copy of an invisible world."[6] Here we find Lewis exploring the implications of the source of values being outside the physical world and the physical world itself a creation by something beyond it. With his love of mythology and his grounding in Homer, Lewis observed that from the time of Socrates, Plato, and Aristotle, the classical world gradually ceased to believe in the old gods and gradually turned them into allegorical ornaments of literature. In the *Aeneid* and the *Iliad*, the gods had mythological reasons for their motives and behavior, but by the time of the *Thebaid* (ca. AD 90), Mars appears as an allegorical device: the god of war who rages because that is what war does. If he did not rage, he would not exist.[7] Of all the allegorical themes that attracted the attention of Lewis, however, none surpassed the inner conflict a person experiences in the choice between good and evil, which is found in the *Thebaid*. Lewis wrote, "Here already in the pagan poet we have in no ambiguous form the favourite theme of the Middle Ages—the battle of the virtues and the vices, the Psychomachia, the *bellum intestinum*, the Holy War."[8] For years, Lewis had been fighting the *bellum intestinum*, the war of the innards, and he had been losing until he came to Christ.

Then he made a remarkable observation that would appear in several of his apologetics books later. The death of the gods into allegorical figures had not happened because of Christianity, for the dissatisfaction with the old gods had been growing since the time of Socrates. Lewis said that "monotheism should not be regarded as the rival of polytheism, but rather as its maturity."[9] In *Surprised by Joy*, Lewis mentioned that once he believed in a God, he then had to determine what kind of God. He expressed this same approach in *The Problem of Pain* and *Mere Christianity*. This had been Augustine's dilemma. Once Lewis realized that all the peoples of the world had always known that some kind of God was there, he had to take the myths seriously and understand their function. He asked: "Where has religion reached its true maturity? Where, if anywhere, have the hints of all Paganism been fulfilled?"[10]

In the end, Jack Lewis decided that Jesus fulfilled all the hints. Lewis had been reading the Gospels and the letters of Paul in the year leading up to his faith in Christ, and he would have noticed that the apostles littered their sentences with the observation that Jesus had fulfilled the Law and the Prophets. It was all there, which in turn gave the Scriptures an authority that he had never seen before. For prophecy to be fulfilled, it must have a source outside the prophet. Thus, it must have a supernatural origin.

Lewis's belief in Christ implied irreconcilable differences with Owen Barfield. Because of his view of an evolved universal consciousness that he identified with the imagination he regarded as conveying truth, Barfield accepted all the heretics and their beliefs as true: Gnostics, Neoplatonists, Cathars, Knights Templars, Rosicrucians—it did not matter. To Barfield, they were more Christian than their orthodox contemporaries.[11] Thus, Barfield did not like Lewis's reliance on the Bible "as the final revelation of Divinity to man."[12] Barfield preferred a continuing process of understanding deity through the imagination of the evolving universal consciousness. He defined Christianity as the acceptance of the incarnation and resurrection of Jesus as the central point of human evolution. The incarnation did not mean God taking flesh; it meant humanity evolving to divinity. He did not believe that the other aspects of the gospel (the creator God, fulfillment of Scripture, atoning death, exaltation, gift of the Holy Spirit, second coming) are essential to Christianity. Thus Barfield regarded the heretics as good Christians.[13] Several years later, Lewis would explain to one of his correspondents that he regarded Barfield's religious ideas as "a kind of Gnosticism."[14]

After his conversion, Lewis never again discussed theology with Barfield, unless it came up accidentally in conversation, and then Lewis would move on quickly. He never shied away from controversy, but he tired of Barfield's efforts to convert him to a system that appalled him. Furthermore, Barfield's logic seems to have tired Lewis. In many ways, arguing with Barfield was like arguing with his father. From time to time, Lewis remarked that he could not understand Barfield's logic in his written essays.[15] Lewis always said it in a kind way, but his difficulty understanding Barfield was not because Barfield had superior intelligence. Jack had no trouble understanding Plato, Aristotle, or Augustine. Rather, Barfield had a tendency to logical fallacies and stream of consciousness that skipped logical steps in an argument.

Lewis's study of the allegorical tradition had played its part in his conversion. As for the *bellum intestinum*, he thought that the internal battle lies at the heart of allegory, but the image of a battle does not best portray the inner struggle with temptation. Lewis realized that without the concept of temptation, all reference to good and evil vanishes away. While Prudentius had depicted the struggle between good and evil as a war, Seneca had portrayed it as a journey. Lewis observed, "Seneca, with his imagery of life as a journey, was nearer to the mark than Prudentius: for Seneca outlined the theme of the *Pilgrim's Progress*, and the *Pilgrim's Progress* is a better book than the *Holy War*."[16] Thus, the journey to the world's end had captivated him. Life is a spiritual journey.

One final word needs to be given on *The Allegory of Love* to indicate its relationship to Lewis's conversion, as well as his career. The word is *imagination*. Lewis began with the classical world in order to explain how allegory works, but he showed also how the old gods declined "from deity to hypostasis and from hypostasis to decoration."[17] It was decoration that let romance enter and freed the poet to inventions beyond what had been known in literature theretofore. Lewis explained:

> Under the pretext of allegory something else has slipped in, and something so important that the garden in the *Romance of the Rose* itself is only one of its temporary embodiments— something which, under many names, lurks at the back of most romantic poetry. I mean the 'other world' not of religion, but of imagination; the land of longing, the Earthly Paradise, the garden east of the sun and west of the moon.[18]

With this final statement, we will be prepared to examine Lewis's first account of his conversion with its full title: *The Pilgrim's Regress: An Allegorical Apology for Christianity, Reason and Romanticism*. Lewis would not write that book, however, for a while.

Life Goes On

In Oxford, Jack began the practice of attending chapel at Magdalen every morning at eight o'clock and then going to breakfast. In the process, he made a new friend, Adam Fox, who served as dean of the chapel and presided over the chapel services each day.

They then ate breakfast together. In far-off China, Warnie finally decided that his faith in Christ was not a mere whim or passing fad, and on Christmas Day 1931, he took Communion at the Bubbling Well Chapel in Shanghai.[19] Minto, on the other hand, had nothing nice to say about the change of atmosphere in her house. The daughter and sister of clergymen, she had escaped religion and had no interest in making a return.

Lewis had not initially warmed to Ronald Tolkien when they first met at an English faculty function, but once they found common ground over Old Icelandic and, even more, over what Tolkien had been secretly writing, they became comrades in the English School. Lewis changed his mind about the syllabus and came over to Tolkien's point of view. Tolkien wanted a greater emphasis on the study of the English language and how it changed from Anglo-Saxon into modern English. By 1931, Tolkien—with the help of Lewis—had carried the day. Part of the problem had arisen because English language pupils had been required to read great portions of Shakespeare and Milton, which Tolkien regarded as too modern, while English literature pupils had been required to endure painfully theoretical studies of philology. Tolkien's proposal involved learning philology through reading the old texts of literature. Lewis and Tolkien had become allies.[20]

Lewis viewed their triumph as a victory over the "junto" that had controlled the English School, but he wondered how long it would take his group to become just as corrupt.[21] The victors in the revolt against the controlling junto started their own celebratory group, which they called The Cave, after the cave in which David gathered his supporters against King Saul (1 Sam. 22:1). The group centered on Tolkien and included Lewis; Coghill; Leonard Rice-Oxley of Keble College; Herbert Francis Brett-Smith, who lectured in English at several colleges; Maurice Roy Ridley of Balliol; and Dyson, who was still at Reading.[22] Once they had achieved their aims in 1931, they continued to meet for ten years for a rousing meal at the end of term.

At some point between his coming to faith in Christ and November 22, 1931, when he wrote a long letter to Warnie, Jack and Tolkien had begun the practice of meeting on Monday morning in Jack's rooms at Magdalen, when possible. Jack had no pupils on Monday, while Tolkien, in his exalted position as professor of Anglo-Saxon, had few teaching duties. In his letter to Warnie, Jack provided the earliest description of a get-together that would grow and blossom into a full fellowship of like-minded men in Oxford who eventually styled themselves the Inklings. They offered criticism of each other's writing and often drifted into discussions of theology or settled into bawdy and puns. For Lewis, the meeting with Tolkien had become the most pleasant spot of the week.[23] The weekly meetings would continue with some regularity until Lewis left Oxford for Cambridge in 1954.

Jack's relationship with Hugo Dyson had also flourished. Though Dyson lived about twenty-five miles away where he taught at the University of Reading, he frequently made the trip up to Oxford to meet with Coghill, Tolkien, and Lewis. Jack spent the night with Dyson and his wife, Margaret, in early November 1931. Jack apparently had told Warnie about Dyson after their late-night talk at Magdalen. Of course, Dyson was always extraordinary company, but Jack was surprised that Margaret was so exceptional. At this point in his life, he had low expectations of women, possibly because of the level of conversation he had endured with Minto and the friends she cultivated. Jack told Warnie that Margaret was so nice that he almost regretted leaving her after dinner to go to Dyson's study for some serious smoking and talk.[24]

In Shanghai, Warnie found himself in the midst of the Japanese attack against the city. Of all things to be reading, Warnie turned to *The Faerie Queene*, to which Jack would devote the concluding chapter of *The Allegory of Love*. The long year of 1932 was a difficult one in Shanghai. Japanese planes bombed the city while a Japanese fleet lay offshore. At the height of the conflict, over a hundred thousand Japanese troops fought to control the city.

A negotiated peace between China and Japan was established in May, but the incident was merely the first of Japan's testing of Chinese strength before the onslaught of a full invasion aimed at the conquest of China. By Christmas of 1932, however, Warnie was back at the Kilns as a private citizen, his retirement effective as of December 21. Captain Lewis managed to retire with retirement pay before the age of forty.[25]

While Warnie was in China, Maureen took a job teaching music at the Monmouth School for Girls in Monmouthshire, where she taught until 1933.[26] Jack thought that Maureen's absence would contribute to Minto's well-being because she would take with her the cause of endless jobs and bickering that her presence seemed to foster.[27] Without Maureen in the house, however, Jack had to rearrange his weekly schedule during term by January 1932 so that Minto would not be alone for too many nights each week. Maureen came home from Monmouth for Friday and Saturday nights, and Jack stayed at the Kilns on Sunday and Wednesday nights.[28] He may have still been meeting with the Mermaids on Monday nights and the Kolbítar on Tuesday nights. On Thursday nights he had been meeting with a philosophy group, but his Thursdays would become otherwise occupied about this time with his new group, the Inklings. Coincident with Maureen's departure, the Kilns acquired a new maid, who could cook and, to Jack's surprise, was actually *allowed* to cook by Minto.[29] As it turned out, Jack confided to Warnie that she did not cook as well or as much as Minto had done, but he asked Warnie not to mention it to Minto, lest a row ensue.[30] Minto ruled with an iron hand, and even the neighbors noticed. Jack's new elderly friend, the Reverend Mr. Foord-Kelcey remarked: "Ah you Irish! I love to listen to Mrs. Moore—wouldn't be happy without a grievance."[31]

During this early period of his life as a Christian, Lewis consumed volumes of devotional material, such as William Law's *A Serious Call to a Devout and Holy Life* (1728) and *An Appeal to All That Doubt or Disbelieve the Truths of the Gospel* (1742), which he preferred.[32] He also told Warnie that he was not impressed with Descartes's proofs for the existence of God. In fact, though Lewis would gain international fame as an apologist, he did not think any proofs for the existence of God were convincing. In this regard, he liked Cecil Harwood's definition of God as "a Being who spends his time having his existence proved and disproved."[33] He thought Anselm's ontological argument could be argued both ways. This argument is deceptively simple: I have in my mind the idea of a most perfect being, than which no greater can be conceived; but a being that actually exists would be greater than one that exists only in the mind; therefore, God exists. Lewis told Warnie that it all depends on who has the idea and where it came from. He thought the origin of mythology demonstrated the earliest form of an idea of God. By 1938, he told his former student Dom Bede (Alan Richard) Griffiths that pure reason in humans does not seem to be convinced by proofs. He thought that tradition and divine guidance had more to do with a conviction that God exists.[34] Former students would play an important part in Lewis's life, and he realized it early on. At the end of 1931, Jack mentioned to Arthur Greeves that he gained a new friend from among his pupils almost every year.[35]

While Warnie was in China, Jack also had the responsibility for the fashioning and installation of a stained-glass window at St Mark's, Dundela. The brothers decided to donate a window to the church in honor of their parents. Jack suspected that other members of the church were attempting to exert some influence on the design of the window behind the scenes. On reflection, he believed that the curate of the church was speaking under directions from Arthur's sister, Lily Ewart, when he suggested adding an image of St Mark's tower to the design. Jack declined the helpful hints.[36]

With his large frame, booming voice, and ruddy complexion, Lewis appeared the picture of good health at first sight. A sickly child plagued by ill health throughout his school years, Lewis continued to succumb to one malady after another throughout the 1930s. Between New Year's Day and Easter of 1932, he spent a total of three weeks in bed with three episodes of influenza.[37] Nonetheless, he kept a cheerful disposition and was thankful for protracted periods when he could catch up on his reading. By 1939, Lewis would confide to Dom Bede Griffiths that he had gone from having flu once a year to having it once a term.[38] He might have added that when he had the flu and was in bed for a week, he often had a relapse and had to go back to bed for another week.[39]

After his Easter vacation bout of flu in 1932, Jack began to look forward to a performance of Wagner's *Siegfried* on May 16.[40] Earlier in the winter, he had told Arthur Greeves that the music of Wagner was still as evocative for him as it had been when they were young.[41] He had hoped that Barfield would join him, but Owen had a conflict. Jack went by himself.[42] He described the performance to Warnie. It was Jack's first visit to the Royal Opera House in Covent Garden. He had wanted to attend a performance of *Siegfried* for twenty years. Unfortunately, his expectation of a Covent Garden performance was too high. He had thought that a Covent Garden performance must be incomparable, but it seemed just like any other performance of an opera in terms of the quality of the singing—two magnificent singers, one has-been, two adequate singers, and two truly bad. What surprised him was that the acting was far better than he had expected.[43]

Lewis continued to enjoy the old pleasures. First, after the performance of *Siegfried*, his love of music experienced a revival. Second, he took his annual walking tour with Barfield and the anthroposophists. In spite of Barfield's and Harwood's running commentary on the thought of Rudolf Steiner, Lewis loved tromping across the countryside. The third great pleasure of life for Lewis was swimming. He did not have his first swim for the year until Sunday, June 12. To his dismay, the draining of the swampy ground at the Kilns by Frederick David Lyddiatt, who had been helping with various jobs there for several years, and a Mr. Knight, who also did some jobs, succeeded in lowering the level of the water in the pond.[44] Jack at least had the satisfaction of being able to tell them, "I told you so," but that pleasure did not make up for the loss of water. A fourth great pleasure came in August when Jack returned to Belfast for a two-week visit with Arthur.

The Pilgrim's Regress

During his two-week visit with Greeves in 1932, C. S. Lewis wrote an account of his conversion as an allegory on the model of John Bunyan's *The Pilgrim's Progress*. How is it possible to write a book in two weeks? To a certain degree, Lewis had been writing his life story since his days at Great Bookham. He knew the important moments. He knew every crisis. He knew when he had experienced major shifts in his understanding of the world and of himself. He knew his own story. This book, *The Pilgrim's Regress*, has been called a spiritual autobiography. In terms of the Christian tradition of which Lewis has become a part, it is his personal testimony, the methodology for the spreading of the Christian faith that Jesus had instructed his disciples to use. A Christian testimony is simply what Christians know from their own experience; or as Lewis wrote to Greeves, "I can describe only what I know."[45] *The Pilgrim's Regress* stands in the tradition of not only *The Pilgrim's Progress* but also Augustine's *Confessions* and the rich heritage of similar accounts of how believers came to faith. In that sense, this book is a spiritual exercise more than a writing exercise.

Instead of *progress*, Lewis spoke of *regress*. By regress, he did not mean a deterioration in the spiritual well-being of the pilgrim. Rather, he meant that once the pilgrim has come to faith, he must return to his everyday world and live in this world as one who has faith in Jesus Christ. The pilgrim is changed in the course of the journey. The story that Lewis had loved for so long—about the journey to the end of the world to find the answer to the heart's deepest longing—turned out to be Lewis's story. The subtitle explained what Lewis hoped to accomplish with this book:

An Apology for Christianity, Reason, and Romanticism. Though some people think of Lewis's apologetics as his logical essays that he undertook during World War II—*The Problem of Pain*, the BBC broadcasts that became *Mere Christianity*, and *Miracles*—his first self-conscious effort at apologetics was in the form of a medieval allegorical tale like *The Faerie Queene*. It is a story, not a philosophical argument.

The apology for Christianity forms the storyline. It is the narrative of how Lewis came to faith, except he has veiled the story in the form of medieval allegory. He would retell the story again twenty years later in straightforward prose as *Surprised by Joy*. By 1932, Lewis had been living every day in the world of medieval allegory for over four years while writing his yet-to-be-completed masterpiece on medieval allegorical courtly love poetry. He probably did not fully appreciate at this point how few modern people can actually understand allegory, but he would in time.

The apology also extends to reason, that dimension of the human spirit that allows people to make rational judgments. It facilitates discernment, evaluation, assessment, calculation, comparison, contrast, and the wide variety of capacities related to thought. Reason is the function of the mind. Through his testimony, Lewis affirmed that God uses the human mind to draw people to himself. God is the author of rationality, and Lewis would identify irrationality with temptation and sin.

Finally, his apology deals with what he called "romanticism" in 1932. By the time the third edition was published in 1943, he regretted the choice of this term. In their "Great War," Lewis and Barfield argued over the meaning of romanticism. Lewis came to realize that the term has many different meanings. He and Tolkien had discussed the problem with the word even before the book's first printing.[46] Lewis intended to draw attention to the relationship between his imagination and the experience he had been calling Joy for ten years. He was presenting an apology for religious experience. He meant to distinguish between a simple aesthetic experience and an experience that comes from a personal encounter with God. He had rejected all of Barfield's arguments for imagination's capacity to know God, but in the end, he had decided that God makes himself known to humans through the imagination.

The central figure in *The Pilgrim's Regress* is John. The nickname for John is Jack. John is Jack Lewis. Since allegory expresses immaterial emotions, values, and qualities by means of a material picture, Lewis needed an image to picture his experience of Joy. He settled on a vision of a beautiful island that John has glimpsed through a hedge. John's journey begins as a search for the elusive island. He is born in Puritania. Many people assumed that Lewis was referring to Ulster with its Puritan background. Ulster, however, is a physical place, and allegory does not reference physical or material things. Puritania could be a metaphor for Ulster, but then it would not be an allegory. The land of Puritania is an allegorical figure for legalism. Lewis's earliest understanding of religion was a matter of rules and punishment.

Lewis decided to include a map of the "world" through which John journeyed in quest of the island. The map includes a legend that indicates all the shires along the way. After Puritania, John goes through Ceremonia, a veiled reference to an orientation toward religious ceremonies. Next, he comes to Orgiastica, where John develops a new interest in sex. On he travels through nineteen different lands. These include Occultica, which pictures Lewis's temporary fascination with the occult, and Zeitgeistheim, the spirit of the age, which displays Lewis's new look in postwar Oxford. He has a stop in Hegaliana, for his Hegelian idealism, and even a visit to Anthroposophia, the land of Barfield's anthroposophy. At last John comes to the Table Land and the great lady at the end of the world: Mother Kirk.

Before John meets Mother Kirk, however, he falls under the influence of a number of other people for a time. Lewis explained to Arthur Greeves that a Mr. Sensible quotes a number of great texts but misses the point of the authors. One of Lewis's main contentions was that ignorance of classical learning had contributed to the rise of atheism, thus John's encounter with Ignorantia.[47]

When he submitted the manuscript of *The Pilgrim's Regress* to Guy Noel Pocock, his editor at J. M. Dent, who had published *Dymer*, Lewis confessed that in addition to his serious intentions, he also had comic passages in which he ridiculed Anglo-Catholicism, materialism, sitwellism, psychoanalysis, and T. S. Eliot.[48] On February 2, 1933, Pocock wrote to say that Dent would publish the new book, but Lewis would have to make some changes. For one thing, in addition to the book's allegorical form, Lewis had filled it with Latin quotations.[49] Jack agreed to translate the Latin into English for the benefit of modern readers who lived in Ignorantia. He also suggested that he could add marginal notes to help guide the reader.[50] By April 12, the book had been typeset, and Jack had corrected the proofs. The book was published on May 25, 1933.[51]

The Inklings

In his preface to *The Allegory of Love*, Lewis thanked Tolkien for reading the first chapter and offering criticism. Lewis wrote the first chapter in 1928. Tolkien, in turn, had shown *The Lay of Leithian* to Lewis, who had offered his criticism. Lewis wrote *The Pilgrim's Regress* in August 1932, and Tolkien finished *The Hobbit* by mid-January of 1933.[52] *The Hobbit* was a diversion or distraction from Tolkien's longstanding project of creating the mythology of Middle-earth. Yet, he had difficulty completing this children's story. He stopped writing for about a year on two occasions.[53] Lewis and Tolkien provided each other the support, encouragement, criticism, and interest in their work that would allow them to write the books for which they became known.

In a letter to the editor of the *Observer* on February 20, 1938, Tolkien declared that he had not based *The Hobbit* on any other book but acknowledged that *Beowulf* and his own "Silmarillion," as yet unfinished, were his primary sources.[54] Yet, *The Hobbit* is unlike *Beowulf* or any of the tales in *The Silmarillion* in its published form. *The Hobbit* represents a departure from the kind of story that Tolkien loved and that he had been trying without success to write in *The Silmarillion*. *Beowulf* and all of the Norse stories that Tolkien loved shared a common plot. Simply stated it is this: the hero fights against impossible odds and dies.

The culture out of which *Beowulf* appeared was grim and dark. The Celtic world, which included the Germanic and Norse peoples as well as the Britons and Irish, indeed most of pre-Christian Europe, believed in dreadful gods who demanded human sacrifice. The Celtic peoples offered their own children, and eventually their slaves, as human sacrifices, which they then devoured in ritual cannibalism. They did not love their gods but feared them. The gods themselves had nothing to look forward to except their own destruction. Alliteration can be a pleasant literary device unless overdone, but it is impossible to overdo the nature of the Norse mythologies. Thus, their stories are characterized by darkness, doubt, depression, dismay, dread, despair, destruction, and death. The stories set a mood of stubbornness, suffering, sorrow, shadow, and sadness. The characters experience treachery, torment, terror, trouble, tears, threat, and treason. The stories are tales of futility, faithlessness, foulness, fear, and folly. These disquieting words are the words used by Tolkien throughout *The Silmarillion*. In the Norse tales, the heroes make their journeys to death and ruin.

The Hobbit represents an entirely different kind of plot. The plot, and later that of *The Lord of the Rings*, comes from a different culture. It is the plot that C. S. Lewis learned to love as a teenager and never outgrew. It is the story of the struggle against all odds to the end of the world for the great prize that ends in victory and a return to home as a changed person. It is a story that comes from a culture with an entirely different kind of God—a God who journeys into time and space as a man in order to battle death itself and rise victorious. It is a story of hope rather than despair.

In all likelihood, Tolkien adopted Lewis's favorite plot in the context of their weekly meetings in the early 1930s when they talked about *The Hobbit*, *The Allegory of Love*, and *The Pilgrim's Regress*. Lewis would be the most likely source for this change of plot because Tolkien would not have come upon this plot by himself. Tolkien hated the literature of England after the Norman conquest in 1066, taking the view that English culture had been "Frenchified." In the end, Tolkien employed Lewis's cherished tale of "there and back again."

Tolkien and Lewis may very well not have been conscious of the departure of *The Hobbit* from Tolkien's normal story plot, but that shift made sense.[55] Tolkien was a devout Christian, and his efforts to reproduce the Norse mythologies with Middle-earth were at odds with his own faith. This may be why he struggled to finish *The Silmarillion*. In any event, his two greatest stories follow the plot of the gospel rather than the Norse edda. For a clear example of the contrast between the gospel plot and the edda plot, compare Tolkien's telling of the *Ring* story (*The Lord of the Rings*) with Wagner's telling of the *Ring* story (*The Ring of the Nibelungen*).

Over the ensuing years, the mutual exchange between Lewis and Tolkien would grow into the group of men who met regularly during university terms and called themselves the Inklings. Exactly when the Inklings first began to meet regularly and who formed the group may never be known. In 1967, Tolkien wrote that he thought they probably acquired the name in the mid-1930s. The group of gathered friends predated their name, which Lewis salvaged from an undergraduate writing club at University College for which he and Tolkien served as faculty advisors but which folded when its members graduated.[56]

In a letter to Janet Spens in which he discussed matters related to *The Allegory of Love*, Lewis mentioned that he belonged to a group of four people who had discussed her idea of the relationship between *The Faerie Queene* and Wordsworth's *Prelude* at the end of Michaelmas term in 1934.[57] In all likelihood, Lewis referred to the Inklings, who would have been discussing Lewis's *The Allegory of Love*, the last chapter of which deals with *The Faerie Queene*. If so, the four members of the group at this early stage probably included Lewis and Tolkien. The other two would probably have come from a small group of three: Nevill Coghill, Hugo Dyson, and Warnie Lewis. Warnie had retired to Oxford on December 21, 1932. He met Dyson on February 18, 1933, and he met Coghill at a dinner on July 26, 1933, at Exeter College, where he and Jack were guests of Tolkien and Dyson.[58]

The group appears to have grown gradually and not intentionally. On Wednesday night, January 25, 1933, a month after Warnie's return from China and retirement, Tolkien invited him and Jack to dinner at Pembroke College. Afterward, they retired to Jack's rooms at Magdalen College, where they talked of language until eleven.[59] Dinner followed by a late-night talk in Jack's rooms would be the pattern for Inklings meetings for years to come, not unlike Jack's late-night talk with Tolkien and Dyson in 1931.

By 1936, the group had a name, and Lewis identified its four members in a letter to Charles Williams: Lewis, Tolkien, Coghill, and Jack's brother, Warnie.[60] The Inklings had two qualifications or matters in common. They had a tendency to write, and they were all Christians. Lewis's letter to Williams was a fan letter after he had read Williams's *The Place of the Lion*. Coghill had introduced Lewis to the book, and Lewis told Tolkien and Warnie about it, all of whom were taken with it. Lewis invited Williams to come for an Inklings meeting any day except Saturday or Sunday in Trinity term after Easter 1936.[61] The invitation suggests that the Inklings had not yet fixed their meeting day, which would become Thursday evenings during World War II. A general reading of Warnie's diary also demonstrates that Thursday evenings were not yet reserved for Inklings meetings. Jack still had Martlets meetings on Thursday evenings as late as the 1933–1934 academic year.[62]

Dyson was probably the next person who gradually became part of the group. What he added to the group is best understood by Warnie's description of Dyson the first time they met in Jack's rooms at Magdalen. Warnie was busy typing when

> in came J's friend Dyson from Reading—a man who gives the impression of being made of quick silver: he pours himself into a room on a cataract of words and gestures, and you are caught up in the stream—but after the first plunge, it is exhilarating. I was swept up by him to the Mitre Tap, in the Turl (a distinct discovery this, by the way) where we had two glasses of Bristol milk a piece and discussed China, Japan, staff officers, Dickens, house property as an investment, and most utterly unexpected "Your favorite reading's *Orlando Furioso* isn't it?" (deprecatory gesture as I get ready to deny this) "Sorry! Sorry! My mistake". As we left the pub., a boy came into the yard and fell on the cobbles. D (appealingly) "Don't do that my boy: it hurts you and distresses us".[63]

Following the dinner at Exeter College where Warnie first met Coghill, a small party of five went to Magdalen to talk until late: Lewis, Tolkien, Dyson, Warnie, and a clergyman whom Warnie did not yet know when he noted the event in his diary.[64] The clergyman may have been simply someone who tagged along, or he may have been Adam Fox, chaplain of Magdalen College, with whom Jack had breakfast every morning following morning prayer. Fox would indeed become a regular member of the Inklings.

The Allegory of Love

Oxford University's Clarendon Press published *The Allegory of Love* on May 21, 1936. Despite Lewis's refusal to condescend to his audience by translating his Latin quotations, the book is remarkably readable and accessible to an educated audience. He assumed that his modern audience would not understand how to read allegory, and his explanation makes allegory accessible. For those who have stumbled over *The Pilgrim's Regress*, the path to comprehending it is by way of chapter 2 in *The Allegory of Love*. Academic books like Lewis's treatment of medieval allegorical courtly love poetry normally enjoy a small printing of a few thousand copies, and after three or four years the publisher discounts the remaining inventory and takes the book out of print. *The Allegory of Love* is still in print after more than eighty years! Such a phenomenon is almost unheard of in scholarly life. Helen Gardner wrote that whether one agreed with Lewis or not, "after reading this book, one's whole imagination of the past has been extended and changed. Lewis recovered for the ordinary reader what had been lost for centuries, the power to read allegory and to respond to the allegorical mode of thinking."[65] Twenty-first-century scholars may disagree with Lewis's views, but they must engage his thought, because he set the standard. If Lewis had done nothing else, he would be a monumental figure in literary criticism for this book. E. T. Donaldson, the great American literary critic who belonged to the new criticism school of Yale, once told Derek Brewer that "he would have 'given an arm and a leg' to have written *The Allegory of Love*."[66]

For those who have read Lewis's later scholarly books and his popular books, however, *The Allegory of Love* provides an introduction to his thought and method. Just as the stories he examined in this book opened the way to his religious conversion, they opened the way to his academic career and his popular writing. Though the sense of longing and desire that Lewis associated with the experience of Joy forms the plot for many of these stories, at the same time they deal with different dimensions of love, from friendship to romantic love. For modern audiences, the most famous of the courtly love stories is also the most familiar, for it continues to be retold—the story of Sir Lancelot and Queen Guinevere. At a time when marriage was nothing more than a business transaction, courtly love involved adultery. Lewis's book traces how courtly love was eventually defeated by "the romantic conception of marriage."[67] In his final chapter, which deals with *The Faerie Queene*—

his favorite of all the allegorical stories of the journey to the end of the world—Lewis cites Spenser, who identified "three kinds of love": *eros*, *storgē*, and *philia*.[68] Lewis would pursue this idea in later writing until he finally wrote *The Four Loves* in 1960, the year his wife died. To Spenser's three loves, Lewis added *agapē*, the divine love taught in the New Testament. After he died, Lewis's lectures on *The Faerie Queene* were edited and published by Alastair Fowler, one of Lewis's former doctoral students.

Lewis would explore the meaning and nature of the four loves in *That Hideous Strength*, *The Great Divorce*, *The Screwtape Letters*, *Mere Christianity*, and *Till We Have Faces*. He explored not only what love is but also what it is not. He explored the corruption of love and the substitutes people choose over love. Yet it all stemmed from *The Allegory of Love*, where he first began to identify and define the issues.

In his explanation of how allegory began and how the ancient gods of Greece and Rome were reduced to allegorical emblems during the ancient period, Lewis developed a scheme for understanding the history of religion and its relationship to God. While studying with W. T. Kirkpatrick, Lewis had been exposed to a materialist understanding of the history of religion as a merely evolutionary concept. In discussing monotheism as the maturity of polytheism rather than its rival, Lewis developed a theistic view of the history of religion.[69] Lewis would incorporate this view into *The Problem of Pain* and *Mere Christianity* at the outset.

In explaining the inner conflict (*bellum intestinum*) over a choice between good and evil, which was a favorite subject of allegory, Lewis raised the whole issue of values, particularly the concepts of right and wrong. In discussing moral conflict and temptation, Lewis necessarily raised an issue that would animate much of his later writing.[70] *The Screwtape Letters*; *The Great Divorce*; *Perelandra*; *The Lion, the Witch and the Wardrobe*; and *A Preface to Paradise Lost* all deal with the problem of temptation in the terms that Lewis first announced in *The Allegory of Love*.

The internal conflict involves the opposite of wholeness. Only in victory over the dark alternative does resolution come and is wholeness achieved. Wholeness is a character issue that Lewis explored in *The Allegory of Love*. Character is what a person must produce from the raw material within that contends for mastery of a person.[71] Lewis described this contention as a struggle between head, breast, and loins.[72] He would develop this idea further during World War II in lectures published as *The Abolition of Man*, in which the head (intellect) and the bowels (emotions) must be mediated by the chest (character).

Lewis's study also forced him to comprehend the entirety of medieval culture and the idea of a culture's worldview, as opposed to an individual's point of view. People have different opinions, but people within a culture have a shared worldview of how they think even about the matters over which they disagree. In a letter to Sister Madelva, who taught English at Saint Mary's College in Notre Dame, Indiana, Lewis wrote of what he inadvertently learned by doing the research necessary to write *The Allegory of Love*: "I found that I had accumulated a certain amount of general information which, tho far from being very recondite, was more than the ordinary student in the school could gather for himself. I then conceived the idea of my 'prolegomena'."[73] His prolegomena was Lewis's famous and popular lectures on the medieval world, which attracted hundreds of students each term over many decades.[74] At last, his prolegomena was published as *The Discarded Image* in 1964, several months after he died.

In his discussion of the allegorical depiction of life as a journey, Lewis described his favorite story. Every culture contains the journey story, but each culture tells it slightly differently, based on its own worldview—what it believes and values. The journey story, and how people are changed by the journey, as Lewis told it, lies at the heart of *The Pilgrim's Regress*; *Out of the Silent Planet*; *Perelandra*; *The Great Divorce*; *The Lion, the Witch and the Wardrobe*; *Prince Caspian*; *The Voyage of the Dawn Treader*; *The Silver*

Chair; *The Horse and His Boy*; *The Magician's Nephew*; and *The Last Battle*. It even forms the plot of *Dymer*, and elements of it appear in *Till We Have Faces*.

Finally, Lewis explored the origins of the literary world of imagination in *The Allegory of Love*. Neither the religious otherworld of heaven nor the adventurer's otherworld of searching for King Solomon's mines, the world of imagination is the land of longing, "east of the sun and west of the moon."[75] In *The Allegory of Love*, Lewis *explained* what he would later *do* in his books that involved traveling from our world to "the other world," which can be reached by a wardrobe, a spaceship, a bus, a coffin, a ring, a picture, and even a train wreck.

Lewis never finished exploring the implications of what he had learned while writing *The Allegory of Love*. It laid out his scholarly and imaginative agenda for the rest of his life. Along the way, it secured his reputation as one of the greatest literary critics of the twentieth century.

Enter Charles Williams

Nevill Coghill had been one of Lewis's most significant Christian friends for over ten years when he published *The Allegory of Love*. Coghill had helped Lewis publish *Dymer* several years before Lewis accepted Coghill's faith. He had enjoyed with Lewis and Tolkien the joys of speaking and reading Old Icelandic with the Kolbítar. He easily became one of the original members of the Inklings, assuring good conversation together at least once a week. At some point in early winter of 1936, Coghill suggested that Lewis read *The Place of the Lion*, by Charles Williams.[76]

It had been a rough winter. Kipling, King George V, and Baron Papworth, the beloved dog of the Kilns, all died within a few weeks of each other. Jack normally had the flu about this time every year, and this may have been the occasion during which he turned to Coghill's recommendation. He wrote to Arthur Greeves about its enormous impact on him. After describing the clever intellectual basis for the book—a connection between Plato's world of ideals with the physical world of images through which the ideals began to suck all the images back into themselves—Lewis described the spiritual impact of the book on him. He said that it made him conscious of the enormous sin of the "abuse of intellect" to which he was especially susceptible. At the same time, it taught him more about humility, a trait he had not theretofore cultivated, than he had ever known before.[77] He recognized it at once as something most unusual—"a *Christian* fantasy."[78] He told Leo Baker that it was a "theological shocker!"[79]

Then Lewis did something completely out of character. On March 11, 1936, he wrote his fan letter to Charles Williams. For many years, Williams had been an editor at Oxford University Press in its offices at Amen House in London. Lewis lavished *The Place of the Lion* with praise, calling it one of the great literary events of his life, and he placed it in the company of the works of George MacDonald, G. K. Chesterton, and William Morris! He had pleasure in reading it as good fantasy, the pleasure of real theological and philosophical stimulation, the pleasure of finding interesting characters, and finally, the unexpected experience of substantial edification.[80] He then invited Williams to come up to Oxford for a weeknight and take part in his little literary club. This invitation constitutes the earliest written notice of the Inklings in which Lewis made clear that it was a Christian group of writers who meet during the week and not on weekends.[81]

In reply, Lewis received a letter from Williams, who had been reading the page proofs of *The Allegory of Love* admiringly. Williams had been about to write to Lewis when Lewis's letter arrived. Williams's reply focused on how thrilled he was to find someone else who shared his vision of romantic theology, which combined erotic love and religion.[82] He did not feel free to accept an invitation to attend an Inklings meeting, because he expected that any discretionary time he would have during the next term would be devoted to trips to Canterbury, where his new play, *Thomas*

Cranmer of Canterbury, was to be produced for the Canterbury Festival. He reciprocated the invitation, however, by insisting that Lewis join him for dinner if he should come to London. He also sent Lewis a copy of *Poems of Conformity* (1917), one of his earliest books of poetry.[83]

Replying to Williams, Lewis wrote to clarify his views and to make clear that he did not share Williams's ideas about erotic love. Lewis was kind and generous, but he made clear that he did not approve of Williams's "blend of erotic and religious feelings."[84] Part of the confusion had arisen because of Lewis's use of the term *romanticism* in the 1930s, including the subtitle to *The Pilgrim's Regress*. The term had too wide-ranging a meaning and was open to misinterpretation. Lewis made clear to Williams, however, that the kind of romanticism Williams thought he had seen in *The Allegory of Love* was not his kind at all.[85] He explained that one kind of romanticism finds its expression in romantic love, which was Williams's notion. Another kind of romanticism finds its expression in mythology, which was Lewis's. Williams was interested in ladies, while Lewis was interested in gods.[86]

Lewis also made clear in this second letter to Williams that Williams's poetry was "excessively *difficult*."[87] When Lewis made a remark like this, he did not mean that he was not smart enough to understand something. He meant that the writer had not written very well. He had made remarks like this to Arthur Greeves for two decades. Through Arthur, he had gradually learned to say it in as kind a way as possible. He had said similar things to Owen Barfield about the logic of his arguments. Almost everyone who commented on Williams's poetry remarked on its incomprehensibility. Part of being a friend for Lewis, however, involved exchanging honest criticism. He often liked people with whom he disagreed about basic beliefs, such as Barfield. He disagreed with Tolkien over church order. He disagreed with Williams over his romantic theology. It is important to note that Lewis's enthusiasm for a friend never caused him to lose his hold on reality. Interestingly, after Lewis died in 1963, Owen Barfield began to refer to Lewis and the Inklings as the romantic theologians, which he did not intend as a compliment.

After setting the record straight, Lewis proceeded to renew his invitation for Williams to attend an Inklings meeting, and he suggested a weeknight between May 18 and May 22, 1936. We have no evidence that Lewis and Williams corresponded again until a year and a half later, when Williams sent Lewis a copy of his new book *Descent into Hell*. In thanking Williams, Lewis renewed the invitation to come to Oxford for a gathering of the Inklings. He suggested either Wednesday, October 20, or Wednesday, October 27, 1937.[88] The invitation suggests that the Inklings were meeting on Wednesday at the time, rather than Thursday, as is often commonly understood. The open invitation to any weeknight the previous year suggests that they were moderately flexible, so long as it was a weeknight and not over the weekend.

Over the next two years, Lewis would write two more brief letters to Williams—probably his last to him. (Both Williams and Barfield, by the method of their professions—publishing and the law—maintained their correspondence files.) On June 7, 1938, Lewis wrote to congratulate Williams on the publication of *He Came Down from Heaven*.[89] On February 22, 1939, while laid up in bed with his annual Hilary term bout with the flu, Lewis wrote to complain to Williams about Oxford University Press and its dithering with the publication of *The Personal Heresy*, which seemed to Lewis to be dragging on and on toward no end.[90] By the beginning of 1939, Lewis and Williams were only cordial correspondents, but by the end of 1939, they would become the closest of friends.

6

From Scholar to Novelist

1930–1939

After his father's death, when Warnie Lewis returned to duty in England, he regularly spent weekends and leave at Hillsboro with Jack, Minto, and Maureen, the maids, the dogs, the cats, and whatever other visitors might have landed on the doorstep. Shotover Hill became a favorite place for the brothers to walk. It stood right on the edge of Headington, but its wildness transported them home to Ireland.[1] In the 1930s, their favorite places to go for a drink or a meal were the Mitre Hotel, where they had always gone in the 1920s, and the Eastgate Hotel, closer to Magdalen College and across the street from the Examination Schools building, where Jack began to lecture to large crowds.[2] They had time to renew the closeness they had experienced before Malvern College, but in time, they began to enrich their relationship by adding to it a number of joint friends. Each brother had his own particular friends, but the two also began to develop a set of shared friends.

The Inklings

In his important book *The Inklings*, Humphrey Carpenter first drew international attention to the group of literary friends who gathered around Lewis and Tolkien. People had known about the Inklings, and the name appeared in print from time to time, but Carpenter was the first person to write a book about the group.[3] Because large sections of Carpenter's book are fictional, however, he managed to create several false impressions about the group. The oft repeated weekly schedule of Tuesday mornings at the Eagle and Child pub for drinks and talk, and the late-night gatherings on Thursday nights in Lewis's rooms at Magdalen for reading what they were writing was not so firm and well-established a pattern as Carpenter suggested. A letter from Charles Williams to his wife suggests that the regular Tuesday morning gatherings probably did not begin until July 29, 1941, when Lewis, Tolkien, Williams, and a few others "unexpectedly colloqued" at Magdalen College.[4] That they gathered unexpectedly and at Magdalen suggests that the routine meetings on Tuesday mornings at the Eagle and Child had not yet begun.

We have very little written evidence about the Inklings in the 1930s. The few primary sources are a small number of letters written by Jack and scattered suggestions in Warnie's diaries. Once World War II began and Warnie was called back to active duty with an eventual promotion to major, Jack wrote to him and kept him abreast of what happened at Inklings gatherings in 1939 and 1940, when Warnie was discharged and returned to Oxford. Tolkien and Williams also made note of the Inklings in a few letters—Tolkien to his son Christopher and Williams to his wife. The scant information that we have paints an irregular picture of the Inklings schedule until the regimen of war forced a routine. Warnie made note of a Monday evening in March 1934 when he and Jack had supper with Tolkien at the Eastgate so that they could all read Wagner's *Walküre* together.[5] Williams mentioned several different weeknights when they met: a Tuesday evening in March and May 1943 and Friday evenings in August and September 1940.[6]

The Inklings slowly grew in numbers over the years. During one of his frequent bouts of flu in 1934 or 1935, Jack had a visit from the new doctor in Headington, named Robert Havard. After discussing his flu for a few minutes, Lewis and Havard quickly embarked on a wide-ranging discussion of ethics and philosophy for half an hour. Soon after that, Havard was invited to his first meeting of the Inklings.[7] Havard would be one of the most regular attendees of the weekly gatherings, though he just as regularly reminded everyone that he was not a literary man.

Life at the Kilns

Jack and Warnie had entirely different experiences of adjusting to family life with Minto and Maureen. Part of the difference involves the motives and expectations of the brothers. For years, living beyond his means with his salary supplemented by generous monthly allowances from his father, Warnie had looked forward to early retirement from the army to live the life of a gentleman. For Warnie, the Kilns represented the modest estate of a country squire who had never done manual labor in his life. With the substantial inheritance that he expected from his father, Warnie had looked forward to a comfortable retirement, free from the cares of the world. Instead, he found that his father had distributed his wealth to his two sons, month by month, for years before his death. The money was almost gone. Selling Little Lea at the height of the Depression meant that the brothers realized only about half what it had been worth two years earlier. The greatest indignity, however, came with the realization that Minto assigned him the kind of manual tasks that an enlisted man would have performed in the army. He also found that his organizational and administrative skills developed during years of active duty in the Royal Army Service Corps were not only ignored but spurned by Minto, who ruled the house according to her own sense of the right way to do things.

Jack, on the other hand, had taken on family life willingly and knowingly as the burden it would prove to be. He was living out the chivalric ideal about which he wrote in *The Allegory of Love* and which he had embraced as a teenager from reading the works of Morris, Malory, Spenser, and MacDonald. In *The Allegory of Love*, Lewis had commented on a famous passage in which Lancelot has lost his horse and must demean himself by riding in a donkey cart in order to fulfill his obligation to rescue Guinevere. When Lewis accepted the duty of caring for Mrs. Moore and her daughter in the place of Paddy Moore, he knowingly and willingly accepted what would have been degradation to a man raised to be an Edwardian gentleman. He had never done "chores" at Little Lea. He had never seen Albert Lewis do the "washing up."

Owen Barfield, though one of Jack's two or three closest friends, confessed that he did not know anything about life at the Kilns and Jack's relationship to Mrs. Moore. Except for their annual walking trips, Barfield saw very little of Lewis between the late 1920s and 1940, when the war put an end to their walking tours. Warnie, on the other hand, maintained a running record of life at the Kilns. In 1930, he thought Minto was still a "good looking" woman, though the few photographs of her do not convey that impression. Many beautiful women do not take good photographs, and Warnie's judgment should be relied upon in this matter, especially since he did not spare his criticism of Minto in his diary.

On the good side, the Kilns was a house full of music, and the Lewis brothers loved music. Maureen's piano and violin practice in her early teens a decade earlier had annoyed Jack at the time, but by the early 1930s, she was an accomplished musician and music teacher. She and Warnie went to a concert in Oxford almost every week when he was on leave.[8] When Warnie retired and moved into the Kilns, Maureen gave him piano lessons, which he enjoyed immensely. Nevill Coghill, Jack's multitalented friend, played the violin, and in February 1934, he and Maureen played

C. S. and Warren Lewis with Mrs. Moore at the Kilns, 1930. Used by permission of the Marion E. Wade Center, Wheaton College, Wheaton, IL.

together in a quintet for a concert at Exeter College, where Coghill was a fellow. The concert was on a Thursday evening, which suggests that Thursday had not yet become the fixed time for the Inklings to gather.[9]

Yet Maureen had her other side. Warnie thought she was terribly naive for a woman of twenty-five in 1930. He made this judgment after she had started to undress in the kitchen in order to try on a dress she was sewing. At this point, Warnie was not yet the venerable old Major Lewis—he was in his mid-thirties! When Minto suggested that she should change in her room, Maureen replied that she had just put on clean underwear that morning![10] By the time Warnie returned from China, he had grown accustomed to Maureen's sometimes outrageous behavior and comments, which he called Maureenisms. In the course of conversation over tea one day, the remark had been made that Guards officers wore stays, to which Maureen reacted: "What! Just like these?" while pulling her frock up to her chin and disclosing an ensemble of chemise, corset, blue knickers, and black silk stockings.[11] Warnie continued to marvel at things Maureen might say or do without any awareness of its inappropriateness. While on their Easter holiday in 1933 at a farmhouse in the Chilterns, she remarked: "I saw the cock jumping on one of the hens [*sic*] back yesterday and giving it a terrible time. Does he often do that?"[12]

In October 1930, Warnie bought a Jowett, an automobile manufactured in England between 1906 and 1954. Everyone at the Kilns learned to drive the car, including Jack, whose driving made Warnie nervous. Warnie, who began driving a motorcycle during World War I, had not driven a car for ten years when he bought the Jowett.[13] Once they all moved to the Kilns, driving became the primary responsibility of Maureen and Paxford, the new odd-job man.

Before going off to China for his last tour of duty before retirement, Warnie moved most of his books into Jack's small study in his rooms at Magdalen College. Warnie regarded Jack's rooms in college as "their" special place away from the Kilns and Minto. There they would nurture and recapture their long-lost childhood closeness. Warnie set up his typewriter in the study and began to work on editing all the Lewis family letters and papers dating back to the mid-nineteenth century. The study became Warnie's new "little end room," complete with a few childhood mementoes from Little Lea.[14] Meanwhile, Jack began writing a novel set in Ulster, which Warnie encouraged, but it was soon cast aside and forgotten.[15] Jack had other work to do and a different novel to write.

A new puppy named Troddles came to the Kilns in January 1932.[16] With the death of Papworth/Mr. Papworth/Baron Papworth/Tykes in 1937, the golden retriever joined the family.[17] The animals were generally understood to be Minto's pets, at least by Minto, and Warnie was charged with caring for them. He, in turn, developed a deep affection for Papworth. Minto also continued to maintain open house to all, whether congenial guests or not. When

Minto's sister-in-law Molly Askins came for an extended stay with her young son Michael in 1935, Jack found many reasons not to like the "insufferable semi-lady woman," but perhaps her worst offense was that she never read stories to her son, which left his "poor imagination" without the benefit of "any natural food."[18]

Jack had taken up cross-country walks as a favorite pastime after he and Warnie had drifted apart in their teenage years. With Warnie moving to the Kilns after his retirement, Jack was eager to share this great pleasure with his older brother, who was not prone to exercise and who had developed a prominent bay window while leading the leisurely life of an officer stationed at the outskirts of the British Empire. Over January 3–6, 1933, Jack and Warnie took a walking tour of the Wye Valley, along the border of England and Wales.[19] These annual walking trips by the brothers and no one else became a regular feature of their life together during the 1930s. It allowed them to get away from the Kilns and its complicated social structure and probably contributed significantly to the renewal of their deep love for each other. This 1933 walking trip also provided Warnie with an unforeseen but most happy benefit. He was delighted to learn that Jack snored, a behavior of which Jack had long accused Warnie. In regard to Jack's serious health problems in his fifties, his snoring suggests that he might have had sleep apnea, which puts undue stress on the heart.[20]

In February 1933, the builders began installing a metal staircase on the outside of the house from Jack's end room so that he could enter and leave by a new door cut against the window frame. The upstairs of the Kilns had three rooms. At the head of the stairs, Maureen's room was to the right. To the left was Minto's room. Beyond Minto's room was Jack's, which could be reached only by going through Minto's room. In his diary, Warnie noted that creating an exterior entrance to Jack's room made the house much more commodious since, until then, the two rooms could only be occupied by men without the separate entrance.[21] The door between Minto's room and Jack's room was locked and the key eventually lost. A locksmith had to be called to open the door after Minto went to a nursing home.

Also in February 1933, Jack and Warnie gave to Mr. Johns, the curate of Holy Trinity Church, a pile of books that they had designated for disposal. They were packing them up for removal when Minto insisted on going through them all, one by one, to be sure they had not included any of her books, adding that she "often wants a book to give away to some one [*sic*] at Christmas." Her behavior infuriated Warnie, who was already annoyed by Minto's behavior toward the curate at tea. She had enjoyed having old Cranny to tea because he had lost his faith, but she did not care for the company of clergy who took it all seriously. They became for her an easy target.[22] At the same time, the domestic situation at the Kilns continued in turmoil with the servants, none of whom seemed to rise to the level of barely adequate. Nellie complained about Ivy because, Warnie surmised, Nellie had a sister who wanted Ivy's job. Warnie blamed Minto for encouraging the chaos by taking sides. Though Fred Paxford had come to the Kilns to do a variety of jobs, Jack and Warnie still undertook the endless labors of cutting and digging their way through the wilderness to lay out garden paths through the woods and across the small estate.[23]

On Easter Sunday 1933, after attending several services in the rural countryside and an Easter Pageant on Good Friday, Jack had an idea for a story. It grew out of the opinion of some of the early church fathers that punishment of the wicked is eternal but intermittent. In that scenario, Jack conceived an excursion from hell to heaven. The idea percolated in his brain before emerging eleven years later as a serial in the *Guardian*, which was then collected as the book *The Great Divorce*.[24] This episode is only one of many that illustrate how Lewis sometimes wrote. He began with an idea that he might turn over in his mind for years before he did anything about it. Finally, the idea burst forth and he wrote furiously in a short period of time, which gives the impression of writing a book in a matter of a few weeks. When he finally began to write, he did not suffer from writer's block. He knew what he had to say.

Warnie regarded Minto's selfishness as amusing or irritating, depending on his mood. After attending a performance of *Midsummer Night's Dream* in June 1933, the entire Kilns household was stuck in the car park as hundreds of cars converged on the exit. Minto decried the selfishness of all the cars trying to push their way out without any regard for others. When they finally got to the gate, she was shocked and disgusted to see the cars trying to edge their way ahead of them. Maureen was driving, and Warnie gave her full marks for her patience and not saying anything in a trying situation.[25]

Warnie's toleration of Minto continued to wear thin as the summer of 1933 groaned on. For one who enjoyed conversation, Warnie grew more and more irritated by Minto's tendency to shout down any attempt at general conversation while she had the floor.[26] She had also taken to relying on the opinion of Paxford, the yard man, who freely expressed his views on all topics without the encumbrance of information. While declaring her judgment on all matters, she regularly began with "Paxford says."[27]

Not surprisingly, Fred Paxford's view of Mrs. Moore differed considerably from that of Warnie Lewis. Writing after the death of C. S. Lewis, Paxford recalled Mrs. Moore as

> a great lady, very fond of Ireland and the Irish and of mothering people. If any of the household was a little off color, out came the thermometer. She was like a mother to Mr. Jack, and he always called her Mintoes. She was also very good to me. . . . She had a good nature. Anyone who came to the Kilns for help nearly always went away with money, and if it was a man, a handful of cigarettes.[28]

Obviously, different people had different experiences of Minto. When Mrs. Moore died and Lewis married a few years later, Paxford would have to adjust to a new regime. Of Mrs. Joy Davidman

Gresham Lewis, Paxford said not a word in his memoir of Lewis. Warnie, on the other hand, had unqualified praise for Joy Lewis.

By September 1933, a Singer had replaced their first car, but Minto did not like it.[29] Warnie noted that on the drive to the sea for their holiday, Minto gave the sort of maddening advice to Maureen about her driving that Albert Lewis might have given: it was absurd and it came too late to be of relevance.[30] On leaving the Kilns, Minto decided that they would drive straight to their destination without stopping for tea. At 3:30 she decided that they would stop for tea at 4:00, but at 3:50 she decided that they would stop for tea immediately. Instead of tea, however, Minto had packed a thermos of the thick, sweet coffee she served after dinner. Warnie did not want to drink it, but given the "electrical" atmosphere between Minto and Maureen by this time, he prudently drank half a cup. Jack lay low.[31] Warnie's diary is filled with daily observations of Minto's regime of this sort, along with his critique of how foolish, selfish, and irritating she could be.

One afternoon during their holiday, Minto managed to get separated from Jack while they were shopping. Having failed to recall their plan, she rushed back to the hotel and demanded in a loud voice for all the inhabitants to hear, "Where's Jack? Where's Jack?" After a raucous time during which Minto raised the alarm that he had met with a terrible accident, Warnie and Minto found him standing on the curb across town where he and Minto had agreed to meet. Maureen observed, "I knew this would happen if Jack was fool enough to let her out of his sight."[32] Warnie was angry, but Jack was angrier. Minto spent the rest of the day playing for sympathy, but none came. She relapsed into her last defense at supper, a depressing monologue on declining into old age. Warnie reflected on this rant in his diary with the observation that it must be a terrible topic for an atheist to contemplate. It would be bad enough for an "atheist of intellect and noble character," but for a "selfish and stupid old woman" like Minto, "it must be sheer hell."[33]

These incidents illustrate how Minto's earlier charm had begun to wear thin by the mid-1930s. Charm soon looked like nothing more than silliness. Lewis had broken with his great friend Leo Baker in the mid-1920s largely over Minto. Minto did not like Baker, and she regularly expressed her opinion of his defects; and Jack perceived that Baker had a dim view of Minto. Jack cut off all contact with Baker until April 1935, when he wrote a long letter of apology seeking reconciliation after hearing from Barfield that Baker was ill.[34] Jack had begun to face the fact that people with whom Minto had conflict were not necessarily to blame, including Maureen.

Warnie eventually found one way to mitigate the oppression he felt from Minto. In 1936, he acquired a necessary accoutrement to his mystique as a country squire. He commissioned the construction of a twenty-foot, two-berth cabin cruiser, which he named the *Bosphorus* in honor of the ship in one of the childhood tales of Boxen written by Jack.[35] He kept the boat at Salter's Boatyard at Folly Bridge in Oxford. The *Bosphorus* was a "ditch crawler," one of a vast fleet of small craft that plied the rivers and canals that crisscross England and lace the Thames Valley. The Thames is bordered by a seemingly endless number of riverside pubs where Warnie could tie up and while away the lazy afternoons. By the mid-1930s, it had become increasingly evident that Warnie had developed a drinking problem. Life with Minto exacerbated his anxiety, and life on the river provided a way of retreat. With the little cabin and its berths, Warnie could stay away from the Kilns for days at a time. Living on his little boat, no one knew where Warnie might be. He was a moving target.[36]

Another Fellow Traveler

At the last stage of his conversion, Lewis had a pupil who shared his atheism but also was on the journey toward becoming a Christian.[37] Alan Richard Griffiths was only eight years younger than Jack and became one of Lewis's first pupils in 1925. After reading

English with Lewis, Griffiths remained around Oxford, living at a cottage in the country that he had bought with two friends. There they sought to live a simple, communal life. Griffiths had become a walking companion for Lewis, as well as a sparring partner. Growing disenchanted with naturalism, he embraced asceticism by 1930.[38] When Griffiths heard of Barfield's desire to edit Coleridge's unpublished works but his father's refusal to continue to fund Owen's failed literary life, Griffiths offered him a hundred pounds a year.[39] Though Barfield decided to enter his father's law practice instead of pursuing Coleridge, Griffiths was invited for Barfield's annual walking tour over Easter of 1932.[40]

Though Griffiths had become a Christian by 1932, Lewis thought he was approaching "unmitigated egoism" and told Barfield that anthroposophy might be his only chance![41] The Easter walk in 1932 disappointed Lewis, who had wanted Griffiths along to balance all the anthroposophists. Griffiths proved the saying that there is no zealot like a convert. Lewis regarded his manner of conversation about religion with Barfield as "appalling severity and egotism" which suggested that all the others were "infallibly damned."[42] Griffiths grew "intolerable" to Lewis, who said, "He displayed a perversity and disingenuousness in argument and cold blooded brutality—religious brutality is the worst kind"; this "revolted" Lewis and the others.[43] By 1934, Griffiths had converted to Catholicism and become a monk at a monastery in the Cotswolds, near Oxford, where Lewis visited him. Griffiths took the new name of Dom Bede Griffiths.

Just as Barfield had sought in vain to convert Lewis to anthroposophy through their disputations, Griffiths sought to convert Lewis to Catholicism. In his letter to Griffiths on April 4, 1934, Lewis discussed a wide variety of issues, including how T. S. Eliot might belong to the group attempting to revise Scholasticism in opposition to idealism, the possibility that divine grace might lead someone outside the Christian faith to be saved by focusing their faith on the aspects of their religion that are true, and the extent to which paganism and pantheism might be stops along the way to Christianity. The main point he wanted to make, however, was that he refused to discuss any of the questions at issue between the Roman Catholic Church and the Church of England.[44] Lewis told Griffiths that one of his most intimate friends for the previous decade was Catholic and that they had many religious conversations. No doubt, he referred to Tolkien. Though they had many differences, Lewis had found that they had "enormous common ground."[45] This enormous common ground would percolate in his mind for several more years until it blossomed as the radio broadcasts that formed *Mere Christianity*. Griffiths, however, would not relent.

In a letter written on February 20, 1936, Lewis laid out the issue as plainly and as kindly as he might. Griffiths wanted to convert Lewis, but Lewis did not want to convert Griffiths. Griffiths believed that Lewis was guilty of damnable errors, while Lewis thought that Griffiths's Catholic beliefs were simply a mass of comparatively harmless human traditions. This collection of traditions could be harmful to some people under certain conditions but did not seem to be harmful to Griffiths. Lewis had no intertest in attacking Griffiths, nor did he want to engage in another "epistolary controversy" like the one he had carried on with Barfield, in which his opponent began with the declaration that no argument would persuade him to change his mind. Lewis and Tolkien derived great edification from talking about common ground, but Griffiths wanted to talk only of differences! Lewis simply would not play along.[46] When Griffiths finally understood that Lewis would not attend to his desire for a knock-down, drag-out fight followed by the utter defeat and capitulation of Lewis, he ceased from his frontal attacks and settled into an important correspondence with Lewis that would last for years. Once Griffiths became an agreeable correspondent, Lewis discussed many important ideas that occupied his mind, from mysticism and prayer to the genesis of books he would write, such as *Out of the Silent*

Planet. Having gone through a religious conversion, Griffiths also provided Lewis with a prayer partner who shared his concern for his students, like George Sayer, whose desire to be liked reminded Lewis of himself when he was younger.

Lewis, Tolkien, and the "New Hobbit"

At the time of his conversion, Lewis wrote to Arthur Greeves that Tolkien and Dyson represented friends of the second class, unlike Arthur and Barfield, who stood as friends of the first class.[47] By February of 1933, when Jack first told Arthur about *The Hobbit*, Tolkien had moved from the second class to the first class. Jack mused that had they known Tolkien during their prewar years, all three of them would have been alike.[48] In many ways, Tolkien moved into the place that Barfield had filled in the 1920s.

On December 19, 1937, Ronald Tolkien wrote to Charles Furth, one of the editors at Allen & Unwin, who had published *The Hobbit*, to say that he had written the first chapter of a new Hobbit story that focused on Bilbo Baggins's birthday party. In the course of the party, Bilbo slipped his magic ring on his finger and disappeared. Unfortunately, Tolkien did not know why Bilbo had disappeared or where he was going. Tolkien assumed Bilbo had run out of money, but he did not know. He stalled.[49] Over the next few months, he decided that the story must center on Bilbo's ring, but he did not know how. He continued to write and added the figures who would eventually become in later rewritings Frodo, Pippin, and Merry. With three draft chapters completed, a journey underway, and mysterious "dark riders" in pursuit, Tolkien still did not know what his new Hobbit story was about, nor did he have a working title.

Meanwhile, Owen Barfield had written a poetic drama that had attempted a retelling of the story of Orpheus and his journey to Hades to bring his wife back to the land of the living. Barfield's play remained unstaged and unpublished, but the fact of it set Lewis to thinking of his favorite Norse/Germanic myth—the story of the ring of power. In recent years, Lewis had returned to the story set to music by Wagner. He had attended performances of several of the four operas that comprised Wagner's *Ring* cycle. He had read the libretto of *Die Walküre* with Warnie and Tolkien. He had already thought of the possibilities of a retelling of the Psyche and Cupid myth himself, but he would not accomplish it for two more decades. In March 1938, as Tolkien struggled to find an idea and plot for his new Hobbit, Lewis wondered to Barfield what someone might make of a retelling of the *Ring*.[50]

We now stand in the path of speculation. The documentary evidence of Tolkien's quandary, Lewis's idea, their weekly meetings, and the sequence of events implies that Lewis first suggested that Tolkien retell their favorite myth with Hobbits. By the end of the summer, Tolkien had worked out the basic plot that explained the origin of Bilbo's magic ring.[51] It was not just a magic ring that rendered the wearer invisible; it was the ring of power fashioned to rule the world—just like the ring in the Norse myth. Sauron, the one who fashioned the ring, sought to recover it—just like Alberich in the Norse myth. Sauron sent out his Ring Wraiths as invincible warriors—just like Wotan's Valkyrie daughters in the Norse myth. The parallels go on and on. Tolkien credited Lewis with encouraging him to continue writing his new Hobbit story whenever he stalled, but he never gave Lewis credit for prompting his thought or stimulating his imagination.

To some degree, Tolkien seems to have harbored mild jealousy of Lewis, judging from comments in some of his letters. He regarded himself as the superior authority on mythology, perhaps unaware of the extent to which Lewis had read and researched the subject in several cultures besides simply the Norse myths. This rivalry would emerge in Tolkien's harsh criticism of The Chronicles of Narnia several years later. To a certain extent, Tolkien is not the most reliable authority on sources and influences on his development of *The Lord of the Rings*, for he declared emphatically that the only thing his ring and Wagner's had in common was that they were both round.⁵² Such a comment was not only false but absurd. In defense of Tolkien, however, it is possible that he meant that his faith assumptions and Wagner's nihilistic assumptions had nothing in common. In his story, Tolkien demonstrated how a Christian telling of a story differs from a nihilistic telling of the same basic story.

The strain of jealousy was unfortunate, but everyone has his or her main flaw. Lewis recognized that his was pride. Warnie knew that his was envy. Lewis often reminded Arthur that his was greed. The jealousy may have kept Tolkien from fully enjoying the enormity of his accomplishment, for while The Chronicles of Narnia has become a children's classic, *The Lord of the Rings* is a monumental literary achievement without parallel in the twentieth century. It not only is great in its own right but has become one of the most influential works of fiction in the modern period.

Out of the Silent Planet

With *The Hobbit* and *The Allegory of Love* behind them, Lewis proposed that he and Tolkien should undertake the writing of the kinds of stories they liked, since no one else was doing it. Lewis said that he would write a space-travel story and suggested that Tolkien should write a time-travel story.⁵³ Tolkien stalled, but Lewis wrote *Out of the Silent Planet*.⁵⁴

Lewis liked the idea of interplanetary travel as a mythology. He had found this approach to science fiction in *Voyage to Arcturus*, a little-known novel by David Lindsay, published in 1920.⁵⁵ That story's point of view was profoundly non-Christian, but Lewis wanted to attempt a space-travel myth from a Christian point of view.⁵⁶ Olaf Stapledon's *Last and First Men* and J. B. S. Haldane's *Possible Worlds* had spurred him to action because of their materialistic views of the universe, but perhaps the strongest incentive to try his hand at science fiction came from a pupil. Sometime around June 1937, Lewis had a conversation with one of his intelligent atheist pupils who pinned all his hopes for significance in the universe on humanity's ability to evolve and begin "planet jumping" forever.[57] The unending march of evolution, combined with technological advances, would allow the successors of the human race to suck the life out of one world after another as they spread across the galaxy, and then on from galaxy to galaxy. The very idea horrified Lewis. It placed humans in the roll of villain that the Martians had played in H. G. Wells's *War of the Worlds*.

Lewis had tarried long in W. T. Kirkpatrick's world of materialistic evolution, and his own logical critique of it had led him to abandon it in favor of a universe guided by a Creator who continued to be involved in the process, imbuing the whole with meaning and purpose. Writing a space-travel novel gave Lewis the opportunity to show what a militant, self-serving exploitation of the universe might look like. In constructing his novel, Lewis found that his academic scholarship sparked his imagination to present a vision of the universe theretofore unseen in science fiction. Rather than build his story around the technology of space travel, he built it around a view of space itself that he had gleaned from the medieval worldview. When he began writing his space-travel novel, Lewis had been lecturing on the medieval worldview for several years based on material he had assembled while working on *The Allegory of Love*. Thus, *Out of the Silent Planet* came from the overflow of Lewis's academic work. Eventually, in 1962 he finally prepared his lectures on the medieval worldview for publication as *The Discarded Image*, but it did not see print until 1964, the year after his death.[58]

The medieval world inherited several contradictory belief systems from antiquity.[59] From the Christians, it inherited a belief in a Creator God who rules the universe and who entered into time and space to experience full humanity as Jesus of Nazareth without ever ceasing to exist outside of time and space in eternal power and perfection. From the pagan philosophers, however, the medievals inherited a vision of a universe filled with a hierarchy of spiritual beings who exercise rule over specific territories. The apostle Paul referred to this pagan understanding when he spoke of powers and principalities (Rom. 8:38; Eph. 6:12). The medieval world synthesized Platonic philosophy with Christian faith by identifying the *daemonia*, the spiritual beings in the hierarchy of the pagans, with the angels in service to God and the demons in service to Satan. Rather than empty space, Lewis wrote about the heavens filled with extraordinary and glorious beings, heavens full of energy and vitality.

Writing about what he knew, as all good novelists must, Lewis combined the medieval cosmology of worlds governed by arch-angels with his love of walking tours across wild landscapes and a philologist named Elwin Ransom, taken to be modeled on Tolkien.[60] The notion of Tolkien on a walking tour was probably received by the Inklings as a private joke, one of many Lewis would insert in his science-fiction trilogy before he was finished. Tolkien enjoyed a stroll across a meadow where he could stop and inspect the flowers and twigs or admire the view before taking a few more steps and pondering the distant hills. In fact, Lewis had taken Tolkien along on one of Owen Barfield's annual walking tours, but it had been a failure. While Lewis and Barfield charged across the countryside in full stride, paying little attention to the scenery as they argued over literature, Tolkien took his time.

A philologist, however, solves an important problem in an interplanetary-travel novel that not all science-fiction stories even recognize. How does an earthling converse with someone from another planet? It is the business of the philologist to understand how language works. It takes Ransom only a few moments after his first encounter with one of the beings covered in thick black hair to realize that the creature is talking, and if it can talk, Ransom can eventually work out what it is saying.[61] Ransom learns that Mars is called Malacandra by its inhabitants and that Earth is called Thulcandra. He learns that Malacandra has three sentient species: *hrossa*, the hairy poets; *séroni*, the pursuers of knowledge; and *pfifltriggi*, the craftsmen. The *eldila* are the semi-invisible/

opaque angelic beings overseen by the *Oyarsa*. The Creator and Ruler of the universe is *Maleldil the Young*. Finally, Ransom learns that the Oyarsa of Thulcandra have rebelled against Maleldil and made war in heaven.

Ransom comes to be on Malacandra through a kidnapping by the two villains: Devine, an oily politician, and Weston, the physicist who built the spaceship. Devine and Weston have been to Malacandra once before, and they surmise that the Malacandrans want a human sacrifice in order to do business. Ransom comes along at just the right time to fit their need for a human to offer. Upon landing on Malacandra, however, Ransom makes his escape, only to find himself alone on a terrifying world, presumably with man-eating aliens.

In *Out of the Silent Planet*, Lewis looked at H. G. Wells's vision of diabolical invaders from Mars from the other way around. Instead of Martians invading Earth, Lewis thought of earthlings invading Mars. He had developed this way of exploring an idea from the other way around when writing to Arthur Greeves to explain an important idea or concept with which Arthur struggled. This approach would later form the basis for *The Screwtape Letters*, and even for his explanation of the most effective approach to apologetics.[62] From H. G. Wells the materialist, Ransom had learned to think of aliens as the most horrible of monsters: "insect-like, vermiculate or crustacean Abominable" with "twitching feelers, rasping wings, slimy coils, curling tentacles" that formed a "monstrous union of superhuman intelligence and insatiable cruelty."[63] As it turns out, humans are the monsters in the universe.

Out of the Silent Planet is one of Lewis's most successful apologetic works. Without resorting to a lecture or philosophical argument, he made the case for the reasonableness of the Christian doctrine of the fall from an original relationship with the Creator of the universe. Along the way, he introduced the concepts of angels inhabiting the universe and Satan (whose name is never used) as the archangel who rebelled against the Creator. This rebellion led to the isolation of Earth from the rest of the universe. Thus, Earth is the silent planet that has cut itself off from the rest of creation. Lewis also realized the problem of using theological language in a popular book for which the general audience would have no understanding. Again, he relied on his philologist to come up with appropriate words to convey the meaning of ideas for which the audience had no concept. Ransom never mentions sin. Instead, he explains that humans have become "bent."

With all that he had managed to say about the Christian faith without actually saying anything about the Christian faith, Lewis was amazed at how few people realized what he had done. In a letter to Sister Penelope at the convent of St Mary in Wantage, near Oxford, Lewis remarked that of approximately sixty reviews of *Out of the Silent Planet*, only two had recognized his literary portrayal of the fall. He told her that he thought the vast ignorance of the Christian faith might actually be an advantage in the evangelization of England, because he saw how "any amount of theology can now be smuggled into people's minds under the cover of romance without their knowing it."[64]

In the dramatic conclusion to the story, the two archvillains have introduced murder to Malacandra and are brought before the Oyarsa for judgment. Weston defends their action on the basis of the materialistic hope of perpetual evolution and planet hopping espoused by Lewis's pupil. On much the same basis, the followers of Darwin in the nineteenth century had justified colonial expansion and domination on the basis of racial superiority. Weston declared that it was his right to conquer the universe.[65] Though he succeeded in presenting the perspective of those who see hope in planet jumping, Lewis did not preach. Ransom does not debate Weston. Instead, the Oyarsa questions Weston, who lays out his beliefs and ambitions. Lewis intended for his readers to "feel" a certain way about Devine's and Weston's ideas, motives, and behavior. Reflection could come later. In this way, *Out of the Silent Planet* succeeds at something Lewis felt strongly about. He believed that a well-told story "works" on the reader without needing to tell the reader what to believe, do, or feel. If the story works, the reader will experience what the storyteller intended. Lewis had learned this important matter about stories from reading many of them, some of which worked and many of which did not.

Literary Criticism and Theory

What Lewis accomplished in writing *Out of the Silent Planet* parallels what he had come to believe about literature in general and what constituted legitimate literary criticism. Even while writing *The Pilgrim's Regress*, *The Allegory of Love*, and *Out of the Silent Planet*, Lewis had begun to write occasional academic articles. For a young scholar who was heavily engaged in writing an important monograph, Lewis was remarkably productive in writing academic articles and giving guest lectures at other universities. During the 1930s, he published

- "A Note on *Comus*," in *The Review of English Studies*, 1932;
- "What Chaucer Really Did to *Il Filostrato*," in *Essays and Studies by Members of the English Association*, 1932;
- "The Personal Heresy in Criticism," in *Essays and Studies by Members of the English Association*, 1934;
- "A Metrical Suggestion," in *Lysistrata*, 1935;
- "Open Letter to Dr. Tillyard," in *Essays and Studies by Members of the English Association*, 1936;
- "Genius and Genius," in *The Review of English Studies*, 1936;
- "Donne and Love Poetry in the Seventeenth Century," in *Seventeenth Century Studies Presented to Sir Herbert Grierson*, 1938; and
- "The Fifteenth Century Heroic Line," in *Essays and Studies by Members of the English Association*, 1939.

By way of comparison, Tolkien produced five small articles during the same period and no scholarly monographs, and Tolkien had a less demanding schedule, since he held a professorial chair. He did, however, write *The Hobbit*.

In addition to his scholarly academic articles, Lewis found himself increasingly in demand as a speaker. By early 1935, he had spoken to societies at Manchester, Birmingham, and Cambridge—all before the recognition that came with the publication of *The Allegory of Love*.[66] By 1939, he had spoken at enough societies to publish these papers as *Rehabilitations and Other Essays*. These invited lectures do not represent the measured, meticulous, analytical tone of his formal, academic writing. Instead, they have a lively, energetic, strident tone and rise to the level of controversy. In his talks, Lewis defended what he valued and attacked what he thought needed attacking. In "Shelley, Dryden, and Mr. Eliot," presented at Bedford College in London, and "William Morris," presented at the Martlet Society of Oxford in 1937, Lewis defended the great romantic poets against the hatred and neglect of romanticism that had grown popular.[67] In "The Idea of an 'English School,'" presented to a joint meeting of the Classical and English Associations, and in "Our English Syllabus," presented to the undergraduate English Society of Oxford, he defended the new English syllabus that Tolkien had proposed. In "High and Low Brows," presented to the English Society at Oxford, he defended the popular books he had enjoyed that increased his ability to enjoy greater literature and life itself. Even more, he championed the notion of true literary enjoyment apart from any current fashion in literary taste.

In addition to these essays, which Lewis expressly described in his preface to *Rehabilitations and Other Essays* as advocating a strong view against prevailing sentiments, he included several other essays without comment. He presented "Bluspels and Flalansferes: A Semantic Nightmare" at Manchester University. He read the paper "Variation in Shakespeare and Others" at a meeting of the Mermaid Club, possibly as early as the late 1920s. He read a paper "Christianity and Literature" to an undergraduate religious society at Oxford. Finally, he included in his collection "The Alliterative Metre," a technical explanation of how traditional Anglo-Saxon and Old Norse alliterative meter works. This paper was much more academic in nature and had been published in 1935 in *Lysistrata*, a short-lived academic journal.

The most well-known work that Lewis undertook in relation to literary criticism broadly in the 1930s involved what he called "the personal heresy." This essay grew into a full-blown controversy between Lewis and Eustace M. W. Tillyard, a Cambridge literary scholar recognized for his work on Shakespeare and Milton. One cannot help but wonder if Eustace Tillyard lent his name to Eustace Scrubb in *The Voyage of the Dawn Treader*. Lewis published the initial blast as "The Personal Heresy" in the academic journal *Essays and Studies by Members of the English Association* in 1934. This essay attacks what had grown into a widespread idea that poetry is essentially the "expression of the poet's personality." Lewis had been thinking about this idea for at least ten years before an advertisement on the cover of a volume of war poems, which promised the reader insight into the inmost feelings of the poets, prompted Lewis to write.[68] In his opening salvo, he attacked Tillyard's insistence, in his book on Milton, that *Paradise Lost* is really about the state of Milton's mind rather than about the fall of the human race. Tillyard wrote a "Rejoinder" to Lewis's essay, to which Lewis responded with "An Open Letter to Dr. Tillyard." In the end, the two men decided to complete their debate with a book that included their first essays along with the further development of their ideas on the subject. This volume was published as *The Personal Heresy: A Controversy* in 1939.

Lewis rebelled against an autobiographical or psychological reading of poetry. Instead, he advocated reading poetry—and he would later add all drama and fiction—on its own terms without considering the author. He did not deny that some forms of literature should be read with an eye to the frame of mind of the author: essays, private letters, and some literature where the lines are blurred between personal writing and imaginative writing.[69] Of imaginative writing, however, Lewis insisted that the reader must dive in and taste the work on its own terms without being bothered by the personality of the author. At this point, Lewis appealed to love and the danger of confusing a love of the personality of T. S. Eliot or D. H. Lawrence or Virgil with what each wrote. He even introduced the three Greek words for love that he had come across when writing his chapter on Spenser in *The Allegory of Love*: *eros*, *philia*, and *storgē*.[70] He would continue to think about the various aspects of love until he wrote *The Four Loves* (1960).

Lewis went on to distinguish "dead poets" from the poetry they wrote. The veneration and affection for the dead poet encompasses emotions and regard that ought to be given to one's neighbor, while the poetry can be enjoyed for its own sake. This controversy arose as English literary scholars continued to establish for themselves a place in the academic world. The study of English literature at a university was only a few decades old, and English faculty members were still trying to determine what they actually did. By making the author the subject of study, one approach to criticism created a specialization for itself not available to the average reader. This is the path of discovering the "secret meaning" to a text that lay in the inner psyche of the author, which only the literary critic was qualified to ferret out.

Lewis took a much more democratic approach to literature, probably based on the enormous enjoyment he had gained from it as an adolescent. In this controversy, as in his later treatments of literary criticism, he often referenced T. S. Eliot for his insistence that only the great poets could properly judge poetry. Lewis would have none of it. Lewis has received mixed reviews over the years for his combative stance in *The Personal Heresy*, which avoided any semblance of careful nuance, but the psychological approach to literary criticism he so despised soon fell out of favor as his view of the matter came to dominate, though he was never acknowledged as a leading force in its demise.

The problem of the personal heresy has probably had a longer life in the United States related to the study of American literature. When I was in college, an American literature professor at the University of South Carolina declared that *The Narrative of Arthur Gordon Pym of Nantucket*, Edgar Allan Poe's only novel, was actually "a journey into Poe's inner psyche." Publishers continue to print new editions of *The Last of the Mohicans*, by James Fenimore Cooper; *The House of the Seven Gables*, by Nathaniel Hawthorne; innumerable collections of the short stories of Poe; and *Tom Sawyer*, by Mark Twain, all of which the public continue to read for pleasure. American literature professors, however, venerated Ralph Waldo Emerson, who never wrote a significant story, poem, or novel. The personal heresy keeps Emerson in print for required reading in American literature classes at American universities. Some literature professors acknowledge the problem with the excuse that Emerson's importance lies in his profound philosophy. Yet, the philosophy department does not read Emerson.

In all this work, Lewis expressed a concern that he felt deeply and that related to his faith in God, and by extension, what kind of universe exists. Lewis thought the time would come when people would once again want an approach to literary theory that was not based on materialism. Lewis explained to Paul Elmer More, one of his academic correspondents, that he aimed at just such a theory in the essays he had begun to publish in the 1930s.[71] With the publication of *The Personal Heresy*, Lewis had begun to demonstrate what a later generation would call the integration of faith and learning, though Lewis never cared for that phrase. Nonetheless, he began to show what it means to think about a discipline from the perspective of faith, just as others in Oxford thought of their disciplines from the perspective of materialism, Marxism, or fascism.

Most of Lewis's published essays began life as lectures. This pattern would continue throughout his career. He liked to try out his ideas with an audience before committing them to print. This approach provided him with constructive criticism to improve the articles, but it also resulted in a dynamic form of writing that arose from his engagement with an audience. Just as he thought that poetry should be read with the ear, he appears to have believed that good written arguments should also appeal to the ear. As a public speaker, Lewis excelled. The number of invitations he received to give lectures away from Oxford reflects his growing reputation as a good speaker during the 1930s. Lewis normally attracted around four hundred undergraduates to his lectures on medieval literature in the vast upper halls of the Examinations Schools building, where he spoke without the benefit of amplification.

Derek Brewer recalled Lewis's lectures as schematic, well organized, and clear, with helpful quotations and illustrations, which made note-taking simple.[72] Lewis spoke from well-organized notes, but not from a detailed manuscript, so that he engaged the audience with his loud, clear voice. His speech retained faint touches of his Ulster background in the way he pronounced his r's and words like *Lat'n*.[73] Gervase Mathew suggested that Lewis's style of lecturing allowed him to forge "a personal link with those who heard him."[74] Unlike the usual Oxford lecturer, who spoke fast in a soft voice, Lewis had a loud, booming voice but spoke slowly "in a deep velvety tone."[75] He punctuated the lectures, on what to many of his audience would have seemed an arcane subject, with jokes and witty remarks. For instance, he characterized the disordered philosophy of Aldous Huxley with a ludicrous remark intended to represent Huxley's view: "Christianity and Buddhism are very much alike, especially Buddhism."[76] Derek Brewer noted that Lewis planned his jokes with great timing so that "the fuse might be lit several minutes before the actual, yet unexpected, explosion."[77] Though Lewis had something of the performer about him when he gave his lectures in his Oxford teaching gown, Alastair Fowler thought he created more the impression of "exploring a thought for the first time."[78] Though Lewis often wrote about the importance of formality and ceremonial, his lectures were so far from that tone that he began his lectures as soon as he entered the room on his way to the rostrum and continued speaking as he strode to the door at the end.[79]

Fowler and many others have noted that Tolkien did not have the same magisterial presence in the lecture hall. Tolkien was not "always easily audible."[80] For that matter, few of those who lectured in the School of English did a very good job until Lewis was joined by Lord David Cecil in 1939. Peter Milward has observed that Lewis soon became the object of envy among his colleagues.[81] This envy may have played as great a part in Lewis's alienation from his Oxford colleagues as his Christianity. They were not envious of Tolkien. In fact, they would give him an even more prestigious professorship after the war. Milward recalled:

> Tolkien spoke in such a small voice, one had to sit close up to his lectern to hear what he was saying, and as I came in from another important lecture, I found myself sitting at the back of the not-so-large classroom without being able to catch a single word. So I had to give up on him and content myself with Lewis.[82]

Tolkien may have begun to feel some sense of irritation, if not full-blown jealousy, at the crowds of undergraduates that Lewis began to attract. After all, Tolkien was the senior man with a professorship. He was older than Lewis. He had been a Christian longer, and to a certain extent he probably thought of Lewis as his disciple. Still, Tolkien drew a respectable crowd to his lectures on *Beowulf*.[83] And even if Lewis had his ten-thousands of admirers, Tolkien had his thousands, as Helen Tyrrell Wheeler testified of him:

His lectures too, usually held in the Taylorian, were packed out largely because of the extraordinary pressure of excitement that swept over his audience when he broke (as he frequently did) into a Bardic rendering of *Beowulf.* Where else in the world would one be able to hear the hypnotic rhythms and crashing, criss-crossing alliterations of this poem delivered with such (we thought) impeccable authenticity of inflection? And if it was not impeccably authentic, then it ought to be, for the effect of spellbound attention was unfailing.[84]

Most of Tolkien's lectures, however, were not on *Beowulf* in the Taylorian but on philology in the small ground-floor rooms of the Examination Schools, which lend themselves more to small group discussion around a table.

Lewis and Mrs. Moore

With the conversion of Jack, the move of the family into the Kilns, and Warnie joining them when he retired, it is time to draw some conclusions about the relationship between Jack and Mrs. Moore before Warnie arrived on the scene. In *C. S. Lewis: A Biography* (1974), Walter Hooper and Roger Lancelyn Green argued that if Lewis had a sexual attraction to Mrs. Moore at first meeting her, it quickly transformed into a longing for a "mother-substitute" that was quite innocent.[85] Humphrey Carpenter took the view in *The Inklings* (1978) that Jack and Mrs. Moore treated each other like mother and son from the beginning of their relationship.[86] Carpenter dismissed the idea that Jack and Janie had a sexual relationship on the practical basis of inevitable talk among the servants and the problem of Maureen living in the house.[87] In his review of *The Inklings*, Lord David Cecil remarked that Lewis and Mrs. Moore had a platonic relationship that involved sacrifice on Lewis's part.[88] Though Cecil was not one of Lewis's most intimate friends, he was one of the Inklings, and he did enjoy a cordial friendship with Lewis that involved Lewis dining with the

Cecils in their home. Cecil's views are probably representative of the impression that Lewis's friends had of his relationship with Mrs. Moore. George Sayer, a former student of Lewis and friend in later life, also took the view in *Jack: C. S. Lewis and His Times* (1988) that Lewis regarded Mrs. Moore "almost as a mother."[89] Sayer observed that on her side, Mrs. Moore mothered Jack.[90]

Opinion about the relationship between Lewis and Mrs. Moore began to change in 1990 with A. N. Wilson's biography of Lewis, *C. S. Lewis: A Biography*. Beginning with his introduction, Wilson began to suggest that something sexual must have been going on between the two.[91] At first, Wilson suggested that the bond between them was of the mothering type that had long been the common view.[92] Then Wilson made the assertion that there could be no doubt that Jack and Janie fell in love when he was convalescing from his war wounds, yet he drew the conclusion without evidence other than that it must have happened.[93] Wilson explained that the public face of the relationship, however, would have to have been that of mother and son.[94] Finally, Wilson revealed his evidence to demonstrate that Lewis had a sexual relationship with Mrs. Moore. In a letter to Wilson, Maureen mentioned that one Sunday she did not want to go to church as usual. One of many arguments ensued between Maureen and her mother, who wanted some peace and quiet for an hour without Maureen in the house. Wilson suggests that the reason Jack and Janie wanted Maureen to go to church was so that they could carry on a sexual affair. Wilson did not quote from the letter but merely interpreted what he thought the implications were.[95]

Wilson's suggestion was powerful enough, in the absence of evidence, to change the way people tended to think about Lewis and Mrs. Moore before his conversion. In *C. S. Lewis: A Life* (2013), Alister McGrath pointed out that George Sayer changed his mind about the possibility of a sexual relationship between Jack and Janie and insisted in the revised edition of his biography that he was "quite certain" they were lovers.[96] McGrath concluded that

Lewis and Mrs. Moore had a complex relationship that included both a sexual dimension of passion and a mother-son dimension of affection.

One of the great differences in how people have viewed the relationship concerns how social values have changed since the 1970s. The sexual revolution of the counterculture of the 1960s was just beginning to gain acceptance in the 1970s, but by the late 1990s, free sexual expression without benefit of marriage had become commonplace. Men and women engaged in sexual relations as casually as going to the movies. In the changing climate, it became easy to assume that Lewis and Mrs. Moore must have been having a sexual affair. All the circumstantial evidence is present. They lived in the same house.

When one examines life in the Moore-Lewis household between 1919 and 1930, however, it grows increasingly difficult to conceive of how Jack and Janie could possibly have been carrying on an affair. They kept open house all the time. People came and stayed for weeks and months on end. They had paying boarders. They always had at least one maid and often more than one. The neighbors were constantly coming in and out of the house. They were under constant surveillance. They simply had no time or place in which to carry on an affair. The only thing that rises to the level of evidence is a passing remark by Maureen that on one occasion, her mother was upset with her for not going to church. In the many years that they all lived together, if Maureen had no other grounds for suspecting a sexual relation between her mother and Jack, then the evidence from silence is overwhelming that nothing ever happened.

We do have strong evidence, however, that Jack's relationship with Mrs. Moore was motivated by the romantic ideal of chivalry and noble obligation that he had found and embraced from the medieval stories he loved. Caring for Mrs. Moore would not be the only area of his life in which Jack had embraced the chivalric ideal. He had chosen to go to war when many of his and Arthur's family and friends had refused to fight. In his letters to Arthur and Warnie, Jack repeatedly lavished contempt on those who took advantage of the Irish exemption from service in World War I. Of course, it is possible that his embrace of the chivalric ideal could have included the adulterous dimension of courtly love found between Sir Lancelot and Queen Guinevere, which he explained in *The Allegory of Love*, but the circumstances of their home life and the absence of any telltale evidence suggests that Jack's relationship with Mrs. Moore followed the example of Reepicheep rather than Lancelot.

University Politics

Flush with their success in revising the English School syllabus, Lewis and Tolkien undertook a broader campaign within the university in 1938 when the chair of the professor of poetry fell vacant. This professorship was not a permanent appointment but a place held for five years before the election of a new professor. Several members of the university nominated Sir Edmund Chambers for the position. Chambers had a well-deserved reputation as a learned but dull scholar. Since Lewis's conversion, it had been his practice to attend chapel every morning during term at Magdalen before breakfast. As dean of divinity at Magdalen, the equivalent of college chaplain, Adam Fox led the morning prayer service, after which he and Lewis went to the dining room of the Senior Common Room for breakfast together.[97] Upon learning of Chambers's nomination one morning, Fox remarked: "This is simply shocking. They might as well make me Professor of Poetry." To this declaration, Lewis replied, "Right, we will."[98]

Though Fox in his chaplaincy position was a fellow of Magdalen, he was not regarded technically as a member of the faculty. The post of professor of poetry, however, was an elective position voted upon by members of the university who held the MA degree, the normal prerequisite to teaching at Oxford. The clergyman did not need academic credentials so much as academic votes.

Fox had become part of the Inklings at some point prior to the election of the poetry chair. The previous year, he had published *Old King Coel*, a book-length poem based on the legendary king of the Britons in Roman times reputed to be the grandfather of Constantine, who was popularized in the old nursey rhyme. The slim volume does not rise to the ranks of great poetry, but it did mean that Fox had actually published a poetry book. Lacking the academic credentials, Fox was promoted as a "practising poet" [*sic*]. In all likelihood, he had read the work in progress at gatherings of the Inklings in the mid-1930s. Lewis and Tolkien nominated Fox, and then the campaigning began.[99] The establishment began to fear that Chambers would not be a strong enough candidate, so they nominated Lord David Cecil, who would become one of the Inklings after 1939 and a good friend of Lewis, as a second candidate, who only succeeded in splitting the vote and giving the election to Fox.[100] Tolkien mentioned the election in a letter to his publisher, Stanley Unwin, with pride, for Fox was a member of Tolkien's "literary club of *practising poets*—before whom the *Hobbit*, and other works (such as *the Silent Planet*) have been read."[101]

First Impressions

In *Light on C. S. Lewis*, Nevill Coghill gave one of the most detailed descriptions of Lewis's appearance of the many that have been written by those who knew him. Unfortunately, Coghill does not mention the age of Lewis for the description that he gave. He knew Lewis from his undergraduate days until his death. The description fits a mature Lewis but not an old Lewis. Coghill and Lewis would not have as much time together after 1939, so perhaps it fits best at this point in his life:

> He was a largish, unathletic-looking man, heavy but not tall, with a roundish, florid face that perspired easily and showed networks of tiny blood-vessels on close inspection; he had a

C. S. Lewis outside an English country church, 1938. Used by permission of the Marion E. Wade Center, Wheaton College, Wheaton, IL.

dark flop of hair and rather pouched eyes; those eyes gave life to the face, they were large and brown and unusually expressive. The main effects were of a mild, plain powerfulness, and over all there was a sense of simple masculinity, of a virility absorbed into intellectual life.[102]

George Watson remembered Lewis as a "short, stocky figure" who looked "less like a wit than a pork butcher of hearty disposition."[103]

7

From Peace to War

1939–1941

C. S. Lewis liked to tell people that he never read the newspapers, which provided him with a platform to discuss all that was wrong with journalism and the popular press. He had developed his prejudice against the press from his childhood when his father repeated what he had read in the newspapers. Albert would critique the papers with his usual flair for the overdramatic, which served him so well in the police court of Belfast. W. T. Kirkpatrick had instilled in young Jack a suspicion and skepticism regarding the press's tendency to favor one political party over another, to either attack or defend the government, and in general to create a market in which to sell papers.

Jack's claim of never reading the newspapers was almost true. He explained that if anything important happened, someone was sure to tell him. Mrs. Moore constantly told him about what she had read in her newspapers, but she had a preference for the kinds of papers that featured the latest scandal and gossip among the rich and famous. During breakfast at Magdalen College, Lewis could expect to hear in some form or other what the papers had to say that day from the perspective of his colleagues.

In fact, Lewis did read the newspapers when something important was happening. During the Irish Civil War in the 1920s, he read the papers.[1] During the great miners' strike in 1926, he also read the papers.[2] The Japanese bombardment of Shanghai in 1932 had forced Jack to read the papers because Warnie had found himself in the middle of the new war brewing in the Far East between Japan and China. Jack explained to Arthur that he loathed the papers' flippancy and "sensational exploitation of things that mean life and death."[3] By January of 1939, Jack was reading the newspapers again.[4] He had actually subscribed to the *Imperial News Bulletin* until November 1939, when he decided to let his subscription lapse. He explained to Warnie, "What's the use of paying 2/- a month to be tormented by prophecies wh. if false are needless misery and if true can't be averted by us?"[5] At the end of May 1941, almost two years into the war, Lewis wrote facetiously to Arthur that one of the biggest differences between the last war and the present war was that both he and Arthur were by then following the news.[6]

The Gathering Cloud

Lewis had expressed his contempt for the Nazi regime in Germany as early as 1933 in the way he presented Hitler's ideology in *The Pilgrim's Regress*. By the time Hitler annexed Austria in March 1938, however, Lewis began to fear war looming. He mentioned his growing concern over the danger of war in a letter to Dom Bede Griffiths in April 1938. Concerned as he was about the danger of war, he was no less concerned that his fortitude and reliance on God had not grown more than it had since his conversion. He realized how much his happiness depended on his physical condition, and he began to realize what part physical affliction might play in one's spiritual growth.[7] This realization would grow as he reflected on the suffering that would come with war. It would become a central theme in his approach to the problem of suffering, which he explored in *The Problem of Pain* (1940).[8]

Between April 1938 and the invasion of Poland in September 1939, Lewis mentioned his dread of the coming of war regularly in his letters to Griffiths, Owen Barfield, Hamilton Jenkin, and Sister Penelope.[9] He felt relief that the coming horror had not caused him to have any doubts about God.[10] He was troubled, however, to realize how terrified he was of the prospect of war, and he asked Griffiths to pray for him for courage.[11] As has been mentioned earlier, Lewis ended World War I with a wound that never fully healed and that caused him pain for years. He also suffered from nightmares.[12] Like so many, if not most, of his generation who had fought, Lewis ended the war with a suppressed case of shell shock, or what today would be called post-traumatic stress disorder. As Hitler flexed his muscle across Europe, all the memories of Lewis's earlier war came flooding back, and he saw what lay ahead. He thought it would be much better to die than to go through another war.[13] In fact, when he wrote *The Screwtape Letters*, death proved to be the way out for the patient.

Nonetheless, Lewis was no pacifist. He believed that his country had a duty to stand up to Hitler and all he represented. Jack expressed himself privately to his friends but also publicly in a letter to the editor of *Theology* magazine.[14] He firmly believed that the defense of the innocent was an important ground for war and that this defense embodied the chivalric spirit of the knight errant.[15] Lewis never strayed far from his love of the chivalric tradition he had found in his books, which had motivated him since his decision to fight in World War I.

His brooding on the coming war also led Lewis to ponder more deeply what part God played in such disasters of human making. His dread of war with all its loss led him to think that only such disasters lead people to escape their worldliness and grasp more eternal things. He thought that human behavior "*forces* God to surgical treatment."[16] In spite of his lack of courage and his sense of impending, overwhelming loss, Lewis grew in his conviction that "whatever misery He [God] permits will be for our ultimate good."[17] To Sister Penelope he wrote, just weeks before the declaration of war, "Whatever evil Satan sets on foot God will always do some good or other by it."[18] This line of disconnected thought sprinkled through his letters over a year to various people demonstrates the way Lewis often thought about a problem or a subject before he actually intended to write about it. It also demonstrates how he was able to write *The Problem of Pain* so quickly on short notice. It had been percolating and only needed an occasion to come out of his brain. As his chronic pain increased in the mid-1930s, Lewis had mentioned his own problem with pain to Leo Baker in his letter of apology in 1936. Lewis thought that physical pain was the worst of evils. Baker was having his own bout with pain at the time, but Lewis had endured chronic pain since his war injuries in 1918. Pain no longer presented the same intellectual difficulties it once had for Lewis before his conversion, but he also realized that his intellect and his feelings were not in harmony over the matter.[19]

The summer of 1939 marked the end of what some have called the long weekend between World War I and World War II. The 1930s had been a settled time for Lewis in which he grew accustomed to domestic life at the Kilns. He did some important scholarly writing that secured his reputation and standing in university culture. He wrote some lighter pieces for his own amusement that garnered mild passing notice from the critics and praise from his friends. He formed a new group of friends with whom he talked literature each week. He usually had two to three servants at the Kilns. He managed at least four vacations almost every year. With Warnie he always took a walking tour every January, no matter how bleak or miserable the weather.[20] Most Easters, he went on a walking tour with Barfield and his anthroposophical friends.[21] Almost every summer, he visited Arthur in Ireland.[22] As we have seen, he went on holiday with Mrs.

Moore and the Kilns household every August or September for several weeks. In the midst of the Great Depression, Lewis had a good life.

As war's dark shadow lengthened, Lewis wondered if he or some of his friends might die in the coming conflict. Though he had lied to his father about the aerial attacks of the German zeppelins during World War I, he knew full well that the coming war would be waged against civilians as much as soldiers. He wrote to Barfield that if they were separated, he wanted him to know how much their friendship had meant to him. He added, "In some ways we've had a corking good time these 20 years."[23]

In August of 1939, Warnie Lewis decided to take his brother and Hugo Dyson on a ditch-crawling trip on the *Bosphorus*. August in the Thames Valley is a glorious time with the gardens all in full bloom. They planned to leave from Salter's Boatyard at Folly Bridge in Oxford on Saturday, August 26, but before the date arrived, Warnie faced recall to active duty from his reserve status.[24] Without Warnie to skipper the craft, Jack and Hugo turned to Dr. Robert Havard, their fellow Inkling, who agreed to take them on the three-day cruise up the Thames. Just three days earlier, Germany and the Soviet Union had signed a nonaggression pact, which heightened the signs of coming war. In his memoir of the trip, Havard observed that along the thirty-mile stretch of navigable water above Oxford, six bridges cross the river, and at each bridge may be found at least one country inn. They stopped at almost all of them along the way to fortify themselves.[25]

They first stopped at The Trout in Godstow, at the far end of Port Meadow from Oxford. Havard recalled that they arrived just before the inn closed, so they must have left late in the day, since The Trout is only about three miles from Folly Bridge. It also means that The Trout must have closed early on a Saturday evening in 1939. They cruised on past Wytham Great Wood where the Thames makes a wide bend and then on southwestward to Newbridge, where Lewis and Dyson stayed at the Rose Revived

Inn while Havard slept on board the *Bosphorus*. On Sunday morning, they journeyed on to Tadpole Bridge, where they tied up to go to church in Buckland a mile away. Lewis and Dyson attended services at the Church of England parish church of St Mary the Virgin while Havard attended St George's Roman Catholic Church. A few miles farther up the river, they stopped for lunch at Radcot, location of the oldest bridge on the Thames. They stopped for supper at Lechlade after passing Kelmscott Manor, the home of William Morris, who had meant so much to Lewis since his days at Great Bookham. After supper, they ventured the short distance to Inglesham and the entrance to the abandoned Thames and Severn Canal.[26]

On Monday morning they began their return trip to Oxford. Then the motor broke down. The foot paths along the river recall the old days when river traffic meant tow ropes pulled by mules and horses. Without a working motor, Lewis and Dyson served duty as the dray horses to pull the *Bosphorus* down river while Havard steered the boat. Then it began to rain. Fortunately, Havard managed to get the motor running again, and they made their way back to The Trout where they stopped for lunch. There they learned that Hitler had invaded Poland. It was September 1, 1939. They all knew that England would soon be at war. Havard said that Lewis was profoundly depressed by the news, but over supper that night at the Clarendon Hotel he managed to quip that at least they now had less chance of dying of cancer.[27]

Even as the ditch crawlers made their way back to Oxford on Monday, Warnie boarded a train to take him back into the army to serve king and country.[28] Why had he not made the trip? As a retired officer, Warnie was placed on the reserve list, and as European acrimony increased, he would have been informed of the likelihood of his recall to active duty. Warnie probably knew he would have to report for duty and needed to put his affairs in order. If the crisis came over the weekend, as it did, he needed to be ready to report immediately. The real question is why Jack would have taken the river cruise without him. He had been anticipating the war for over a year. He knew Warnie would have to go. Perhaps he could not stand the thought of sitting idly by and watching his brother go off to what they both knew would be a dreadful war from which Warnie might not return.

The Changing Homefront

When Warnie left for his posting at Catterick in Yorkshire, a small group of three schoolgirls arrived at the Kilns, the first of a series of evacuees from London who would stay at the Kilns during the war.[29] The number of girls who would stay at the Kilns normally ranged from three to four, but they came and went throughout the war. Life was changing rapidly for Lewis. He expected it to change more. He was almost four years younger than Warnie. Jack was forty years old and the government had announced that able-bodied men up to the age of forty-one were liable for duty. Jack reported in the first of many letters to Warnie during the opening of the war that the president of Magdalen College had laughed "to scorn the alarms raised" by his fears about active service.[30]

Lewis recalled the bleak emptiness of Oxford during the Great War, when only a few elderly dons and a smattering of halt, lame, and Irish undergraduates inhabited the vast, lonely colleges of Oxford. In anticipation of the closure of the Oxford colleges for the duration of the war, Lewis packed up all his thousands of books and had them carted down to the cellars of New Building to make way for whatever use the government would make of his rooms. In his second letter to Warnie, he reported that one of the most reminiscent features of the last war had reappeared—"the information which always comes too late to prevent you doing an unnecessary job."[31] No sooner had he carried his entire library down several flights of stairs to the cellars than he received word that the government would not require his rooms. In fact, college life would go on with a new batch of freshers coming up to Oxford to begin their studies within the month![32] Young men under twenty would not be drafted. They could begin their university studies or work a job until they were older.[33] The Nazis would not be given the satisfaction of closing the universities.

At first, the war did not have a great impact on Lewis's weekly routine. Since coming up to Oxford as an undergraduate, Lewis had been a "joiner," which probably would have surprised anyone who had known him at Malvern College. He moved in and out of a variety of groups over the years. As the war began, he had a full schedule. On Monday evenings, he read Dante with Colin Hardie.[34] This experience probably led to Hardie's inclusion in the Inklings, but it also probably had an influence on Lewis's developing thoughts on temptation that he would explore in *The Screwtape Letters*, *Perelandra*, and *The Great Divorce*. On Tuesday evenings, he and Adam Fox met with the undergraduate Student Christian Movement chapter, which had met on Monday afternoons and would move its meeting time to Friday afternoons by the winter of 1940.[35] During the war, Lewis would begin to discover that schedules were written in sand. By February 1940, he was meeting with Hardie and the Dante Society on Tuesday evenings, an appointment he still kept by mid-war.[36] The Inklings normally met on Thursday evenings, but this meeting time was subject to change as they sometimes met on Friday or Wednesday, when circumstances demanded.[37] He met with the Gibbon Club on Friday evenings at least by the beginning of 1940.[38] Lewis really did not have time for a war. His schedule was full.

Lewis had never cared for his parish rector, the Reverend Thomas Eric "Peter" Bleiben. He viewed Bleiben as too liberal, and he patiently awaited the time when Bleiben would move on to a more prestigious and lucrative parish than Holy Trinity in Headington Quarry. Alas, Bleiben announced in church that he had intended to move to another parish, but in light of the war, he felt it his duty to remain in Headington. He had also begun the war by praying that God would prosper the "righteous cause" of their nation. Though Lewis subscribed to the justice of fighting the Nazis, he thought it an impertinence to inform God of the matter.[39]

Along with this news, intended to give his brother a laugh, Lewis added what he thought might become some really good news. Charles Williams, whom he had tried several times to lure up to Oxford for a meeting with the Inklings, had moved to Oxford along with the staff of the London branch of the Oxford University Press.[40] Williams would reside in Oxford during the week throughout the war but spend the weekends in London with his wife and son, who refused to relocate to the university town. The blitz probably seemed less dangerous than the academic snobbery they feared. In his first letter home to his wife upon moving to Oxford, Williams announced that Lewis had given him the use of his college rooms for the weekend while he got settled. Williams found the rooms waiting for him with a tea tray laid out for him including tea, milk, and an electric kettle.[41]

In the end, Williams lodged with the Spalding family on South Parks Road near Parson's Pleasure. Ruth Spalding, one of the Spalding daughters, had produced Williams's play *Seed of Adam* at the University Church of St Mary the Virgin, at which time Williams made her acquaintance. Through the Spaldings, Williams got to know Dorothy L. Sayers better. They had met before the war, but she was a friend of the Spaldings and stayed with them when she visited Oxford.

In his characteristically idiosyncratic manner, Williams referred to the Inklings as "Magdalen" in letters to his wife, presumably because they usually met in Lewis's rooms at Magdalen College.[42] Williams does not appear to have been enthralled with the Inklings at first. In fact, Williams had more than one literary circle to which he belonged. Once a week, he met Basil Blackwell, Christopher Fry, and Gerard Hopkins for lunch at the Eastgate Hotel.[43] Blackwell not only owned the famous Blackwell's Bookshop but also directed its publishing arm. Fry was a prominent playright, and Hopkins was the nephew of the poet and a gifted translator.

Charles Williams outside the Spaldings' home, Oxford. Used by permission of the Marion E. Wade Center, Wheaton College, Wheaton, IL.

Still, Williams was drawn to Lewis and began to make room for the Inklings. The meeting times had not yet completely settled into the routine of Thursday night and Tuesday morning, which would become standard during World War II. When the Inklings met on Friday evening, August 30, 1940, Williams had not been to a Friday meeting for two weeks and would not attend again for another two weeks. He told his wife that "fortunately" he had something better to do. While acknowledging that Lewis and his friends were good for the mind, he thought all enjoyment required "centredness."[44] He seemed to be sending a cryptic message to his wife that he would much prefer to be back in London with her on a Friday night. Williams's desire to be home in London on Friday night may be why the Inklings eventually settled on Thursday evening as their regular meeting time. As the months passed, Lewis also found that his Friday evenings had to be spent traveling to speak in far-flung parts of the kingdom.

The continued operation of the university during the war would form the theme of an important message that Lewis would deliver from the pulpit of the University Church of St Mary the Virgin just over a month after the declaration of war on October 22. Canon T. R. Milford had appreciated *The Pilgrim's Regress*, and with the anxiety and restlessness among undergraduates who were perplexed as to their duty, Lewis seemed just the right person to speak to them from the perspective of a don and ex-soldier who had been wounded. Lewis spoke at Evensong to a large congregation. Milford mimeographed the sermon ahead of time in order to distribute copies at the service under the title "'None Other Gods': Culture in War-Time." It was published later that year in pamphlet form as "The Christian in Danger." Today it is known as "Learning in War-Time."[45]

In this lecture, for it is not really a sermon, Lewis began by defining a university as "a society for the pursuit of learning" and then asked two basic questions: (1) Why would one begin an education with so little chance of completing it? (2) How can someone occupy himself with the pursuit of learning when lives and liberty are at stake in a great war?[46] He then proceeded to turn the question on its head, a standard plan of attack for Lewis. He essentially asked what war has to do with it. In a world where everyone is moving toward either heaven or hell, how could anyone attend to anything except the religious duty of evangelism? In a world in which death is a certainty for everyone, how could there be any place for learning or art or literature or any other aspect of human culture? One aspect of Lewis's conversion that he expressed in *The Pilgrim's Regress* is that the Christian life consists in doing most of the things a person did before becoming a Christian. Lewis insisted that if we attempted to suspend our intellectual or aesthetic life, we would only end by substituting a worse cultural life for a better.

If we do not develop our ability to think rationally, we will think irrationally. If we abandon aesthetic satisfaction, we will sink to sensual satisfaction.[47]

Despite his earlier rebuke of his rector, Lewis said that he did believe their cause to be righteous and therefore a religious duty. While his audience might be called upon to die for their country, they should never think of living at all for their country. God's claim on us is higher than the claim of culture. Nonetheless, cultural life will exist alongside the church, and Christians with the capacity have a duty to pursue learning. Lewis argued that "good philosophy must exist, if for no other reason, because bad philosophy needs to be answered."[48] In the end, it was a question not of whether the undergraduates of 1939 would have time to finish their program of study but of what they would make of their time while they had the opportunity to study.

By September 10, Oxford had its first air-raid warning. The drills were taken seriously, and families moved quickly to a place of safety. Shelters quickly appeared all over England. In most cases, these involved sand bags piled over a sheet-metal frame. Americans had their first exposure to these air-raid shelters through the film *Mrs. Miniver* (1942). Jack and Warnie were not satisfied with the standard air-raid shelter. Having lived through the trenches on the Western Front, they knew what high explosives could do, and the power of bombs had increased significantly over the previous twenty years. The air-raid shelter at the Kilns could withstand anything that Hitler could throw at them. The Lewis brothers meant to be safe. Their "dug-out" actually tunneled into the side of Shotover Hill with most of the massive hill above it. It was "not a nasty, dirty, wet hole, filled with the ends of worms and an oozy smell, nor yet a dry, bare, sandy hole with nothing in it to sit down on or to eat."[49] No. It was a concrete-and-brick reinforced home in the side of the hill of which Bilbo and Frodo Baggins would have been proud. Jack eventually referred to this little corner of his estate as Dug-Out Mound.[50]

Warnie and Jack went to enormous expense, but they would be safe if the war came to them. Because of Jack's forebodings of war, they had time to make preparations. John Lawlor recalled that Oxford had begun testing its air-raid sirens in June of 1939.[51]

At the Kilns, Jack took his young evacuees swimming in the pond, which he noted was cleaner than he had ever before seen it in September. Because the girls did not all have bathing suits, they had to take turns. Jack supervised and told the girls when it was time to take turns. At this announcement, a head would disappear beneath the water only to emerge ten yards further away and yell, "What?" Down again it went and popped up twenty more yards away to yell, "I can't hear what you said!"[52] The girls proved much more cooperative with their first air-raid drill, but Jack thought that the blackout was the greatest trouble he would face. He had experience with blackout curtains from the Great War in Great Bookham, where they had to guard against any flicker of light that could be seen by the zeppelins above. Jack told Warnie that the blackout curtains at the Kilns were just a "series of old rags." They worked fine, but they caused extra labor for Jack to arrange them properly. To his great relief, he set up the curtains every night by himself and took them down again in the morning without help, and apparently without supervision from Mrs. Moore.[53] In the course of the war, the rags were replaced by old army blankets that stood as permanent fixtures on the curtain rods. When Joy Davidman came to live at the Kilns years later, the blackout curtains still hung on the curtain rods.

Two weeks into the war, Jack wrote to Arthur to say that his nerves were "staggered," but his faith remained sound. He did not doubt that God would ultimately bring good from all the suffering they faced if they used the war properly. He had the ghastly feeling that he had been through it all before—that he had fallen asleep at the end of the last war to dream a lovely dream, only to awake to the war once again.[54] In terms of how the war might affect him personally, Lewis wrote, "It has come in the nick of time:

I was just beginning to get too well settled in my profession, too successful, and probably self complacent [*sic*]."[55] Such thoughts filled his head in the days and months before he received his first request from someone else for him to write a book, this time on the problem of suffering.

Lewis wanted to be of some use to the war effort besides teaching late-adolescent boys before they entered the army. He suggested to George Gordon, president of Magdalen College, that he could be an instructor in the Army Educational Corps. It made sense to Jack. He had served in the army as an officer and was almost killed. More harrowing than that, he had taught adolescent boys for fifteen years. Gordon only laughed again and said that Lewis would be wasted in such a position. He said that Lewis would do better in the Ministry of Information.[56] By September 18, Jack had carried two-thirds of his books from the cellar to his rooms, where he had the satisfaction of placing them on the shelves and the irrational feeling that one of the minor horrors of the war was now over.

At the Kilns, Jack's favorite evacuee was taken home by her mother and replaced with a Jewish Austrian refugee who he was told was a difficult child, but Jack did not find her so. Minto thought the girls were troublesome, but Jack thought they had only discovered that Maureen was "ragable"; the girls could wind her up.[57] By now, Maureen was teaching music at Oxford High School.[58] Jack found the girls much more pleasant than Minto's relatives who had come to stay for long periods throughout the 1930s. In fact, he told Sister Penelope that he found the girls delightful, for he had never appreciated children until the war brought them to him.[59] The difficulty lay not with the girls but with Minto. She was alarmed by the Russo-German Pact and was determined to buy a revolver. She created a trying atmosphere for Jack, but he found that if he did not contradict her, things went more smoothly.[60] He made the best of the situation and tried to carry on. For company on his daily walks, Jack had Bruce and Poggio, the current Kilns dogs.[61]

October found Warnie assigned to the No. 3 Base Supply Depot, in Le Havre, France. Throughout the fall of 1939 and the winter of 1940, the war remained silent. Each side spent its time preparing for the great assault to come. It was called the Phony War. As for Jack, he lost his university lectureship, which brought with it a stipend of two hundred pounds a year. All university lectureships were canceled, so he had not been singled out, but the loss stung just the same.[62]

It was also in October 1939 that Ashley Sampson asked Lewis to write a book for Centenary Press, a division of Geoffrey Bles, in its Christian Challenge series.[63] Lewis's acceptance of this invitation began a relationship between him and the Geoffrey Bles publishing house that would continue for the rest of his life and beyond. Sampson intended for the Christian Challenge series to reach people outside the church; therefore, this book marked a new direction in Lewis's writing that would bear much fruit. Sampson had read *The Pilgrim's Regress*, and on the basis of that work, he asked Lewis to write a book for unchurched laypeople on the problem of pain and suffering.[64] *The Pilgrim's Regress* is arguably Lewis's least accessible book, including his academic books. Why Sampson thought Lewis could communicate with theologically immature people on the basis of *The Pilgrim's Regress* remains a mystery. Perhaps he had seen *Out of the Silent Planet* and knew what Lewis could do. By November, however, Lewis was reading to the Inklings from this work in progress, which he would call *The Problem of Pain*.[65] He dedicated it to "The Inklings," and it was published in October 1940.[66] When Sampson saw the pamphlet with Lewis's sermon, he decided to include it in an anthology he was editing, *Famous English Sermons* (1940).[67]

Shortly before his birthday in November 1939, Lewis went to hear Adam Fox deliver his inaugural lecture as professor of poetry. The grand occasion called for a grand venue, so he spoke in the Divinity School, the ground floor of the original university library building, above which is the Duke Humfrey's Library and around which stands the fabled Bodleian Library. Lewis had never been in the room before in his more than twenty years' association with Oxford University. He wrote to Warnie that it was the most beautiful room in Oxford and perhaps all of England.[68] Begun in 1420, it was completed in 1483, one of the last architectural wonders of the medieval English world, with its widely spreading vaulted arches and great walls of clear rather than stained glass. Fox did not deliver a great lecture, but he did not embarrass. A few months later, however, Lewis returned to the room to hear Sir Edmund Chambers, whom Fox had defeated in the contest for professor of poetry. Chambers delivered the Sidney Lee Lecture, and Lewis could not contain his glee to Warnie because the esteemed scholar was "so portentously dull that I think even his supporters must have been ashamed of him."[69]

When January 1940 arrived and Warnie was far away in France, unable to keep the annual walking tour appointment with his brother, Jack enlisted Cecil Harwood to walk across the county of Somerset from Minehead to Porlock and about.[70] In his forty-first year, Lewis still loved miserable, wet, cold, windy weather and despised hot weather. His letters to Warnie during the first winter of the war luxuriate in how much he loved the wretched weather. Meanwhile, Warnie was in the hospital in France for some unnamed reason. In a letter of commiseration, Jack recalled that his most pleasant memories of Malvern and the army were the times he spent in the hospital and infirmary. While convalescing from trench fever in Le Tréport in 1918, Jack first decided "that beer was not an utterly unpleasant drink."[71] By early February, Warnie was back in the hospital again with a high fever.[72]

Williams and *Paradise Lost*

On January 29, 1940, Lewis and Tolkien gave up their usual Monday morning time together to go hear Charles Williams lecture on Milton. Lewis had arranged to get Williams added to the university's list of lecturers whose lectures throughout a term the undergraduates were not required to attend but might attend for their own amusement.[73] Lewis and Tolkien met Williams at Magdalen College and escorted him to the Divinity School, where he spoke. Williams reported to his wife that Lewis had called his lecture "the most important thing that has happened in the Divinity School for a hundred years, or is likely to happen for the next hundred."[74]

At some point during the war, and perhaps by the time he gave this lecture, Williams began to join Lewis and Tolkien for their Monday morning drink and talk. Much has been written about Tolkien's resentment of this intrusion into his friendship with Lewis, but it is possible that Tolkien did not feel the sting until long after Williams was dead. All of Tolkien's private remarks about Williams during his lifetime were positive.[75] In 1944, Tolkien wrote to his son Christopher and mentioned his Monday morning meeting with Lewis and Williams, but could not recall much of "the feast of reason and flow of soul, partly because we all agree so."[76] In all likelihood, Tolkien soured on Williams as his own friendship with Lewis waned in the 1950s, and perhaps Williams became a convenient person to blame, along with Joy Davidman.[77] Tolkien's negative remarks about Williams all date from after Lewis's death.[78] When he went to hear the lecture on *Paradise Lost*, Tolkien was great friends with Williams. It is interesting to note that by the war years, the Lewis brothers had given Tolkien the affectionate nickname of Tollers, but Williams remained one the few people Lewis ever knew who never received one of his nicknames.

The next week in his letter to Warnie, Jack was quoting from Milton's *Paradise Lost*.[79] Williams had reignited Lewis's love of *Paradise Lost*, which he had first experienced at Great Bookham during the last war. Jack's letters for months to come were punctuated by quotations from *Paradise Lost*. He began rereading and annotating the book for tutorials, and he wrote Warnie that owing to Williams's lectures, he found the parts about the war in heaven much better than he had before.[80] When University College of North Wales invited Lewis to deliver the Ballard Mathews

Lectures in 1941, he informed the principal that he would lecture on *Paradise Lost*.[81] Lewis expanded the three lectures and published them in 1942 as *A Preface to Paradise Lost*, which he dedicated to Charles Williams. The dedication took the form of a page-long letter in which Lewis praised Williams and described the effect of his Milton lecture at the Divinity School.[82]

In March 1940, Lewis published "Dangers of National Repentance" in the *Guardian*, a weekly newspaper that promoted the views of the High Church wing of the Church of England.[83] Though Lewis did not regard himself as High Church, he would publish a number of articles in the *Guardian* in the years to come, including his series that became *The Screwtape Letters* and a second series that became *The Great Divorce*. He wrote to Warnie that he supposed publishing in the *Guardian* represented a milestone in his "ecclesiastical career," and he was right.[84]

As the war continued largely at an international diplomatic level before May 1940, Lewis viewed the European scene with dismay. That Stalin and Hitler had patched up the irreconcilable differences between communism and fascism to their mutual advantage in the division of Poland demonstrated just how shallow a dictator's convictions can be. For the moment, Lewis was concerned over what stance Franco would take in Spain. He feared the use of Christianity as a tool of the state. He suggested to Warnie that Franco's brand of Christendom might represent the Catholic version of what "Ulster Orangeism" represented to Protestantism.[85] Jack had a much more critical view of the politicization of Protestantism in Northern Ireland than Tolkien ever gave him credit for having. Jack and Warnie both agreed that honest Catholicism was far preferable to any form of Christian totalitarianism that might break out in the world of conflict as they saw it.[86]

Family and Friends in Wartime

After much fretting that it might not come off, the annual walk with the anthroposophists came at the beginning of April. Barfield,

Harwood, and Field made up the party as usual, along with Jack, but this time Hugo Dyson joined them at their base in Minehead on the Bristol Channel with its back to the vast expanse of Exmoor. Dyson had come down to visit his in-laws who lived in the neighborhood. Dyson's war wounds to his leg, which required him to use a cane, prevented him from taking part in the long walks, but he more than compensated by his contribution to the chatter when everyone returned to the inn at night.[87] At the end of this joyous walking tour, Jack learned that Hitler had invaded Denmark and taken the country in one day without serious resistance.[88]

In the ten years since his conversion, Lewis had helped two of his former pupils as they slowly made their way along the journey to faith: Dom Bede Griffiths and George Sayer, who would become his biographer. Jack observed to his brother that both of these had converted to Catholicism. Now he found that a third of his former pupils was far along the same road, and this time it was a woman. Mary Shelley Neylan had been involved in a progressive education school that did not believe in discipline or rules for children, yet she had begun to question if her group was on the right track. Jack was asking Warnie and Griffiths to pray for her, because she kept asking Jack questions and he did not know what to say.[89] Lewis had ten good years of preparation as a Christian in which to learn how to talk to people about their faith rather than to debate them, as would have been his old habit. For the rest of the war, he realized that his task was not to win an argument with people but to help them answer the questions that churned within them. He still enjoyed a good public debate, no holds barred, with a strident opponent who meant to defeat him. He still loved to debate his friends over obscure points of theology about which neither was quite sure. Most people, however, struggled with uncertainty and perplexity. Most simply needed help thinking through their questions.

Jack kept Warnie informed of all the gossip from the Kilns. Maureen had brought home a male friend who Minto and Jack thought was dreadful. Minto referred to him as "that little black bounder" and Jack called him Maureen's "ugly little friend."[90] Lewis was always glad to see him leave. His name was Leonard James Blake, and he served as director of music at Worksop College, in Nottinghamshire. Lewis had a dim view of Blake and provided an anecdote to Warnie to illustrate his manner. When someone asked rhetorically in conversation why women wore lipstick that only succeeded in making their lips greasy, Blake interjected that he used Vaseline on his lips twice a day.[91] His awkwardness notwithstanding, Maureen married Leonard Blake on August 27, 1940.[92]

As the Phony War wore on everyone's nerves in the spring of 1940, Lewis dwelt more and more on the Christian obligation to forgive one's enemies and to pray for them. He spent time in prayer for Hitler, Stalin, Mussolini, and several of his Oxford acquaintances that fit the category of enemies. In letters to Warnie and Dom Bede Griffiths, Jack discussed the difficulty of these instructions from the Lord himself.[93] Worse yet, the Lord expects us to love our enemies! In discussing this problem with Warnie, Jack drew upon a reference from Spenser's *The Fairie Queene* that he had mentioned in *The Allegory of Love*. The Greeks had three primary words for love: "Eros = sexual love, Storge = family affection, Philia = friendship."[94] Lewis then told Warnie something he had not included in his book. He observed that the New Testament adds a fourth kind of love, *agapē* or charity, which the classical Greek world hardly mentioned at all. Lewis saw this expression of love as an act of the will rather than sentiment.[95] He would expound this idea at length twenty years later in *The Four Loves*.

The army evacuated Warnie from France in the first week of May 1940, and he went home to the Kilns for a brief visit before reporting for duty at Wenvoe Camp, near Cardiff, Wales.[96] Then, on May 10, Germany invaded the Netherlands, Belgium, and Luxembourg. By June 14, the Germans had pushed through

France and occupied Paris. On June 22, the French signed an armistice with Germany. Meanwhile, the British Expeditionary Force was pinned down in the coastal town of Dunkirk, France, near the Belgian border, with a complement of over 330,000 troops. Between May 27 and June 4, the British successfully evacuated most of the troops. The rescue of the British Expeditionary Force stands as one of the most heroic and glorious moments in the entire history of warfare in recorded time. The parents of Britain simply went in little boats and brought their children home. The Phony War was over. People had died in the hundreds of thousands by June.

Jack usually mentioned Minto's declining health in his letters to Warnie in the first year of the war. She seemed always to be in "poor form" from one or more of her ailments. Though Jack escaped his usual bout of flu in Hilary term, he came down with it by the beginning of July, and his weakness lingered for days afterward.[97] He did not complain, for illness was a routine matter with Lewis by this stage of his life. He enjoyed his confinement by reading things he had meant to read but normally could not for lack of time. On May 14, Anthony Eden had called on all able-bodied men under the age of sixty-five to join the Local Defence Volunteers (LDV), which Jack promptly did. With his flu, however, he had to convalesce. His slow recovery meant that he could not stand for more than half an hour, so he did not resume his LDV duties until August. His assignment was to patrol Oxford in the dark of the blackout between one thirty and four thirty on Saturday morning. He was amused by the debate over whether it was Friday night or Saturday morning.[98] Following a Friday evening Inklings meeting, he set out. He enjoyed his initial patrol, spent mostly in smoking, sitting in a college pavilion, and talking, but he tired of carrying a rifle again after more than twenty years.[99] Soon after beginning his duties, he had his own uniform, which he thought made him look "an absolute ass."[100] As the war progressed, the LDV would become the Home Guard.

The Birth of Screwtape

Jack's illness kept him away from church for many weeks. When he did return on July 21, he went to the midday Communion service, where the Reverend Arthur William Blanchett preached. Blanchett was the curate at Holy Trinity Church in Headington, and the Reverend Thomas Eric "Peter" Bleiben was the rector.[101] The sermon was not one of Blanchett's best, and as Jack's mind wandered, he came up with an idea for a book. He explained in his weekly letter to Warnie that it would be called "As One Devil to Another" and would involve a series of letters of advice from an elderly retired devil to a young devil just starting out his career with his first "patient."[102] As the idea matured, the name changed to *The Screwtape Letters*, but the infernal temptations that arise in church pews would retain a place of prominence. As he considered the experience of temptation, he decided that he would depart from his Low Church orientation and make confession to a priest, which he did the last week of October 1940.[103] Lewis would say his confessions to Father Walter Adams of the Anglican community of Saint John the Evangelist in Oxford until Adams died in 1952.[104]

We know very little of what transpired between Lewis and Adams during the confessional, for that is the nature of confession, but from time to time Jack made reference to something that had been said. His prayers for others had grown "irksome" as his circle widened, and he had more people on his prayer list. Adams advised him not to try to pray for everyone every night but to stretch it out. Lewis advised Mary Neylan that this change had turned an irksome duty into a delight.[105] On another occasion, Lewis explained to Neylan that it was a mercy to him to hear the voice of another person to liberate him from the "labyrinths" of his own conscience.[106] Lewis had developed the tendency in his youth and young adulthood to overanalyze himself, which can become a particularly acute problem for a private person like him. He did not seek absolution—just someone to talk to.

The best of all possible news came just after Jack wrote to Warnie on August 17, 1940. Instead of a letter in reply, Warnie himself turned up at the Kilns, having been transferred to the reserves and officially retired from the regular army. Like his younger brother, he would continue to do his bit. He joined the 6th Oxford City Home Guard Battalion as a private soldier.[107] By May, his service had switched allegiances from the army to the navy in the Upper Thames Patrol. He lived on board the *Bosphorus*, which he painted battleship gray as he plied the waters of the Thames Valley on the lookout for German spies, saboteurs, and related dangers. He even bought a blue peaked cap to emphasize that he was now part of the navy.[108]

The Problem of Pain

In October 1940, the Centenary Press of Geoffrey Bles published *The Problem of Pain*. In brief, the problem of pain or suffering or evil may be stated this way: If there is a good, loving, all-powerful God, then why do bad things happen? Sometimes the question is extended: Why do bad things happen to good people? Lewis began addressing the problem by recalling his own reflections on the question from the other way around when he had thought about it as an atheist. Lewis wrote to Griffiths a few years later that his mother's death, his unhappy experience of boarding school, and the horrors of World War I had made the problem of suffering quite personal to Lewis and that his atheism was based on it.[109] The universe is a cold, inhospitable place, and on our planet all the creatures prey on one another. For conscious creatures, life involves pain, and for humans, their reasoning capacity allows them to heighten the experience of pain by the ability to anticipate pain and death. Reason also allows humans to expand their ability to inflict pain on others. The atheist Lewis concluded that no spirit stands behind the universe unless it is an indifferent spirit or an evil spirit. This view, however, raises an enormous problem that most people never notice. If the universe is so bad, then how did humans ever come to think that it was made by a "wise and good Creator"?[110] With this question, Lewis turned the debate around.

Lewis argued that religion does not have its origin in observing the universe. Rather, religion in all its forms comes as a result of revelation. In dismissing Christianity in a letter to Arthur Greeves during World War I, Lewis had taken a naturalistic approach to the history of religion. Now he borrowed from much of that history, but he gave it a different interpretation. He said that all the developed world religions have the same three elements in their development. First comes the experience of the *numinous*, a concept Lewis got from Rudolf Otto's *The Idea of the Holy*. The term essentially refers to the universality of spiritual experience and embraces the combination of fear, dread, and awe. The fear goes beyond apprehension of physical danger, for the fear involves something that cannot be seen but is felt, something that is dangerous yet attracts. Lewis would use this concept but not this term to describe how mortals experience Aslan in The Chronicles of Narnia. Is he safe? He has swallowed whole worlds![111] It is important to understand that the experience is not a psychological project but the actual encounter with something that elicits the feeling.

The second element in the development of religion involves morality. Morality implies the consciousness of "I ought" or "I ought not." It is not simply a desire but a sense of right and wrong. Moral consciousness involves a major "jump" beyond the simple facts of life which have no moral value. People are aware not merely of a moral law but also of disobeying this law. In ancient pagan religion, the numinous and moral consciousness were not united in religion. The gods were feared, but they did not dabble in morality.[112]

The third stage in the development of religion occurs when humans comprehend that the numinous is the source and "guardian of the morality to which they feel obligated."[113] This union of the universal spirit and morality has not taken place in all religions everywhere: "Non-moral religion, and non-religious morality, existed and still exist."[114] Lewis suggested that only the Jews made this jump "with perfect decision."[115] The identification of numinous power with morality might only be madness, or it might be revelation. The descendants of Abraham declared that the awful, dreadful spirit who exercised unlimited power is a *"righteous"* God who loves righteousness.[116]

The fourth element in the development of religion involves a historical event. This event is the incarnation of the all-powerful, righteous God in human form as Jesus. Lewis declared this claim to be so shocking that it allows for only two possible responses. Either Jesus was "a raving lunatic of an unusually abominable type, or else He was, and is, precisely what He said."[117] If the latter, then everything else said about him becomes credible—including his death and resurrection, which somehow create a positive change in humanity's relation to God. Christianity is not a philosophical reflection on the origin and nature of the universe; it is the historical conclusion of God's spiritual preparation of humanity. The problem of pain does not exist until the assurance of the ultimate love and goodness of reality comes with the development of religion.[118]

Lewis next examined the idea of an all-powerful God. He cautioned against falling into the trap of the Scholastics of the Middle Ages, who pondered whether God could do impossible things. Lewis said that it was important to distinguish between the intrinsically possible and the intrinsically impossible. He said that we may attribute miracles to God but not nonsense. An example of pseudological nonsense would involve the problem of whether God can make a rock so big that he cannot move it. Thus, Lewis examined what kind of world an all-powerful God could create in which people like us could have free will to act. A world with consistent laws of nature is necessary for people to know how to act. In such a world, nerve endings, or "pain-fibres" as Lewis called them, tell how close to a fire we may come before we pass from safety to danger. Thus, pain serves a helpful purpose and is not necessarily evil. God could have created a world in which all action is regulated in such a way that no wrong action could take place, but this would be a world without free will, and evil thoughts would be impossible.[119]

Having dealt with the problem of a good God and an all-powerful God, Lewis then turned to the problem of a loving God. The real problem is that "we want, in fact, not so much a Father in Heaven as a grandfather in heaven—a senile benevolence who, as they say, 'liked to see young people enjoying themselves' and whose plan for the universe was simply that it might truly be said at the end of each day, 'a good time was had by all'."[120] To correct this view, Lewis turned to the four Greek ideas related to love without actually using the Greek words. Only recently had he discussed the four loves in a letter to Warnie. In fact, he had been thinking about all of the matters in *The Problem of Pain* for a few years as he saw the coming war. In the rest of the book, Lewis began to sketch out the idea that had come to console him and prepare him for the war he dreaded. God would bring some good out of the misery of war, but God would also use the pain people would experience toward their spiritual healing. In our pain, God gives us himself. Lewis knew of himself that he did not tend to surrender to Christ when all was rosy with the world. Only in the return to the horrors of war with which he was well acquainted did he throw himself on Christ. Thus, he concluded: "God whispers to us in our pleasures, speaks in our conscience, but shouts in our pain: it is His megaphone to rouse a deaf world."[121]

Many of the essential ideas that Lewis introduced in *The Problem of Pain* would prove useful to him when he began his radio talks for the BBC the following year. In particular, he dealt in a different way with the development of religion, which he discussed more comparatively, and with the problem of morality, or right and wrong. He would also expand on the idea of what to make of the claims of Jesus to deity. These claims have often been refuted by modern skeptics who point out that Jesus never claimed to be the Son of God. Instead, he always insisted that he was the Son of Man. In fact, he frequently told people not to tell anyone that he was the Messiah. This confusion arises from modern audiences' unfamiliarity with the Bible. "Son of Man" was the divine title for the appearance of God in human form at the end of time as righteous Judge and King, based on the apocalyptic vision of Daniel found in Daniel 7:13–14. *Messiah* was a royal term that referred to the human descendant of King David who would rule an everlasting kingdom. At his trial, Jesus admitted that he was the Messiah, a claim for which the Sanhedrin could turn him over to the Romans for execution as a rebel against Rome. Then Jesus said that he was also the Son of Man who would come on the clouds of heaven, making clear that he meant the one prophesied by Daniel. At these words, the high priest tore his garments, for he had heard unspeakable blasphemy—unless it was true (Matt. 26:62–66).

Even as *The Problem of Pain* appeared in print, Lewis had begun to develop his idea about demonic correspondence. According to George Sayer, Lewis's former pupil who became a Christian and later wrote a masterful biography of Lewis, the manuscript of *The Screwtape Letters* grew quickly. Lewis wrote one letter a week and submitted the full manuscript to the *Guardian* in February 1941.[122] It may be helpful to recall that the writing of *The Screwtape Letters* and Warnie's return to the Kilns all took place during the very worst days of the great aerial conflict known as the Battle of Britain, when the small, young Royal Air Force defended Britain against the overwhelming onslaught of the German Luftwaffe. The Battle of Britain lasted from July 10 until October 31, 1940. The next dreadful stage of the war involved the nighttime bombing raids known as the blitz, which lasted from September 7, 1940, through May 11, 1941.

8

From Academic Work to War Work

1941

The publication of *The Problem of Pain* opened new doors and created new demands for C. S. Lewis. On February 7, 1941, Dr. James W. Welch, director of religious broadcasting for the BBC, wrote to Lewis after reading his new book. He invited Lewis to speak on the BBC to an audience that he estimated at over a million people on some topic about Christianity from a layman's point of view.[1] Lewis immediately accepted, with the provision that it would have to be during the summer vacation. He suggested a talk about the objective reality of right and wrong.[2] Lewis next heard from Eric Fenn, Welch's assistant head, who proposed that Lewis deliver a series of four talks on Wednesday evenings in either August or September. Lewis agreed and said that he preferred August dates.[3] By May 12, he had completed an outline for his talks and sent it to Fenn for his approval.[4]

About the time that Lewis agreed to speak on the BBC, another invitation came, this one from the Reverend Maurice Edwards, chaplain in chief of the Royal Air Force (RAF). The Very

Reverend Walter Robert Matthews, dean of St Paul's Cathedral in London, had funds available for a lectureship, and he offered to make the lectureship available to the RAF to pay Lewis to speak at air bases. Lewis said that he was willing to give it a try but that the age for service duty was bound to be raised, and he would be called back into the army.[5] On a rainy night sometime in the first half of 1941, Edwards called on Lewis in his rooms at Magdalen College with his advisor, Charles Gilmore, to convince Lewis to speak and to work out the details. Lewis still believed that he would be called back into the army, but the chaplains convinced him to take on this extra responsibility, which would prove to be a huge demand on his time and energy.[6] He wrote to Sister Penelope on May 15 that he had given some talks at the RAF base in Abingdon, but he thought he had been a complete failure.[7] Others thought differently, and Lewis would continue to speak at RAF bases across Britain throughout the war. Lewis's popularity had just begun to rise dramatically, for since he began speaking at RAF bases, *The Screwtape Letters* began to appear in serial form in the *Guardian* on May 2 and would continue to appear each week for another thirty weeks.[8] His books had reached a modest audience, but the *Guardian* reached a mass audience. By the time he began his BBC broadcasts in August, he would already have a following.

Broadcast to Iceland

A year earlier, during the third week of April 1940, Lewis had read Christopher Dawson's *Beyond Politics*. What struck Lewis about the book was the distinction Dawson drew between the ideal of freedom and the ideal of democracy. The idea of democracy as propounded by Rousseau and embodied in the French Revolution placed its emphasis on the "general will" of the community over against the individual. The idea of freedom as expressed by the English placed its emphasis on the rights of the individual over against the will of the whole. Dawson traced modern English notions of freedom to the Nonconformists of the seventeenth century, who sought religious liberty, and to the English aristocracy, which asserted its rights over against the crown. Dawson concluded that without freedom, modern democracy and modern dictatorship are "twin children of the Revolution" with their emphasis on the community or collective or state.[9]

Jack told Warnie that he thought this view explained a great deal about the difference between the English and the European democracies. The French offered no exemption from military service for a conscientious objector, but the English did, even if reluctantly. This also explained the political alliance in the seventeenth and eighteenth centuries in England between the great nobility and the nonconformist merchant class. It was never the marriage of convenience as some supposed but a marriage of conviction. This view also explained to Jack why he and Warnie felt so strongly about freedom but less so about democracy.[10] These observations would not have risen to much more than a passing interest, except they became the thesis of C. S. Lewis's first radio broadcast in May 1941.

In one of Charles Williams's lectures, he had imitated a cockney accent while reading Homer, but he had forewarned his audience in all seriousness that he did not do a cockney accent very well. Lewis wrote to Warnie about the event, which he thought was very funny because Williams had an extreme cockney accent without realizing it. Lewis remarked, "It is painful to reflect that each of us is presumably if not under the same, yet under equal, delusion about the sound of his own voice."[11] Lewis found his forecast to be true about himself when he heard the first recording of his voice played back to him the first week of May 1941. In a letter to Arthur Greeves, he confessed, "I was unprepared for the total unfamiliarity of the voice; not a trace, not a hint, of anything one could identify with oneself—one couldn't possibly guess who it was."[12] Then he realized that people who had done awful mock imitations of him speaking had actually done very good imitations of him. Perhaps to his dismay, he realized that he had completely lost his Irish accent, as his mother had always hoped.

The cause for the recording, and the importance of Christopher Dawson's book for Lewis's thought, was a request that came to Lewis from the Joint Broadcasting Committee. This organization had been set up by the government to broadcast to the populations living under German occupation. It was the British approach to propaganda. In this case, however, they wanted Lewis to broadcast a message to a conquered population living under British occupation! On the day that Hitler invaded Belgium, Luxembourg, and the Netherlands, British forces made a surprise invasion of Iceland and began a military occupation of the island that sat strategically midway across the North Atlantic. Iceland had been part of the vast Danish Empire, which also included Greenland and the Faroe Islands, for over a thousand years. Germany had occupied Denmark on May 4, 1940, and it would have been only a matter of time before the Germans occupied Iceland and made it a naval base. In these circumstances, the Joint Broadcasting Committee wanted Lewis to say something that would make the people of Iceland feel better about being invaded by the British.[13]

What very few people would have known at the time is that the Joint Broadcasting Committee was an agency of the ultrasecret Secret Intelligence Service, sometimes called Military Intelligence and also known in fiction as the Secret Service and MI6. The files of the Secret Intelligence Service remain closed, so we do not know any details of how Lewis came to be approached about a broadcast to Iceland. Speculation produces only possibilities. With the large crowds of undergraduates that Lewis had attracted to his lectures for fifteen years, any number of Oxford graduates who might have found themselves in Military Intelligence when the war came would have known of Lewis's interest in Old Icelandic and the Norse settlers of Iceland. C. E. "Tom" Stevens, who would become a regular member of the Inklings after the war, was involved in intelligence work during the war. Stevens was a fellow and tutor in ancient history at Magdalen from 1933 who would have known all about Lewis's interests and his skill at public speaking.[14] Possibly Lord David Cecil mentioned Lewis to his brother, Lord Cranborne, who was high in Churchill's government and may have passed his name along. The most fascinating speculation arises from a "cryptic" remark by Lewis in a letter to his old friend A. K. Hamilton Jenkin just before the outbreak of war. Lewis informed him that he would be delivering lectures in Cambridge once a week during the term and that he should let Lewis know of any "commissions" he might have for Bletchley.[15] Bletchley is a small town halfway between Oxford and Cambridge where the Secret Intelligence Service established a code breaking operation just before the war. All wild speculation.

What we do know is that Lewis recorded his talk on two 78 rpm records the first week of May and that the two records were taken to Iceland. We do not know if the talk was ever broadcast, for Britain transferred control of Iceland to the Americans in July 1941 before the United States entered the war under the pretext that Iceland is technically in the Western Hemisphere and fell under the provisions of the Monroe Doctrine. The transfer of jurisdiction freed up British troops to go where they were needed, and it tied the United States closer to the European war before Pearl Harbor. Lewis's hitherto unknown talk was discovered in Iceland at a used bookshop and sold on eBay, thereby falling into my hands. Unfortunately, only one of the two records is known to have survived. The surviving disk has side 1 and side 3. To be played over the radio, a recorded talk would have needed two turntables. Side 1 would have been on the first turntable, and as soon as it finished, side 2 would have begun on turntable 2 while the first disk was flipped to be ready to play side 3. While side 3 played on disk 1, the second disk would have been flipped to side 4, and in this way the talk could be heard seamlessly before more advanced means of recording were developed.

Label of Lewis's *Norse Spirit* recording for
broadcast to Iceland

After mentioning his early fascination with Norse mythology,
Lewis moved to discuss how the Norse idea of freedom influenced
the English as he traced the theme through English literature. He
contrasted this Norse/English tradition with democracy as such,
and with the continental tradition of society. His thoughts on
Dawson's ideas about freedom and democracy help us picture the
missing strands of Lewis's argument. The recording does not have
the quality of a BBC recording, and a number of words on the first
side are impossible to understand:

Side 1

I am not quite certain why I have been asked to address the
people of Iceland, but I do know why I have accepted the invitation. I have done so in order to repay a great debt. If I seem
to you in the whole to be talking of things of a very ancient
history, you must forgive me. I am trying through you to thank
your ancestors.

My imaginative life almost begins with an awakening to
Norse mythology which came when I was about fourteen.

When I came to my conception of it, it was then romantic and in many ways erroneous, depending on a period of translation by our English books which could hardly be otherwise. But when years later I began at Oxford to learn your language, I found nothing in my earlier love that had to be thrown away. That language still seems to be one of the sharpest and strongest of humankind, one of the best adapted for carrying out the ideal of the old poets:

> Let your words at the feast be strewn [?],
> but let them cut like a sword.
> Let —— —— still listen to it,
> and still touch my heart as perhaps no other can.

This experiment in rhyme is not so uncommon among Englishmen as you might suppose. In every generation since the beginning of the eighteenth century, there have been some who felt a kind of compass needle in them pointing to the North— the essayist and dramatist Sir William Temple, the poet Grey, William Morris. What is the explanation? I do not think it —— to point out our kinship by blood and our early connections. All that, of course, is true. We too are a Baltic people. Our first great poem, *Beowulf*, celebrates Danish heroes. We had Norsemen as kings, but blood explains little. I myself am of Welsh descent, and if blood were all, I ought to find my natural food in —— ——, but in fact, the —— is as insipid to me as the other is intoxicating.

If the northern enchantment caught so many Englishmen, it is because of a real, though subtle, affinity of temper between the two [men?] which then informs in addition to blood kinship, ——. The affinity is easy to feel but difficult to define. One starting point is the fact, recognized I think by all scholars, that whenever a medieval Englishman translated a French romance, he made it a little less courtly; he brought it a little nearer to earth. The farmyard and the castle are nearer to the English person than in the original. And this compliment runs all through our literature straight down —— ——, but they are really very earthy people, the vulgar counterpart, England sets on —— romance. —— —— all be heroes —— ——, but the —— —— people lies in their peasant —— and common ——. Whenever —— ——

Side 2 (missing)

Side 3

But heaven forbid I should mention Dickens only to speak ill of him. His very name recalls me at once to what is perhaps the strongest of all affinities between these two antic [antique?] islands. To speak of Dickens is to think of Bumble the beadle, and that carries our mind at once to a whole crowd of thick-headed magistrates, interfering philanthropists, tyrannical administrators of the Poor Law, and the like. Have you ever noticed the fact that in Dickens, in Shakespeare, in Fielding, in the whole range of English literature, a person in petty authority, a minor official hardly ever appears except to be made ridiculous? There seems to be a deep conviction in our minds that the man who carries some wand of office is more likely than other men to be half knave and wholly fool.

I need not remind you of the similar spirit in Old Icelandic. The very origins of Iceland lie in the impeccable independence of those who went there from Norway because they would not be dragooned at home, would not be brought up to bent and made into a tiny little medieval monarchy on the pattern of the other European countries. I would not like to be hasty in giving this spirit a name. It is not democracy, for it dislikes interfering officialdom in a democratic form of government, at least as much as under any other. It is not in essence the revolutionary spirit. Revolution, in the sense of innovation, is not what it seeks. It generally demands to be left alone and shuts its front door in your face. It is not exactly individualism, for it is quite compatible with the most self-effacing loyalty to a family, a patch of ground, or a chief. But it likes to choose its own chief and to choose him for what he really is: his wisdom, his courage, his beauty, or the fact that he is an old friend. I think it is a little —— to admit the claims of high descent than to admit those of official status, because they seem a little more intrinsic to the man. It does not assert the rights of man in the abstract, but the rights of a particular man. In the long run, it can be described as personal realism. It brings every situation between two people back to what those two people really are. If Bumble or Harald Fairhair wants to be treated as the better man, he must show he is the better man. Its favorite formula in our language is, "and who the devil are you, anyway?"[16]

Side 4 (missing)

The Inklings appear to have known about Lewis's radio talk, for Tolkien made a telling remark in a letter to his son Michael on June 9, 1941. After ranting about how he had spent his whole life studying Germanic matters, which to his mind included England and Scandinavia, and how he had been attracted to the Germanic ideal rather than the classical ideal as an undergraduate (unlike some people who did Greats), he complained, "But no one ever calls on me to 'broadcast', or do a postscript! Yet I suppose I know better than most what is the truth about this 'Nordic' nonsense."[17] He seems offended that Lewis, rather than he, had been invited to give a radio broadcast. Anyone who had heard Tolkien speak would never have asked him to broadcast, regardless of his knowledge of the subject. It is highly likely, however, that Tolkien did not know that his friend's knowledge of Norse mythology and society had also gone back to his school days.

Tolkien also viewed the old tales differently than Lewis did. Tolkien was interested in the language and how it changed. Lewis was interested in the stories and what they revealed about the people who told them. The difference is reflected in how they walked across the countryside. Tolkien wanted to examine the details of a flower or twig, while Lewis wanted to take in the whole landscape.

Tolkien could not have spoken on the Norse influence on English literature for a very important reason beside the fact that he did not speak well. Tolkien had little knowledge of English literature after 1400, and he did not care for much written after 1066.

War Work

Lewis found himself extremely busy during the war as he accepted more and more projects from other people that he would not have undertaken on his own. His major academic project, the volume on English literature in the seventeenth century, sat where he left it before the war began. It would have to wait until after the war for him to make any more headway on it. He told Arthur Greeves that he was so busy, he hardly had any time for reading. Then he mentioned five books he had just read.[18] Fortunately for Lewis, who saw food as a subject of infinite interest "and every meal a high light," by May 1941 he had not yet gone hungry due to rationing.[19] By 1943, however, Lewis would notice that everyone looked thinner.[20]

Nonetheless, the effects of rationing had begun to show as early as April 1940, when the menu began to change at Magdalen College. The finer cuts of meat that Magdalen had been accustomed to serving for five centuries grew increasingly difficult to obtain. The Magdalen dining hall resorted to cuts of meat that never would have appeared on Albert Lewis's table. Offal, those bits of entrails and intestines that make their way into such dishes as steak and kidney pie, had become standard. Lewis sent this news to Warnie not as a complaint, for Warnie and Jack actually preferred the working man's cuts of meat.[21] By August of 1940, however, matters had grown more serious. The German U-boats were sinking the ships with vital food supplies from Canada and the United States. This growing food shortage led to a calamity at Magdalen College. Dinner went from five courses to three, and no meat was served on Friday.[22] Before the war, dinner at Magdalen had been quite a grand affair, which explains in part how Jack

Lewis managed to gain so much weight. George Sayer recalled dinner in hall at Magdalen from the days he was Lewis's pupil before the war. The servants served the meal to the high table from large silver dishes, from which the fellows helped themselves. The five courses began with soup followed by an entrée or fish course. Then came a meat, game, or poultry course. Next came the pudding. Finally, the meal ended with a savory. The meal sometimes included oysters, smoked salmon, or caviar but almost always was accompanied by French or German wine.[23] The war put an end to dinner as it had been known.

On Sunday, June 8, 1941, Lewis preached again for Evensong at the University Church of St Mary the Virgin. This sermon was "The Weight of Glory."[24] He had also accepted Sister Penelope's invitation to speak to the Junior Sisters at the Anglican convent of St Mary in Wantage, near Oxford.[25] By the summer, Lewis was too busy "travelling the country" and speaking at various RAF bases to accept any requests to write book reviews for journals and newspapers, which had long been part of his normal academic work as a fellow.[26] By October, he was hardly home for more than three consecutive nights, and he claimed that travel plans for his "missionary journies [*sic*]" to RAF bases were as complicated as the maps of Saint Paul's missionary journeys.[27]

Lewis appears to have spoken without manuscript or notes when he visited RAF bases. When addressing the airmen and officers of the heavy bomber squadrons based in Norfolk, he expressed his opposition to compulsory chapel attendance. Among other evils, Lewis believed that compulsory attendance hardened people against religion.[28] During that visit, he spoke at the morning worship service in the main aerodrome and later at a satellite station. In the evening, he spoke at another service, where attendance was voluntary. For the morning service, he essentially gave an apologetic for the validity of theology as a map to direct us toward God. In other words, he understood the frame of mind of his audience and a general resentment toward having this Oxford don imposed on them. For the evening service, he did something quite different. He actually preached.

The chaplain had warned Lewis that the evening service would have a low attendance and that few airmen would be present. Some officers would attend because they would have come from the middle and upper classes, where church attendance was still regarded as a sign of good breeding. As it turned out, the chaplain had underestimated the response to Lewis, for "the chapel was uncomfortably crowded."[29] Lewis took as his text, "If anyone would come after me, let him deny himself and take up his cross and follow me" (Mark 8:34). He then told in graphic detail the story of the arrest, trial, torture, and crucifixion of Jesus, along with the mocking and betrayal he endured. Lewis then made the story personal by describing what it had cost him to follow Christ in Oxford, where he had been rejected and castigated by other members of the faculty. Even in his own home, his desire to attend the early church service was assailed as selfish and intended only to inconvenience the other members of the household. He was attacked within his own home as a fanatic who had lost all sense of proportion.[30] Lewis's comprehension of the words of Jesus about being crucified with him, and the words of Paul in Roman 6 about dying with Christ, had become Lewis's primary way of understanding the meaning of the death of Jesus and the doctrine of the atonement.

During the long vacation of summer, Lewis lectured at RAF bases around the country. Each trip lasted two or three days, and then he was home for two or three days before heading out again. For Lewis, who had always loved train travel, trips on crowded trains filled with troops became a great chore and uncomfortable for his arthritic body. By summer's end, he had been to Perthshire, in central Scotland; Shrewsbury, in the West Midlands; and Cumberland, in the northwest of England. He was so busy during the summer and fall of 1941 that he did not have time to write to Greeves between May 25 and December 23.[31]

C. S. Lewis at RAF Chaplaincy School, 1944. Used by permission of the Marion E. Wade Center, Wheaton College, Wheaton, IL.

Not all of these trips were equally Spartan. When he lectured in Hereford, the Right Reverend Richard Godfrey Parsons, bishop of Hereford, and his wife invited Lewis to stay with them at the Bishop's Palace, parts of which date to the twelfth century.[32] In 1943, he stayed at Chicksands Priory and marveled at how the aristocracy lived.[33]

In addition to speaking before the men and women at the RAF bases, Lewis also spoke at the RAF Chaplains School in Cambridge, which was housed at Magdalene College and run by Charles Gilmore. Normally, Lewis lectured on the last day of each course of study.[34] Gilmore feared that inviting Lewis might have been a mistake when Lewis chose as his title "Linguistic Analysis in Pauline Soteriology." The chaplains in training did not necessarily have a theological background. Some had ministry and theological training, but the others came from all walks of life. My philosophy professor in seminary had been one such volunteer.[35] He had been a physicist at Oxford before the war. The chaplains in training devoured dogmatic, authoritarian speakers who offered easy, stock answers to hard questions. Lewis seemed to Gilmore to be off his game that first day. He had trouble choosing the right words to say. He gave all the clues of a man uncomfortable speaking in public. Then he "said something about prostitutes and pawnbrokers being 'pardoned in Heaven, the first by the throne.'"[36] After that, he owned the field. Lewis knew how to read his audience. These world-toughened chaplains had seen it all, to their way of thinking, but Jack Lewis had lived for twenty years in Headington with the family and friends of Janie Moore.

BBC Broadcast

In August 1941, Lewis went to London weekly to give the four radio talks that he named "Right and Wrong: A Clue to the Meaning of the Universe." His fifteen-minute broadcasts took place each Wednesday evening of that month from seven forty-five to eight. Lewis received so many letters arising from the talks that the BBC scheduled a fifth talk on September 3 to allow him to answer the many questions and objections.[37] Many people tend to think of these first BBC broadcast talks as philosophical apologetics. Austen Farrer, Lewis's friend and one of the foremost Anglican theologians of the twentieth century, observed that the radio broadcasts that became *Mere Christianity* are actually expositions of doctrine.[38] Farrer is almost right. Lewis did expound doctrine in much of his later broadcast series, but in this first cycle, he dealt with all the little obstacles to belief in God that had confronted a teenage boy in Great Bookham and a young scholar in postwar Oxford. Those familiar with the slow, laborious journey by which Lewis first struggled to understand how people could have a sense of right and wrong in a materialist universe and only at last came to believe that Jesus Christ is the Lord of glory will recognize that the first BBC broadcast series is simply the personal testimony of C. S. Lewis and his conversion to theism. At the end of the fourth talk, he remarked, "I am not yet within a hundred miles of the

God of Christian theology."[39] This first set of talks has the feel of philosophy for many people simply because Lewis laid out the process so logically and in order. For Farrer, however, it is doctrinal because the track of Lewis's conversion, and the order in which he explained why right and wrong are clues to the meaning of the universe, follows the order of the creeds. Such a rational approach to religious belief came as a shock to many people, but conversion is often the result of a long process.

The first set of broadcasts had such a powerful response that the BBC decided to ask Lewis to prepare a second series of five talks to be given on January 11 and 18, and February 1, 8, and 15 in the winter of 1942. An unforeseen consequence of the broadcasts was the "enormous pile of letters from strangers" that Lewis felt obliged to answer because they had serious questions.[40] The mail problem would only grow larger. Nonetheless, Lewis immediately wrote to Eric Fenn to accept the invitation. He would title his talks "What Christians Believe."[41]

While preparing his *Paradise Lost* lectures, he had completed his thirty-one week series of letters from Uncle Screwtape in the *Guardian* and sent the typed manuscript off to his publisher to produce a book while sending the handwritten original to Sister Penelope, in case the publisher was bombed by the Germans![42] He delivered his lectures at University College on the evenings of December 1–3, 1941, but he realized that he had too much material for three lectures and began plans to turn the lectures into the book that would be published as *A Preface to Paradise Lost*.[43]

The Devil and C. S. Lewis

For at least two years, Lewis had his mind on *Paradise Lost* in one way or other. It began with Charles Williams's lecture in January 1940. *Paradise Lost* deals with the temptation of Adam and Eve by Satan. It focuses on Satan as the great enemy of humanity because of his rebellion against God. For several years prior, Lewis had struggled with the problem of temptation and how to deal with it. We have glimpses of his thoughts on the matter from his letters to Arthur Greeves, Dom Bede Griffiths, and Owen Barfield. Against the backdrop of *Paradise Lost*, Lewis conceived the idea of *The Screwtape Letters* in July 1940. Then, in March 1941, he took the invitation to give a series of lectures at University College as an opportunity to examine *Paradise Lost* as a scholar from a Christian point of view. He was writing *The Screwtape Letters* as he wrote his lectures on *Paradise Lost*. What is more, by November 1941, before he delivered his lectures on *Paradise Lost*, he had begun writing *Perelandra*, which is a retelling of Satan's temptation of Eve without the fall.[44] This would be his second science-fiction novel at a time when science fiction was not considered legitimate literature. In fact, it did not yet have a commonly agreed-upon name. Lewis called it "scientifiction" and himself a "scientifictionist."[45] He would not be finished with the diabolical theme of temptation until he wrote *The Great Divorce* in 1944.[46]

The interplay of these projects demonstrates again how the popular work of Lewis came from the overflow of his scholarly work. His literary scholarship stimulated his creative imagination, which became a vehicle for his theological reflection and philosophical insight. In this regard his academic work provides a case study in how a Christian scholar can engage a subject from a Christian point of view without betraying his or her discipline. As happened with *The Allegory of Love*, Lewis's study of *Paradise Lost* spawned a much larger body of work.

The Screwtape Letters

Like *The Problem of Pain* and the BBC radio broadcasts, *The Screwtape Letters* belongs to the Christian devotional form of personal testimony, approaching that of *The Pilgrim's Regress*. The letters are confessional in nature, like Augustine's *Confessions*, Patrick's *Confession*, and Bunyan's *Grace Abounding*. Furthermore, they came at a time when Lewis had decided to begin voicing his confession to a priest as an aid in dealing with temptation. Yet these testimonies are veiled in nonpersonal, reasoned discourse. Though they are confessional, Lewis is not the subject. Not until he wrote *Surprised by Joy* could he bring himself to give a straightforward testimony. He told Fenn at the BBC that "testifying" was simply not his gift.[47] As *Surprised by Joy* demonstrates, he was mistaken.

Lewis always insisted that he was not a theologian, and the professionally credentialed theologians also insisted that he was not a theologian, but, of course, he was a theologian. A theologian is not a person who has studied systematic theology but a Christian who thinks about God. And Lewis spent a great deal of time thinking about God. He thought of God not simply as a concept but as a person with whom he spent a great deal of time and before whom he often felt ashamed. Yet Lewis never intended to do the work of a systematic theologian. As Dennis Beets has often emphasized, Lewis was a pastoral theologian who aimed at bringing comfort to people who were confused and afflicted.

The Screwtape Letters enjoyed enormous popular success, but in 1948, Lewis mentioned that it was the book that he enjoyed writing the least.[48] In these letters, Lewis wrote from the other way around, a technique he had thought about since his years in Great Bookham. In this case, however, writing from the other way around meant thinking along diabolical paths as he laid himself bare to his own most susceptible spiritual flaws.[49] He did not write about murder, rape, and grand larceny. He wrote about snobbishness, peevishness, selfishness, and pride.

In *The Screwtape Letters*, Lewis recounted episodes in his life where the temptation was real and when he felt ashamed of himself. His letters to Warnie tell us how he felt about his church, about the people filling the pews, about the rector and curate, and about the terrible hymns. Warnie's memoir of his brother confirmed that the domestic situation at the Kilns that caused Jack so much stress and gloom is reflected in his books.[50] Jack's diary from the 1920s tells us how he felt about Arthur Greeves embarrassing him in front of his new friends. His letters to Arthur tell us about his boyhood distractions, his arrogance, his intellectual snobbery, and his spiritual pride.

Jack's letters to Warnie at the beginning of the war reveal how Minto's conversation, manner, complaints, and selfishness irritated him. He regularly told Warnie of Minto's particularly irrational and ludicrous statements. While discussing an appropriate epitaph on the gravestone of Minto's friend Alice Hamilton Moore, Minto interrupted Jack to say, "Dates will live."[51] He had no idea what she meant. When Maureen and one of her friends decided to go out on the frozen pond, Minto warned them to be careful not to slip because "it's simply *like ice*."[52] A letter from Warnie had produced relief in Minto "because of her usual inability to imagine any causes for silence except major disasters."[53] As Jack's friendship with Sister Penelope grew, he asked for prayer for Jane, a name by which no one ever called Mrs. Moore, and revealed his honest assessment of her: "an unbeliever, ill, old, frightened, full of charity in the sense of alms, but full of uncharity in several other senses."[54] To Sister Penelope, Lewis could say of the Kilns, "We are not a very happy house."[55] Tolkien and Barfield knew nothing of the strain of life with Minto, but Warnie reflected on Jack's and his experience of her during the last twenty years of her life:

> She was a woman of very limited mind, and notably domineering and possessive of temperament. . . . In twenty years I never saw a book in her hands; her conversation was chiefly about herself, and was otherwise a matter of ill-informed dogmatism: her mind was of a type that [Jack] found barely tolerable elsewhere.[56]

Consistent with Jack's description of domestic relations at the Kilns in his letters and diary, Warnie described Mrs. Moore's management of the house as "an autocracy that developed into stifling tyranny," for she was the sort of person who thrives "on crisis and chaos; every day had to have some kind of domestic scene or upheaval, commonly involving the maids."[57] All of these kinds of dynamics appear in *The Screwtape Letters* and *The Great Divorce* as points of attack for temptation.

The Screwtape Letters do not deal only with Lewis's temptations. He also spoke prophetically of trends he saw that afflicted or tempted others in church and in society. He specifically mentioned "the inner ring" that had caused him such pain as a boy and that he had experienced again in the Senior Common Room at Magdalen College from T. D. Weldon and his lot. Several of the ladies he knew in Belfast and Headington also make veiled appearances. Yet how can any of these assertions really be true? Lewis was a staunch critic of what he called the "personal heresy," which alleged that the author was the subject of the book. For this biography to see Lewis in so many of his books seems to be the worst case of the "personal heresy." It would be if this biography saw Lewis in *Out of the Silent Planet* or *Till We Have Faces*, which are pure works of fiction. Lewis made several exceptions to his charge of the "personal heresy," and books like Augustine's *Confessions* fall within the exception because they are represented to be about the author. It is also important to distinguish works like *The Pilgrim's Regress, Surprised by Joy,* and *A Grief Observed,* which are biographical in nature, from fictional works like *The Screwtape Letters* and *The Great Divorce,* which are only informed by what Lewis learned and observed from his experience. In short, though the latter books contain glimpses of Lewis, they are not *about* Lewis so much as they are about temptations with which Lewis was acquainted and with which many people can identify. In the preface to the 1961 edition of *Screwtape,* Lewis acknowledged that he had learned how temptation works through his own heart.[58]

A Preface to Paradise Lost

Unlike *The Screwtape Letters* and the radio broadcasts that became *Mere Christianity,* Lewis's *A Preface to Paradise Lost* is not about him; it is about Milton's *Paradise Lost* (1667, 1674). *Paradise*

Lost is the last great, popular epic poem written in English. Milton wrote it during the same period in which John Bunyan wrote *The Pilgrim's Progress* (1678), the last great, popular allegory written in English. Both wrote in a time of revolution—and not just military and political, with the upheavals of the English Civil War and the Restoration of the monarchy and the Glorious Revolution. It was a time that transformed the English language; *you* replaced *thou* and *ye*. As he had done in *The Allegory of Love* with the allegorical form, Lewis explained how epic poetry works in *A Preface to Paradise Lost*, so that a generation unfamiliar with it could appreciate it. He also wrote to contend for his approach to literary criticism in contrast to the kind of criticism exemplified by T. S. Eliot, Lewis's great nemesis.

The first paragraph of *A Preface to Paradise Lost* deserves to be quoted in full in order for the reader to see how Lewis began his case for literary criticism based on the text rather than on external philosophical opinions and theories. Every academic discipline can be, and has been from time to time, hijacked by a political, social, philosophical, or religious agenda distinct from the discipline. The humanities are susceptible to this problem, but not necessarily more so than the sciences or the professions. The way to untangle this distortion of an academic discipline is to go back to the heart of the discipline. In the case of *Paradise Lost*, Lewis rejected various approaches to its study that were not studies of the poem but attempts to make a statement about something else. He wrote:

> The first qualification for judging any piece of workmanship from a corkscrew to a cathedral is to know *what* it is—what it was intended to do and how it is meant to be used. After that has been discovered the temperance reformer may decide that the corkscrew was made for a bad purpose, and the communist may think the same about the cathedral. But such questions come later. The first thing is to understand the object before you: as long as you think the corkscrew was meant for opening tins or the cathedral for entertaining tourists you

can say nothing to the purpose about them. The first thing the reader needs to know about *Paradise Lost* is what Milton meant it to be.[59]

With these words, Lewis proceeded to give an introduction to how epic poetry "works" so that it could be understood by a culture that has not known epic poetry for centuries.

This book was groundbreaking at the time and led to a resurgence of the study of *Paradise Lost* in colleges and universities across the English-speaking world. Academic books rarely stay in print for more than a few years, but *A Preface to Paradise Lost* has remained in print since 1942. Lewis set the standard, and whoever deals with *Paradise Lost* most go back to Lewis and engage his ideas, whether one agrees with him or not. In many ways, his book begins as an apologetic for the very long narrative poem—the kind of poem he had written with *Dymer*, but one that had been out of fashion for centuries. He had first undertaken such a public defense of the long poem at a Martlets meeting in 1920. As president of the Martlets that year, Lewis was also asked to read his paper on narrative poetry again at the joint meeting with the Cambridge Martlets later in the academic year. Lewis's adversary in his paper was Edgar Allan Poe, who had written on several occasions, in reference to *Paradise Lost*, that the long poem cannot sustain a unity of effect.[60]

Lewis fell in love with epic poetry when he first went to study with W. T. Kirkpatrick in Great Bookham at the age of sixteen. Kirkpatrick put Lewis to work translating Homer's *Iliad* from Greek, and Lewis devoured it with relish. He would also read the *Odyssey*, the sequel to the *Iliad*, and then Virgil's *Aeneid* in Latin. He had also read *Beowulf*, the Anglo-Saxon epic with pre-Christian origins, and *The Song of Roland*, the French epic of Charlemagne's time. In 1916, Lewis had written to Arthur Greeves that if he wanted to understand *Beowulf*, he had to forget all his ideas of what a book is for someone in the twentieth century and put himself in the position of the people for whom *Beowulf* was told.[61] Lewis despised approaches to literary criticism that imposed a set of modern values on a piece of literature. In *A Preface to Paradise Lost*, he helped the modern reader understand how to approach the epics of Greece, Rome, France, and Britain from the perspective of the original writer and, of equal importance, the perspective of the original audience.

Lewis spent the first half of the book distinguishing between primary epic, of which the *Iliad* and the *Odyssey*, *The Song of Roland*, and *Beowulf* are examples, and secondary epic, of which the *Aeneid* and *Paradise Lost* are examples. He insisted that the two terms refer to chronology and not value judgment. The primary epics, or earlier epics, were oral and not written at first. Their audiences listened to a grand recitation that would have lasted for hours, possibly over several days. With this observation, Lewis made clear that in antiquity, all poetry was spoken and musical in nature. To a certain degree, he believed all poetry speaks to the ear. The epics had a grave tone to them that told of noble warriors who came to a tragic end. Recited on the occasion of a great gathering in the banquet hall, the primary epic had a quality, lost to the modern world, that embraces the ideas of solemnity (but not gloom) and ceremonial.[62] This original context for the presentation of primary epic required a certain technique in order to sustain the poem and hold the attention of the audience.

Primary epic makes use of the repetition of stock phrases. The same phrases are heard over and over throughout the long poem. Thus, in the *Iliad*, the god Poseidon is never only Poseidon; he is "Poseidon shaker of the earth." The sea is never only the sea; it is the "wine-dark sea."[63] The repetition serves as ritual, elevating the poetry above the speech of the marketplace and reinforcing the solemnity and ceremonial of the epic. It makes it special. The stock phrases create a familiarity so that the audience is reminded of what has been and anticipates what will come. Lewis explained that "the general result of this is that Homer's poetry is, in an unusual degree, believable."[64] In *Beowulf* the repetition is also there, but with slight variations, as in Hebrew poetry.

Secondary epic emerges with a literate audience; it is meant to be read from a book. Virgil was its first great proponent, during the rule of Caesar Augustus, the first Roman emperor. Whereas primary epics had no great subject other than the heroic tragedy of the principle figure of the story, secondary epics address some great theme. For Virgil in his *Aeneid*, the great theme was the heroic origin of Rome herself. It is a tale of nationalism, unlike the *Iliad*, in which Trojans receive equal honor with Greeks. In secondary epic, the central figures carry the weight of destiny or eternity. Primary epics dealt with the immediate, while secondary epics dealt with far-ranging consequences that affect many people for generations to come.[65]

In style, the secondary epic has an even grander and more elevated solemnity and ceremonial than the primary epic. Composed for a reading audience, however, the newer form does not depend on the stock phrases of oral technique. Instead, Milton turned to words and sentence constructions that were slightly unfamiliar or anachronistic. He used proper names that evoked strong emotional responses, and words that relate to sense experience, such as darkness, light, flowers, and sexuality, in order to create an atmosphere of sensual excitement.[66] Lewis spoke of Milton manipulating his audience. Edgar Allan Poe referred to the poet creating an effect in the audience. It is what a film director strives to do with cinematic tools.

In the second half of *A Preface to Paradise Lost*, Lewis defended his approach to literary criticism and the artistry of Milton against the recent trend in literary theory represented by I. A. Richards, D. G. James, and T. S. Eliot. His opponents deplored the stock responses to moral questions they found in *Paradise Lost*. Lewis countered that society would do well to recover Milton's stock responses to pride, treachery, pain, and death.[67] In his biography of his former tutor, George Sayer agreed with Helen

Gardner that Lewis had waxed too moralistic in *A Preface to Paradise Lost*, perhaps because he devoted chapters to "The Doctrine of the Unchanging Human Heart," "Milton and St. Augustine," "Hierarchy," "The Theology of *Paradise Lost*," "Satan," "Satan's Followers," "The Mistake about Milton's Angels," "Adam and Eve," "Unfallen Sexuality," and "The Fall."[68] Unless one follows the path of the critics whom Lewis wrote to refute, however, these are precisely the matters that a critic of Milton should discuss, because Milton was concerned with morality.

In chapter 13, Lewis finally came to one of the main points he wanted to make. He discussed the tendency since the time of William Blake and Percy Shelley for critics to regard Satan as the hero of *Paradise Lost*. Lewis put this idea in its place through an examination of the self-delusion of Satan as one who regarded himself as the injured party, and by reference to Milton's theology. Lewis declared, "We know from his prose works that [Milton] believed everything detestable to be, in the long run, also ridiculous; and mere Christianity commits every Christian to believing that 'the Devil is (in the long run) an ass'."[69] Lewis said that we see the same ridiculous trait of the "Sense of Injured Merit" in a variety of familiar situations: the spoiled child, the film star, politicians, and minor poets.[70] He showed what this sin looks like in his popular works. He depicted this sin with a would-be poet in *The Great Divorce*.[71] He devoted letter 21 to the issue of perceived injury in *The Screwtape Letters*, where he described situations from his own life:

> Now you will have noticed that nothing throws him into a passion so easily as to find a tract of time which he reckoned on having at his own disposal unexpectedly taken from him. It is the unexpected visitor (when he looked forward to a quiet evening), or the friend's talkative wife (turning up when he looked forward to a *tête-a-tête* with the friend), that throw him out of gear.[72]

The desire for recognition, and the resulting sense of injury in its absence, had been a concern of Lewis since the summer of 1930—a year before his faith in Jesus Christ.[73]

In book 1 of *Paradise Lost*, Satan proudly declares of his situation when excluded from the presence of God,

Here we may reign secure, and in my choice
to reign is worth ambition though in Hell:
Better to reign in Hell, than serve in Heaven.

In all likelihood, Milton intended to contrast the attitude of Satan with a famous Scripture passage:

For a day in your courts is better
    than a thousand elsewhere.
I would rather be a doorkeeper in the house of my God
    than dwell in the tents of wickedness. (Ps. 84:10)

Satan has played the fool. Hell is still hell. Lewis and Milton would have been familiar with the passage from Homer's *Odyssey* in which Odysseus visits Hades and finds Achilles fawned over by the dead. Odysseus observes of Achilles's situation that being dead must not be so bad, to which Achilles replies: "Glorious Odysseus: don't try to reconcile me to my dying. I'd rather serve as another man's labourer, as a poor peasant without land, and be alive on Earth, than be lord of all the lifeless dead."[74] Milton's Satan has played the fool.

Lewis admitted that Satan was the "best drawn of Milton's characters," but this fact does not make him Milton's hero.[75] What the critics who saw Satan as the hero failed to notice about all literature is that good characters are extremely difficult to create, while evil characters are a simple matter. In January 1939, many months before the war started and before Williams gave his lecture on *Paradise Lost*, Lewis had written to his old college friend A. K. Hamilton Jenkin to discuss the very issue. He had reasoned that we have no difficulty imagining people worse than we are, because of our ability to conceive doing terrible things that we never actually carry out. On the other hand, we have no frame of reference for imagining someone better than us.[76] In his first letter to Sister Penelope in the summer of 1939, Lewis had repeated the same observation while commenting on Charles Williams's rare success in portraying convincing good characters: "The reason they are rare in fiction is that to imagine a man worse than yourself you've only got to stop doing something, while to imagine one better you've got to do something."[77] The very fact of temptation allows us to imagine evil. We do not really know what it feels like to be better than we are, and when novelists "guess at it," they tend to blunder.[78]

Perelandra

While preparing the lectures that became *A Preface to Paradise Lost*, Lewis began writing *Perelandra*, a sequel to *Out of the Silent Planet*. It was the book that he most enjoyed writing and his favorite among his own books.[79] He first mentioned it in a letter to Sister Penelope on November 9, 1941, in which he revealed that he had gotten Ransom to Venus, the world that the Oyarsa called Perelandra.[80] The friendship between Lewis and Sister Penelope began when the patristics scholar and Anglican nun wrote a fan letter to Lewis after reading *Out of the Silent Planet* in 1939. In a letter to Arthur Greeves at the end of December, he explained the plot: "The idea is that Venus is at the Adam-and-Eve stage: i.e. the first two rational creatures have just appeared and are still innocent. My hero arrives in time to prevent their 'falling' as *our* first pair did."[81] Perelandra (Venus) has an entirely different experience from Malacandra (Mars), because intelligent life is brought forth on Perelandra after the incarnation. Never having fallen, like humans on Thulcandra (Earth), the people on Perelandra have no need of redemption, yet they benefit from the incarnation.[82]

The idea for the book did not begin, however, with the thought of writing a story inspired by *Paradise Lost* but without the fall. It actually began with the mental image of floating islands and the desire to create an imaginary world where such things might be found. Only then did the retelling of the temptation of Adam and Eve develop, driven by the need for something to happen.[83] The inspiration for Lewis's fiction often grew from a mental picture drawn up by the imagination, but he stressed the importance of something actually happening in a story. He loved stories, and this may account for why he took such a dim view of much of the fad in modern fiction in the 1920s and 1930s.[84] So many novels won critical praise though in them nothing happened. *Perelandra* took the turn it did because Lewis was already interested in the story behind *Paradise Lost*.[85]

By May 11, 1942, Lewis had completed the draft of *Perelandra* and promised to send Sister Penelope a copy of the manuscript as soon as his handwritten copy was typed. He also asked if he might dedicate the novel to the sisters of her community.[86] Their formal name was The Community of St. Mary the Virgin (CSMV), but Lewis dedicated the book "To SOME LADIES at WANTAGE."[87] Unsure of what this dedication meant, the Portuguese translator rendered it "To Some Wanton Ladies."

Perelandra is not personal testimony, and it is not about C. S. Lewis. Nonetheless, it provides an example of how Lewis wrote about what he knew. First of all, he knew about *Paradise Lost* and the fall. He knew about temptation and how subtle it can be. He knew the medieval cosmology and its relation to Plato's hierarchy and how the medieval mind had sought to synthesize the two. He also knew how to have fun with his friends. He actually placed himself in the first chapter of the story as a friend of Ransom who is called upon to return and help at the end of the story. Ransom lives in a cottage near Worchester, which is the country of Great Malvern where Lewis attended the hated Malvern College. Lewis also used much of the imagery of spiritual warfare he had employed in the broadcast talks, such as our world as "enemy-occupied territory."[88]

Ransom's cottage observes the wartime blackout so familiar to Lewis. Ransom asks Lewis to be ready to come at a moment's notice when he receives word that Ransom has returned from Venus. Lewis reminds Ransom that in time of war, Lewis might be dead by then, to which Ransom replies that there are four or five people whom Lewis can entrust with the mission. Ransom also asks that Lewis bring a doctor. To ensure that the Inklings do not miss this allusion to them, Lewis suggests that he will bring "Humphrey."[89] Humphrey was the nickname by which Dr. Robert Havard was known to the Inklings. Havard was an apt example of someone who might be dead a year hence, for he had been called up to active duty as a military surgeon in the navy. In 1943, while on sea duty, he grew a beard that came in red, so Lewis dubbed him "the Red Admiral" in addition to his two other nicknames— "Humphrey" and "the Useless Quack."[90] Largely through the influence of Tolkien, Havard was reassigned later to duty in Oxford with a malaria research unit. For Tolkien's success in pulling strings, Lewis would dub him "The Lord of the Strings."[91]

On another level, Lewis had grown increasingly concerned by the tendency of many people to confuse science with philosophical ideas about science, which led to the emergence of a mythology based on science. To say that science studies the physical universe is a scientific statement. To say that only the physical universe exists is a philosophical statement with no basis in science. To say that science makes observations of the physical world through the five senses is a scientific statement. To say that only things that can be known through the five senses exist is a philosophical statement with no basis in science. Yet many intelligent people confuse their philosophical ideas about nonscientific concerns with science.

In *Perelandra*, Lewis sought to show how such a thing can happen and what its trajectory might be through the vehicle of his archfiend, Dr. Weston. In *Out of the Silent Planet*, Weston had voiced the views of the standard materialist, but in *Perelandra*, Lewis showed how such views can take on a mythological but demonic view of science. With the completion of *Perelandra* and the weekly articles that became *The Great Divorce*, Lewis completed his interest in writing about *Paradise Lost*. With the scientific theme in *Perelandra*, however, he would begin a new project to critique the uninformed development of a mythology of science that he found terrifying.

C. S. Lewis: Man of Affairs

With so many things going on and so many demands upon his time outside his job, 1941 was the worst possible time for C. S. Lewis to have the honor of being elected vice president of Magdalen College. Nonetheless, it happened. Lewis was an odd choice for this office. He certainly did not aspire to high administrative positions. To the contrary, the thought would have repelled him, but Lewis had a profound sense of duty. His talents did not lie with administration, and surely his colleagues would have known so after fifteen years. To make matters worse, President Gordon fell ill during Lewis's term of office, and the management of college affairs fell to Lewis. He suddenly found himself inundated by official correspondence, college and university committee meetings, phone calls, and interviews. The only relief to this burden was the president's secretary, who took dictation.[92]

In spite of his booming voice and emphatic tone, Lewis was far from authoritarian in his dealings with undergraduates. His tendency was to grant their requests without delay, just as he tended to excuse his pupils from a weekly tutorial without bothering to ask why they needed to be absent.[93] One of his colleagues noted, however, that his year of service was not without its ration of chaos:

> It is the function of the vice president to allot rooms for meetings or private entertainment. Lewis carried a little diary in which he sometimes entered the arrangements, more often not. Consequently two societies might find themselves holding

lectures simultaneously. The efficient kitchen staff usually sorted out conflicting dinners.[94]

When possible, Warnie did his best to help organize the engagements. Given the many other demands upon him during his year as vice president, it is not difficult to understand why he asked to be relieved after serving only one year of what was normally a two-year term.[95]

With all of these many responsibilities that he had taken on, primarily at the request of others, the last thing Lewis needed was another weekly obligation. Yet, at the end of Michaelmas term in 1941, Lewis accepted another duty. Stella Aldwinckle served as a chaplain within the Oxford Pastorate. In her ministry to the ladies of Somerville College, undergraduate home of Dorothy L. Sayers before the Great War, Miss Aldwinckle had heard the concern that none of the religious clubs at the university seemed to be addressing the questions of agnostics and atheists. The agnostics and atheists believed that Oxford needed a new club, so Aldwinckle organized a club to provide "an open forum for the discussion of the intellectual difficulties connected with religion and with Christianity in particular."[96] *The Problem of Pain* had just been published, and Aldwinckle decided that Lewis, who had moved from atheism to Christianity, was just the person to lead the new club as its president.

Lewis agreed to serve, which meant that he would give up one night every week during term, with Aldwinckle serving as chairman. She took care of all the arrangements involved in setting up and publicizing a weekly meeting open to the whole university. Thus, Lewis's limited managerial skills were not taxed further. The resulting Socratic Club met on Monday evenings from eight fifteen until ten thirty. Aldwinckle and Lewis, who were joined by L. W. Grensted, the former Nolloth Professor of the Philosophy of the Christian Religion, planned the programs one or two terms in advance. Each meeting involved the presentation of a formal paper with a response, followed by a period of open questions. If the paper was presented by a Christian, then the response came from an atheist or agnostic, and vice versa.[97] Often, Lewis gave the Christian response. When an atheist responded to a Christian, Lewis sometimes interjected himself into the match if he thought the Christian was not up to the challenge. On one occasion when Michael Foster presented a paper "Belief and Reason in Philosophy," A. J. Ayer gave the atheist response.[98] Ayer, one of the leading lights of logical positivism and one of the most formidable opponents of Christianity from a philosophical perspective, dealt harshly with the paper without much rebuttal from Foster. Lewis then entered the fray, and according to Ayer, they "engaged in a flashy debate, which entertained the audience but did neither of us much credit, while Foster sat by, suffering in silence."[99] Lewis would remain actively involved, usually giving the Christian responses himself, until he left for Cambridge in 1954.[100]

9

From Personal Testimony to
Philosophy of Science

1942–1944

Lewis began 1942 by delivering his second set of BBC Sunday evening talks on January 11 and 18, and February 1, 8, and 15.[1] In this set, he completed his testimony by describing the movement from belief in some sort of God to belief in the God of the Bible, who entered into creation as Jesus Christ. He called this series "What Christians Believe." Portions of it echo what he had already written in *The Problem of Pain*. There he had discussed the three stages of development of religion and added a fourth stage found in Christianity: the historical event of the incarnation of God as Jesus.[2] In *The Problem of Pain*, his presentation uses the language of Rudolf Otto and his "experience of the *Numinous*."[3] Though he repeated the idea of four stages in "What Christians Believe," he modified the stages and made the language more colloquial to speak of God sending humans "good dreams" and "hammering into the heads" of the Jews what kind of God he was.[4]

What Christians Believe

In both *The Problem of Pain* and "What Christians Believe," Lewis discusses the alternatives of monism and dualism while dealing with the problems of evil, universal sin, Satan, and temptation. In both, he deals with the necessity of God coming into the world to deal with sin. In both, he explores why Jesus died for our sins. In both, asserting the deity of Christ, Lewis includes the familiar proposal that Jesus must be a liar, a lunatic, or Lord.[5]

In both the book and the BBC series, he took the time to distinguish between the biblical teaching that Jesus died for our sins and theologies constructed to explain how the death of Jesus works. In *The Problem of Pain*, Lewis called Anselm's satisfaction theory a "legal fiction," probably because it was based on the feudal system rather than on any passages in the Bible.[6] In "What Christians Believe," Lewis insisted that theories about the atonement are not Christianity but only human attempts to explain how the atonement works. We do not have to understand how the death of Christ saves us; we have to believe that his death saves us.[7] Dom Bede Griffiths, who continued to be upset with Lewis's resistance to his efforts to bring him round to Rome, rebuked Lewis for not affirming Anselm's theory of the atonement whereby Christ made restitution for the injury done to God's honor by the sin of Adam. Calvin modified Anselm's theory slightly as the penal substitution theory. Lewis simply replied that he had called it "historical fiction" because it has no basis in the New Testament and was never affirmed throughout the patristic period of the early church.[8]

Charity

Speaking on the BBC had meant a modest fee for Lewis. Mrs. Janie Moore ran the Kilns with a firm hand, overseeing its management, and appears to have made the financial decisions regardless of the source of the money. Furthermore, she looked for every possible way to add a little income to the purse. On the other hand, she had no interest in ideas or literature. So Jack's writing of books may have seemed an idle amusement to her. She would have known from *Spirits in Bondage* and *Dymer* that there is no money to be made from books. *The Pilgrim's Regress* would have been an absolute mystery, and *The Allegory of Love* would have been a huge bore. By the time people began buying Lewis's books, Minto may not have realized that money was changing hands. Otherwise, it is impossible to understand how Lewis got away with what he did.

On February 9, 1942, Lewis wrote to Eric Fenn at the BBC to direct him to distribute his fees for speaking to four recipients: a Miss Webb in Gloucester, the Clergy Widows Fund, a Miss Burton in Buckingham, and the Society of St John Evangelist in Oxford. Lewis's new confessor belonged to the last. Clergy Widows were always in need. The other two represent the growing number of people who began to write to Lewis with their problems. On February 24 alone, he wrote thirty-five letters to his new following.[9] Miss Burton had begun corresponding with Lewis after the appearance of *The Problem of Pain*. While she needed money, Lewis wrote to Sister Penelope that he thought Miss Burton was in greater need of visiting and counsel, better done by the sister than by him.[10] Lewis would attract the kind of female attention that he described as "a tragic, tormented person of the Brontë type, living in torment, ironic, unbalanced—emphatically not a person to meet if one is of the opposite sex."[11]

The total disbursement from the BBC came to fifty guineas.[12] It is highly unlikely that Minto would have allowed this extravagant benevolence had she known about it. As his royalties and fees grew, Lewis arranged to have his fees distributed directly to his intended beneficiaries without the checks ever coming to the Kilns. He asked Ronald Boswell at John Lane, the Bodley Head to send his royalty from *Perelandra* directly to the Clergy Widows Fund.[13] He had begun this practice with the sixty-two pounds he had received from the *Guardian* for *The Screwtape Letters*.[14] In November 1942, he asked Fenn to send his check for the third BBC talks to a Mrs. Boshell.[15] Unfortunately, Lewis had not reckoned on his tax liability. Though he had given away the money, he still had to pay tax on the earnings! Owen Barfield came to his rescue and set up a charitable trust to be administered by Barfield into which Lewis contributed the proceeds from his publications and other fees until the time of his marriage in 1957. By means of a deed of covenant, Lewis paid into the trust and avoided his tax liability. Barfield named the trust the Agapargyry (from the Greek *agapē*, for love, and *argyrion*, for money). They often shortened this word in conversation to *agapod*, *agapony*, or even better, the *ag*.[16]

When seventeen-year-old Derek Brewer went up to Oxford in 1941, he found that his scholarship did not cover all his expenses, and his family could not help him. He told his troubles to Lewis, who was his tutor. Brewer reports that Lewis persuaded Magdalen to make a grant to Brewer of twenty pounds. This would have been the year when Lewis served as vice president, so he might have had the influence to arrange a grant. It is more likely that the twenty pounds actually came from Lewis. As the college representative for the Student Christian Movement, Brewer found that he had the responsibility to ask for contributions toward the organization's charities, to which Lewis readily gave a one-pound note.[17]

In February 1942, the BBC asked Lewis if he would make a third series of broadcasts that fall. He quickly agreed without having in mind what he would talk about this time. He had exhausted his testimony in terms of obstacles to faith that he had worked through. The third series of talks would be quite different. He invited Fenn to make the trip to Oxford to discuss with him what the subject might be.[18]

Literary Friends

Lewis's published writing had the unintended consequence of the flood of unwanted correspondence, but it had the benefit of opening new friendships with people who would matter to him. The first of these had been Charles Williams, who appreciated *The*

Allegory of Love. Next came Sister Penelope, who had read *Out of the Silent Planet.* In April 1942, Lewis received his first letter from Dorothy L. Sayers, who was far better known at the time for her Lord Peter Wimsey detective stories. Until then, Lewis had not thought very highly of Sayers. He called her *Zeal of Thy House* "pretty bad."[19] He did not like *Gaudy Night* at all.[20] Of course, it would have been odd if he had, since he never cared for detective fiction.[21] His first assessment of *The Mind of the Maker* was that it was "good on the whole."[22] Sayers had written to ask Lewis to contribute a volume on love and marriage to a series she planned to edit designed to prepare Britain for the postwar experience. His discussion of love and marriage in *The Screwtape Letters* had prompted her invitation. Lewis declined, but he invited her to lunch in Oxford in the first week of June. Thus began a long literary friendship. Barbara Reynolds has speculated that this initial exchange between Lewis and Sayers led to his treatment of marriage in *That Hideous Strength.*[23]

Dorothy L. Sayers never hesitated to suggest more work for Lewis. A formidable lady who had taken up apologetics before Lewis, she had also turned her attention to religious drama and then to radio drama. She did not suffer fools gladly, and her wit and keenness of mind were the equal of his. He found in her a worthy correspondent, and their letters to each other are a delight to read. In the midst of his third series of radio broadcasts, which she no doubt heard, she suggested that he adapt *The Screwtape Letters* as radio drama! He declined.[24]

Charles Williams also came to know Sayers. Both wrote plays for the Canterbury Festival, and they had mutual friends, the Spaldings, in Oxford. Williams was not a great admirer of Sayers at first. He thought her plays had little style.[25] Upon receiving a letter of praise from Sayers after she read his *The Figure of Beatrice,* however, Williams confided to his wife that he began to admire Sayers as a human being, if not a playwright, which he had never done before.[26] Then he decided he should be polite to Sayers after she sent another, much longer and effusive, letter about *The Figure of Beatrice*. He even thought he might suggest to her that she publish the letter as an *Open Letter* to him.[27] Williams boarded with Sayers's friends in Oxford, and when she came to visit them, she also visited with Williams. He complained to his wife that he had to sit up until one thirty in the morning talking with Sayers because she loved conversation.[28]

This account of his relations with Sayers may sound crass and vulgar, but he did not have the advantage of an Albert Lewis for a father or an Oxford education to secure his future. Williams had to scrape for a living. He accepted hack writing jobs to add a little to his meager wages at the Oxford University Press. His novels were not the roaring success of *The Hobbit* or Lewis's religious books. If Dorothy L. Sayers could help him, and she certainly could, he would let her. In the end, Williams's *Beatrice* changed the direction of her life and would solidify her friendship with C. S. Lewis. *The Figure of Beatrice* is a study of Dante, and after her war work, Sayers would learn Italian so that she could translate Dante's *Divine Comedy* into English.

Though Lewis refused to discuss theology with Owen Barfield after his conversion, he continued to reply to Daphne Harwood—Cecil Harwood's wife and a devoted anthroposophist and disciple of Rudolf Steiner—when she wrote to Lewis about his errors and how she hoped he would come to the truth of anthroposophy. He replied in good nature to all her points. When she wrote to him—apparently after reading Screwtape's comments on falling in love in *The Screwtape Letters*—to lament his "increasing Authoritarianism," Lewis finally took off his gloves. She appears to have rebuked him for relying on the Bible as his authority instead of a higher light. He wrote in reply: "As for 'increasing Authoritarianism'—well! If that doesn't take the bun!! When you have heard half as many sentences beginning 'Christianity teaches' from me as I have heard ones beginning 'Steiner says' from you and Cecil & Owen & Wolf—why then we'll start talking about authoritarianism!"[29] After making a few more points about the unsustainability of romantic love alone as a basis for marriage, he ended by declaring that "Eros won't do without Agape."[30] The comment indicates the way Lewis continued to think about ideas he had explored in *The Allegory of Love* that he would finally expound in *The Four Loves*. Daphne Harwood soon gave up on converting Lewis.

Lewis continued to crisscross the kingdom to speak to the RAF officers and men in the spring of 1942. He regarded the typical airbase as a "place of Nissan [*sic*] huts and loud speakers." The Nissen hut, known to Americans as the Quonset hut, is a prefabricated half-cylinder building covered in a skin of corrugated steel roofing. Lewis spoke in Plymouth in the west and then in "our grim eastern counties" in April.[31] In July, he accepted an invitation to deliver a talk entitled "Christianity Is Not a Patent Medicine" at a base at Yatesbury, Wiltshire.[32] By then, he had developed the practice of having a smaller, follow-up meeting after his major address in order to converse with the more serious attendees. He had to interrupt these duties in the middle of April to be present as godfather for the baptism of Sarah Neylan, the daughter of Mary Shelley Neylan who had become a Christian following a long series of letters and conversations with Lewis after she had been his pupil.[33] Then, on April 22, he delivered a lecture titled "Hamlet: The Prince or the Poem?" for the Annual Shakespeare Lecture to the British Academy.[34]

Christian Behavior

By the end of June, Lewis was hard at work writing his third BBC series of talks. In this series, he shifted the subject from Christian belief to Christian behavior. He chose to call it *behavior* because he thought that terms like *ethics*, *morals*, and *morality* had been spoiled for the modern world.[35] He sent a provisional outline to Eric Fenn and suggested that they meet in Oxford to discuss his plans in mid-July. The first book of Lewis's BBC talks was released by the Centenary Press of Geoffrey Bles on July 13, 1942, as

Broadcast Talks. It included the first two series of his talks: "Right and Wrong: A Clue to the Meaning of the Universe" and "What Christians Believe."[36] By July 29, Lewis had finished writing the eight talks of his new series and sent the manuscript to Fenn in longhand because he thought it would be too expensive to pay to have it typed.[37] This decision suggests that Warnie was in no condition at the time to undertake his brother's typing.

Lewis broadcast his third BBC series on Sunday afternoons between September 20 and November 8, 1942. Partway through this series, Oxford University Press released *A Preface to Paradise Lost* on October 8.[38] Amid all the demands on his time in addition to his full-time job and growing need to care for Mrs. Moore, who was entering senility and continuing to decline in health, Dom Bede Griffiths had offered the not-very-helpful advice that Lewis should retire into "private life." Shirking responsibility was not an option for Lewis, who had always felt the noble obligation in the strongest possible way. He would do his duty, even if others did not, but he added, "God is my witness, I don't *look* for engagements."[39] In fact, his many engagements cost him dearly. In late November, he was invited by Delmar Banner, a prominent portraitist, to visit the Lake District and meet Beatrix Potter, whom Lewis greatly admired, but he could not consider it.[40] She died soon afterward.

The hectic life of Lewis in 1942 is reflected in the letters he wrote to friends that year. He did not write to Arthur Greeves but once, in December. He wrote one very brief note to Barfield, in August, acknowledging a poem that Barfield had sent, and then another quick note primarily about setting up his trust. He was certainly writing letters, most of which were lost or discarded, but these were to total strangers who had questions to ask or complaints to raise. The letters took up an enormous amount of his time. The American edition of *The Collected Letters of C. S. Lewis* devotes 142 pages to the letters we have from 1940. By comparison, it has only 48 pages for 1941 and just 39 pages for

1942. The extra work was crushing him. The load would not lighten as the war wore on.

As the War Wore On

In January 1943, Jack began the year with what was by then a rare letter to Greeves to request an address, and he gave Arthur the news. Minto was laid up again with a terrible case of her varicose ulcers. Warnie had lost weight. Jack was busy "writing, writing, writing—letters, notes, exam papers, books, lectures."[41] He confessed that the "great luck" he had with his books had given him "much pleasure," though he lamented the number of letters that he had to write on account of his success. Finally, he confided that the rheumatism in his right hand—his writing hand—had grown so severe that he had not been able sleep on his right side for over a year.[42] Lewis wrote everything in longhand with a steel-nib pen and bottle of ink, which only heightened the pain in his arthritic hand. He told Mary Neylan a few days later that he was having trouble forming legible letters.[43]

In 1935, Lewis had been invited to write the volume on the sixteenth century for a major multivolume history of English literature. Eight years later, he had not yet begun to write it. Douglas Bush completed his volume on the seventeenth century by January 1943.[44] Lewis had accepted and completed a number of writing assignments after he had agreed to write the volume for the Oxford History of the English Language series, which he began to refer to as OHEL. The first week of February, however, he received just the incentive he needed to begin work on the volume that had not yet stirred his interest. George Macaulay Trevelyan, master of Trinity College in Cambridge, invited him to bring the Clark Lectures in the next academic year.[45] The lectures would represent only a small part of the completed volume, but preparing them provided Lewis with the structure and deadline he needed to begin work.

An unforeseen consequence of war was that many of Lewis's colleagues under forty took leave of absence to help with the war effort in other places. Among those who left was T. D. Weldon, who had irritated Lewis for years. With the absence of Weldon and his circle, whom he also referred to as the "Leftists," life at Magdalen got "pleasanter and pleasanter."[46] In fact, it was much nicer than during peacetime because "the stormy spirits are away."[47] Though away, Weldon and William James Millar Mackenzie kept an eye on affairs at the college and inserted themselves when they could. Early in the war, Jack had written to Warnie that they managed to obtain leave "from whatever absurd office they [were] now in" to return to Magdalen for a "Modern Subjects Scholarship" meeting to ensure that Lewis would not "fill the place up with duds" while they were away.[48] The unexpected appearance for the scholarship meeting seemed a small price to pay for a little peace in college.

The Abolition of Man

At the end of 1942, Lewis had an important writing project—another one he had not intended but the result of yet another invitation. He was invited to deliver the Riddell Lectures at the University of Durham to be given at the end of February 1943. The invitation afforded him the opportunity to deal with a new threat to reason and values that was spreading unnoticed through the popular culture. Oxford University Press published his series of three lectures on January 6, 1943, as *The Abolition of Man*.[49] Normally, lectures are published after their presentation, but in this case, Lewis would not deliver the lectures until after their publication.

The Riddell Memorial Lectures were established in 1928 in honor of Sir John Buchanan-Riddell by his son Sir Walter, principal of Hertford College, Oxford. Both father and son were devout Christians, and the lectureship was founded to explore the relationship between religion and contemporary thought. Lewis actually delivered the lectures not at the University of Durham in Durham but in the Physics Lecture Theatre at King's College in Newcastle, which at that time was a constituent college of the

University of Durham.[50] Many distinguished scholars and thinkers have presented the lectures, including Christopher Hill, John Baillie, Alasdair MacIntyre, and Michael Polanyi.

At the beginning of World War II, Warnie Lewis left off keeping his diary, but on Monday, February 22, 1943, he picked up his pen again to record the trip he made with his brother to northern England for the lectures. Warnie wrote nothing about the lectures but devoted himself to recording the packing on Monday and the places they visited along the way. It was the first vacation the brothers had together since before the war. As the train passed through York making its way north, they admired the distant cathedral, which had been spared from the bombing. This was the route that Warnie had taken at the beginning of the war to his post at Catterick. Next, they passed through Durham before reaching Newcastle. Jack gave his first lecture that evening after tea. The next morning, they returned to Durham, a city that had been ruled by the prince-bishops of Durham in the Norman period, and the two wandered the precincts of Durham Cathedral and Durham Castle, the original residence of the bishops. The brothers had assumed that Durham was a dirty industrial town rather than the medieval jewel of "exquisite beauty" that they found.[51] They had an enchanting time together discovering one of the loveliest towns in England. They deeply regretted not making Durham their base instead of Newcastle. Upon arriving back in Newcastle, Jack went off to give his second lecture while Warnie explored for the best place to find a drink. On Thursday, they wandered through Newcastle, which Warnie thought had the same flavor as Belfast. After tea, Jack gave his last lecture, following which he dined with the rector of the university. Warnie explored more of the city, dined alone, and passed the rest of the evening at the Douglas bar.[52]

Why would Warnie not have attended his brother's lectures? Warnie deplored philosophy, and he knew that these lectures would focus on the despised subject. Warnie had expressed his final word on philosophy after rereading *Dymer* in 1934 and concluding that it was only philosophy disguised as poetry. He resolved that if he were emperor of the world, he would "start a pogrom against philosophers."[53]

Fifty years after the "Abolition of Man" lectures, two of the most significant philosophers of the English-speaking world delivered commemorative lectures to pay tribute to Lewis for these remarkable lectures. Basil Mitchell, who served as vice president of the Socratic Club under Lewis and who succeeded him as president when he moved to Cambridge, held the Nolloth Chair of Christian Philosophy at Oxford. John Lucas also held a fellowship in philosophy, at Merton College, Oxford. Lucas pointed out that in the midst of war, with civilization at stake, Lewis did not take the time in his three lectures to demonstrate an understanding of the views of his opponents and how they arrived at those views. After the war, however, the climate had changed, and many critics thought that Lewis's lectures seemed "not very courteously written."[54] In *The Inklings*, Humphrey Carpenter took Lewis to task for not giving his opponents "a chance." Carpenter declared that *The Abolition of Man* was "not an argument but a harangue."[55] Basil Mitchell, on the other hand, did not rebuke Lewis for insensitivity to his opponents or failure to note their good points. Mitchell recognized that Lewis was doing more than merely critiquing moral subjectivism or, as it is commonly known today, moral relativism. He was critiquing the very nature of education, as his subtitle made clear: *Reflections on Education with Special Reference to the Teaching of English in the Upper Forms of Schools.*[56]

The idea for these lectures arose in the course of Lewis's weekly tutorials. He discovered that some of his pupils had been taught in their English literature textbooks that all values are only subjective feelings. Universal values do not exist. This idea posed a direct contradiction to Lewis's conversion experience, in which his long journey from atheism to faith in Christ began with the problem of universal values, or "Right and Wrong as a Clue to the Meaning of the Universe." He could not let this challenge go unmet. About the same time, he received a review copy of *The Control of Language*, a new English textbook by Alec King and Martin Ketley, which taught the subjectivist view.[57] These authors would provide an ideal illustration of the effect of the problem, but they were victims of the problem and not its originators. Lewis did not even refer to them or their book by name. He called them Gaius and Titius, and their textbook *The Green Book*. The title may be an allusion to the Blue Book and Brown Book associated with Ludwig Wittgenstein, a former logical positivist who developed linguistic analysis, the philosophical movement that lay behind the moral subjectivism in vogue at the time.

King and Ketley had used a story about Coleridge to explain the view that all values are subjective. No doubt the story would have kindled old memories for Lewis, because much of his "Great War" with Owen Barfield had centered on discussions of Coleridge! Coleridge encountered two tourists at a waterfall. One called the waterfall sublime while the other called it pretty. Coleridge approved the first judgment but dismissed the second. For Lewis, this story would have had particularly powerful meaning because of his own conversion experience. The idea of the sublime is the view that something can elicit awe and wonder. Lewis's experience of Joy was just this sort of experience. He had spent years grappling with it and recognizing that it was not a subjective experience of his own feelings but an experience of something outside himself that acted upon him. King and Ketley gave a different view that would have horrified Lewis:

> Gaius and Titius comment as follows: 'When the man said *This is sublime*, he appeared to be making a remark about the waterfall. . . . Actually . . . he was not making a remark about the waterfall, but a remark about his own feelings. What he was saying really was *I have feelings associated in my mind with the word "Sublime,"* or shortly, *I have sublime feelings*.'[58]

285

Before moving to his argument, Lewis sorted out the illogic of their assertion. A person who calls something sublime could not be having sublime feelings (a sense of awe and wonder about himself); such a person would be having *humble* feelings if he called something else sublime.

In *The Abolition of Man*, Lewis provided a case study in how to think about an academic discipline from a Christian perspective as he also demonstrated how one discipline (philosophy) may have an impact on another discipline (literature or science) without anyone noticing. From his own experience with W. T. Kirkpatrick, Lewis knew how all sorts of ideas about philosophy, science, God, and the nature of knowledge had slipped into his head while Kirkpatrick tutored him in Homer and Greek. Considering the ideas that King and Ketley had slipped into their textbook on literature, Lewis could foresee the similar effect on a boy—

> a boy who thinks he is 'doing' his 'English prep' and has no notion that ethics, theology, and politics are all at stake. It is not a theory they put into his mind, but an assumption, which ten years hence, its origin forgotten and its presence unconscious, will condition him to take one side in a controversy which he has never recognized as a controversy at all.[59]

Lewis was alarmed at how education was becoming merely conditioning, and those who dominated education had become the conditioners. In what they thought was their effort to remove emotion from judgment, the authors only succeeded in teaching nothing about how to tell a good piece of writing from a bad piece of writing. They had abandoned their own discipline. The point Lewis made in his first lecture was that emotions should not be ignored but trained, because "without the aid of trained emotions the intellect is powerless against the animal organism."[60]

Building on a central idea that he had discussed in *The Allegory of Love*, Lewis explained that the head represents the intellect, and the belly represents the brute animal impulse. Between the two lies the chest, which represents the mitigating power of character, or magnanimity, to mediate between cold, calculating intellect (represented by the North in *The Pilgrim's Regress*) and unbridled animal appetite (represented by the South in *The Pilgrim's Regress*). By denying the reality of objective values, *The Green Book* would only produce "Men without Chests."[61]

In the second lecture, Lewis explored the concept of the *Tao*, a Chinese expression for the harmony of the universe that involves the idea of objective value—that some things are true and some things are false. He used an Eastern term rather than a Christian term to stress the idea of the universal recognition of objective values, even though every culture will have its own selective attitudes that are unique. What might appear to be a weakness is actually a strength of his argument, for Lewis focuses his attention on the phenomenon of ideologically based values—those unique attitudes that arise distinct from universal values. *The Green Book* represents the effort to base values on facts, but facts do not beg, steal, or borrow values. Lewis faults King and Ketley not for being skeptical of values but for not being skeptical enough about a set of fashionable, avant-garde values that had gained uncritical acceptance by the generation between World War I and World War II.

In his final lecture, Lewis turned his attention to the absence of values behind decision-making that affects vast populations, both in the present and for all generations to come. He spoke ten years before the identification of DNA by Watson and Crick and more than fifty years before the mapping of the human genome, but he knew about the Nazi experiments in eugenics and the perfection of the master race. We live in a world in which humans have become the object of experimentation. Lewis knew that rather than breeding better roses or dogs or pigs, biological science would soon have the capability to alter humans. Without an objective set of values guiding the development of science, those making the decisions would do so based on the current ideological fad.

The final triumph of human effort over nature would result in *the abolition of man*.[62] By the time Lewis delivered these lectures, he was almost finished writing a fictional version of these ideas in his last science-fiction novel, *That Hideous Strength*.[63]

New Directions in Writing

Two of Lewis's books were published in April 1943. Geoffrey Bles released *Christian Behaviour: A Further Series of Broadcast Talks* on April 19. The next day, John Lane, the Bodley Head released *Perelandra*.[64] After accepting so many invitations to speak and to write, however, Lewis finally began to learn to say no. He declined a request from Eric Fenn to share his personal testimony on the BBC; Lewis explained that what he would say would simply be repeating his previous talks.[65] He had given his personal testimony in his first two talks without ever saying so. Next, he refused to speak about *Paradise Lost*, explaining to Fenn that it would waste his time to tell people they would enjoy reading it when both he and Fenn knew they would not.[66] Not until June did Fenn succeed in suggesting a fourth series to which Lewis would agree. He also agreed to take part in a BBC program called "The Anvil" on July 22, 1943, which involved a panel discussion of religious subjects led by James Welch.[67]

Still, Lewis was not yet impervious to the power of suggestion. Dorothy L. Sayers sent to him an advance copy of *The Man Born to Be King: A Play-Cycle on the Life of Our Lord and Saviour Jesus Christ* in mid-May 1943. The BBC had broadcast the plays once a month between December 1941 and October 1942. Lewis, who did not care for the radio, had only heard one of the plays. The letter accompanying the book included a long section in imitation of *The Screwtape Letters* designed to convey Sayers's irritation at having to spend so much time arguing with atheists. She closed the letter with the observation that "there aren't any up-to-date books about Miracles."[68] It was a clear challenge. In his reply to her gift, Lewis told her that he was "starting a book on Miracles."[69] Walter Hooper has suggested that Sayers's suggestion was just the encouragement Lewis needed to write his most philosophically sophisticated book.[70]

At the Kilns, Minto continued to suffer from varicose ulcers on her legs and was in a great deal of pain. They had begun to keep chickens and rabbits to supplement their food ration midway through the war.[71] By the summer, Lewis had to cancel several of his RAF engagements because of Minto's condition. The two maids made matters worse, for both Muriel and Margaret had serious mental-health issues. Rather than providing help to Lewis, they required help. Such had been the perpetual problem with the maids that Minto had hired for over twenty years. Lewis confided to Sister Penelope that "there is never any time when *all* these three women are in good temper."[72] The great relief to Lewis came in July 1943 when June Flewett, an evacuee from London whose father was senior classics master at St Paul's School, came to live at the Kilns until the end of the war.[73] After the war, she studied at the Royal Academy of Dramatic Arts in London and changed her name to Jill for the stage. She later married Clement Freud, the grandson of Sigmund Freud. With June at the Kilns, Warnie began to flourish.[74] The day before she left the Kilns in 1945, Warnie wrote a vivid description of why he and Jack loved her so much:

> She is not yet eighteen, but I have met no one of any age further advanced in the Christian way of life. From seven in the morning till nine at night, shut off from people of her own age, almost grudged the time for her religious duties, she has slaved at the Kilns, for a fraction of 2d. an hour; I have never seen her other than gay, eager to anticipate exigent demands, never complaining, always self accusing [*sic*] in the frequent crises of that dreary house. Her reaction to the meanest ingratitude was to seek its cause in her own faults. She is one of those rare people to whom one can venture to apply the word "saintly".
> . . . From a personal selfish point of view I shall feel the loss of June very keenly: for in addition to her other virtues, she is

a clever girl, and with her gone, it means that when J is away, there is no one to talk to in this house.[75]

In many ways, June held the Kilns together with Jack on the road so much of the time, Minto descending further into senility, the maids in a constant state of hysteria, and Warnie slipping into serious alcoholism, unbeknownst to June. Yet, Jack managed to write six chapters of his book on miracles by the end of September.[76] And by December 1943, he had finished writing *That Hideous Strength* and the scripts for his fourth radio talk series, "Beyond Personality."[77]

That Hideous Strength, *Miracles*, and *The Abolition of Man* were all written within the same time frame, and all look at the problem of science left to its own devices without an overarching value system to guide and restrain it. Lewis made clear in his preface to *That Hideous Strength* that he hoped to make the same point in the novel that he had made in *The Abolition of Man*.[78] He had been fascinated by science since he was a boy. He had no quarrel with science or technology. He assured Arthur C. Clark that he regarded them as neutral. His problem lay with the philosophy that many of the public and a growing number of scientists tended to confuse with science.[79] He had written to Mary Neylan in 1940 that he had no quarrel with psychology so long as it remained a science and did not set itself up as a philosophy that made comments on metaphysical questions outside its methodological sphere.[80] He had touched on the problem in his first two science-fiction novels, but it became the major focus of his work in 1943. While he did not think every scientist was a "Weston," like his character in *Out of the Silent Planet* and *Perelandra*, he did believe that more and more scientists had fallen into that trap. He reminded Clark that he lived among scientists in Oxford.[81] At Magdalen, he dined with them every day. In 1942, Magdalen College elected Sir Henry Thomas Tizard, who was a chemist, as president to succeed George Gordon. What Lewis called "scientism," rather than science, was his objection. Most of his writing in the second half of the war aimed at this problem.

"Beyond Personality"

By December 1943, Lewis had completed the scripts for his last series of radio broadcasts. At the end of Michaelmas term, he had grown too busy with his many obligations and deadlines to meet with the Inklings. On December 9, Tolkien wrote to his son Christopher that he had not seen Lewis for weeks![82] In light of *The Abolition of Man*, *Miracles*, and *That Hideous Strength*, the most striking thing about the fourth series of BBC talks is that Lewis switched his metaphors and illustrations from the war imagery found in the earlier talks to scientific imagery. He had mentioned scientific ideas in his earlier talks, but not often. The last talks emphasized science and dispensed with war imagery.

The seven talks that he gave on Tuesday evenings at 10:20 began on February 22 and ran through April 4, 1944.[83] A 10:20 broadcast meant that Lewis would have to take a late train back to Oxford and not be home until three o'clock in the morning, only to face tutorials the next morning. Under the circumstances, the BBC agreed that Lewis could prerecord three of his seven talks. For this reason, we now have the recordings of Lewis delivering talks 2, 6, and 7. The BBC published them in its weekly magazine, *The Listener*, two days after their broadcast.[84] Lewis named these talks "Beyond Personality: The Christian View of God." To Sister Penelope, Lewis wrote that his talks were on the doctrine of the Trinity, and when he published all of the talks as *Mere Christianity* in 1952, he changed the subtitle of this last section to "Or First Steps in the Doctrine of the Trinity."[85]

While adapting the radio talks to a book format, Lewis added four chapters—3, 6, 9, and 10—to the original seven talks.[86] He began his discussion of the Trinity by distinguishing biological life from spiritual life. Along the way, he mentioned insects, space, and the relationship between matter and energy. In the second chapter, he mentioned multiple dimensions of space and the implications of more than four dimensions. He also spoke of geologists, zoologists, and laboratory science. In the third chapter, he addressed time and Einstein's theory of relativity without mentioning Einstein or his theory. Nonetheless, they are there, along with Augustine and the idea that time is a dimension of matter so that a nonphysical being is not subject to a physical quality like time. In the fourth chapter he discussed infections. In the fifth, he examined procreation and human lineage. In the sixth, he returned to Einstein's understanding of the relationship of space, matter, and time to explore the value of the universe as we find it for the promotion of life.

Not until the seventh chapter did Lewis dispense with using scientific illustrations within a culture saturated with scientific ideas to explain what Christians believe. He spoke theologically about what it means that God is tripersonal. In the eighth chapter, he returned to scientific imagery as he considered the possibility of extraterrestrial beings and the immensity of the universe. Again, in chapter 9, Lewis left off any scientific language as he explored the implications of what it means to be born again. In the tenth chapter, he resumed scientific metaphors as he spoke of natural causes and psychology in order to explain free will. Finally, in the last chapter, Lewis talked about evolution, natural selection, and how regeneration is an entirely different concept. He may have had Owen Barfield in mind while writing the last chapters, for Barfield saw human evolution into immortality as the heart of his understanding of spirituality. And why might Lewis have used scientific imagery in nine of his chapters but not in the other two? In these two chapters, Lewis summed up the theological points he was making. In chapter 7, he crystalized his explanation of the Trinity, and in chapter 9, he explained the new birth.

The world was changing. From his pupils Lewis had learned just how fast it was changing. The world had been electrified since his boyhood. Gramophones had been replaced by radios. Technology abounded, and the world was in love with the success of science. Lewis had to speak the language of his audience in order to warn them that unsound philosophy had crept in under the guise of science while no one was paying attention. It was not the use of science that bothered Lewis but its misuse. The danger lay not with the sciences but with the humanities, which had fallen to pieces after World War I and abandoned their function in preserving the concepts of right, wrong, true, false, and beautiful. Poetry no longer made sense, music no longer had melodies, novels no longer had plots, paintings no longer were pictures, and the vast public ceased to be interested in the arts.

That Hideous Strength

C. S. Lewis had an amazing ability to write under the most trying of circumstances. His brother noted how Minto constantly interrupted his writing with little chores at the Kilns. Various of his pupils and friends observed his ability to pick up his pen immediately after an interruption and begin writing again as if nothing had intervened to shake his train of thought. Alastair Fowler thought that Lewis's writing ability had to do with the way he composed in his head before he ever began writing. We have observed how he first had developed ideas for books that he did not begin writing until later. Fowler speculated that he could do this because of his remarkable memory, which allowed him to quote long passages or to recall the substance of a page. Fowler told the story of how Lewis challenged Kenneth Tynan

> to choose a number from one to forty, for the shelf in Lewis's library; a number from one to twenty, for the place in this shelf; from one to a hundred, for the page; and from one to twenty-five for the line, which he read aloud. Lewis had then to identify the book and say what the page was about.[87]

George Watson said that Lewis had the opposite of writer's block. The words always seemed to flow from his pen. Watson once asked him if he ever found it difficult to write. Lewis replied, sometimes "when I come back in the evening after dinner, I tell myself I am too tired and shouldn't write anything. But I always do."[88] Yet Lewis started many writing projects that he never completed. Sometimes he tired of them. Sometimes he did not know what would happen next. This would seem to be writer's block, except it never kept him from writing. Most remarkably, he worked on multiple projects at the same time in a grand literary juggling act. It had been that way for years. While writing *The Allegory of Love*, he wrote *The Pilgrim's Regress* and several important academic articles. It had been that way with *The Screwtape Letters*, *Perelandra*, and *A Preface to Paradise Lost*. While he was writing *Miracles*, he also wrote *That Hideous Strength*.

The central plot of *That Hideous Strength* came to Lewis in a discussion with his friend A. K. Hamilton Jenkin in 1923 as they conceived a horror story in which a scientist discovered the technique for keeping alive the brain and nerve endings of a corpse.[89] Lewis did nothing with the idea at the time, but as with so many other ideas he had, he kept it filed away in his own brain until he had a use for it. He realized that such a story belongs to the horror form of science fiction. Another plot feature came in 1931 when Jack and Warnie returned to the Whipsnade Zoo with Minto and Maureen. There they saw the bears, which Jack particularly loved, and he set his heart on having one, which he would have named "Bultitude," as a pet at the Kilns.[90] In 1963, in a slim biography in a series about Bodley Head authors, Lewis's friend Roger Lancelyn Green, who collaborated with Walter Hooper over a decade later in the first full-length biography of Lewis, declared emphatically that W. T. Kirkpatrick "supplied the basis for the character of MacPhee in *That Hideous Strength*."[91] This declaration has entered the tradition of understanding Lewis and is repeated by most of Lewis's biographers as a fact.[92]

Though Lewis finished writing it in December 1943, *That Hideous Strength* takes place after the war has been won by Britain.[93] This sense of hope shined through a year before the Allies would land in Normandy on D-Day. Once again, Lewis did not write about himself, but he wrote about what he knew. He set the story in a small university town with an ancient lineage. Given the time frame in which he wrote, the University of Durham may have inspired the setting of the University of Edgestow, even though the physical description of the university and its grounds does not fit Durham. The idea of the third, smaller university after Oxford and Cambridge does fit. In his preface, Lewis remarked that it had no resemblance to Durham, except for its smallness.[94]

Corporate sin is not a concept that many modern conservative Christians like to admit, even though it fills the pages of the Old Testament, from the flood to the tower of Babel, to Sodom and Gomorrah, to Egypt, to Israel and Judah. Lewis, however, had a profound understanding of how individual sin increases exponentially where two or more are gathered. In *That Hideous Strength*, he showed what "the inner ring" looks like. He had warned of it in *The Abolition of Man*. Long before that, he had experienced it as a boy in school. He had found it in the Senior Common Room at Magdalen, where his adversary Weldon held sway. He certainly saw it in the ideology of Nazism in Germany, communism in the Soviet Union, and fascism in Spain. In *That Hideous Strength*, Lewis gave two examples of corporate sin with the informal inner ring at Bracton College and the formal institution of the National Institute of Co-ordinated Experiments (NICE). In his last broadcast talk, Lewis had made the point that being nice is not the intended goal for humanity.

The entrance to Bragdon Wood from Bracton College conjures up mental images similar to the experience of walking through Magdalen College across the bridge into Addison's Walk. The imagination fabricates ideas from the whole of experience, borrowing where it will. Charles Williams had been reading his long poem on King Arthur at the Inklings meetings, which probably accounts for the sudden and shocking appearance of Merlin out of Bragdon Wood.[95] Lewis never cared for Williams's poetry or criticism, but he adored the novels, which Lewis called "theological shockers."[96] *That Hideous Strength* is like a Williams novel in the way it blends the normal flow of life with the sudden introduction of the angelic and demonic. It is not a "normal" science-fiction tale, though it includes the same kind of scientific horror found in *Frankenstein*. Spiritual dynamics have always characterized science fiction since Mary Shelley and Edgar Allan Poe, but legendary figures like Merlin seem alien to the genre. By the twenty-first century, however, this element would almost become a requirement of science-fiction movies.

Though this book completes the Ransom trilogy, Ransom hardly appears in the story. He remains in the background. The central figure is Jane Studdock, who wanted a career as a scholar but "was not perhaps a very original thinker."[97] She was like Mr. Dick in *David Copperfield*, who could not finish his memorial; she could not write her dissertation. Daphne and Cecil Harwood wrote to Lewis with concern over how he had dealt with the issue of a married woman pursuing a career. He replied that he had intended an entirely different issue: the problem of anyone following an "*imagined* vocation at the expense of a real one."[98]

He may have been serious. He said that if he had intended to address the idea of giving up a promising career, he would have portrayed Jane as someone who had written a brilliant thesis on Donne instead of someone who had nothing to say. He knew something about pursuing an imagined career, for he had imagined himself a poet until he was thirty. If Lewis can be found in any of the characters of his science-fiction novels, his personal experience of giving up a career as a poet and taking on Jesus Christ best informed the development of Jane in *That Hideous Strength*. It may or may not have been significant that Lewis referred to Mrs. Moore by her given name of Jane in his letters to Sister Penelope. He also mentioned the idea to Arthur Greeves of dedicating the book to their friend Jane McNeill, whose Ulster accent they mocked behind her back by calling her "Tchannie."[99]

Jane had wanted to go to university but had to remain home to care for her widowed mother.[100]

Without doubt, Lewis was a traditionalist. He believed in traditional roles of men and women. He thought that a woman's place was in the home and that women were not really the intellectual equals of men. According to what he told Charles Williams, their minds were not "meant for logic or great art."[101] But Lewis had made that remark at the beginning of the war, when his greatest exposure to female logic was Minto, Minto's friends, and the maids whom Minto hired.

Since then he had discovered that Sister Penelope had one of the keenest minds for Greek scholarship that he knew. In 1944, when she published a translation of *The Incarnation of the Word of God* by Athanasius, the fourth-century bishop of Alexandria, Lewis wrote the introduction, and Sister Penelope dedicated the book to him. He discovered that Dorothy L. Sayers could match him wit for wit and usually come out ahead. He had learned that Helen Gardner had a keen intellect and broad knowledge of his subject. Lewis had not yet changed his mind about women because, like Tolkien's Treebeard, he had never changed his mind quickly. But he had come face-to-face with a number of examples of the kind of woman he had never thought existed, coming from his Edwardian background in Belfast and the cloistered colleges of Oxford. Of his description of women in *That Hideous Strength*, Dorothy L. Sayers remarked that Lewis wrote a lot of "shocking nonsense about women and marriage" not because he was a bad theologian "but because he [was] a rather frightened bachelor."[102] In the 1950s, he would meet a woman who completely changed his views of the sexes.

While the first two science-fiction novels had contained fleeting glances of Tolkien, Havard, and the Inklings, in *That Hideous Strength* Lewis gave himself free rein to include his friends. Ransom refers to "one of Barfield's 'ancient unities.'"[103] In chapter 9, Camilla quotes from Charles Williams's poem *Taliessin through*

Logres.[104] Lewis made numerous references to Numinor, eldils, and Middle-earth from Tolkien's unfinished "new Hobbit" book.[105] No doubt, Williams would have been thrilled at such exposure, but Tolkien was not. He was highly offended. In a letter in 1955, Tolkien referred to Lewis's use of *Númenor*, which Lewis had misspelled *Numinor*, as a clear case of plagiarism.[106] Tolkien offered an excuse for why Lewis misspelled the word, but none was necessary. Lewis was a gifted misspeller of words, like his brother, and could misspell words with ease in at least six languages.

Dorothy L. Sayers did not care for the figure of Ransom in the final book of the trilogy for the same reason that Lewis had said that Satan was the best-drawn character in *Paradise Lost*.[107] By the third volume, Ransom's goodness had outgrown Lewis's experience of goodness and seemed artificial. Nor did she like "that Merlin stuff."[108] More significantly, Sayers took issue with Lewis's attempt to identify Ransom with the Fisher King of the Holy Grail tradition by virtue of his wounded heel. Percival was the wounded king who protected the Grail. Because of his wound, he could do little more than fish. Wagner's *Parsifal* is based on one strand of the legend tradition. In *That Hideous Strength*, Ransom's sister left him a fortune when she died, which allowed him to buy a great house that became his base, with the condition that he adopt her married name, Fisher-King.[109] It was not a subtle allusion. Sayers pointed out that the legendary Fisher King was wounded between the thighs and not the heel![110] While he was still writing the book, however, Lewis had told E. R. Eddison that the wounded heel had to do not with the Fisher King story at all but with the reference to Satan in Genesis 3:14–15 and the enmity between him and the woman's seed—"He shall bruise your head, and you shall bruise his heel."[111]

Tolkien and Sayers were purists about literary matters and could not abide mixing different strands of literary tradition. Tolkien despised The Chronicles of Narnia because in the first story, Lewis had intermingled Father Christmas with fawns. It is not clear that Tolkien ever bothered to read all of the Narnia stories. Lewis, on the other hand, looked at literature on a grand scale over thousands of years. He understood better than most critics the way different strands of literary tradition actually do mingle over centuries and millennia. An example of this mingling can be seen with the lost sword that is restored to its rightful owner that appears with King Arthur, with Siegfried, and with Theseus all the way back in ancient Greece. This element figures prominently in *The Lord of the Rings* with Aragon and the sword that only the rightful king can wield. The "return of the king" motif is also an ancient tradition of the *Sibylline Oracles* of late classical Rome. Tolkien himself did not hesitate to borrow Plato's Atlantis myth and transport it to Númenor.[112] Though Tolkien did not read widely, he certainly knew the background to these elements of his own stories.

Ransom's wound that would not heal may have had associations for Lewis even closer to home. Mrs. Moore's varicose ulcers on her leg would not heal. They had plagued her and, by extension, Lewis for several years. Lewis also knew from his own experience what it meant to have a wound that would not mend. His battle wound from May 1918 had never fully healed. When the shell exploded and sent shrapnel tearing through his body, it left him with lingering health issues that continued to plague him. The surgeon tending him also failed to remove all the shrapnel. While he was writing *That Hideous Strength*, busy with a brutal schedule and incessant demands from all his duties, the old shrapnel wound caused enough pain for him to seek a medical opinion.[113] The shrapnel lay quiet for twenty years until the late 1930s, but after that, during the whole of the war, it caused him pain. By the time he began his last broadcasts in 1944, he had scheduled an operation during the summer vacation to remove the shrapnel.[114] The first week of July, Lewis had his surgery at a nursing home on the Banbury Road.[115] On July 16, when he wrote to his young goddaughter, Sarah Neylan, Lewis described the ordeal and gave his opinion of nursing home care: "I didn't have a bad time in the

Home but they didn't give me enough to eat and they washed me all over as if I wasn't old enough to wash myself. Have you ever met a hospital-nurse? They are very strong-minded women."[116]

J. R. R. Tolkien always insisted that Lewis had not influenced his writing of *The Lord of the Rings* in any way, except for his encouragement. We have seen that Tolkien adopted Lewis's journey story in contrast to the normal Norse tale that Tolkien tried to write in *The Silmarillion*. We have already seen that Lewis probably gave Tolkien the suggestion to retell the story of the Nibelung ring of power. We also know that Tolkien stalled in his writing during the war, unsure of where the story was going. Frodo's wound, whose debilitating effect grew over time, became a central feature of the ending of the story. It is highly likely that Lewis's wound to his chest near his shoulder, which Tolkien probably did not know about until the operation, suggested to Tolkien the prominence of Frodo's wound that could not heal in this world, like Ransom's wound.

Before his surgery, however, Lewis managed to give the 1944 Clark Lectures at Cambridge University. He delivered the lectures on four Wednesday afternoons beginning on April 26 and going through May 17.[117] He left Oxford by train each Wednesday early enough to arrive for his five-o'clock lecture, and then he stayed afterward with the master of Trinity College in the Master's Lodge. *Lodge* is a misleading term when speaking of Trinity, one of the grandest of the grand colleges of Oxford and Cambridge. Lewis described the lodge as "an Elizabethan palace, room opening out of room like at Hampton Court."[118] The hospitality of Cambridge would have contrasted sharply with his lodgings at the RAF camps across Britain. Lewis arrived back in Oxford on Thursday in time to preside at the Inklings. Tolkien, who received his most helpful attention from Lewis in their Monday morning meetings, began to miss the Thursday night meetings. After Lewis's first lecture in Cambridge, Tolkien wrote to his son Christopher that he had been too tired to attend the "Lewis séance."[119]

Cover of *The Saturday Review*, April 8, 1944, in which *Perelandra* was reviewed

Five years into the war, Lewis was as busy as ever and the stress of the Kilns had only increased, though some of the physical demands had been relieved by June Flewett. He found that he spent his vacations on trains going to RAF bases and his terms in committee meetings.[120] With a reduction in the faculty on account of the war, everyone had to take on more committee responsibilities. Lewis had always enjoyed train travel, but the congestion of trains during the war was a different matter. All trains were troop trains, especially since the Americans had arrived in preparation for the Allied invasion of Europe. The troop buildup of Americans had been tremendous, and there were even American officers at Magdalen College! The one great bright spot of all the travel in overcrowded trains was that Lewis had time to read—time he would not have had in college or at the Kilns. He also gained increased recognition in the United States, where his books enjoyed brisk sales. In January 1944, *Current Biography* included a one-and-a-half-page sketch of Lewis, with an unflattering photograph. The sketch included mentions of *Dymer* and *The Pilgrim's Regress*, and quotations from positive reviews of *The Allegory of Love*, *A Preface to Paradise Lost*, *The Screwtape Letters*, *Out of the Silent Planet*, and *The Problem of Pain*. The conclusion of the entry remarked on how little was known of Lewis's private life, though he was thought to be a recluse "so shy that he has been known to lock himself in his study whenever a woman was reported on the way to visit the College."[121] One can only wonder what the source of the gossip might have been. In April 1944, *The Saturday Review* featured a drawing of Lewis on the cover with a full-page review of *Perelandra*.[122]

10

From War to Peace

1944–1945

As Lewis prepared for his surgery to remove the shrapnel from his body, the Allies prepared to invade Europe. During the early morning of June 6, 1944, the invasion force left the ports of southern England and made the six-hour voyage across the English Channel to land on the beaches of Normandy at dawn. Though Lewis mentioned the war in his radio broadcasts, *The Screwtape Letters*, *Perelandra*, and other articles and talks, he rarely discussed the war in his letters. He talked about the home front, rationing, his war work, and what the war meant on a day-to-day basis, but he did not talk about North Africa, Singapore, Burma, Italy, U-boat attacks on convoys, or any of the many military aspects of the war. He did not fret about what he could not control. He focused his mental and emotional energy on his duty and his family. He had not written about military campaigns for the most part since Norway in 1940.[1] On September 6, 1944, however, he broke his silence on military matters in a letter to Sister Penelope. He had learned to tell her things that weighed on his mind, especially things at the Kilns. After five years of war, he told her, "I never in my most sanguine moments dreamed that the invasion of Europe wd. go so well."[2]

A Ministering Angel

In the same letter in which he unburdened himself about his personal news, he mentioned his surgery, and he told her that Minto had suffered a stroke and lost the use of her left arm.[3] Between Jack's grueling lecture schedule with the RAF, his surgery and convalescence in the summer, and Minto's varicose ulcers and debilitating stroke, the situation at the Kilns would have grown helpless by summer 1944 if it had not been for June Flewett. She had been accepted by the Royal Academy of Dramatic Art (RADA) to begin her studies during the fall term, but she had decided to delay her entry so that she could stay at the Kilns and help. As much as Lewis loved to have June in the house, he knew that her best interests lay in returning to London and beginning her studies. He wrote to June's mother the day before he wrote to Sister Penelope to urge Mrs. Flewett to make June begin her studies.[4] June refused all the urging to get on with her life. She would remain at the Kilns for the duration of the war.

Years later, as Lady Jill Freud, June recalled what life had been like at the Kilns during the war. Minto had always flown into a rage when her daughter, Maureen, or one of the maids had not done something exactly the way she, Minto, would do it. Jill Freud described this obsessive insistence as a "ritual" that had to be done exactly the same way day after day. The ritual included caring for the chickens: "The hens had to have their doors closed 15 minutes after dusk and they had to have them opened in the morning 15 minutes before sunrise. So when it was my responsibility, I had to get up at half past five in the morning in the summer in order to open them up—as if it mattered."[5] Freud also described the maddening way that Minto hoarded basic staples, like butter and flour. She did not obtain more butter than any other family, which at the Kilns was about a half pound a week. Instead, she would not allow the family to use the butter. She kept it safe in the refrigerator as she built up her stockpile, but she never used her hoard. No one ate the store of butter. The hoarding of flour was so bad that it got infested with weevils and was ruined.[6]

June had her share of verbal abuse from Minto when she dared violate a ritual. She had offered to cook fish pies. Normally, Minto insisted on doing the cooking, which became impossible during her trouble with varicose ulcers and her stroke. Minto could only lie in bed and rage against June for using her mother's recipe instead of Minto's.[7] Nor did she treat Warnie very nicely.

Freud recalled that she never saw Warnie when he was not completely sober. She later realized that he had a drinking problem, but during the war, when he binged, he went away.[8] The *Bosphorus* may have provided a friendly home away from home for his binges while June was in residence at the Kilns, but a contributing factor to Warnie's sobriety was the new project he undertook. After a lifetime of interest in the reign of Louis XIV, Warnie began writing a book on the era of the Sun King that would be published in 1953 as *The Splendid Century: Some Aspects of French Life in the Reign of Louis XIV*. He read chapters to the Inklings, to the approval of Tolkien.[9]

As generous of spirit as June was, her primary motive in remaining at the Kilns was probably not to make life easier for poor Minto. A devout Catholic who had come from a parochial school, June had a great admiration for C. S. Lewis, whose wartime books had meant so much to so many. It was some months, however, before she realized that Jack, who was so easy to chat with and for whom she was developing a teenage crush, was C. S. Lewis. To her horror, she realized that the great man could see into her soul and knew her every fault! "Madly in love," Flewett would have done anything for him.[10] Looking back on the situation fifty-five years later, she thought that everyone in the house must have known, but they probably did not. Minto was too self-centered, and the brothers were too naive. Jack could have taken advantage of the pretty, vivacious girl on the brink of womanhood, but Freud said that he was too honorable for anything like that. Instead, they talked about books together, and he encouraged her intellectual development.[11]

Keeping Up with Friends

We have forty-seven letters that Lewis wrote in 1943. From 1944, we have forty-four, and they are shorter. The American edition of Lewis's collected letters devotes fifty-four pages to the letters of 1943 but only thirty-five to the letters of 1944. He wrote to Barfield only once in 1943 and once in 1944. He wrote to Arthur Greeves only three times in 1943 and three times in 1944. Lewis wrote to Dorothy L. Sayers four times in 1943 but not at all the following year. Sister Penelope received six letters in 1943 but only three in 1944. E. R. Eddison had six letters from Lewis in 1943 but only two in 1944.

Barfield and Greeves were his dear friends, but Lewis had learned the art of making new friends who shared common interests. During the war, his new friends included Williams, Sayers, Sister Penelope, and Eddison. They all provided a different enrichment to Lewis. Sister Penelope had a profound intellect that went along with her spiritual depth. Sayers shared the common concern for the representation of the Christian faith in the popular culture. Eddison shared his interest in science fiction but, more precisely, in creating imaginary worlds. Correspondence with these three fed him spiritually, emotionally, and intellectually during the war. These are the people he went out of his way to meet in that difficult time.

Lewis had chanced upon Eddison's novel *The Worm Ouroboros* in the fall of 1942. He was smitten by it. Lewis said that this novel had given him the experience that rarely happens after someone reaches middle-age—"the sense of having opened a new door."[12] He was effusive in his praise. Eddison's books were works of art. No other author reminds us of Eddison. Nowhere else can Eddison's achievement be found. It was the sort of thing Lewis had said about Tolkien and Williams. Lewis sent one of his rare fan letters to Eddison in November 1942 having written it in sixteenth-century English—the English of Wyatt, Spenser, and Shakespeare, about whom Lewis was writing for the Oxford History of the English Language series.[13] Perhaps, the language was a test. Eddison would either be charmed or repulsed. Apparently, he was charmed, and he replied in like manner, which began their regular correspondence, always in sixteenth-century English.

The friendship blossomed, and Lewis invited Eddison to dine with him at Magdalen College on February 17, 1943. After dinner, they were joined in Lewis's rooms for a gathering of the Inklings. Eddison read "Seven against the King" to the group.[14] Lewis regularly invited visitors to an Inklings meeting. Advising Eddison that since the beginning of the war, the fellows no longer wore their black gowns in hall, he added that they had declined to be "hobbinols." A hobbinol was a rustic, and this term may be the origin of Tolkien's hobbits.[15]

Owen Barfield was also invited to an Inklings meeting several times over the years. A tradition among people who write about Lewis says that Barfield was one of the Inklings, but it is difficult to make the case. Without actually declaring that Owen Barfield belonged to the group, Humphrey Carpenter, in *The Inklings* (1978), suggested as much. In his fictional account of what might have happened at their gatherings, Carpenter remarked that some of the Inklings had dropped out by the dark days of World War II. He mentioned that Adam Fox rarely came, but Carpenter failed to note that Fox had moved to London to become a canon of Westminster Abbey. Carpenter added, "Owen Barfield very occasionally turns up on his visits from London, where he still works as a solicitor."[16] He left the impression that Barfield had once been a regularly attending member of the Inklings until his move to London. In his 1977 biography of Tolkien, Carpenter was more blunt, naming Barfield definitely as a member who could rarely attend because of his work in London.[17] Oddly enough, Carpenter did not mention Adam Fox or Charles Williams in the biography. Without question, Barfield attended some of the Inklings gatherings, but can we accurately say that Barfield belonged to the group?

In his first letter to Williams in 1936, C. S. Lewis mentioned that he, Warren, Nevill Coghill, and Tolkien had "a sort of informal club called the Inklings: the qualifications (as they have informally evolved) are a tendency to write, and Christianity."[18] Though Barfield easily qualified on the first score, his anthroposophical convictions as a disciple of Rudolf Steiner placed him outside the bounds of orthodox Christianity. Nonetheless, opinions differed about his stand in relation to the faith. Warnie considered him a "baffling thing, a practicing Christian who is a believer in reincarnation."[19] While Barfield claimed to be a Christian and was baptized in 1948, he and Lewis differed radically over their understandings of what it means to be a Christian. Lewis thought it was "maddening" when an anthroposophist set himself up to be a Christian.[20]

After Lewis's conversion, he and Barfield no longer discussed philosophy, metaphysics, and especially theology.[21] The Inklings tended to drift into a discussion of theology regularly when they got together. Though they had wide-ranging opinions, they shared a common faith that Barfield did not. Their robust arguments aimed at light, but Barfield aimed at converting people to anthroposophy. As Lewis and most of the Inklings were interested in converting people to Christianity, Barfield and they stood at cross-purposes. While discussions of theology with Tolkien led to a deeper understanding of faith for Lewis, discussions with Barfield about theology served no purpose since Barfield had his mind made up from 1922.

The strongest evidence that Barfield belonged to the Inklings comes in a letter from Jack to Warnie at the beginning of World War II. In February 1940, in two different letters to Warnie in

France, Jack mentioned Barfield in connection with the Inklings. In the first, he remarked that the diversity of the Inklings included most of the professions: Warnie was a soldier, Fox was a clergyman, Havard was a doctor, and Barfield was a lawyer.[22] This last statement suggests that Barfield was "one of us." The second letter mentioned that Barfield had visited Oxford on a Thursday night, which Jack regretted. Lewis remarked that though Barfield knew *most* of the Inklings and got along well with them, Jack preferred to have Barfield all to himself.[23] The remark is odd if Barfield were one of the group—he would have known all the group instead of most members.

In December 1941, however, Lewis wrote to Dom Bede Griffiths to explain who were "The Inklings" to whom he had dedicated his new book, *The Problem of Pain*. Griffiths had tried throughout the 1930s to convert Lewis to Catholicism. Lewis in turn refused to discuss the differences between the Church of England and the Church of Rome with Griffiths. This history lies behind the way Lewis explained the ecclesiastical pluralism of the Inklings:

> Williams, Dyson of Reading, & my brother (Anglicans) and Tolkien and my doctor, Havard (your Church) are the 'Inklings' to whom my *Problem of Pain* was dedicated. We meet on Friday evenings in my rooms: theoretically to talk about literature, but in fact nearly always to talk about something better. What I owe to them all is incalculable. Dyson and Tolkien were the immediate causes of my own conversion. Is any pleasure on earth as great as a circle of Christian friends by a good fire?[24]

As much as Lewis loved Barfield, cared for him, and enjoyed his company, Lewis did not number him among his Christian friends. Barfield simply did not fit.

As Barfield remarked on a number of occasions, one of the fundamental differences between him and Lewis was that Lewis continued to develop after his conversion, but Barfield proudly observed that he "never changed at all."[25] Barfield believed that humanity as a whole is a spiritual unity that evolves and will continue to evolve, especially in its relation to God. Whereas Lewis believed that God's specific revelation to humanity reached its completeness with the Bible and the coming of Christ, Barfield believed that the incarnation and resurrection of Jesus represent the central point of shared human evolution. Jesus was simply the first to reach this stage of evolution. This was Barfield's understanding of what it meant to be a Christian.[26] Thus, he always felt uneasy with Lewis's theology, which he thought made too many rash generalizations, such as the idea that no Christian could believe in reincarnation. Barfield believed in reincarnation, among many other heterodox beliefs. Barfield also disliked Lewis's reliance on the Bible as God's final revelation.[27] While he liked Lewis's literary and philosophical writings, Barfield did not like Lewis's religious writings in the main. He only listened to two of Lewis's BBC talks during the war, aimed as they were at "mere Christianity."[28]

Barfield also differed from Lewis in his literary tastes. Barfield did not care for Norse mythology or William Morris.[29] He had not read as widely as Lewis. His primary interests after they met focused on anthropology, sociology, philosophy of language, and philosophy of history from an anthroposophical point of view. His literary concerns, such as his interest in Coleridge's understanding of imagination, were to demonstrate Rudolf Steiner's ideas through literary theory. None of these interests and disinterests fitted with the people who called themselves the Inklings. In fact, in an essay written in 1971, Barfield specifically excluded himself as a member because of what he called their "romantic theology."[30] He explained that he distanced himself from the Inklings because their theology was so at odds with his, even though they were Catholics and Protestants, for they were all orthodox as regards the creeds.

Dr. Robert Havard, known as "Humphrey," one of the most faithful attendees of Inklings gatherings, who had first joined the group after treating Lewis for flu in 1934 or 1935, listed the members as Lewis, Warnie, Tolkien, Coghill, Wrenn, Cecil, Dyson, Hardie, Fox, and Williams.[31] To this group, he added Commander Dundas-Grant, who joined the group during the war.[32] He did not include Owen Barfield in his list or his discussion of the Inklings. Havard explained that the outlook of the Inklings "was broadly traditional Christianity, taking their tone largely from Lewis himself, but the membership was indifferently distributed between Church of England and Roman Catholic."[33]

Nevill Coghill wrote about the Inklings in his contribution to *Light on C. S. Lewis*. He took pride in introducing Lewis to the writings of Charles Williams, which led Lewis to write to Williams and begin their great friendship. Williams became a member of the Inklings when he moved to Oxford during World War II. Reflecting on the two Inklings closest to Lewis, Coghill wrote, "I believe Williams was the only one of us, except perhaps Ronald Tolkien, from whom Lewis learnt any of his thinking."[34] Of course, Barfield had an enormous influence on the development of Lewis's thinking, as Coghill knew. Coghill had been one of the new Christian friends Lewis made at Oxford after World War I when he also became friends with Barfield. Even if he had not known of Barfield's influence through personal experience, which is most unlikely, he would have known from reading *Surprised by Joy*, to which he refers in *Light on C. S. Lewis* when discussing Lewis's conversion to Christianity. Had Barfield been regarded by the Inklings as a member instead of an occasional visitor, Coghill could not have neglected to include him in the small circle of Inklings who influenced Lewis's thinking.

Of his own connection with the Inklings, Barfield spoke in a recorded conversation with Walter Hooper and Kim Gilnett at the C. S. Lewis Summer Institute in Oxford in July 1988.[35] Lewis regarded Barfield as one of his three best friends, alongside Arthur Greeves and Warren, his brother. Their friendship began in Oxford, but after graduation and a failed attempt to earn his living as a writer, Barfield settled into his father's legal practice in London. The Inklings began after Barfield's departure from Oxford. Barfield spoke of the Inklings in connection with Warren's relationship to his more famous brother. He said that Warren "also used to attend the meetings of the little group they called 'the Inklings,' which met every week in Lewis's room. I only went once in a dozen times when I wasn't living in Oxford."[36] In another essay published in 1971, Barfield had declared that he seldom attended an Inklings meeting.[37] The war period would have been a more difficult time for Barfield to get away because he had taken on a part-time job with the Inland Revenue.[38] His visits were so rare, in fact, that he never heard any of Tolkien's readings of *The Lord of the Rings*, which were regular fare from the late 1930s throughout the war years.[39] It is also important to note that Barfield said "they" called their group the Inklings. While a member might sometimes refer to fellow members that way, Barfield never said. "*We* called *our* group the Inklings." He always referred to the Inklings in the third person. He spoke of Lewis's Inkling friends, rather than his own friends, and said that they did not like Lewis's wife, Joy.[40] He referred to Charles Williams as Lewis's friend, but if Barfield had been an Inkling, would Williams not have been his friend as well?[41]

No doubt, Barfield was a welcome guest on the rare occasions when he found himself in Oxford on a mid-workweek evening when the Inklings were gathering. Those visits, however, were too rare for him to enjoy or to contribute the kind of interaction and influence that Diana Glyer describes in *The Company They Keep*, which examines the influence of the Inklings operating on several levels.[42] Barfield was friend and legal advisor on business matters to Lewis but does not appear to have been regarded by the Inklings as one of them. Lewis had many friends who were not Inklings, including Arthur Greeves and Austen Farrer. Lewis also belonged to other groups. He had closer friends outside the Inklings with whom he confided on matters he never told the Inklings. Barfield

Cecil Harwood, C. S. Lewis, Walter O. Field, Eric Beckett, and
Alan Hanbury-Sparrow on a walking tour in Wales; photo by
Owen Barfield, ca. 1935. Used by permission of the Marion
E. Wade Center, Wheaton College, Wheaton, IL.

belonged to the circle of annual walking-tour friends that included
Cecil Harwood and "Wof" (Walter Ogilvie) Field. Lewis appears
never to have mentioned the Inklings in letters to any of his other
friends except Dom Bede Griffiths, who had asked about them.
His different circles of friends sometimes knew one another, but
they did not all belong to each other.

The Inklings played an important part in Lewis's writing
throughout the 1930s and 1940s. A popular conception abides regarding Lewis's writing style. Alastair Fowler reported that "when
things went well Lewis would write only a rough copy and a fair
copy (with one or two corrections per page). And that was it,
except for scholarly books like the OHEL volume, which were
tried out first as lectures."[43] He certainly gave the impression of
writing that way, but Fowler does not include the extra step. Lewis
"tried out" almost everything on the Inklings before he wrote
his final draft. He dedicated *Rehabilitations* to Hugo Dyson. He

dedicated *The Problem of Pain* to the Inklings.[44] He dedicated *The Screwtape Letters* to Tolkien. *Out of the Silent Planet* was dedicated to Warnie, and *A Preface to Paradise Lost* to Charles Williams. He dedicated the books to the people who heard him read them aloud and with whom he discussed them. The point of the meetings was to offer and receive helpful criticism.

Not everyone liked what he heard at an Inklings meeting. Dyson grew weary of Tolkien's new Hobbit. Tolkien did not care for Lewis's letters from a demon. Almost everyone had trouble with Williams's poetry and theology. Lewis wrote to Warnie in November of 1939 that Charles Wrenn, a regular presence at Inklings gatherings, expressed a strong desire at one meeting to burn Charles Williams at the stake. At least, Wrenn said that a conversation with Williams helped him understand why the inquisitors felt it their duty to burn heretics. After the meeting, Lewis and Tolkien agreed that just as some people at school were "eminently kickable," Williams was "eminently combustible."[45] Lewis admitted that Williams suffered from affectations that were really "honest defects of taste."[46] He also allowed that Williams's extraordinary imagination, which Hugo Dyson called "clotted glory from Charles," could appear both silly and vulgar, owing to a shortage of discipline in Williams's writing. None of that mattered, however, because Lewis thought him "a lovely creature" and was proud to be his friend.[47]

Lewis faulted Williams's undisciplined mind for some of the ideas that crept into his theology when they belonged more properly to his novels.[48] Lewis wished that Williams would focus his dynamic imagination on writing novels, which Lewis greatly admired, and avoid writing criticism, which Lewis thought he did poorly. He agreed with T. S. Eliot on perhaps only one thing—the obscurity of Williams's poetry.[49] Lewis told Williams that he should be beaten with a birch rod for it. Lewis told Barfield that he had argued with Williams about it, but to no avail.[50] In that sense, Williams did not derive the benefit of the Inklings criticism that Lewis received. Lewis sought helpful criticism, but Williams smiled on. Worse than his poetry, however, were his plays. Lewis thought they were "the least valuable part of his work."[51] The inferior work did not matter to Lewis; the novels made up for them all. And when Williams spoke, it was as though he had drawn all around him into one of his novels. It was the old feeling Lewis had gotten from Norse mythology. By 1945, Lewis could say to Sister Penelope that Williams was his "dearest friend."[52] Lewis's prodding may have led to Williams's decision to begin writing *All Hallows' Eve*, which he read at the Inklings meetings.[53]

The friendship between Lewis and Williams grew up around Williams's novels. Williams, in turn, recognized Lewis's great intellect and his contribution to scholarship. In many ways, however, they were as different as Lewis and Greeves. Williams was self-educated, which accounts in large measure for the lack of intellectual discipline that so bothered Lewis. His mind was brilliant but untrained. A great deal has been observed and written about the enormous appeal Williams had to the ladies. Of course, in due time, the same could be said of Lewis. The difference appears to be that Williams tended to cultivate the appeal. In fact, he enjoyed cultivating his standing among people who had standing. At the Inklings meeting on Thursday evening, November 30, 1944, Lord David Cecil addressed Williams as Charles. In a letter to his wife, Williams reveled in the realization that he was "on Christian name terms" with Lord David, the son of the fourth Marquess of Salisbury and grandson of Queen Victoria's prime minister. By the end of the evening, he proved so bold as to address Lord David simply as David.[54]

Perhaps, the familiarity says something about the nature of the Inklings, a group that cut across social classes. The many social barriers in England at the time made such a group highly unlikely. The Catholic and Protestant mix was unusual. So was the English and Irish mix. Lord David was not the only member of the aristocracy, for Nevill Coghill was the son of a baronet and grew up in a great country house. Like Frodo Baggins, Tolkien was an orphan. The Lewis brothers were solidly middle-class, the sons of a barrister. Humphrey Havard was also a professional man. Adam Fox was a clergyman. Warnie and James Dundas-Grant were both military men. Only half of the Inklings were literary academics. In that sense, it was never the subversive group within the university that some critics made it out to be. It was a company of friends who liked stories, poetry, and Jesus.

Along with Lewis, Williams and Cecil were by far the most prolific writers of the group. Cecil had returned to Oxford in 1939 as a fellow in English at New College. During the war, he published *The English Poets* (1941), *The Oxford Book of Christian Verse* (1941), *Men of the RAF* (1942), *Hardy the Novelist: An Essay in Criticism* (1942), *Anthony and Cleopatra* (1944), and *Poetry of Thomas Grey* (1945). The last three of these books began as named lectureships: the Clark Lectures, the W. P. Ker Memorial Lecture, and the Warton Lecture. During the same period, Williams published *Witchcraft* (1941), *The Forgiveness of Sins* (1942), *The Figure of Beatrice* (1943), *The Region of Summer Stars* (1944), *All Hallows' Eve* (1945), and *The House of the Octopus* (1945). The average academic would do well to accomplish this much in an entire career.

Despite their common interests, the Inklings differed in many of their critical judgments. Lewis's well-known contempt for T. S. Eliot and his modern poetry ripples through much of his academic criticism. It would be a mistake, however, to assume that all of the Inklings took this view. Lord David Cecil had known and liked Eliot for years. They both attended Lady Ottoline Morrell's famous literary teas in the 1920s. Cecil approved of Eliot's poetry. So did Charles Williams! Williams also knew Eliot—who edited Williams's novels at Faber and Faber—and for some time had threatened to bring Lewis and Eliot together in order to sort out their differences.[55] Perhaps the obscurity of Williams's poetry and the fact that some of the greatest critical literary minds of the twentieth century could not make heads or tails of it gave Williams common cause with Eliot. Yet, Eliot found Williams's poetry just as obscure as Lewis did.

Hugo Dyson came to the Inklings not to read his work like Lewis and Tolkien but to talk. Dyson's quick wit could always be counted on in a running commentary on events. When he heard about Williams's Milton lectures, which dealt with virginity, Dyson replied, "The fellow's becoming a common chastitute."[56] Coghill's presence at the Inklings became rarer and rarer as the war dragged on. Lewis and Dyson discussed his habitual absence and confessed to each other: "We 'got on better without him'. His Leftism, and his 'Producing' and his, I fear, unsoundness in religion, are producing a rift."[57] Lewis was not sure that a rift really mattered in the case of Coghill, since he was always accepting invitations but not keeping the engagements.

Coghill's time had become increasingly devoted to the Oxford University Dramatic Society (OUDS), of which he became the driving force for thirty years. When the war began, Coghill's involvement with the OUDS changed. The club had outstanding debts to different shops and tradesmen of Oxford in excess of a thousand pounds, which was an enormous sum for undergraduates in 1939. Coghill assumed the responsibility to pay off the debt and keep the club going during the war. He approached the vice chancellor, none other than his friend George Gordon of the English faculty, who also served as president of Magdalen College. Gordon bestowed on Coghill authority to sell and manage the assets of the club and to raise the money as best he could by producing profitable plays.[58] Thus, to Lewis's annoyance, Coghill was always producing plays.

To further complicate his life, Coghill had the demanding responsibility of proctor of the university in 1940–1941. In this capacity, he exercised discipline over the university's wayward undergraduates. The proctor's constabulary, known as Bulldogs, feared that mild-mannered Coghill was not up to the job, forgetting that he had served with distinction during the last war. Having seen Coghill in action, one of the skeptical Bulldogs reported, "We've never had a better Proctor."[59] In addition, Coghill held the post of sub-rector at Exeter College, comparable to Lewis's one-year post as vice president at Magdalen, for most of the war years.[60] In *That Hideous Strength*, Lewis gave to Curry, the leader of the progressive element at Bracton College, the post of sub-warden, comparable to the position held by Lewis and Coghill, which in the wrong hands could wield untold power and do manifold damage.[61] Coghill's absence from Inklings meetings in the war years was not simply lack of interest. He was a busy man, too. Like Lewis, he had his own war work. His friendship with Lewis, however, continued apart from regular Inklings meetings. They dined together at Exeter and Magdalen throughout the war.[62] He was always good company and a stimulating conversationalist for Lewis, though their literary tastes differed at points. Lewis said of Coghill after the war, "No man whom I have ever met describes another man's work better than Mr. Coghill (his descriptions of Kafka always seemed to me better even than Kafka)."[63]

Lewis made the effort to attend Coghill's plays when he could, but he had little free time between his war work and Minto's demands at the Kilns. He went to see several short plays, including one by Yeats, in December 1939.[64] He took June Flewett to see Coghill's production of *Measure for Measure* in June 1944, in which Richard Burton appeared as Angelo.[65] Coghill, however, had no memory of Lewis ever attending.[66] Coghill's theatrical involvement, university duties, and college responsibilities left little time for the Inklings and little room for memories.

While Lewis remained the most prolific writer of the Inklings, others regularly read to the group their works in progress. Before he left Oxford for Westminster Abbey in 1942, Adam Fox read from his poem "Paradisal," based on Blenheim Park in winter.[67] Williams read from his nativity play, *The House by the Stable*, and from his Whitsun play, *Terror on Night*.[68] Hugo Dyson wrote a book with John Butt titled *Augustans and Romantics (1689–*

1839), which Lewis spent a week proofreading for him.[69] Humphrey Havard, who always insisted that he was not a literary man, was enticed by Lewis to write a paper on the experience of physical pain, which Lewis included as an appendix to *The Problem of Pain*.[70] On another occasion, he read an account of his mountain climbing experience.[71] Of course, Tolkien regularly read chapters from his "new Hobbit."[72]

When Lewis finished writing *That Hideous Strength* in 1943, he assumed that Tolkien would publish *The Lord of the Rings* shortly after. It was not published until nine years later. Tolkien had been offended that Lewis had mentioned some of Tolkien's Middle-earth creations in his science-fiction book. The incident illustrates the way in which Tolkien was more like Hugo Dyson than like Lewis. By 1945, Dyson had written only two scholarly books: *Pope: Poetry and Prose* (1933), which was actually an edited book, and *Augustans and Romantics* (1940), which he coauthored. Tolkien had not actually written any. He had contributed a glossary of terms in Middle English to be used with Kenneth Sisam's *Fourteenth Century Verse and Prose* in 1922. He had edited an edition of *Sir Gawain and the Green Knight* with E. V. Gordon in 1925. His 1936 long essay "Beowulf: The Monsters and the Critics" is regarded as a classic in Beowulf studies. Other than these, he published a number of poems of little note and a few introductions to the works of others. Lewis had always known what Tolkien could do, but he had never done it. Lewis defended Tolkien as "a very great man," saying in 1944 that "his published works . . . ought to fill a shelf by now."[73] They ought to have done so, but they did not. Like many brilliant people who did well in school, settled into academic careers, and were recognized as great scholars and honored with professorships, Tolkien did precious little publishing in his field.

While Lewis devoted energy and time to encouraging Tolkien in hopes of eventually seeing the completion of *The Lord of the Rings*, Tolkien offered little encouragement to Lewis.[74]

Tolkien did not care for *The Great Divorce*.[75] He had not cared for the way all the Arthurian mythology "ruined" *That Hideous Strength*.[76] He had not cared for *The Screwtape Letters* and wondered why Lewis had dedicated it to him.[77] During a very trying time when Lewis had taken on an enormous number of extra duties, he received little encouragement from Tolkien.

The Great Divorce

By May 1944, Lewis was deep into writing what would eventually be published as *The Great Divorce*.[78] By July, he had completed the manuscript and hired Barbara Wall, to whom he would dedicate the book, to type it for him. His hiring a typist suggests that Warnie was in no condition to help with the typing at this point. Alternatively, Warnie could have been so busy with Jack's fan mail that an extra hand was needed. On July 31, Lewis sent the manuscript to the publisher.[79]

The publisher was the *Guardian*, the church newspaper that had published *The Screwtape Letters* before it became a book. The *Guardian* published this new series as "Who Goes Home? Or The Grand Divorce" in weekly installments from November 10, 1944, until April 13, 1945.[80] In the end, the first title had to be dropped because another book already had the title *Who Goes Home?*[81] Lewis confided to Dom Bede Griffiths that he feared the serial lacked a "musical or architectural unity." Once the ghosts arrive in heaven, the episodes could have taken place in any order. Nothing builds on a previous episode. Lewis thought it had spiritual unity, but he was not sure that spiritual unity alone would make a good book.[82] It was published by Geoffrey Bles: The Centenary Press in January 1946, though the copyright page erroneously gives the publication date as November 1945.[83] In February 1948, the BBC made a recording of Lewis reading the preface to *The Great Divorce*.[84]

Lewis first conceived the idea of a story about inmates in hell making an excursion to heaven during an Easter vacation in 1933.[85] While most of his writing the previous two years had focused on the confusion of materialist philosophy with science and the dangers of relativistic values, this series continued his reflections on the experience of temptation that he had explored in *The Screwtape Letters* and *Perelandra* while studying *Paradise Lost*. Lewis made no attempt in this series to provide a theology of heaven and hell, because the story is not about those destinations. It is about the road to heaven or hell. He made clear in his preface that not all roads lead to heaven. Instead, all roads fork, and people must make a decision at each fork. Lewis didn't write about what might happen in heaven and hell. Instead, he wrote about how people might be set back on the right path in this life. In that light, he took his inspiration from *The Pilgrim's Progress*, a book to which he became devoted long before he was a Christian.

In his preface, Lewis reminded his readers that *The Great Divorce* was a work not only of fiction but also of fantasy. He had a particular expression for this kind of story: *supposal*. In *The Allegory of Love*, he had explained that the geographical places in Chrétien de Troyes's *Lancelot* "are mere romantic supposals."[86] The way Lewis described heaven and hell did not even rise to the level of speculation. He was not concerned with conditions in the afterlife. Instead, he focused on how people deal with the choices presented to them in temptation during this life. Lewis depicted people who face the *bellum intestinum* that he discussed in *The Allegory of Love*, the inner war, the battle between right and wrong. Like so many of his stories, this one involves a journey, just like the stories he fell in love with as a teenage boy in Great Bookham.

Williams had been writing and talking about Dante's *Divine Comedy* when Lewis began working on *The Great Divorce*. In *The Divine Comedy*, the Roman poet Virgil serves as Dante's guide through hell and purgatory. Beatrice guides him through heaven. In *The Great Divorce*, Lewis has George MacDonald as his guide. The works of MacDonald had guided Lewis to faith in Christ. As *The Great Divorce* opens, Lewis has been wandering for hours in the rain, in perpetual twilight that never becomes night. The description anticipates the land of Narnia, where it is always winter but never Christmas. The scene of a dingy part of town that could only be called "slums" reaches its most dismal prospect when Lewis describes the bookshops as the kind that sell the works of Aristotle. When he read this line to the Inklings, it would have produced a laugh. Lewis was always railing against Aristotle, whom he called the philosopher of divisions in *The Allegory of Love*. With tongue in cheek, Lewis described what hell would be like for a book lover like him who also loved a pitch-black night during his air-raid warden patrols so that he could see the stars.

In *The Screwtape Letters*, Lewis explored the infernal thinking behind temptation, but more importantly, the presence of God's grace in times of temptation. In *The Great Divorce*, Lewis explored the impact of temptation and how people think about it. He described what it looks like to nurture our own worst flaws. In the face of temptation, however, he shows how God offers a way of escape from our self-centeredness. God offers choices about how to respond to temptation. This book is not about choices we have after death; it is about choices we have before we die. When the confrontation comes, it is a confrontation with oneself: "Friend," said the Spirit. "Could you, only for a moment, fix your mind on something not yourself?"[87]

The Fifth BBC Series

Lewis's broadcast talks had met with such success that the BBC endeavored to export Lewis to the rest of the empire. R. S. Lee, the overseas religious broadcasting organizer for the BBC, wrote to Lewis in October 1944 to tell him that the director of religious broadcasting in Australia wanted Lewis to broadcast down under. Since the BBC had recorded only a few of the talks, it would mean repeating what he had already done. Lewis did not like the idea of repeating his earlier broadcasts, since they had already been published in book form. If given six months, however, he agreed to prepare a new set of talks.[88]

As it turned out, the Australia Broadcasting Commission did not want a new series. They wanted a rebroadcast of "Christian Behaviour." They wanted Lewis to record the talks at the BBC in London before November 19. Lewis declined. He realized that most listeners would not have read his book, but those who had might feel "tricked." He could not do it with any conviction, and he thought it would damage his "future utility."[89] Undeterred, Lee wrote again to say that the Australians would be disappointed, but their disappointment would be alleviated if Lewis would agree to proceed with a new series of talks. On reflection, Lewis withdrew his earlier offer to prepare a fresh series. He had given it much thought and realized that he had nothing more to say on the radio. He had finished.[90]

Once Lewis had given his final word on the subject, Lee wrote to him again in December. Lee needed six talks for Lent to broadcast to the BBC's Pacific, African, North American, and General Overseas services. Lee proposed "The Sin of Man," "God's Plan for Man," "The Incarnation," "The Nature of Christ's Sacrifice," "The Life in Grace," and "Christ the Lord of Life."[91] In a brief reply, Lewis declined, yet again. While a good plan in itself, it was Lee's plan and not his plan. Besides, it overlapped with much he had already done. Lewis would not do a fifth series of wartime radio broadcasts for the kingdom, the empire, or the Americans.[92]

The Last Year of the War

Despite the success of the Allies in the Battle of the Bulge during Christmas, 1945 began with a sad note at the Kilns. The time had come for June Flewett to commence her studies at the Royal Academy of Dramatic Arts in London. She left the Kilns on January 3.[93] Lewis would pay her tuition.

With Macmillan's American publication of *The Screwtape Letters, The Problem of Pain, Out of the Silent Planet, Perelandra,* the three volumes of broadcast talks, and even *The Pilgrim's Regress*, Lewis was beginning to enjoy a degree of popularity in the United States. It also meant that his fan-mail load increased dramatically. Along with the increased revenue stream came invitations to visit the United States on a lecture tour. To all of these suggestions Lewis replied emphatically that a trip to America was "out of the question."[94] His reason was simple. He had an elderly, invalid "mother" who required his attention, and he could not be away from home for more than a few days at a time.[95] The loss of June had made the problem of caring for Minto all the more acute.

Even as June left, a new arrival came to the extended family. Maureen Moore Blake gave birth to her son, Richard Francis Blake, on January 8, 1945.[96] Lewis became his godfather, a role he fulfilled for an increasing number of children.[97] Jack wrote to June and her mother with news at the Kilns in the first days of her absence: the hens asked after her, Warnie grew more depressed, the cats had stopped fighting following the calamity of June's departure, Bruce was wet, the potatoes were criticized (by Minto) as either overdone or underdone, and Maureen's husband Leonard managed to keep up his appetite "wonderfully."[98] Lewis missed her.

Nonetheless, the war went on, and Lewis's war work with it. After June was gone, he traveled to Rochester to speak.[99] The Rochester airfield housed the Short Brothers' aviation factory, which built seaplanes and the Stirling four-engine bomber. It also housed a flight training school of the RAF.

Miracles

Lewis finished writing his book on miracles by February 1945, though it would not be published until May 1947.[100] In it he combined several themes he had discussed and written about over a number of years. At the heart of *Miracles*, Lewis expressed his concern for the reality of the supernatural. He had written to

Dom Bede Griffiths about the importance of supernatural experience in 1936.[101] Of course, his own experience of Joy, which he identified with Rudolf Otto's treatment of numinous experience, provided him with personal evidence of the supernatural, but he would not discuss personal experience in a book that was perhaps his most philosophical. His view of the supernatural involved not only belief in the existence of the supernatural but also personal experience with the supernatural. He had told Sister Penelope in 1939 that he had no real interest in the distinctions often drawn between the High Church party and the Low Church party within the Church of England. His real concern was the distinction "between religion with a real supernaturalism & salvationism on the one hand and all watered-down and modernist versions on the other."[102] Though Lewis described his conversion experience as intellectual rather than emotional, it had a definite mystical dimension.[103]

In 1943, he told Sister Penelope that writing his book about "the Supernatural" had resulted in chapters that were for him "hymns on Nature."[104] On May 10, 1945, two days after the German surrender, Lewis explained this idea further to Griffiths. Writing a book on miracles, which to a certain extent involves an invasion of nature, had made him "realise Nature" in a way he had never done before. This statement sounds particularly astonishing for a man like Lewis, who had reveled in nature since his teenage years. He explained how he felt:

> You don't *see* Nature till you believe in the Supernatural: don't get the full, hot, salty tang of her except by contrast with the pure water from beyond the world. Those who mistake Nature for the All are just those who can never realise her as a *particular creature* with her own flawed, terrible, beautiful individuality.[105]

With the war over, Lewis complained to Sister Penelope that the real enemy of God was "religion" that denied the supernatural—

"the vague slush of humanitarian idealism, Emersonian Pantheism, democratic politics and material progressiveness with a few Christian names and formulae added to taste like salt and pepper."[106] He longed to see this kind of materialistic religion "stamped out!"[107]

The first chapter of *The Problem of Pain* had contrasted a naturalistic or materialist view of reality with a religious or supernaturalist view.[108] In his fourth radio broadcast, "What Lies behind the Law," Lewis contrasted the materialist and religious views.[109] In *Out of the Silent Planet*, the materialist view of Weston comes face-to-face with the supernatural reality of the Oyarsa. In *The Great Divorce*, the apostate bishop clings to his materialistic interpretation of religion, even when confronted with the supernatural reality of hell and its inmates alongside heaven and its citizens.[110] The heavenly Spirit confronts him with the question "When, in our whole lives, did we honestly face, in solitude, the one question on which all turned: whether after all the Supernatural might not in fact occur?"[111] The heavenly Spirit declares that he and the ghostly bishop had not considered the question because "we were afraid of crude salvationism."[112] Lewis continued this theme in *Miracles*.

Lewis began *Miracles* with a scant chapter of just over two pages in which he declared that the question of miracles cannot be solved by sensory experience (what we see, hear, smell, touch, or taste), the primary tool of experimental science. Empirical data must always be interpreted, and alternative explanations for miracles can always be proposed. We tend to interpret the data according to our philosophical presuppositions. For instance, Einstein refused to accept the empirical evidence of quantum theory and big bang theory because they clashed with the philosophical claims of Aristotle that had governed science for over two thousand years. Lewis explained that one must first determine if miracles are possible from a philosophical point of view before declaring that the miracles of the Bible could not occur.

In chapter 2, Lewis devoted eight pages to distinguishing the naturalist from the supernaturalist. He did not accept David Hume's eighteenth-century definition of miracle as a violation of the laws of nature, a view that had become widely accepted in popular culture. Lewis had devoted a great deal of attention in *The Problem of Pain* to explaining why God does not violate the laws by which he governs the universe. Lewis defined miracle as "an interference with Nature by supernatural power."[113] The naturalist believes that nothing exists except nature, or the physical universe; therefore, no supernatural power exists that can interfere with nature. The supernaturalist believes that, in addition to nature, something else exists. Lewis showed that people use the word *nature* in a variety of ways. For the naturalist, nature is the closed, interlocking system of cause and effect. Even though quantum theory, chaos theory, big bang cosmology, and DNA genetics now demonstrate the openness of the universe, a naturalistic point of view continues to have great sway in the twenty-first century. Lewis gave the example of quantum theory, an area of science largely unknown by even learned people before the late twentieth century, to suggest the openness of the universe.[114] The closed universe has no place for free will. The supernaturalist agrees with the naturalist that something must be the original basic fact. Instead of nature, however, the supernaturalist believes that the original fact is the supernatural power that caused nature in the first place. For purposes of his examination of miracles, Lewis focuses on belief in one God as the supernatural power, since polytheistic religions do not normally espouse belief in a Creator of nature. Lewis proposed that supernaturalism, multiple natures completely unconnected with entirely different physics, might exist. God would be the only point of contact between such natures or worlds or universes.

If naturalism is true, then miracles cannot exist, but if supernaturalism is true, then they may. For naturalism to be true, everything within nature must be explained by the total system of nature. If something exists that cannot be explained by the physical system of cause and effect, then the philosophy of naturalism has been falsified.[115] Quantum theory, with its observation of the indeterminate behavior of subatomic particles, demonstrates that the universe is not a closed, determinate system of cause and effect. If nature has a "back door" at its lowest level of organization, perhaps it also has a "front door opening on the Supernatural."[116]

What we know about the universe, we infer from our observations. The mind interprets sensory data. In this sense, all scientific knowledge "depends upon the validity of reasoning."[117] The reasoning of a person in a psychologically irrational state lacks validity and tends to be open to doubt by others. On this basis, Lewis proposed a rule: "*No thought is valid if it can be fully explained as the result of irrational causes.*"[118] He then commenced an examination of human reason as a whole. Naturalism explains human reason as the consequence of irrational causes. The mind is simply one other thing in the universe that is a result of the total system, which is only brute matter. The thoughts of the scientist may have the advantage of group psychosis to validate them, but in the naturalistic system, rationality is caused by irrationality as mind evolves from brute matter.

Lewis admitted that an argument can be made for the development of rationality by chance and that this trait was inherited. Those who inherited the trait had an advantage over brutes without rationality in the competition for survival. With this advantage, the rational overwhelmed the brute. The problem with this explanation is that it is based on inference. One must assume the validity of inference in order for the argument to work. It is a circular argument. Trusting in argument at all requires the assumption of the validity of reason. The naturalist may accept the validity of reason on pragmatic grounds, but Lewis will not allow that the naturalist can make truth claims on this basis.

Lewis did not deny that consciousness or other mental activity arises within the processes of nature. He argued strictly about the problem of reason. Reason has power over nature—as Lewis had argued in *The Abolition of Man*—and not necessarily for the good. Nature, on the other hand, has no power over reason. To this extent, rational thought has a degree of independence from nature. Lewis then argued that this kind of independence of rationality must have its origins in Reason, a Reason that must exist outside the closed system of nature. The explanation for the rationality of human reason lies outside the total system of nature: "Each has come into Nature from Supernature: each has its tap-root in an eternal, self-existent, rational Being, whom we call God. Each is an offshoot, or spearhead, or incursion of that Supernatural reality into Nature."[119] Thus, human reason is the example of the interference with nature by a supernatural power.

It is interesting to note that Lewis does not deny or refute the idea of the evolution of animals in *Miracles* or elsewhere. In *The Problem of Pain*, he remarked, "If by saying that man rose from brutality you mean simply that man is descended from animals, I have no objection."[120] On the other hand, he strenuously objected to the proposal that God had nothing to do with it. In "What Christians Believe," the second series of radio broadcasts, Lewis began his last talk by pointing out that "people often ask when the next step in evolution—the step beyond man—will happen."[121] This question lay behind Barfield's anthroposophy. Lewis simply said that it had already happened, but it was not evolution ascending to God; rather God descended to us to change us. In his very last radio talk, "New Men," at the end of series 4, Lewis discussed evolution again and argued that "the next step" was not like the previous steps of evolution. It was not a physical change like a bigger brain. It was a spiritual change—"a change from being creatures of God to being sons of God."[122]

Lewis did not argue with the concept of evolution, which he did not see as a contradiction of Scripture so long as it allowed for the involvement of God in the creation of life. He did object, however, to the insertion of a philosophical point of view into the science which declared that God could not be involved in the evolution of life. In December 1944, Lewis responded to a letter of complaint from Captain Bernard Acworth, founder of the Evolution Protest Movement. Lewis explained:

> I am not attacking or defending Evolution. I believe that Christianity can still be believed, even if Evolution is true. That is where you and I differ. Thinking as I do, I can't help regarding your advice (that I henceforth include arguments against Evolution in all my Christian apologetics) as a temptation to fight the battle on what is really a false issue: and also on *terrain* very unsuitable for the only weapon I have.[123]

Lewis's battle was with naturalism in all of its forms, of which unguided natural selection, as opposed to evolution, was just one.

Miracles is probably Lewis's most philosophical book, though written for a popular audience rather than for trained philosophers. Lewis understood that apologetics is not meant for career philosophers but for everyone. In the first scholarly treatment of Lewis's apologetics by a philosopher, Richard B. Cunningham identified what set Lewis apart from the professional theologians and philosophers of the mid-twentieth century:

> Does apologetics consist of academics talking to academics; of arid, abstruse, systematic rehashing of perennial problems within a limited, esoteric, theological eddy? Or should the apologist wade into the mainstream of life, confronting modern problems and encouraging the masses of men, gaining a hearing for the Christian faith by any possible method? Is there a place for living and vital, imaginative and poetic, Christian apologies, which are aimed not at academics but at men in the street who worship the gods of the marketplace?[124]

Lewis did what he did during the war only because those who were trained to do it tended to write merely for one another.

Lewis's argument that human reason is evidence for the involvement of God within nature may seem simple or unconvincing to many, but he recognized an enormous problem that has troubled many who hold to naturalism. In *Miracles*, he quoted J. B. S. Haldane, one of his adversaries, who said on the same subject, "If my mental processes are determined wholly by the motions of atoms in my brain, I have no reason to suppose that my beliefs are true . . . and hence I have no reason for supposing my brain to be composed of atoms."[125] Perhaps more fascinating is the view of Charles Darwin on the subject. A year before he died, he wrote to a correspondent about what troubled him most about his theory of natural selection:

> Nevertheless, you have expressed my inward conviction, though far more vividly and clearly than I could have done, that the Universe is not the result of chance. With me the horrid doubt always arises whether the convictions of man's mind, which has developed from the mind of the lower animals, are of any value or at all trustworthy. Would any one trust in the convictions of a monkey's mind, if there are any convictions in such a mind?[126]

Naturalism was always the great enemy for Lewis, and *Miracles* was the summation of his response to it during World War II. With the completion of the manuscript of *Miracles*, his war work was almost over.

The End of the War

After the Battle of the Bulge during Christmas 1944, the Allies pushed on into Germany from the west while the Soviet troops pushed toward Berlin from the east. As the Red Army fought the remains of the German Wehrmacht and Waffen-SS through the streets of Berlin, Hitler committed suicide on April 30. Admiral Karl Dönitz succeeded Hitler as head of state, but the Third Reich was finished. General Alfred Jodl surrendered all German forces unconditionally on May 8, 1945. The war was over.

Everyone had known that the end was coming soon. Preparations were underway for life after the war. Charles Williams had picked up adjunct lecture work during the war with so many English fellows away with war duties, but they would be coming back. Williams would not gain an appointment as a reader at Oxford. It had been a dream of his, but it was never a realistic dream.[127] The Oxford University Press would move its wartime offices back to Amen House in London, and Williams would leave behind the dreaming spires of Oxford. Lewis and Tolkien had anticipated Williams's departure and the loss it would mean to their Tuesday mornings and Thursday evenings. They decided to publish a *Festschrift* in Williams's honor with contributed chapters from his friends to mark his departure from Oxford. Lewis, Tolkien, and Barfield already had in mind what they would contribute.[128]

When news of the surrender finally came, and Britain celebrated VE Day (victory in Europe), Lewis told Griffiths that he did not know exactly how to feel in the light of the miraculous provision by which so many had escaped harm even in the midst of the devastation.[129] When peace came, life went on largely as it had before. Lewis still had his tutorials. Minto still needed him to come when she called. The Inklings would still drink on Tuesday mornings at the Eagle and Child, and they would congregate in his rooms at Magdalen to talk late into Thursday evening. The Socratic Club would meet again on May 14, when he was scheduled to speak, appropriately enough, on "Resurrection."[130]

Just as Lewis bore his physical pain in silence, Williams had experienced severe abdominal pain in 1945 without the knowledge of his friends. On Monday, May 14, the day of the Socratic Club meeting, Williams was admitted to the Radcliffe Infirmary for an operation.[131] Lewis went to see him at the Radcliffe on Tuesday morning and took him a book to read. When he arrived, he learned that Williams had died. The Radcliffe is only a few short blocks from the Eagle and Child in St Giles. Lewis walked to join his friends for their usual Inklings gathering and give them the horrible news. He had difficulty making them understand that

Williams was dead.[132] Of that experience he wrote, "The world seemed to us at that moment primarily a *strange* one."[133]

Warnie Lewis had been in Jack's rooms at Magdalen working on his book about the age of Louis XIV when a call came from the Radcliffe Infirmary to tell Jack that Williams had died. A woman gave Warnie the message, but he did not know who she was. He was stunned. Jack, while leaving Magdalen to visit his friend, had told him that morning that Williams was in the hospital for an operation. Neither brother was prepared for their friend's death. Warnie wrote in his diary, "There will be no more pints with Charles: no more 'Bird and Baby': the blackout has fallen, and the Inklings can never be the same again."[134]

Tolkien went home and immediately wrote to Mrs. Williams to say that Father Gervase Mathew, a new addition to the Inklings, would say Mass for Williams, with Tolkien serving at Blackfriars on Saturday, May 18.[135] Williams's funeral was conducted on Friday, May 17, at Saint Cross Church, around the corner from where Williams had lodged with the Spaldings on South Parks Road. He was buried in the Saint Cross churchyard near Kenneth Grahame, author of *The Wind in the Willows*. After the funeral, Lewis and Dyson went to Addison's Walk, where Lewis had walked with Dyson and Tolkien some fifteen years earlier. Dyson, who normally kept the world in an uproar of hilarity also had a profound depth of spiritual sensitivity. As they sat together, Dyson said:

> Our Lord told the disciples it was expedient for them that He should go away for otherwise the Comforter would not come to them. I do not think it blasphemous to suppose that what was true archetypally, and in eminence, of His death may, in the appropriate degree, be true of the deaths of all His followers.[136]

It was what Lewis needed to hear.

Lewis wrote to Owen Barfield that Williams's death was the first severe loss he had ever experienced. Perhaps he had been too young for his mother's death to affect him severely. His father's death left him feeling guilty that he had not treated him better, but it did not leave Jack with a deep sense of loss. Yet, in the wake of Williams's death, Lewis gained a stronger belief in immortality, which had never been a great issue with him in his conversion experience. The loss also "swept away" all his dread and horror at funerals, coffins, and graves. He found that he no longer had his old feelings about ghosts and would not mind if Williams turned up. He included in his letter to Barfield a summary of what Dyson had said to him, possibly as a word of testimony to his faith, for though he knew that Barfield did not hold to historic Christianity, Lewis was not even sure that he could be called a theist.[137]

To Mary Neylan, Lewis confessed that the death of Williams brought him grief but that he found his faith was "ten times stronger than it was a week ago."[138] He found that the old talk about feeling closer to someone than ever before was not just talk. It was the way Lewis felt, but of all people, he could not put it into words.[139] Lewis was experiencing the implications of how he understood the efficacy of the death of Christ. Those who have faith in Christ are crucified with Christ across time and space through the Holy Spirit. Christ is in them and they are in Christ by the Holy Spirit. Since Williams and Lewis were both in Christ, they enjoyed the communion of the saints. For those in Christ, the barrier of time and space, death and the grave, lose their power. To know Christ is to know that all those in him are not far away and not separated for long.

When he wrote to Mrs. Williams a few days after the funeral, Lewis said that he felt his friendship with Williams was not ended. He repeated again what Dyson had said and reaffirmed his confidence in the life that is assured in Christ beyond death. A month earlier, he would have thought such words were a "silly sentiment." Suddenly he knew better.[140] To Sister Penelope, he also repeated Dyson's words and added that Williams's death had "made the next world much more real and palpable."[141] He had heard

widows and bereaved mothers talk about how they felt the near-
ness of the one they had lost, and Lewis always thought such talk
was just "sentimental hyperbole."[142] Now he knew better. Life in
Christ is supernatural.

Conclusion

Lewis learned that he was still learning. He was discovering how
Christ affected him in the present day. He had discovered spiritual
resources to accomplish a Herculean task during the war when
one demand after another piled on him. Just when he needed
someone who could encourage him in all the writing he would do
during the war—and without realizing at the time that he needed
someone like him—Charles Williams appeared in Oxford. Just as
suddenly, Williams was gone. The loss was tremendous because
Lewis would never again have a friend quite like Williams. Yet he
found that he was all right. He would miss Williams, but his death
did not crush Lewis. He found that the things he believed about
Jesus Christ actually mattered in day-to-day experience. What he
believed was not only true; it made a difference in life.

Life would go on after the war. Lewis would continue to grow
and find new work to do. He could return to the things he wanted
to do. He had spent six years doing his duty and writing what
other people wanted him to write. He had written what he would
never have written on his own. Yet the apologetics that he wrote
when he put his own work on the shelf has endured as a legacy
affecting millions of lives. He had attacked the philosophical assumptions of his age and made his voice heard. Under the influence of W. T. Kirkpatrick, he had thought he would become a
philosopher, but once he had made his mark at Oxford, he realized
that he loved stories more than philosophy. With the war over, he
was free to study and teach about stories again. He could complete his massive account titled *English Literature in the Sixteenth
Century*. Perhaps he might even write some stories.

Epilogue

C. S. Lewis denied having an emotional conversion. He stressed the part played by reason. Some people have interpreted him to mean that his conversion did not involve his emotions. His lengthy discussion of the relationship between the head and the belly in *The Abolition of Man* should impress upon us the extent to which he valued the totality of what it means to be human and the wholeness of a person, involving the intellect and the emotions mediated by character. An emotional conversion during the first half of the twentieth century was understood in relation to ecstatic experiences as in the Azusa Street Revival of 1906, when people began speaking in tongues. An emotional conversion meant the kind of experiences associated with the revival meetings of Billy Sunday, which had their counterparts in the Salvation Army meetings in England. In that sense, Lewis did not have an emotional conversion, but his conversion involved his emotions.

The part in his conversion played by his intellect would have remained fruitless except for the recurring experience of deep longing that seized him when he least expected it. While his mind carried on a dogged examination of reality, his emotions experienced something coming at him from the outside. Then he realized that his values, and value itself, were coming at him from outside. His reason and his emotions were in harmony in his conversion.

The remarkable thing about his conversion, however, is the effect it had on his character. Before his conversion he never had any intellectual interest in immortality or life beyond the grave. His conversion was not about going to heaven when he died, though he accepted that aspect of it gratefully as part of the bargain. His conversion centered on knowing the truth about reality. When he discovered the truth, he realized that Truth was a personal being who created everything and then entered into that creation. He not only knew about God with his reason but also met God with his emotions. He experienced Joy. And God changed him.

Lewis examined the relationship of intellect, emotions, and character in *The Abolition of Man*. He had actually introduced the interplay in *The Pilgrim's Regress* a decade earlier, as its subtitle indicates: *An Allegorical Apology for Christianity, Reason and Romanticism*. After giving the Riddell lectures at Durham in 1943, published as *The Abolition of Man*, Lewis issued a third edition of *The Pilgrim's Regress* in 1943 with a new preface, in which he explained that by romanticism he meant the experience of "intense longing," which he called Joy in *Surprised by Joy*.[1] This experience involves the feelings of pain and delight at the same time. What we have with his preface is an example of how Lewis grew in his understanding over time. Reflecting on the issue of relative values that prompted *The Abolition of Man*, he grew in his understanding of the relationship between reason and emotion in general and in his own experience in particular. He continued to become more self-aware.

Owen Barfield frequently commented that he never changed his mind about anything but Lewis was always changing his mind. To change the mind is the meaning of the word in the Bible that is usually translated "repentance." Lewis was always submitting his life to Christ to be changed. He was always renewing his mind. He understood the New Testament concept of the atonement as involving dying with Christ. He continually submitted habits and attitudes to be killed, as he graphically portrayed in *The Great Divorce*. How this happened appeared in little ways over many years.

In his early years as an undergraduate and later as a young fellow at Magdalen, Lewis made many offhand remarks about other undergraduates at Oxford or fellows at Cambridge whose vulgar (i.e., unsophisticated and socially inferior) speech betrayed them as not real gentlemen. They were not the sort with whom he could become seriously acquainted. He was a snob and had been for years. After his conversion, however, he began to change. His attitude toward other people began to change. By 1939, he could love the company of a funny little man with the crudest of cockney accents. Charles Williams became his dearest friend. Such a change in Lewis is remarkable.

Barfield accused Lewis of insincerity in his "Open Letter to Dr. Tillyard" (published in 1936), in which Lewis spoke graciously and humbly of Tillyard.[2] Barfield claimed that Lewis was guilty of a *pastiche voulu*—a feigned imitation designed to win Tillyard's approval.[3] At the conclusion of his "Open Letter," Lewis had acknowledged that he was "engaged with an 'older and a better soldier,'" and he ended by writing that even if Tillyard thought him "too pert you will not suspect me of malice. If you honour me with a reply it will be kind; and then, God defend the right!"[4] Barfield is correct that the passage does not sound like the old Jack Lewis he knew when he was still in Oxford, but Barfield was commenting on something Lewis wrote some six years after Barfield moved to London. More significantly, it was five years after Lewis's conversion to faith in Christ. How far apart the two friends had grown in the interval is reflected in Barfield's observation in the same essay that "a great change" took place in Lewis between 1930 and 1940 but that Barfield thought it had nothing to do with Lewis's conversion.[5] I think Barfield was mistaken. After his conversion, Lewis grew more courteous toward his opponents in debate and controversy. His conversion tended to encourage his appropriation of the medieval ideal of courtly combat into his own mode of thought and behavior. His involvement in the Socratic Club demonstrates this aspect of Lewis, for he remained a vigorous and formidable debate opponent, but always with courtesy.

At the time of his conversion, Lewis wrote to Arthur Greeves about his struggle with temptation, the *bellum intestinum* that formed a central focus of *The Allegory of Love*. By the time that internal war came again, he had become so self-aware and spiritually aware of others, he could write powerfully about the experience of temptation in *The Screwtape Letters* and *The Great Divorce* in a way that helped other people see their own shortcomings as nice people. Lewis himself had become a nice person, though he would have deplored such a designation. Perhaps it would be nicer to say that he had become a pleasant person to be around. He was no longer the young man who constantly found fault with his father.

After his conversion, Lewis had deep remorse for how he had treated his father. To his credit, he felt both shame and remorse. Yet grace came to him. In almost every letter he wrote to his brother at the beginning of the Second World War, he had some little reference to a funny event that reminded him of his father. These comments were different from those in his letters in the 1920s, in which he ridiculed his father with contempt. In the later letters, his comments were laced with an affectionate longing for someone he now missed. Such is the way of grace.

The change in Lewis's character did not occur without him being aware of it. Lewis's uncomplaining surrender to Mrs. Moore's bonded servitude baffled his brother, but we know from Jack's letters that he hated to be interrupted. He hated for his time to be intruded upon by someone else. We also know from his letters that he was glad he could perform the duties to Mrs. Moore that he had failed to perform for his father. He was not doing penance. He did not feel guilt. Instead, he had embraced the New Testament value of forbearance (not insisting on one's own rights) and the model of Christ in serving others. He also knew that his greatest temptation had always been toward pride. In his letters to Arthur Greeves during his middle years after his conversion, he regularly apologized for his arrogance, which had been so pronounced when they were young, with the hope that he did not behave that way anymore. The biblical value in opposition to pride is humility. It is one of the hallmarks of courtly love that Lewis explored in *The Allegory of Love*. It went along with his embracing the chivalric ideal of duty. He had no sense of duty to his father before his conversion, and he deeply regretted that for the rest of his life.

One of the first things that began to happen in Lewis's life in the context of his conversion was reconciliation with Warnie, Arthur Greeves, and Leo Baker. Jack had drifted away from his primary relationships between his teenage years and his early twenties. He rarely wrote to his brother or to Greeves in the 1920s until the final stage of his conversion mounted into a crisis. He wanted to be close to Warnie and Arthur again. He changed his mind about what was important and how he judged people. Reconciling with Leo Baker took a few years longer, but growth takes time.

The other striking thing about the middle years of C. S. Lewis is the way his youth prepared him for his life's work, both professionally and as a Christian. The books he read for fun when he lived with W. T. Kirkpatrick became his livelihood. Because he had read so deeply and so widely for pleasure as a teenager, he was able to do the English literature degree at Oxford in one year, which opened the way for his fellowship at Magdalen College. He knew this about himself, and in his letters he commented on why his literature studies had been relatively easy during a year that was emotionally draining. The stories he loved as a teenager became his scholarly specialty and the basis for the academic reputation he established with the publication of *The Allegory of Love* and *A Preface to Paradise Lost*. The medieval world that he once described to Greeves in his letters would occupy his teaching and writing through the end of his life with his last two scholarly books, both published posthumously: *The Discarded Image* and *Spenser's Images of Life*.

The apologetic writing that Lewis undertook during World War II also depended upon his experience at Great Bookham with Kirkpatrick. Kirk gave Lewis the intellectual reasoning he needed to provide a foundation for his atheism, but at the same time, he gave Lewis the critical tools that would tear his atheism to pieces from the inside. When Lewis wrote about materialism, he did so from the point of view of a materialist who understood materialism inside out. He would regularly write about seeing something from the other way round. He grasped this way of thinking from experience. He knew the materialist objections to Christian faith because they had been *his* objections. He could never have written *The Problem of Pain*, *Mere Christianity*, *The Abolition of Man*, or *Miracles* if he had not already thoroughly fathomed the territory he covered. He understood it not only as a well-read Christian but also as someone who had viewed Christianity with hostile skepticism.

As someone who had been there and back again, Lewis was versed in the journey of life that had first stabbed his heart in the stories of Morris, Malory, Spenser, Bunyan, and MacDonald. He learned that the journey was his story too. He understood that he was still in the midst of his own journey, and he did not know what would come next. As a self-aware Christian, however, he knew his own story well enough to tell it, however obliquely, in *The Pilgrim's Regress*, then to objectify this same story in his broadcast talks, and then to pick out episodes of his own experience and the experiences of others he knew to present as mirrors for the readers of *The Screwtape Letters* and *The Great Divorce*. Lewis's atheism prepared him to be an apologist. Though he lived a relatively dull and ordinary life, his spiritual journey has managed to speak to millions of other people, perhaps because most of us also live rather dull and ordinary lives.

During his middle years, Lewis also learned to deal with the demands that come with relationships. In the 1920s, when he tired of an acquaintance or when maintaining a relationship proved inconvenient at a distance, he simply let it go. Mrs. Moore's gaiety and geniality declined steadily as she aged. Her physical complaints increased yearly as her mood grew more irritable. Life at the Kilns became one long, tense squabble between Mrs. Moore, Maureen, and the maids who came and went with shocking regularity. No one would work for Mrs. Moore for long. In this environment, Warren Lewis turned to alcohol to numb the distress. Amid this deteriorating situation, Lewis had to keep an even temper and hold the house together. It all took its toll on him. Until his conversion, Lewis's strategy for dealing with unpleasantness had been flight, avoidance, and disengagement. He had used this strategy with his father and brother. After his conversion, he poured himself into his relationships in spite of the shortcomings of those he cared about. He had even learned that he had shortcomings of his own.

By 1945, however, Lewis knew that one episode of his life had come to an end. He had begun turning down invitations to speak on the BBC a year before the end of the war because he knew he had finished what he had to say about the big matters that concerned him. He had done his duty. He had accomplished what he set out to do. He had no more interest in writing apologetics. *Perelandra* had been the book he most enjoyed writing. Perhaps he could finally return to fiction. In 1945, however, he did not know what would come next. He would discover that what came next already had its foundation laid in what had gone before, but the last stage of his journey would be through entirely different territory than he had previously traveled.

In 1939, Lewis was a vigorous man who had just entered middle age. By 1945, however, he felt like a man entering old age. Mrs. Moore had seen a steady decline in her health, but so had Lewis. Throughout the 1920s and 1930s, the man who had hated organized sports relished ten- and twenty-mile romps across the countryside. Throughout the war years, his demanding schedule meant that he had to abandon his long daily walks and major walking tours. He always smoked to excess, and except for

Warnie's binges, he tended to drink as much as his brother. Even his beloved tea, which he drank four to six times a day, meant that he was consuming too much caffeine for a man whose physician cousin had told him that he had advancing kidney problems. In terms of his diet, Lewis was not being cavalier with his health. He seriously thought that smoking was good for his lungs, which always tended to sickliness, and alcohol was good for his constitution. Without his regular, vigorous exercise, which he had pursued for pleasure rather than health, Lewis's body began to decline.

In the face of all he went through while maintaining an ordinary routine that might lead someone to discouragement, if not despair, Lewis did not become a complainer. In fact, he stopped being a complainer. In his pre-conversion letters to his brother and to Greeves, Lewis complained about almost everything with ease. It almost appears that he complained simply to stay in practice, but that aspect of his character all but disappeared by wartime. He was experiencing what the New Testament calls sanctification— the process by which the Holy Spirit works in a life over time, gradually to change a person to reflect the character of Christ. Lewis was experiencing the supernatural in himself.

In the last stage of his life, Lewis would see many changes to his routine. Lewis liked routine. He did not like change. Yet the last years of his life would be one long series of major changes. Mrs. Moore would die. He would leave the familiarity of Oxford for Cambridge. Freed from his wartime writing obligations, he would devote more time to his teaching and academic writing. He would change the focus of his nonacademic writing. He would marry, and then fall in love—in that order. He would grow old. He would give up old pleasures of twenty-mile walks and swimming in icy water. And he would continue to change his mind.

Notes

Chapter 1: Return to Oxford

1. Walter Hooper, ed., *The Collected Letters of C. S. Lewis*, vol. 1 (New York: HarperSanFrancisco, 2004), 374. Lewis informed Arthur Greeves of this information about his wounds.

2. Hooper, *Letters*, 1:417. Jack mentioned these continuing problems seven months after his injuries, and he would mention them in his letters and diary throughout the 1920s.

3. Hooper, *Letters*, 1:372.

4. Hooper, *Letters*, 1:386–87.

5. Hooper, *Letters*, 1:369. Mrs. Moore did not receive confirmation of her son's death until September. See 1:400.

6. Hooper, *Letters*, 1:387.

7. Hooper, *Letters*, 1:391.

8. "Memoirs of the Lewis Family, 1850–1930," ed. Warren Hamilton Lewis (Marion Wade Center Collection, Wheaton College), 6:19.

9. "Memoirs," 6:38.

10. Hooper, *Letters*, 1:403–4.

11. Hooper, *Letters*, 1:416.

12. Hooper, *Letters*, 1:418.

13. Hooper, *Letters*, 1:421.

14. Hooper, *Letters*, 1:423.

15. Hooper, *Letters*, 1:416.

16. "Memoirs," 6:85.

17. "Memoirs," 6:44–45.

18. "Memoirs," 6:73.

19. "Memoirs," 6:74.

20. "Memoirs," 6:79.

21. Hooper, *Letters*, 1:378.

22. Hooper, *Letters*, 1:389.

23. Hooper, *Letters*, 1:392.

24. "Memoirs," 6:31.

25. Hooper, *Letters*, 1:396.

26. "Memoirs," 6:38.
27. Hooper, *Letters*, 1:399.
28. Hooper, *Letters*, 1:400.
29. "Memoirs," 6:48.
30. Hooper, *Letters*, 1:409.
31. Hooper, *Letters*, 1:410.
32. Hooper, *Letters*, 1:443.
33. "Memoirs," 6:98.
34. Hooper, *Letters*, 1:443.
35. Hooper, *Letters*, 1:443.
36. Hooper, *Letters*, 1:446.
37. Hooper, *Letters*, 1:457.
38. Hooper, *Letters*, 1:453–54.
39. "Memoirs," 6:103.
40. "Memoirs," 6:104.
41. "Memoirs," 6:106, 119.
42. "Memoirs," 6:93.
43. C. S. Lewis, *Surprised by Joy* (London: Bles, 1955), 176–77.
44. Hooper, *Letters*, 1:425–26.
45. Hooper, *Letters*, 1:448.
46. Hooper, *Letters*, 1:426.
47. Hooper, *Letters*, 1:444.
48. "Memoirs," 6:108.
49. "Memoirs," 6:113.
50. "Memoirs," 6:118.
51. Hooper, *Letters*, 1:438.
52. Hooper, *Letters*, 1:434. He loved Homer and Virgil, about whom he wrote in *A Preface to Paradise Lost*. Cicero and Demosthenes, on the other hand, he had referred to as "The Two Great Bores." See Lewis, *Surprised by Joy*, 137.
53. Hooper, *Letters*, 1:408.
54. A. N. Wilson, *C. S. Lewis: A Biography* (New York: Norton, 1990), 62.
55. Hooper, *Letters*, 1:304.
56. Hooper, *Letters*, 1:296.
57. Hooper, *Letters*, 1:444.
58. Hooper, *Letters*, 1:429–30.
59. Hooper, *Letters*, 1:430.
60. Hooper, *Letters*, 1:435.
61. Hooper, *Letters*, 1:430, 441, 448, 453, 526, 528.
62. Hooper, *Letters*, 1:438.
63. Hooper, *Letters*, 1:432–33.
64. Hooper, *Letters*, 1:441.
65. Hooper, *Letters*, 1:453.
66. Lewis, *Surprised by Joy*, 116.

67. Hooper, *Letters*, 1:455.
68. Lewis, *Surprised by Joy*, 121.
69. Hooper, *Letters*, 1:455.
70. Hooper, *Letters*, 1:451–52. This information, which is included in an explanatory section by Walter Hooper, comes from the extensive collection of Lewis family papers edited by Warren Lewis. See "Memoirs," 6:118, 123, 129.
71. Hooper, *Letters*, 1:463.
72. Walter Hooper, ed., *All My Road before Me: The Diary of C. S. Lewis, 1922–1927* (New York: Harcourt Brace Jovanovich, 1991), 252.
73. In his letter to Arthur on February 9, 1919, Jack remarked that "the family" was surprised to see how handsome Arthur was from his photograph. See Hooper, *Letters*, 1:433.
74. The name does not appear in print prior to the first correspondence with Arthur after his Oxford visit. See Hooper, *Letters*, 1:460. It is believed that the name derives from her love of a candy named "Minto." See Wilson, *C. S. Lewis*, 92. Marjorie Lamp Mead and Clyde S. Kilby provided this explanation in Kilby and Mead, eds., *Brothers and Friends: The Diaries of Major Warren Hamilton Lewis* (New York: Harper & Row, 1982), 35n56. Apparently, "Minto" was a Jack Lewis derivative of Nuttao's Peppermint Candy.
75. Hooper, *Diary*, 252.
76. Hooper, *Letters*, 1:265.
77. "Memoirs," 6:115.
78. Hooper, *Letters*, 1:456–57.
79. "Memoirs," 6:125.
80. "Memoirs," 6:128.
81. "Memoirs," 6:145.
82. Hooper, *Letters*, 1:461.
83. "Memoirs," 6:160.
84. "Memoirs," 6:161.
85. Hooper, *Letters*, 1:462. In an amplification, Hooper quotes this passage from Albert's diary in "Memoirs," 6:167.
86. "Memoirs," 6:162.
87. Hooper, *Letters*, 1:462.
88. Hooper, *Letters*, 1:463.
89. Hooper, *Letters*, 1:463.
90. Hooper, *Letters*, 1:465.
91. Leo Baker, "Near the Beginning," in *C. S. Lewis at the Breakfast Table*, ed. James T. Como (New York: Macmillan, 1979), 3.
92. Baker, "Near the Beginning," 4.
93. Baker, "Near the Beginning," 4. The precise term he used was "ebullient."
94. Baker, "Near the Beginning," 7–8.
95. Baker, "Near the Beginning," 6.

96. Baker, "Near the Beginning," 3.
97. Baker, "Near the Beginning," 6.
98. Baker, "Near the Beginning," 6.
99. Baker, "Near the Beginning," 6.
100. Baker, "Near the Beginning," 7, 9.
101. Hooper, *Letters*, 1:474n7.
102. Hooper, *Letters*, 1:477.
103. Hooper, *Letters*, 1:488n36.
104. Hooper, *Letters*, 1:477n14.
105. Hooper, *Letters*, 1:479.
106. Hooper, *Letters*, 1:476, 478.
107. Hooper, *Letters*, 1:495.
108. Hooper, *Letters*, 1:473, 495.
109. Hooper, *Letters*, 1:488.
110. Hooper, *Letters*, 1:487, 493–94, 497, 499.
111. Hooper, *Letters*, 1:494.
112. Lewis, *Surprised by Joy*, 193.
113. Several people have undertaken studies of Lewis's conversion. Two particularly helpful ones are David C. Downing, *The Most Reluctant Convert* (Downers Grove, IL: InterVarsity Press, 2002), and Joel Heck, *From Atheism to Christianity: The Story of C. S. Lewis* (St. Louis, MO: Concordia, 2017).
114. Hooper, *Letters*, 1:485.
115. Hooper, *Letters*, 1:505.
116. Hooper, *Letters*, 1:492.
117. Hooper, *Letters*, 1:492n46.
118. Hooper, *Letters*, 1:494.
119. Hooper, *Letters*, 1:505.
120. Hooper, *Letters*, 1:507.
121. Hooper, *Letters*, 1:513.
122. Hooper, *Letters*, 1:509.
123. Hooper, *Letters*, 1:509.
124. Hooper, *Letters*, 1:520.
125. Hooper, *Letters*, 1:511–12.
126. Hooper, *Letters*, 1:512.
127. Hooper, *Letters*, 1:517.
128. Hooper, *Letters*, 1:522.
129. Hooper, *Letters*, 1:528.
130. Hooper, *Letters*, 1:522.
131. "Memoirs," 6:254.
132. Hooper, *Letters*, 1:526.
133. Hooper, *Letters*, 1:527.
134. Hooper, *Letters*, 1:529n35.
135. Hooper, *Letters*, 1:530–31.
136. Hooper, *Letters*, 1:533.

137. Hooper, *Letters*, 1:534.
138. Hooper, *Letters*, 1:564–65.
139. Walter Hooper, ed., *The Collected Letters of C. S. Lewis*, vol. 2 (New York: HarperSanFrancisco, 2004), 67.
140. Hooper, *Letters*, 1:534.
141. Hooper, *Letters*, 1:535.
142. Hooper, *Letters*, 1:535.
143. Hooper, *Letters*, 1:536.
144. Hooper, *Letters*, 1:539–40.
145. "Memoirs," 6:292.
146. Hooper, *Letters*, 1:543.
147. Hooper, *Letters*, 1:547–48.
148. Lewis, *Surprised by Joy*, 191.
149. Hooper, *Letters*, 1:544.
150. Hooper, *Letters*, 1:549, 551.
151. "Memoirs," 6:320.
152. "Memoirs," 6:320.
153. Hooper, *Letters*, 1:564.
154. Hooper, *Letters*, 1:554.
155. Hooper, *Letters*, 1:557.
156. Hooper, *Letters*, 1:555.
157. Paul Carus published *The Gospel of Buddha* in 1894 following his attendance of the Parliament of the World's Religions in 1893. Intent on discovering a new religion based on modern science, Carus rewrote what Buddhist texts he could find and inserted them into his book modeled on the line of the New Testament Gospels.
158. Hooper, *Letters*, 1:567.
159. Hooper, *Letters*, 1:567–68.
160. Hooper, *Letters*, 1:568.
161. Hooper, *Letters*, 1:569.
162. Hooper, *Letters*, 1:570–84.
163. "Memoirs," 7:84–85.
164. Hooper, *Letters*, 1:586.
165. Hooper, *Letters*, 1:588.
166. "Memoirs," 7:96.
167. Hooper, *Letters*, 1:591–92.
168. Hooper, *Letters*, 1:594–96.
169. Hooper, *Letters*, 1:596–98.
170. Hooper, *Letters*, 1:600–602.

Chapter 2: From Philosophy to Literature

1. Walter Hooper, ed., *All My Road before Me: The Diary of C. S. Lewis, 1922–1927* (New York: Harcourt Brace Jovanovich, 1991), 54, 110, 111, 152.
2. Hooper, *Diary*, 81.

3. Alister McGrath, *C. S. Lewis: A Life* (Carol Stream, IL: Tyndale, 2013), 74.
4. Hooper, *Diary*, 17. Such a crisis arose when Lewis first began keeping his diary.
5. Hooper, *Diary*, 17n13.
6. Jack's sickliness continued throughout his early days in Oxford. Hooper, *Diary*, 18, 22, 52, 61, 62, 66, 87, 103, 104, 121, 126, 133, 134, 139, 155, 157, 159, 161, 165, 192, 224, 229, 249, 250, 251, 268, 279, 281, 283, 284, 307, 314, 324, 331, 337, 345, 350, 358, 382, 386, 395, 414, 415, 425, 435, 442, 451, 456; Walter Hooper, ed., *The Collected Letters of C. S. Lewis*, vol. 1 (New York: HarperSanFrancisco, 2004), 714, 722, 749, 768, 792, 800, 883, 892, 922, 937, 939, 956, 961.
7. Hooper, *Diary*, 29–30.
8. Mrs. Moore's ailments increased year after year. Hooper, *Diary*, 18, 29, 32, 35, 36, 40, 41, 52, 54, 71, 74, 77, 84, 95, 123, 128, 130, 135, 139, 140, 145, 146, 149, 151, 161, 170, 196, 200, 222, 228, 256, 272, 278, 279, 283, 303, 304, 306, 307, 323, 328, 345, 351, 354, 355, 359, 364, 365, 366, 367, 369, 372, 381, 387, 389, 397, 407, 414, 422, 423, 430, 439, 447, 455; Hooper, *Letters*, 1:927, 952, 960.
9. Lewis continued to be drawn to Shotover Hill until he finally moved there. Hooper, *Diary*, 24, 50, 51, 63, 66, 67, 68, 69, 73, 77, 121, 124, 127, 139, 142, 154, 206, 236, 259, 285, 289, 299, 323, 331, 332, 349, 354, 394, 396, 405, 422, 427, 428, 429, 430, 431, 436, 440, 441, 446, 447, 450, 451, 452.
10. Hooper, *Diary*, 22.
11. Hooper, *Diary*, 41.
12. Hooper, *Diary*, 40.
13. Hooper, *Diary*, 34.
14. Hooper, *Diary*, 35.
15. Hooper, *Diary*, 26–27.
16. The poem appeared in *The Beacon*, 3, no. 31 (May 1924): 444–45, and may also be found in Lewis's *Collected Poems*.
17. Hooper, *Diary*, 30.
18. Hooper, *Diary*, 34.
19. Hooper, *Diary*, 37.
20. Hooper, *Diary*, 44. He also read H. Crichton Miller, *The New Psychology and the Teacher* (Hooper, *Diary*, 62); W. H. R. Rivers, *Instinct and the Unconscious* (Hooper, *Diary*, 64); R. H. Hingley, *Psychoanalysis* (Hooper, *Diary*, 70); Havelock Ellis, *Psychology of Sex* (Hooper, *Diary*, 75). For an examination of Lewis and Freud, see Armand M. Nicholi Jr., *The Question of God: C. S. Lewis and Sigmund Freud Debate God, Love, Sex, and the Meaning of Life* (New York: Free Press, 2002).
21. Hooper, *Diary*, 45.
22. Hooper, *Diary*, 48.
23. Hooper, *Diary*, 134.

24. Hooper, *Diary*, 48.
25. Hooper, *Diary*, 51.
26. Hooper, *Diary*, 49.
27. Hooper, *Diary*, 54.
28. Hooper, *Diary*, 49.
29. Hooper, *Diary*, 57.
30. Hooper, *Diary*, 76.
31. Hooper, *Diary*, 67.
32. Hooper, *Diary*, 72, 73.
33. Hooper, *Diary*, 75.
34. Hooper, *Diary*, 74, 114.
35. Hooper, *Diary*, 78.
36. Hooper, *Diary*, 79, 80, 81.
37. Hooper, *Diary*, 79.
38. Hooper, *Diary*, 96.
39. Hooper, *Diary*, 80.
40. Hooper, *Diary*, 85–86.
41. Hooper, *Diary*, 91.
42. Hooper, *Diary*, 94.
43. Hooper, *Diary*, 96.
44. Hooper, *Diary*, 97.
45. Hooper, *Diary*, 100–101.
46. Hooper, *Diary*, 108.
47. Hooper, *Diary*, 104.
48. Hooper, *Diary*, 108.
49. Hooper, *Diary*, 112.
50. Hooper, *Diary*, 113.
51. Hooper, *Diary*, 138.
52. Hooper, *Diary*, 145.
53. Hooper, *Diary*, 118.
54. Hooper, *Diary*, 119.
55. Hooper, *Diary*, 120.
56. Hooper, *Diary*, 120.
57. Hooper, *Diary*, 121.
58. Hooper, *Diary*, 121–22.
59. Hooper, *Diary*, 140–41.
60. Hooper, *Diary*, 141.
61. Hooper, *Diary*, 127.
62. Hooper, *Diary*, 128.
63. Hooper, *Diary*, 154.
64. Hooper, *Diary*, 135.
65. Hooper, *Diary*, 136.
66. Hooper, *Diary*, 142.
67. Hooper, *Diary*, 143.
68. Hooper, *Diary*, 148.

69. Hooper, *Diary*, 148.
70. Hooper, *Diary*, 152.
71. Hooper, *Diary*, 156.
72. Hooper, *Diary*, 157, 155.
73. Hooper, *Diary*, 177.
74. Hooper, *Diary*, 180.
75. Hooper, *Diary*, 183.
76. Hooper, *Diary*, 185–86.
77. Hooper, *Diary*, 189.
78. Hooper, *Diary*, 190–91.
79. Hooper, *Diary*, 192n7, 193n8–9. See also C. S. Lewis, *Selected Literary Essays*, ed. Walter Hooper (Cambridge: Cambridge University Press, 1969). Hooper includes many of Coghill's minutes in the preface.
80. C. S. Lewis, *Surprised by Joy* (London: Bles, 1955), 201.
81. Lewis, *Surprised by Joy*, 201.
82. Reynolds Price, *Ardent Spirits: Leaving Home, Coming Back* (New York: Scribner, 2009), 128.
83. Hooper, *Diary*, 195.
84. Price, *Ardent Spirits*, 128.
85. Hooper, *Diary*, 198.
86. Hooper, *Diary*, 201.
87. Hooper, *Diary*, 202.
88. Hooper, *Diary*, 202.
89. Hooper, *Diary*, 203–4.
90. Hooper, *Diary*, 205.
91. Hooper, *Diary*, 214.
92. Hooper, *Diary*, 210.
93. Hooper, *Diary*, 212.
94. Hooper, *Diary*, 213.
95. Hooper, *Diary*, 220.
96. Hooper, *Diary*, 219.
97. Hooper, *Diary*, 221.
98. Lewis, *Surprised by Joy*, 191–93.
99. Hooper, *Diary*, 222–24.
100. Hooper, *Diary*, 224.
101. Hooper, *Diary*, 81, 82, 84, 86, 87, 89, 91, 93, 227, 263, 402.
102. Hooper, *Diary*, 229.
103. Hooper, *Diary*, 229–30.
104. Hooper, *Diary*, 231.
105. Hooper, *Letters*, 1:605.
106. Hooper, *Diary*, 225, 233, 235.
107. Hooper, *Letters*, 1:607–8. He had heard the rumor from Edgar Frederick Carritt, Lewis's philosophy tutor. See Hooper, *Diary*, 234.
108. Hooper, *Letters*, 1:609–11.
109. Hooper, *Diary*, 238.

110. Hooper, *Diary*, 242.
111. Hooper, *Diary*, 243–45.
112. Hooper, *Diary*, 245–46.
113. Hooper, *Diary*, 247.
114. Hooper, *Diary*, 247.
115. Hooper, *Diary*, 254.
116. Hooper, *Diary*, 255.
117. Hooper, *Diary*, 257, 258.
118. Hooper, *Diary*, 258.
119. Hooper, *Letters*, 1:613.
120. Hooper, *Diary*, 261.
121. Hooper, *Letters*, 1:613.
122. Hooper, *Letters*, 1:613.
123. Hooper, *Diary*, 262–63.
124. Hooper, *Diary*, 261, 266.
125. Hooper, *Diary*, 265.
126. Hooper, *Diary*, 269, 271.
127. Hooper, *Diary*, 266. Portions of these early attempts survive in Warnie Lewis's collected papers of the Lewis family. See "Memoirs of the Lewis Family, 1850–1930," ed. Warren Hamilton Lewis (Marion Wade Center Collection, Wheaton College), 8:163.
128. Hooper, *Diary*, 270.
129. Hooper, *Diary*, 271.
130. Hooper, *Letters*, 1:614–15.
131. Hooper, *Diary*, 278.
132. Lewis, *Surprised by Joy*, 196.
133. Hooper, *Diary*, 281.
134. Hooper, *Diary*, 282–83.
135. Hooper, *Diary*, 283, 285.
136. Hooper, *Diary*, 285.
137. Hooper, *Letters*, 1:619.
138. Hooper, *Diary*, 288.
139. Hooper, *Diary*, 290.
140. Hooper, *Diary*, 291.
141. Hooper, *Diary*, 292.
142. Hooper, *Diary*, 294, 296; Hooper, *Letters*, 1:620–24.
143. Hooper, *Diary*, 297–98.
144. For an examination of their dispute, see Lionel Adey, *C. S. Lewis's "Great War" with Owen Barfield* (Victoria, BC: University of Victoria, 1978). Adey's study concludes that Barfield's influence will be far more long-lasting because of his 1926 book *Poetic Diction*. In 1978, he regarded Lewis's time as having passed and his apologetic works as having lost their appeal.
145. Lewis, *Surprised by Joy*, 205.
146. Hooper, *Diary*, 301.

147. Lewis, *Surprised by Joy*, 205–7.
148. Hooper, *Diary*, 301.
149. Hooper, *Diary*, 317.
150. Hooper, *Diary*, 305.
151. Hooper, *Diary*, 314.
152. Hooper, *Diary*, 314.
153. Hooper, *Diary*, 317.
154. Hooper, *Diary*, 328.
155. Hooper, *Diary*, 318.
156. Hooper, *Diary*, 320.
157. Hooper, *Diary*, 323.
158. Hooper, *Diary*, 320.
159. Hooper, *Diary*, 335.
160. Hooper, *Diary*, 336–37.
161. Hooper, *Diary*, 338.
162. Hooper, *Diary*, 339.
163. Hooper, *Diary*, 343.
164. Hooper, *Diary*, 343.
165. Hooper, *Diary*, 348.

Chapter 3: From Undergraduate to Fellow

1. Walter Hooper, ed., *The Collected Letters of C. S. Lewis*, vol. 1 (New York: HarperSanFrancisco, 2004), 640.
2. Hooper, *Letters*, 1:642.
3. Hooper, *Letters*, 1:642–46.
4. Hooper, *Letters*, 1:646.
5. Hooper, *Letters*, 1:648.
6. Hooper, *Letters*, 1:649.
7. Walter Hooper, ed., *All My Road before Me: The Diary of C. S. Lewis, 1922–1927* (New York: Harcourt Brace Jovanovich, 1991), 358.
8. Hooper, *Diary*, 359.
9. Hooper, *Letters*, 1:650–51.
10. Hooper, *Letters*, 1:652.
11. Hooper, *Letters*, 1:653.
12. Hooper, *Letters*, 1:668–69.
13. Hooper, *Letters*, 1:654.
14. Hooper, *Letters*, 1:657–60.
15. Hooper, *Letters*, 1:660–62.
16. C. S. Lewis, *Surprised by Joy* (London: Bles, 1955), 210.
17. Hooper, *Letters*, 1:662–63.
18. Hooper, *Letters*, 1:663–64.
19. A. N. Wilson, *C. S. Lewis: A Biography* (New York: Norton, 1990), 101–2.
20. C. S. Lewis, *Dymer*, 2nd ed. (London: Dent, 1950), x. Lewis remarked that when he wrote *Dymer*, he was "an extreme anarchist."

21. For the definitive critical analysis of *Dymer*, and all of Lewis's poetry, see Don W. King, *C. S. Lewis, Poet: The Legacy of His Poetic Impulse* (Kent, OH: Kent State University Press, 2001).
22. Hooper, *Letters*, 1:674.
23. Hooper, *Letters*, 1:664–65.
24. Hooper, *Letters*, 1:670.
25. Hooper, *Letters*, 1:671.
26. Hooper, *Diary*, 394.
27. Hooper, *Diary*, 403. In his diary, Lewis stated only that Hardie took him to the meeting. Joel Heck has suggested that the reference is to Colin Hardie, the brother of Frank Hardie, who would become active with the Inklings in the 1940s. Colin, however, belonged to the English faculty and had no philosophical training like Lewis. Frank, on the other hand, was a philosopher with whom Lewis spent a good deal of time. See Joel D. Heck, *From Atheism to Christianity: The Story of C. S. Lewis* (St. Louis: Concordia, 2017), 118n17. Heck gives an excellent account of Lewis's conversion experience.
28. Hooper, *Diary*, 20, 28, 57, 82, 84, 411, 418, 432.
29. Lewis explained the term in the preface to the second edition of *Dymer* in 1950. See C. S. Lewis, *Dymer*, 2nd ed. (London: Dent, 1950), xi.
30. Lewis mentioned conversations and his own ponderings about Christina dreams in his diary throughout the period 1922–1927. See Hooper, *Diary*, 20, 28, 57, 82, 84, 269, 277, 282, 285, 289, 294, 411, 418, 419, 432, 662–64, 670, 672, 673, 675, 679–80, 682, 699, 701, 715, 758, 794, 861, 911, 924–30, 932, 935, 977.
31. Hooper, *Diary*, 411.
32. George Sayer, *Jack: C. S. Lewis and His Times* (New York: Harper & Row, 1988), 132.
33. C. S. Lewis, *Mere Christianity* (New York: HarperSanFrancisco, 2001), 25.
34. Hooper, *Letters*, 1:699.
35. Hooper, *Letters*, 1:732, 735–36.
36. Hooper, *Diary*, 409, 445.
37. Hooper, *Letters*, 1:732n84.
38. Hooper, *Diary*, 465.
39. Hooper, *Diary*, 381.
40. Hooper, *Letters*, 1:701–2.
41. Hooper, *Diary*, 393.
42. Hooper, *Diary*, 379.
43. Lewis, *Surprised by Joy*, 211.
44. Hooper, *Diary*, 401.
45. Hooper, *Diary*, 382.
46. Hooper, *Diary*, 393.
47. Hooper, *Diary*, 396.
48. Hooper, *Diary*, 396.

49. Hooper, *Diary*, 397.
50. Hooper, *Diary*, 403.
51. Hooper, *Diary*, 405, 406, 414.
52. Hooper, *Diary*, 406.
53. Hooper, *Diary*, 418.
54. Hooper, *Diary*, 306.
55. Hooper, *Letters*, 1:706–10.
56. A proof is a prepress copy of a book on which corrections are marked before the book is corrected, printed, and released. In 1926, Lewis would have received his proof as individual, unbound sheets. A proof copy is the author's last chance to find typographical errors and make minor modifications.
57. Hooper, *Diary*, 410.
58. Hooper, *Diary*, 414.
59. Hooper, *Diary*, 400.
60. Hooper, *Diary*, 412.
61. Hooper, *Diary*, 418.
62. Hooper, *Diary*, 390, 400, 407.
63. Hooper, *Diary*, 419.
64. Lewis, *Surprised by Joy*, 205.
65. Hooper, *Diary*, 421.
66. Hooper, *Diary*, 422.
67. C. S. Lewis, *The Pilgrims Regress*, 3rd ed. (London: Bles, 1943), 5.
68. Hooper, *Diary*, 430.
69. Hooper, *Diary*, 457.
70. Hooper, *Diary*, 431–32.
71. Hooper, *Letters*, 1:685–86.
72. Hooper, *Diary*, 432.
73. Hooper, *Diary*, 439.
74. Hooper, *Letters*, 1:686–87.
75. Hooper, *Letters*, 1:693.
76. Walter Hooper, ed., *The Collected Letters of C. S. Lewis*, vol. 3 (New York: HarperSanFrancisco, 2007), 1605n13.
77. Hooper, *Letters*, 3:1605.
78. Hooper, *Letters*, 3:1609.
79. Owen Barfield, *Owen Barfield on C. S. Lewis*, ed. G. B. Tennyson (Middletown, CT: Wesleyan University Press, 1989), 8.
80. Hooper, *Letters*, 3:1615.
81. Hooper, *Letters*, 3:1617–18.
82. Hooper, *Letters*, 3:1606n14.
83. Hooper, *Letters*, 3:1642–43.
84. Hooper, *Letters*, 3:1611.
85. Hooper, *Letters*, 3:1612.
86. Hooper, *Letters*, 3:1613.
87. Hooper, *Letters*, 3:1620.

88. Hooper, *Letters*, 3:1622.
89. Hooper, *Letters*, 3:1635.
90. Hooper, *Letters*, 3:1636–37.
91. The documents include "Clivi Hamiltonis Summae Metaphysices contra Anthroposophis" (known as "Summa"), by Lewis; "Replicit" and "Autem" ("Reply" and "Further Observations"), by Barfield; "Replies to Objections" and "Note on the Law of Contradiction," by Lewis; "De Bono et Malo" ("Of Good and Bad"), by Lewis; "De Toto et Parte" ("Of the Whole and the Part"), by Barfield; and the unfinished "Commentarium in de Toto et Parte" (Commentary on "Of the Whole and the Part"). For a complete examination of the "Great War" documents, see Lionel Adey, *C. S. Lewis's "Great War" with Owen Barfield* (Victoria, BC: University of Victoria, 1978).
92. Hooper, *Letters*, 3:1643n98.
93. Walter Hooper, ed., *The Collected Letters of C. S. Lewis*, vol. 2 (New York: HarperSanFrancisco, 2004), 107–8.
94. Harry Lee Poe and Rebecca Whitten Poe, eds., *C. S. Lewis Remembered* (Grand Rapids, MI: Zondervan, 2006), 35. Barfield expressed this view at the C. S. Lewis Summer Institute in Oxford, July 1988, during a plenary session, when he was interviewed by Kim Gilnett and Walter Hooper. Barfield made a similar point of emphasis at a meeting of the Oxford C. S. Lewis Society, November 19, 1985. See Barfield, *C. S. Lewis*, 106–7.
95. In *Mere Christianity*, Lewis noted that he was helped on his way to Christianity by people who were not themselves Christians. See p. 190.

Chapter 4: From Idealist to Christian
1. Walter Hooper, ed., *The Collected Letters of C. S. Lewis*, vol. 1 (New York: HarperSanFrancisco, 2004), 676.
2. Hooper, *Letters*, 1:683n12.
3. Hooper, *Letters*, 1:713.
4. Hooper, *Letters*, 1:718–19.
5. Hooper, *Letters*, 1:731.
6. Hooper, *Letters*, 1:731.
7. Hooper, *Letters*, 1:736.
8. Hooper, *Letters*, 1:753.
9. Hooper, *Letters*, 1:699, 749, 754, 764, 766–67.
10. Hooper, *Letters*, 1:779.
11. Hooper, *Letters*, 1:763.
12. Conversation between Emrys Jones and Harry Lee Poe during the C. S. Lewis Summer Institute, July 2002.
13. Hooper, *Letters*, 1:786.
14. Hooper, *Letters*, 1:790.
15. C. S. Lewis, "Learning in Wartime," in *The Weight of Glory*, ed. Walter Hooper (New York: Touchstone, 1996), 48. He would state an

associated idea in *The Abolition of Man* a short time later: "The right defence against false sentiments is to inculcate just sentiments." C. S. Lewis, *The Abolition of Man* (New York: Macmillan, 1955), 24.

16. Hooper, *Letters*, 1:795–96.
17. Hooper, *Letters*, 1:798–99.
18. Hooper, *Letters*, 1:800.
19. Hooper, *Letters*, 1:804.
20. Hooper, *Letters*, 1:807.
21. Hooper, *Letters*, 1:809.
22. Hooper, *Letters*, 1:818.
23. Hooper, *Letters*, 1:822.
24. A. N. Wilson, *C. S. Lewis: A Biography* (New York: Norton, 1990), 128.
25. Hooper, *Letters*, 1:823–25.
26. Hooper, *Letters*, 1:829.
27. Hooper, *Letters*, 1:840–43.
28. Hooper, *Letters*, 1:890–91.
29. Hooper, *Letters*, 1:868–69.
30. Hooper, *Letters*, 1:838.
31. Hooper, *Letters*, 1:838.
32. Hooper, *Letters*, 1:880.
33. J. R. R. Tolkien, *The Lays of Beleriand*, ed. Christopher Tolkien (Boston: Houghton Mifflin, 1985), 150.
34. Tolkien, *Lays of Beleriand*, 151.
35. Humphrey Carpenter, *Tolkien: A Biography* (Boston: Houghton Mifflin, 1977), 85, 92.
36. Tolkien, *Lays of Beleriand*, 151.
37. Carpenter, *Tolkien*, 117, 146.
38. Hooper, *Letters*, 1:855.
39. Hooper, *Letters*, 1:832, 855, 858.
40. Hooper, *Letters*, 1:834.
41. Hooper, *Letters*, 1:860.
42. Hooper, *Letters*, 1:873.
43. Hooper, *Letters*, 1:850.
44. Hooper, *Letters*, 1:853–54.
45. Hooper, *Letters*, 1:858–59.
46. Hooper, *Letters*, 1:862.
47. Hooper, *Letters*, 1:872–73.
48. Hooper, *Letters*, 1:877.
49. Hooper, *Letters*, 1:877.
50. Hooper, *Letters*, 1:878.
51. Hooper, *Letters*, 1:882–83.
52. Hooper, *Letters*, 1:881.
53. C. S. Lewis, *Surprised by Joy* (London: Bles, 1955), 211–15.

54. Alister McGrath, *C. S. Lewis: A Life* (Carol Stream, IL: Tyndale, 2013), 137–46. McGrath argues for a conversion during Trinity term, 1930, but I have suggested Hilary term, 1930.

55. Hooper, *Letters*, 1:887.

56. Hooper, *Letters*, 1:898.

57. Hooper, *Letters*, 1:898.

58. Hooper, *Letters*, 1:899.

59. Hooper, *Letters*, 1:906.

60. Hooper, *Letters*, 1:911–12.

61. Hooper, *Letters*, 1:917–18.

62. Hooper, *Letters*, 1:940.

63. Hooper, *Letters*, 1:897.

64. George Sayer, *Jack: C. S. Lewis and His Times* (New York: Harper & Row, 1988), 141.

65. Wilson, *C. S. Lewis*, 122.

66. Wilson, *C. S. Lewis*, 122.

67. Clyde S. Kilby and Marjorie Lamp Mead, eds., *Brothers and Friends: The Diaries of Major Warren Hamilton Lewis* (New York: Harper & Row, 1982), 68–69.

68. Kilby and Mead, *Brothers and Friends*, 69.

69. Kilby and Mead, *Brothers and Friends*, 70.

70. Kilby and Mead, *Brothers and Friends*, 71.

71. Hooper, *Letters*, 1:943.

72. Hooper, *Letters*, 1:956.

73. Hooper, *Letters*, 1:944–45.

74. Kilby and Mead, *Brothers and Friends*, 73.

75. Owen Barfield, *Owen Barfield on C. S. Lewis*, ed. G. B. Tennyson (Middletown, CT: Wesleyan University Press, 1989), 105. Barfield made the remark to a meeting of the Oxford C. S. Lewis Society, November 19, 1985.

76. Kilby and Mead, *Brothers and Friends*, 76.

77. Kilby and Mead, *Brothers and Friends*, 76.

78. Hooper, *Letters*, 1:947–48.

79. Kilby and Mead, *Brothers and Friends*, 79–80.

80. Hooper, *Letters*, 1:950. By January 1931, he had read, in addition to *Phantastes* and *Lilith*, *Fairy Tales*, *Diary of an Old Soul*, and *What's Mine's Mine*.

81. Hooper, *Letters*, 1:952.

82. Hooper, *Letters*, 1:954.

83. Hooper, *Letters*, 1:957.

84. Hooper, *Letters*, 1:957–58.

85. Hooper, *Letters*, 1:958.

86. Kilby and Mead, *Brothers and Friends*, 84.

87. Hooper, *Letters*, 1:967.

88. Hooper, *Letters*, 1:969.

89. Hooper, *Letters*, 1:970.
90. Hooper, *Letters*, 1:974.
91. Hooper, *Letters*, 1:976.
92. Clive Hamilton [C. S. Lewis], *Dymer* (New York: E. P. Dutton, 1926), ii.
93. Hooper, *Letters*, 1:976–77.
94. Walter Hooper, ed., *All My Road before Me: The Diary of C. S. Lewis, 1922–1927* (New York: Harcourt Brace Jovanovich, 1991), 379; Lewis, *Surprised by Joy*, 211.
95. Hooper, *Letters*, 1:977. In *Surprised by Joy*, Lewis gave a brief synopsis of his thought about how the story of Jesus differed from myth and history, yet was similar to both. See Lewis, *Surprised by Joy*, 221–22.
96. Hooper, *Letters*, 1:970.
97. Hooper, *Letters*, 1:975.
98. Hooper, *Letters*, 1:970–71.
99. Kilby and Mead, *Brothers and Friends*, 86–88.
100. Lewis, *Surprised by Joy*, 223. Alister McGrath has speculated that the conversion might have taken place the following year on a return visit to the zoo, when Jack's elderly friend, Edward Foord-Kelcey, drove him there by car in June 1932 and when the bluebells were in bloom. McGrath raises this question, because in describing how lovely Whipsnade Zoo had once been before modernization, he mentioned the bluebells. In the passage, however, Lewis appears to be remembering Whipsnade in the old days rather than necessarily on the day of his final conversion. Even if he were thinking of the day of his conversion, Lewis tended to conflate time and space so that he associated the beauty of the flowers with the day of his awakening to faith. See McGrath, *C. S. Lewis*, 153–56.
101. Kilby and Mead, *Brothers and Friends*, 89.

Chapter 5: From Poet to Scholar

1. C. S. Lewis, *The Allegory of Love* (London: Oxford University Press, 1936), dedication.
2. Owen Barfield, *Owen Barfield on C. S. Lewis*, ed. G. B. Tennyson (Middletown, CT: Wesleyan University Press, 1989), 73.
3. Barfield, *C. S. Lewis*, 73–74.
4. Barfield, *C. S. Lewis*, 76–77.
5. Joel D. Heck, *From Atheism to Christianity: The Story of C. S. Lewis* (St. Louis, MO: Concordia, 2017), 123.
6. Lewis, *The Allegory of Love*, 45.
7. Lewis, *The Allegory of Love*, 50–51.
8. Lewis, *The Allegory of Love*, 54–55.
9. Lewis, *The Allegory of Love*, 57.
10. C. S. Lewis, *Surprised by Joy* (London: Bles, 1955), 221.
11. Barfield, *C. S. Lewis*, 114.
12. Barfield, *C. S. Lewis*, 113.

13. Barfield, *C. S. Lewis*, 114.
14. Walter Hooper, ed., *The Collected Letters of C. S. Lewis*, vol. 2 (New York: HarperSanFrancisco, 2004), 703.
15. Hooper, *Letters*, 2:106.
16. Lewis, *The Allegory of Love*, 69. John Bunyan wrote several accounts of his spiritual pilgrimage. The most famous of these is his allegorical account, *The Pilgrim's Progress*, which has been printed more than any book except the Bible. Lewis had read *The Pilgrim's Progress* a number of times and was reading it again during the last two years of his conversion. A second book by Bunyan, written in straightforward prose, like Lewis's *Surprised by Joy*, was *Grace Abounding*. A third book, another allegory, was *The Holy War*, which in some ways is Bunyan's version of *Paradise Lost*. The full title is *The Holy War Made by Shaddai upon Diabolis, For the Regaining of the Metropolis of the World; or, The Losing and Taking again of the Town of Mansoul*. Lewis did not believe the war imagery as effective as the journey.
17. Lewis, *The Allegory of Love*, 75.
18. Lewis, *The Allegory of Love*, 75–76.
19. Clyde S. Kilby and Marjorie Lamp Mead, eds., *Brothers and Friends: The Diaries of Major Warren Hamilton Lewis* (New York: Harper & Row, 1982), 92.
20. Humphrey Carpenter, *Tolkien: A Biography* (Boston: Houghton Mifflin, 1977), 137.
21. Hooper, *Letters*, 2:9.
22. Hooper, *Letters*, 2:306, 365.
23. Hooper, *Letters*, 2:16.
24. Hooper, *Letters*, 2:16.
25. Kilby and Mead, *Brothers and Friends*, 95–96.
26. Hooper, *Letters*, 3n5.
27. Hooper, *Letters*, 2:4.
28. Hooper, *Letters*, 2:44.
29. Hooper, *Letters*, 2:31.
30. Hooper, *Letters*, 2:44.
31. Hooper, *Letters* 2:38.
32. Hooper, *Letters*, 2:5.
33. Hooper, *Letters*, 2:7.
34. Hooper, *Letters*, 2:233.
35. Hooper, *Letters*, 2:25.
36. Hooper, *Letters*, 2:19.
37. Hooper, *Letters*, 2:47, 49, 54, 77.
38. Hooper, *Letters*, 2:258.
39. We do not know how often Lewis was ill, but he often pled illness as his excuse for failure to write and complete a task in a timely manner. Hooper, *Letters*, 2:98, 102, 173, 174, 208, 210, 213, 222, 228, 240 247, 253.

40. Hooper, *Letters*, 2:77.
41. Hooper, *Letters*, 2:51.
42. Hooper, *Letters*, 2:78.
43. Hooper, *Letters*, 2:84.
44. Hooper, *Letters*, 2:80, 15.
45. Hooper, *Letters*, 2:93.
46. Hooper, *Letters*, 2:103.
47. Hooper, *Letters*, 2:103.
48. Hooper, *Letters*, 2:94.
49. Hooper, *Letters*, 2:94–95.
50. Hooper, *Letters*, 2:98–99.
51. Hooper, *Letters*, 2:109–10.
52. Hooper, *Letters*, 2:96.
53. Humphrey Carpenter, ed., *The Letters of J. R. R. Tolkien* (London: Allen & Unwin, 1981), 32. Tolkien described the process of writing *The Hobbit* in a letter to the editor of the *Observer* printed on February 20, 1938. For a history and critical analysis of the text of *The Hobbit*, see John D. Rateliff, *The History of the Hobbit*, 2 vols. (Boston: Houghton Mifflin, 2007).
54. Carpenter, *Letters of Tolkien*, 31.
55. Lewis was well aware of the way the Norse stories reflected a dreadful culture. In "First and Second Things," written during World War II, Lewis described the point of Norse mythology. The Vikings served gods whose backs were against the wall and knew that they would be defeated in the end. The gods would fall; thus, the Germanic poetry idealized heroic stands in fighting against all odds. Lewis indicated that it was both paradoxical and foolish of the Nazis to attempt to revive their pre-Christian mythology but to get it all wrong. See C. S. Lewis, "First and Second Things," in *God in the Dock*, ed. Walter Hooper (Grand Rapids, MI: Eerdmans, 1970), 278–79.
56. Tolkien provided the background to the name in a letter to William Luther White, dated September 11, 1967. See William Luther White, *The Image of Man in C. S. Lewis* (Nashville: Abingdon, 1969), 221–22.
57. Hooper, *Letters*, 2:154.
58. Kilby and Mead, *Brothers and Friends*, 97, 105–6.
59. Warren H. Lewis Diaries Collection, Marion E. Wade Center, Wheaton College, Wheaton, IL, vol. 15 (1933), 30.
60. Hooper, *Letters*, 2:183.
61. Hooper, *Letters*, 2:183.
62. Kilby and Mead, *Brothers and Friends*, 125–26.
63. Kilby and Mead, *Brothers and Friends*, 97–98.
64. Kilby and Mead, *Brothers and Friends*, 106.
65. Helen Gardner, "Clive Staples Lewis 1898–1963," *The Proceedings of the British Academy*, 51 (1966): 423.

66. Derek Brewer, "C. S. Lewis: Sixty Years On," in *C. S. Lewis Remembered*, ed. Harry Lee Poe and Rebecca Whitten Poe (Grand Rapids, MI: Zondervan, 2006), 70.
67. Lewis, *The Allegory of Love*, 298.
68. Lewis, *The Allegory of Love*, 339.
69. Lewis, *The Allegory of Love*, 57.
70. Lewis, *The Allegory of Love*, 58–59.
71. Lewis, *The Allegory of Love*, 61.
72. Lewis, *The Allegory of Love*, 96.
73. Hooper, *Letters*, 2:141.
74. A prolegomena is a critical introduction to a subject. The word is related to the word *prologue*.
75. Lewis, *The Allegory of Love*, 75–76.
76. Hooper, *Letters*, 2:180, 183.
77. Hooper, *Letters*, 2:180.
78. Hooper, *Letters*, 2:181.
79. Hooper, *Letters*, 2:198.
80. Hooper, *Letters*, 2:183.
81. Hooper, *Letters*, 2:183.
82. Hooper, *Letters*, 2:184.
83. Hooper, *Letters*, 2:184–85.
84. Hooper, *Letters*, 2:185.
85. Hooper, *Letters*, 2:185.
86. Hooper, *Letters*, 2:186.
87. Hooper, *Letters*, 2:186.
88. Hooper, *Letters*, 2:219.
89. Hooper, *Letters*, 2:227.
90. Hooper, *Letters*, 2:249.

Chapter 6: From Scholar to Novelist

1. "Memoirs of the Lewis Family, 1850–1930," ed. Warren Hamilton Lewis (Marion Wade Center Collection, Wheaton College), 11:8, 10, 15, 28.
2. "Memoirs," 11:3, 10, 12, 17, 22, 29, 30, 31, 33, 154; Clyde S. Kilby and Marjorie Lamp Mead, eds., *Brothers and Friends: The Diaries of Major Warren Hamilton Lewis* (New York: Harper & Row, 1982), 145.
3. Walter Hooper and Roger Lancelyn Green mentioned the Inklings in several places in their early biography of Lewis. See Green and Hooper, *C. S. Lewis: A Biography* (New York: Harcourt Brace Jovanovich, 1974), 173, 184, 186–87. In recent years, several important studies have been written about the Inklings, each of which has its strengths. See Diana Pavlac Glyer, *The Company They Keep: C. S. Lewis and J. R. R. Tolkien as Writers in Community* (Kent, OH: Kent State University Press, 2007); Harry Lee Poe and James Ray Veneman, *The Inklings of Oxford* (Grand Rapids, MI: Zondervan, 2009); Colin Duriez, *The Oxford Inklings* (Oxford: Lion, 2015); Philip Zaleski and Carol Zaleski, *The Fellowship: The*

Literary Lives of the Inklings (New York: Farrar, Straus and Giroux, 2015); Roger White, Judith White, and Brendan N. Wolfe, eds., *C. S. Lewis and His Circle* (New York: Oxford University Press, 2015); Diana Pavlac Glyer, *Bandersnatch: C. S. Lewis, J. R. R. Tolkien, and the Creative Collaboration of the Inklings* (Kent, OH: Black Squirrel, 2016).

4. Roma A. King Jr., ed., *To Michal from Serge: Letters from Charles Williams to His Wife, Florence, 1939–1945* (Kent, OH: Kent State University Press, 2002), 119.
5. Kilby and Mead, *Brothers and Friends*, 145.
6. King, *To Michal from Serge*, 89–90, 151, 158.
7. Robert E. Havard, "Philia: Jack at Ease," in *Remembering C. S. Lewis*, ed. James T. Como, 3rd ed. (San Francisco: Ignatius, 2005), 349–50. This book is the third edition of the book previously published as *C. S. Lewis at the Breakfast Table* (New York: Macmillan, 1979). Roger Lancelyn Green and Walter Hooper stated incorrectly that Havard joined the group in 1940. See Green and Hooper, *C. S. Lewis*, 187.
8. "Memoirs," 11:20, 22, 27, 31.
9. Kilby and Mead, *Brothers and Friends*, 173.
10. "Memoirs," 11:89.
11. Warren H. Lewis Diaries Collection, Marion E. Wade Center, Wheaton College, Wheaton, IL, vol. 15 (1933), 61.
12. W. H. Lewis Diaries, 15:112.
13. "Memoirs," 11:143.
14. "Memoirs," 11:154.
15. "Memoirs," 11:117.
16. Walter Hooper, ed., *The Collected Letters of C. S. Lewis*, vol. 2 (New York: HarperSanFrancisco, 2004), 44.
17. Hooper, *Letters*, 2:214.
18. Hooper, *Letters*, 2:171.
19. Kilby and Mead, *Brothers and Friends*, 96.
20. W. H. Lewis Diaries, 15:23.
21. W. H. Lewis Diaries, 15:41.
22. W. H. Lewis Diaries, 15:45.
23. W. H. Lewis Diaries, 15:51.
24. W. H. Lewis Diaries, 15:117.
25. W. H. Lewis Diaries, 15:129–30.
26. Warren H. Lewis Diaries Collection, Marion E. Wade Center, Wheaton College, Wheaton, IL, vol. 16 (1933), 76.
27. W. H. Lewis Diaries, 16:77.
28. Fred W. Paxford, "'He Should Have Been a Parson': Observations of a Gardener," in *We Remember C. S. Lewis*, ed. David Graham (Nashville: Broadman & Holman, 2001), 123.
29. The Singer Motor Company manufactured cars until it was absorbed into the Rootes Group in 1956. The name continued until 1970, when it was dropped following acquisition by Chrysler.

30. W. H. Lewis Diaries, 16:106.
31. W. H. Lewis Diaries, 16:107.
32. W. H. Lewis Diaries, 16:128.
33. W. H. Lewis Diaries, 16:130–31.
34. Hooper, *Letters*, 2:161.
35. Kilby and Mead, *Brothers and Friends*, 174; C. S. Lewis, *Boxen*, ed. Walter Hooper (New York: Harcourt Brace Jovanovich, 1985), 61ff.
36. Kilby and Mead, *Brothers and Friends*, 174.
37. C. S. Lewis, *Surprised by Joy* (London: Bles, 1955), 212.
38. Walter Hooper, ed., *The Collected Letters of C. S. Lewis*, vol. 1 (New York: HarperSanFrancisco, 2004), 881.
39. Hooper, *Letters*, 1:908.
40. Hooper, *Letters*, 2:55.
41. Hooper, *Letters*, 2:56.
42. Hooper, *Letters*, 2:72.
43. Hooper, *Letters*, 2:73.
44. Hooper, *Letters*, 2:135.
45. Hooper, *Letters*, 2:136.
46. Hooper, *Letters*, 2:178–79.
47. Hooper, *Letters*, 1:969.
48. Hooper, *Letters*, 2:96.
49. Humphrey Carpenter, *Tolkien* (Boston: Houghton Mifflin, 1977), 185.
50. Hooper, *Letters*, 2:223.
51. Carpenter, *Tolkien*, 187.
52. Carpenter, *Tolkien*, 202.
53. Humphrey Carpenter, ed., *The Letters of J. R. R. Tolkien* (London: Allen & Unwin, 1981), 378.
54. For focused treatments of Lewis's science-fiction trilogy, see David C. Downing, *Planets in Peril* (Amherst, MA: University of Massachusetts Press, 1992), and Sanford Schwartz, *C. S. Lewis on the Final Frontier: Science and the Supernatural in the Space Trilogy* (New York: Oxford University Press, 2009).
55. Hooper, *Letters*, 2:151, 236.
56. Hooper, *Letters*, 2:236–37, 254–55.
57. Hooper, *Letters*, 2:216, 262.
58. C. S. Lewis, *The Discarded Image* (Cambridge: Cambridge University Press, 1964).
59. Lewis, *The Discarded Image*, 12.
60. Carpenter, *Letters of Tolkien*, 89.
61. C. S. Lewis, *Out of the Silent Planet* (New York: Macmillan, 1977), 55.
62. Hooper, *Letters*, 2:426–27; C. S. Lewis, "Christian Apologetics," in *God in the Dock*, ed. Walter Hooper (Grand Rapids, MI: Eerdmans, 1970), 93.
63. Lewis, *Out of the Silent Planet*, 35.
64. Hooper, *Letters*, 2:263.

65. To understand the Western attitude toward Asia and Africa in the second half of the nineteenth century, it is helpful to recognize how social Darwinism arose as the logical conclusion to Darwin's theory of natural selection. The full title of his ground-breaking book is *On the Origin of Species, or the Preservation of Favoured Races in the Struggle for Life*. Racism justified by science became institutionalized into the national policy of the European powers and expressed itself in the United States as Manifest Destiny.

66. Hooper, *Letters*, 2:152.

67. Before each of the essays in his collection, Lewis mentioned the general occasion of the lecture, but he neglected to give dates or other details. See C. S. Lewis, *Rehabilitations and Other Essays* (London: Oxford University Press, 1939). Walter Hooper provided the date of the Martlet address in C. S. Lewis, *Selected Literary Essays*, ed. Walter Hooper (Cambridge: Cambridge University Press, 1969), xix.

68. E. M. W. Tillyard and C. S. Lewis, *The Personal Heresy: A Controversy* (London: Oxford University Press, 1939), 1.

69. C. S. Lewis, "An Open Letter to Dr. Tillyard," *Essays and Studies by Members of the English Association*, 21(1936): 161–62.

70. Lewis, "Open Letter to Dr. Tillyard," 165.

71. Hooper, *Letters*, 2:157.

72. Almost everyone who commented on Lewis's lecture style made mention of how easy it was to take notes from him. Not only was his lecture clear: it was given in a slow enough cadence to catch all that he said.

73. Derek Brewer, "The Tutor: A Portrait," in Como, *Remembering C. S. Lewis*, 133.

74. Gervase Mathew, "Orator," in Como, *Remembering C. S. Lewis*, 190.

75. George Watson, "The Art of Disagreement: C. S. Lewis (1909–1963)," in *C. S. Lewis Remembered*, ed. Harry Lee Poe and Rebecca Whitten Poe (Grand Rapids, MI: Zondervan, 2006), 78.

76. Watson, "The Art of Disagreement," 78.

77. Brewer, "The Tutor," 133.

78. Alastair Fowler, "C. S. Lewis: Supervisor," in Poe and Poe, *C. S. Lewis Remembered*, 108.

79. Fowler, "C. S. Lewis: Supervisor," 108.

80. Fowler, "C. S. Lewis: Supervisor," 108.

81. Peter Milward, "What Lewis Has Meant for Me," in Poe and Poe, *C. S. Lewis Remembered*, 187.

82. Milward, "What Lewis Has Meant for Me," 187.

83. Carpenter, *Tolkien*, 117.

84. Helen Tyrrell Wheeler, "Wartime Tutor," in Graham, *We Remember C. S. Lewis*, 51.

85. Green and Hooper, *C. S. Lewis: A Biography*, 56, 62.

86. Humphrey Carpenter, *The Inklings* (Boston: Houghton Mifflin, 1979), 9.
87. Carpenter, *The Inklings*, 12.
88. David Cecil, "Oxford's Magic Circle," *Books and Bookmen* 24, no. 4 (1979): 11.
89. George Sayer, *Jack: C. S. Lewis and His Times* (New York: Harper & Row, 1988), 70.
90. Sayer, *Jack*, 71.
91. A. N. Wilson, *C. S. Lewis: A Biography* (New York: Norton, 1990), xvi.
92. Wilson, *C. S. Lewis*, 53.
93. Wilson, *C. S. Lewis*, 58.
94. Wilson, *C. S. Lewis*, 59.
95. Wilson, *C. S. Lewis*, 66.
96. Alister McGrath, *C. S. Lewis: A Life* (Carol Stream, IL: Tyndale, 2013), 75.
97. George Sayer is particularly helpful in understanding the routine of life at Magdalen College. As one of Lewis's former pupils, he knew by experience how things were done, as did everyone at Magdalen. He assimilated the tradition himself, and his descriptions came not from research in books but from memory of his own life as an undergraduate. See Sayer, *Jack*, 110–17. Each college at Oxford has its own way of doing things, and life at Magdalen was quite different from the life I knew at Regent's Park, a modest little college in St Giles.
98. Adam Fox, "At the Breakfast Table," in Como, *Remembering C. S. Lewis*, 187.
99. Carpenter, *Letters of Tolkien*, 36.
100. Fox, "At the Breakfast Table," 187; Wilson, *C. S. Lewis*, 157.
101. Carpenter, *Letters of Tolkien*, 36. Tolkien had mentioned his local literary club to Unwin before. See p. 29.
102. Nevill Coghill, "The Approach to English," in *Light on C. S. Lewis*, ed. Jocelyn Gibb (London: Bles, 1965), 57.
103. Watson, "The Art of Disagreement, 77.

Chapter 7: From Peace to War
1. Walter Hooper, ed., *The Collected Letters of C. S. Lewis*, vol. 1 (New York: HarperSanFrancisco, 2004), 464, 500, 502.
2. Walter Hooper, ed., *All My Road before Me: The Diary of C. S. Lewis, 1922–1927* (New York: Harcourt Brace Jovanovich, 1991), 289, 382, 384, 385, 387, 388, 389, 393, 394, 395, 416.
3. Walter Hooper, ed., *The Collected Letters of C. S. Lewis*, vol. 2 (New York: HarperSanFrancisco, 2004), 54.
4. Hooper, *Letters*, 2:244.
5. Hooper, *Letters*, 2:303.
6. Hooper, *Letters*, 2:485.
7. Hooper, *Letters*, 2:225–26.

8. For an excellent monograph on the impact of World War II on the writing of Lewis and Tolkien, see Colin Duriez, *Bedeviled: Lewis, Tolkien and the Shadow of Evil* (Downers Grove, IL: InterVarsity Press, 2015).
9. Hooper, *Letters*, 2:225, 231, 232, 233, 234, 240, 248, 250, 251, 258, 260, 262.
10. Hooper, *Letters*, 2:258.
11. Hooper, *Letters*, 2:234.
12. Of his nightmares, see Hooper, *Letters*, 1:678, 699, 923, 937–38; Hooper, *Diary*, 383, 412, 420, 426, 443, 456. Of his wounds, see Hooper, *Diary*, 240, 249, 386.
13. Hooper, *Letters*, 2:258.
14. Hooper, *Letters*, 2:233–34, 250–52.
15. Hooper, *Letters*, 2:234, 252.
16. Hooper, *Letters*, 2:232.
17. Hooper, *Letters*, 2:258.
18. Hooper, *Letters*, 2:262.
19. Hooper, *Letters*, 2:196.
20. Hooper, *Letters*, 2:91, 111, 115, 239–40. Warnie Lewis discussed the annual January walking tours in his diaries. See Clyde S. Kilby and Marjorie Lamp Mead, eds., *Brothers and Friends: The Diaries of Major Warren Hamilton Lewis* (New York: Harper & Row, 1982), 76, 96, 132, 136, 167, 171, 174–75.
21. Hooper, *Letters*, 2:71–74, 107, 160, 222–23, 241.
22. Hooper, *Letters*, 2:111, 131, 165, 190, 215.
23. Hooper, *Letters*, 2:232.
24. Robert E. Havard, "Philia: Jack at Ease," in *Remembering C. S. Lewis*, ed. James T. Como, 3rd ed. (San Francisco: Ignatius, 2005), 353. This book is the third edition of the book previously published as *C. S. Lewis at the Breakfast Table* (New York: Macmillan, 1979).
25. Havard, "Philia," 354.
26. Havard, "Philia," 354–55.
27. Havard, "Philia," 355–56.
28. Hooper, *Letters*, 2:270.
29. Hooper, *Letters*, 2:270, 274.
30. Hooper, *Letters*, 2:271.
31. Hooper, *Letters*, 2:272.
32. Hooper, *Letters*, 2:272.
33. Hooper, *Letters*, 2:274.
34. Hooper, *Letters*, 2:288, 292.
35. Hooper, *Letters*, 2:287, 296, 330.
36. Hooper, *Letters*, 2:348, 552.
37. Hooper, *Letters*, 2:283, 288, 297, 336, 343, 350, 358, 359, 404, 410.
38. Hooper, *Letters*, 2:344.
39. Hooper, *Letters*, 2:272.
40. Hooper, *Letters*, 2:272.

41. Roma A. King Jr., ed., *To Michal from Serge: Letters from Charles Williams to His Wife, Florence, 1939–1945* (Kent, OH: Kent State University Press, 2002), 15, 18.
42. King, *To Michal from Serge*, 186.
43. Letter from Christopher Fry to Neil Tyler, April 1, 1982, Harry Lee Poe collection.
44. King, *To Michal from Serge*, 89–90.
45. Walter Hooper, introduction to *The Weight of Glory*, by C. S. Lewis, ed. Walter Hooper (New York: Touchstone, 1996), 18.
46. C. S. Lewis, "Learning in War-Time," in Lewis, *The Weight of Glory*, 41.
47. Lewis, "Learning in War-Time," 44.
48. Lewis, "Learning in War-Time," 48.
49. J. R. R. Tolkien, *The Hobbit* (Boston: Houghton Mifflin Company, 1966), 9.
50. Hooper, *Letters*, 2:304.
51. John Lawlor, *C. S. Lewis: Memories and Reflections* (Dallas: Spence, 1998), 18.
52. Hooper, *Letters*, 2:273.
53. Hooper, *Letters*, 2:273.
54. Though he made this remark to Arthur in a letter, the thought came from Hugo Dyson. See Hooper, *Letters*, 2:278.
55. Hooper, *Letters*, 2:274.
56. Hooper, *Letters*, 2:275.
57. Hooper, *Letters*, 2:279.
58. Hooper, *Letters*, 2:416n275.
59. Hooper, *Letters*, 2:451.
60. Hooper, *Letters*, 2:276.
61. Hooper, *Letters*, 2:371, 418.
62. Hooper, *Letters*, 2:280.
63. C. S. Lewis, *The Problem of Pain* (London: Centenary, 1940), vii.
64. Hooper, *Letters*, 2:289n152.
65. Hooper, *Letters*, 2:289.
66. Walter Hooper, "A Bibliography of the Writings of C. S. Lewis: Revised and Enlarged," in Como, *Remembering C. S. Lewis*, 391.
67. Hooper, *Letters*, 2:253n112.
68. Hooper, *Letters*, 2:293. In the film *Harry Potter and the Goblet of Fire*, the divinity school is the room in which Professor McGonagall teaches Ron Weasley to dance, while the Duke Humfrey's Library is where the Hogwarts library scenes were all filmed.
69. Hooper, *Letters*, 2:355.
70. Hooper, *Letters*, 2:317–21.
71. Hooper, *Letters*, 2:333.
72. Hooper, *Letters*, 2:343.
73. Hooper, *Letters*, 2:335.
74. King, *To Michal from Serge*, 42.

75. Humphrey Carpenter, ed., *The Letters of J. R. R. Tolkien* (London: Allen & Unwin, 1981), 67, 71, 79, 81, 93, 102, 103, 105, 122.
76. Carpenter, *Letters of Tolkien*, 102.
77. Carpenter, *Letters of Tolkien*, 341.
78. Carpenter, *Letters of Tolkien*, 341, 349, 361–62.
79. Hooper, *Letters*, 2:338.
80. Hooper, *Letters*, 2:357.
81. Hooper, *Letters*, 2:472–73.
82. C. S. Lewis, *A Preface to Paradise Lost* (London: Oxford University Press, 1942), v–vi.
83. Hooper, *Letters*, 2:367.
84. Hooper, *Letters*, 2:367.
85. Hooper, *Letters*, 2:368.
86. Hooper, *Letters*, 2:368.
87. Hooper, *Letters*, 2:382–85.
88. Hooper, *Letters*, 2:388–89.
89. Hooper, *Letters*, 2:378–79, 392.
90. Hooper, *Letters*, 2:325, 405.
91. Hooper, *Letters*, 2:430.
92. Hooper, *Letters*, 2:1023.
93. Hooper, *Letters*, 2:391, 408.
94. Hooper, *Letters*, 2:408.
95. Hooper, *Letters*, 2:408.
96. Hooper, *Letters*, 2:412.
97. Hooper, *Letters*, 2:421, 422.
98. Hooper, *Letters*, 2:425–26, 432, 433.
99. Hooper, *Letters*, 2:433.
100. Hooper, *Letters*, 2:434.
101. In the Church of England, a rector is the senior pastor of a parish church, and the curate is the associate pastor.
102. Hooper, *Letters*, 2:426.
103. Hooper, *Letters*, 2:452.
104. Hooper, *Letters*, 2:1015.
105. Hooper, *Letters*, 2:507.
106. Hooper, *Letters*, 2:551.
107. Hooper, *Letters*, 2:437.
108. Hooper, *Letters*, 2:486.
109. Hooper, *Letters*, 2:747.
110. Lewis, *The Problem of Pain*, 1–3.
111. Lewis, *The Problem of Pain*, 4–5.
112. Lewis, *The Problem of Pain*, 9–10.
113. Lewis, *The Problem of Pain*, 10.
114. Lewis, *The Problem of Pain*, 11.
115. Lewis, *The Problem of Pain*, 11.
116. Lewis, *The Problem of Pain*, 11.

117. Lewis, *The Problem of Pain*, 11–12.
118. Lewis, *The Problem of Pain*, 12–13.
119. Lewis, *The Problem of Pain*, 14–21.
120. Lewis, *The Problem of Pain*, 28.
121. Lewis, *The Problem of Pain*, 81.
122. George Sayer, *Jack: C. S. Lewis and His Times* (New York: Harper & Row, 1988), 164.

Chapter 8: From Academic Work to War Work
1. Walter Hooper, ed., *The Collected Letters of C. S. Lewis*, vol. 2 (New York: HarperSanFrancisco, 2004), 469–70.
2. Hooper, *Letters*, 2:470.
3. Hooper, *Letters*, 2:470–71.
4. Hooper, *Letters*, 2:484.
5. Hooper, *Letters*, 2:471–72.
6. Charles Gilmore, "To the RAF," in *Remembering C. S. Lewis*, ed. James T. Como, 3rd ed. (San Francisco: Ignatius, 2005), 310. This book is the third edition of the book previously published as *C. S. Lewis at the Breakfast Table* (New York: Macmillan, 1979).
7. Hooper, *Letters*, 2:485. George Sayer placed the beginning of the RAF talks after his first BBC broadcasts, but this was probably a guess. Most likely, he did not have access to the letter to Sister Penelope of May 15, 1941, in which Lewis mentioned giving RAF talks in Abingdon near Oxford. See George Sayer, *Jack: C. S. Lewis and His Times* (New York: Harper & Row, 1988), 171.
8. Hooper, *Letters*, 2:483.
9. Hooper, *Letters*, 2:398.
10. Hooper, *Letters*, 2:398.
11. Hooper, *Letters*, 2:360.
12. Hooper, *Letters*, 2:486.
13. I first wrote of the discovery of this recording for the online version of *Christianity Today* with a tongue-in-cheek title that alluded to a James Bond novel: "On His Majesty's Secret Service." Unfortunately, the editor changed the title to the misleading assertion "C. S. Lewis Was a Secret Agent." From time to time, editors changed the titles of articles written by Lewis. For instance, Lewis disliked the title "Onward, Christian Spacemen," which *Show* magazine gave to one of his articles in 1963. Walter Hooper has since renamed the article "The Seeing Eye." See C. S. Lewis, *Christian Reflections*, ed. Walter Hooper (London: Bles, 1967), xiv.
14. Diana Pavlac Glyer, *The Company They Keep: C. S. Lewis and J. R. R. Tolkien as Writers in Community* (Kent, OH: Kent State University Press, 2007), 242. Stevens proposed using the opening phrase of Beethoven's Fifth Symphony ("da da da daa"), which is Morse Code for the letter *V* (for victory), as the BBC's theme during the war. See

Philip Zaleski and Carol Zaleski, *The Fellowship: The Literary Lives of the Inklings* (New York: Farrar, Straus and Giroux, 2015), 356.

15. Hooper, *Letters*, 2:246.
16. C. S. Lewis, *Norse Spirit in English Literature* © copyright CS Lewis Pte Ltd., transcribed by Harry Lee Poe on May 24, 2016. Reprinted with permission.
17. Humphrey Carpenter, ed., *The Letters of J. R. R. Tolkien* (London: Allen & Unwin, 1981), 55. I am indebted to Holly Ordway for calling my attention to this remark, which she discovered in her own research on Tolkien.
18. Hooper, *Letters*, 2:487.
19. Hooper, *Letters*, 2:487.
20. Hooper, *Letters*, 2:579.
21. Hooper, *Letters*, 2:403.
22. Hooper, *Letters*, 2:432.
23. Sayer, *Jack*, 113–14.
24. Hooper, *Letters*, 2:489.
25. Hooper, *Letters*, 2:478.
26. Hooper, *Letters*, 2: 490.
27. Hooper, *Letters*, 2:492.
28. Stuart Barton Babbage, "To the Royal Airforce," in *C. S. Lewis: Speaker and Teacher*, ed. Carolyn Keefe (Grand Rapids, MI: Zondervan, 1971), 67–68.
29. Babbage, "To the Royal Airforce," 74.
30. Babbage, "To the Royal Airforce," 76.
31. Hooper, *Letters*, 2:504.
32. Hooper, *Letters*, 2:517n27.
33. Hooper, *Letters*, 2:588.
34. Gilmore, "To the RAF," 312–13.
35. Eric Rust was a remarkable man. He often said that Christ comes to people in different ways. He said that Christ came to him through his father, whom he described as an uneducated fundamentalist, but a man full of faith and love. After the war, Rust taught Hebrew and Old Testament theology at Oxford before migrating to the United States, where he taught philosophy at The Southern Baptist Theological Seminary for many years. His books on science and faith were some of the very few published in the mid-twentieth century when Protestant clergy and theologians neglected science under the influence of Karl Barth.
36. Gilmore, "To the RAF," 313.
37. Hooper, *Letters*, 2:492.
38. Austin Farrer, "The Christian Apologist," in *Light on C. S. Lewis*, ed. Jocelyn Gibb (London: Bles, 1965), 31.
39. C. S. Lewis, *Broadcast Talks* (London: Centenary, 1942), 27; cf. C. S. Lewis, *Mere Christianity* (New York: HarperSanFrancisco, 2001), 25.
40. Hooper, *Letters*, 2:504.

41. Hooper, *Letters*, 2:490–91.
42. Hooper, *Letters*, 2:493.
43. Hooper, *Letters*, 2:494.
44. Hooper, *Letters*, 2:496.
45. Hooper, *Letters*, 2:584, 593, 630.
46. I first wrote on the relationship between Lewis's interest in *Paradise Lost* and his books *A Preface to Paradise Lost*, *The Screwtape Letters*, *Perelandra*, and *The Great Divorce* in "The Influence of C. S. Lewis," in *Shaping a Christian Worldview*, ed. David S. Dockery and Gregory Alan Thornbury (Nashville: Broadman & Holman, 2002), 92–108.
47. Hooper, *Letters*, 2:568.
48. Hooper, *Letters*, 2:830.
49. Sayer, *Jack*, 165.
50. W. H. Lewis, ed., *Letters of C. S. Lewis* (London: Bles, 1966), 13.
51. Hooper, *Letters*, 2:297. Alice Moore and Janie Moore share a common gravestone in the churchyard of Holy Trinity Church in Headington near where Jack and Warnie lie buried with a common gravestone.
52. Hooper, *Letters*, 2:331.
53. Hooper, *Letters*, 2:328.
54. Hooper, *Letters*, 2:496.
55. Hooper, *Letters*, 2:635.
56. W. H. Lewis, *Letters*, 12.
57. W. H. Lewis, *Letters*, 21–22.
58. C. S. Lewis, *The Screwtape Letters and Screwtape Proposes a Toast* (London: Bles, 1961), 12.
59. C. S. Lewis, *A Preface to Paradise Lost* (New York: Oxford University Press, 1961), 1.
60. Walter Hooper, "To the Martlets," in Keefe, *C. S. Lewis*, 44–45. Lewis referred to Poe's famous essay on how he wrote "The Raven." See Edgar A. Poe, "The Philosophy of Composition," *Graham's Magazine*, 28, no. 4 (April 1846): 163–67. Poe wrote:

    What we term a long poem is, in fact, merely a succession of brief ones—that is to say, of brief poetical effects. It is needless to demonstrate that a poem is such, only inasmuch as it intensely excites, by elevating, the soul; and all intense excitements are, through a psychal necessity, brief. For this reason, at least one half of "Paradise Lost" is essentially prose—a succession of poetical excitements interspersed, *inevitably*, with corresponding depressions—the whole being deprived, through the extremities of its length, of the vastly important artistic element, totality, or unity, of effect. (p. 164)

61. Walter Hooper, ed., *The Collected Letters of C. S. Lewis*, vol. 1 (New York: HarperSanFrancisco, 2004), 244.
62. Lewis, *A Preface to Paradise Lost*, 13–19.

63. Lewis, *A Preface to Paradise Lost*, 22.
64. Lewis, *A Preface to Paradise Lost*, 23.
65. Lewis, *A Preface to Paradise Lost*, 33–39.
66. Lewis, *A Preface to Paradise Lost*, 40–41.
67. Lewis, *A Preface to Paradise Lost*, 52–56.
68. Sayer, *Jack*, 180.
69. Lewis, *A Preface to Paradise Lost*, 95. Lewis had also used the expression "mere Christianity" in the opening of chapter 25 of *The Screwtape Letters*. He would use it again when he published the anthology of his radio broadcasts as *Mere Christianity* in 1952.
70. Lewis, *A Preface to Paradise Lost*, 96.
71. C. S. Lewis, *The Great Divorce* (London: Centenary, 1945), 15–16. Lewis had spent much of his youth as the Tousle-Headed Poet and the friend of the Tousle-Headed Poet or the enemy of the Tousle-Headed Poet. He knew the type.
72. C. S. Lewis, *The Screwtape Letters* (New York: HarperSanFrancisco, 2001), 111.
73. Hooper, *Letters*, 1:926, 928–31, 932–33.
74. Homer, *The Odyssey*, trans. A. S. Kline, bk. 11, https://www.poetryin translation.com/PITBR/Greek/Odyssey11.php#_Toc90267984.
75. Lewis, *A Preface to Paradise Lost*, 100.
76. Hooper, *Letters*, 2:245–46.
77. Hooper, *Letters*, 2:263.
78. Lewis, *A Preface to Paradise Lost*, 101.
79. Hooper, *Letters*, 2:830. This was his view in January 1948. He often said it was his favorite book. See also 2:600, 645.
80. Hooper, *Letters*, 2:496.
81. Hooper, *Letters*, 2:504.
82. Hooper, *Letters*, 2:667.
83. C. S. Lewis, Kingsley Amis, and Brian Aldiss, "The Establishment Must Die and Rot . . . ," in *C. S. Lewis Remembered*, ed. Harry Lee Poe and Rebecca Whitten Poe (Grand Rapids, MI: Zondervan, 2006), 236.
84. Walter Hooper, ed., *All My Road before Me: The Diary of C. S. Lewis, 1922–1927* (New York: Harcourt Brace Jovanovich, 1991), 241.
85. Hooper, *Letters*, 2:236–37.
86. Hooper, *Letters*, 2:520.
87. Hooper, *Letters*, 2:520n37.
88. C. S. Lewis, *Perelandra* (London: John Lane, The Bodley Head, 1943), 11.
89. Lewis, *Perelandra*, 29.
90. Robert E. Havard, "Philia: Jack at Ease," in Como, *Remembering C. S. Lewis*, 359.
91. Humphrey Carpenter, *The Inklings* (London: Allen & Unwin, 1978), 177.
92. Hooper, *Letters*, 2:504.

93. Derek Brewer, "The Tutor: A Portrait," in Como, *Remembering C. S. Lewis*, 150.
94. Hugh Sinclair, "Forgetful Rudeness," in *We Remember C. S. Lewis*, ed. David Graham (Nashville: Broadman & Holman, 2001), 116.
95. Sinclair, "Forgetful Rudeness," 115.
96. Stella Aldwinckle, *The Socratic Digest*, 1 (1942–1943): 6.
97. Walter Hooper, "Oxford's Bonny Fighter," in Como, *Remembering C. S. Lewis*, 242–45.
98. In Como, *Remembering C. S. Lewis*, 299.
99. A. J. Ayer, *Part of My Life: Memoirs of a Philosopher* (London: Harcourt Brace Jovanovich, 1977), 297.
100. Ayer, *Part of My Life*, 293–308. At the end of his essay on the Socratic Club, Walter Hooper provided a complete list of all the Socratic Club programs with speakers and titles, from January 1942 until the end of June 1954.

Chapter 9: From Personal Testimony to Philosophy of Science

1. Walter Hooper, ed., *The Collected Letters of C. S. Lewis*, vol. 2 (New York: HarperSanFrancisco, 2007), 506.
2. C. S. Lewis, *The Problem of Pain* (London: Centenary, 1940), 4–12.
3. Lewis, *The Problem of Pain*, 4.
4. C. S. Lewis, *Broadcast Talks* (London: Centenary, 1942), 49–50.
5. Lewis, *The Problem of Pain*, 11–12; Lewis, *Broadcast Talks*, 50–51.
6. Lewis, *The Problem of Pain*, 74–76.
7. Lewis, *Broadcast Talks*, 52–53.
8. Hooper, *Letters*, 2:531.
9. Hooper, *Letters*, 2:509.
10. Hooper, *Letters*, 2:519.
11. Hooper, *Letters*, 2:519–20.
12. Hooper, *Letters*, 2:508. A guinea was twenty-one shillings or one pound and one shilling. The pound was worth a little more than four dollars, making his fee a little over two hundred dollars at the time.
13. Hooper, *Letters*, 2:509.
14. Hooper, *Letters*, 2:483.
15. Hooper, *Letters*, 2:534. Mrs. Boshell lived in the little bungalow that Mrs. Moore had built in the garden at the Kilns for her friend Mrs. Alice Moore, who had since died. For an account of Mrs. Boshell, see Walter Hooper, "What about Mrs. Boshell?," in *C. S. Lewis Remembered*, ed. Harry Lee Poe and Rebecca Whitten Poe (Grand Rapids, MI: Zondervan, 2006), 36–51.
16. Owen Barfield, "C. S. Lewis as Christian and Scholar," in Poe and Poe, *C. S. Lewis Remembered*, 31–32.
17. Derek Brewer, "The Tutor: A Portrait," in *Remembering C. S. Lewis*, ed. James T. Como, 3rd ed. (San Francisco: Ignatius, 2005), 132. This

book is the third edition of the book previously published as *C. S. Lewis at the Breakfast Table* (New York: Macmillan, 1979).
18. Hooper, *Letters*, 2:509–10.
19. Hooper, *Letters*, 2:469.
20. Hooper, *Letters*, 2:505.
21. Hooper, *Letters*, 2:64, 67–68.
22. Hooper, *Letters*, 2:469.
23. Barbara Reynolds, "C. S. Lewis and Dorothy L. Sayers," in Poe and Poe, *C. S. Lewis Remembered*, 197.
24. Hooper, *Letters*, 2:533.
25. Roma A. King Jr., ed., *To Michal from Serge: Letters from Charles Williams to His Wife, Florence, 1935–1945* (Kent, OH: Kent State University Press, 2002), 198.
26. King, *To Michal from Serge*, 219.
27. King, *To Michal from Serge*, 222.
28. King, *To Michal from Serge*, 226.
29. Hooper, *Letters*, 2:512.
30. Hooper, *Letters*, 2:513.
31. Hooper, *Letters*, 2:516–17.
32. Hooper, *Letters*, 2:523–25.
33. Hooper, *Letters*, 2:517–18.
34. Hooper, *Letters*, 2:520n38.
35. Hooper, *Letters*, 2:528.
36. Hooper, *Letters*, 2:524.
37. Hooper, *Letters*, 2:525.
38. Hooper, *Letters*, 2:531.
39. Hooper, *Letters*, 2:532.
40. Hooper, *Letters*, 2:537–38.
41. Hooper, *Letters*, 2:550.
42. Hooper, *Letters*, 2:539.
43. Hooper, *Letters*, 2:551.
44. Hooper, *Letters*, 2:548.
45. Hooper, *Letters*, 2:552.
46. Hooper, *Letters*, 2:336, 354.
47. Hooper, *Letters*, 2:579.
48. Hooper, *Letters*, 2:370.
49. Walter Hooper, "A Bibliography of the Writings of C. S. Lewis: Revised and Enlarged," in Como, *Remembering C. S. Lewis*, 393.
50. J[ohn] D. Lucas, "Restoration of Man: A Lecture Given in Durham on Thursday, October 22nd, 1992 to Mark the Fiftieth Anniversary of C. S. Lewis's *The Abolition of Man*," accessed April 10, 2020, users.ox.ac.uk.
51. Clyde S. Kilby and Marjorie Lamp Mead, eds., *Brothers and Friends: The Diaries of Major Warren Hamilton Lewis* (New York: Harper & Row, 1982), 178–79.

52. Warren H. Lewis Diaries Collection, Marion E. Wade Center, Wheaton College, Wheaton, IL, vol. 18 (1943), 181–84.
53. Kilby and Mead, *Brothers and Friends*, 161.
54. Lucas, "Restoration of Man."
55. Humphrey Carpenter, *The Inklings* (London: Allen & Unwin, 1978), 221–22.
56. Basil Mitchell, "C. S. Lewis on the Abolition of Man," in Poe and Poe, *C. S. Lewis Remembered*, 175.
57. George Sayer, *Jack: C. S. Lewis and His Times* (New York: Harper & Row, 1988), 182.
58. C. S. Lewis, *The Abolition of Man* (New York: Macmillan, 1955), 14.
59. Lewis, *The Abolition of Man*, 16–17.
60. Lewis, *The Abolition of Man*, 33–34.
61. Lewis, *The Abolition of Man*, 34.
62. Lewis, *The Abolition of Man*, 77.
63. Hooper, *Letters*, 2:544, 571.
64. Hooper, *Letters*, 2:569.
65. Hooper, *Letters*, 2:568.
66. Hooper, *Letters*, 2:571–72.
67. Hooper, *Letters*, 2:581–82.
68. Barbara Reynolds, *The Letters of Dorothy L. Sayers: 1937–1943; From Novelist to Playwright*, vol. 2 (New York: St. Martin's, 1997), 413.
69. Hooper, *Letters*, 2:573.
70. Hooper, *Letters*, 2:573.
71. Hooper, *Letters*, 2:579.
72. Hooper, *Letters*, 2:587, 601.
73. Hooper, *Letters*, 2:1033.
74. Hooper, *Letters*, 2:596.
75. Kilby and Mead, *Brothers and Friends*, 181.
76. Hooper, *Letters*, 2:591.
77. Hooper, *Letters*, 2:596.
78. C. S. Lewis, *That Hideous Strength* (London: John Lane, The Bodley Head, 1945), 7.
79. For an examination of Lewis's objection to confusing materialistic philosophies with science, see Michael D. Aeschliman, *The Restitution of Man* (Grand Rapids, MI: Eerdmans, 1983).
80. Hooper, *Letters*, 2:372–73.
81. Hooper, *Letters*, 2:594.
82. Humphrey Carpenter, ed., *The Letters of J. R. R. Tolkien* (London: Allen & Unwin, 1981), 65.
83. Hooper, *Letters*, 2:603.
84. Justin Phillips, *C. S. Lewis at the BBC* (London: HarperCollins, 2002), 306.
85. Hooper, *Letters*, 2:603.
86. Phillips, *C. S. Lewis at the BBC*, 306–7.

87. Alastair Fowler, "C. S. Lewis: Supervisor," in Poe and Poe, *C. S. Lewis Remembered*, 106–7.
88. George Watson, "The Art of Disagreement: C. S. Lewis (1898–1963)," in Poe and Poe, *C. S. Lewis Remembered*, 79.
89. Walter Hooper, *All My Road before Me: The Diary of C. S. Lewis, 1922–1927* (London: HarperCollins, 1991), 238.
90. Kilby and Mead, *Brothers and Friends*, 88.
91. Roger Lancelyn Green, *C. S. Lewis* (London: The Bodley Head, 1963), 17–18.
92. A. N. Wilson, *C. S. Lewis: A Biography* (New York: Norton, 1990), 190; Sayer, *Jack*, 184; Philip Zaleski and Carol Zaleski, *The Fellowship* (New York: Farrar, Straus and Giroux, 2015), 328; Rowan Williams, *"That Hideous Strength*: A Reassessment," in *C. S. Lewis and His Circle*, ed. Roger White, Judith Wolfe, and Brendon Wolfe (New York: Oxford University Press, 2015), 96–97.
93. Hooper, *Letters*, 2:596.
94. Lewis, *That Hideous Strength*, 7.
95. For an excellent treatment of direct and indirect ways that the Inklings influenced one another, see Diana Pavlac Glyer, *The Company They Keep* (Kent, OH: Kent State University Press, 2007). Many others have noted the influence of Williams with his Arthurian themes. See Zaleski and Zaleski, *The Fellowship*, 326; Sayer, *Jack*, 177; Wilson, *C. S. Lewis*, 189.
96. Hooper, *Letters*, 2:198.
97. Lewis, *That Hideous Strength*, 10.
98. Hooper, *Letters*, 2:670.
99. Hooper, *Letters*, 2:596. The book is dedicated to J. McNeill, but owing to the wartime scarcity of paper, the publisher placed the dedication at the bottom of the back of the half-title page below the list of Lewis's published books.
100. Hooper, *Letters*, 2:127n59.
101. King, *To Michal from Serge*, 27.
102. Barbara Reynolds, ed., *The Letters of Dorothy L. Sayers*, vol. 3 (Swavesey, UK: Dorothy L. Sayers Society, 1998), 375.
103. Lewis, *That Hideous Strength*, 321.
104. Lewis, *That Hideous Strength*, 237. Lewis also continually refers to Logres, the pre-Roman name for Britain, which Williams used. See pp. 245, 354, 356, 361, 362, 456, 458–62.
105. Lewis, *That Hideous Strength*, 246, 248, 326, 335, 350, 351, 359, 362.
106. Carpenter, *Letters of Tolkien*, 224. Tolkien suggested that Lewis misspelled the word because he had only heard it spoken, presumably in Inklings meetings. One should also note that Lewis was a notoriously poor speller who could misspell words in a number of languages, which has always given me hope.
107. Reynolds, *Letters of Sayers*, 3:177.

108. Reynolds, *Letters of Sayers*, 3:264.
109. Lewis, *That Hideous Strength*, 137.
110. Reynolds, *Letters of Sayers*, 3:265.
111. Hooper, *Letters*, 2:571.
112. Carpenter, *Letters of Tolkien*, 361.
113. Hooper, *Letters*, 2:624.
114. Hooper, *Letters*, 2:603.
115. King, *To Michal from Serge*, 210.
116. Hooper, *Letters*, 2:619.
117. Hooper, *Letters*, 2:552; Carpenter, *Letters of Tolkien*, 74.
118. Hooper, *Letters*, 2:616.
119. Carpenter, *Letters of Tolkien*, 76.
120. Hooper, *Letters*, 2:568.
121. "Lewis, C(live) S(taples)," *Current Biography* 5, no. 1 (January 1944): 24–26. Though brief, this entry may be the first published biography of Lewis.
122. Leonard Bacon, "The Imaginative Power of C. S. Lewis," *The Saturday Review* 27, no. 15 (April 8, 1944): cover, 9. The wood engraving of Lewis on the cover was executed by Frances Obrien Garfield.

Chapter 10: From War to Peace
1. Walter Hooper, ed., *The Collected Letters of C. S. Lewis*, vol. 2 (New York: HarperSanFrancisco, 2004), 400.
2. Hooper, *Letters*, 2:625.
3. Hooper, *Letters*, 2:624.
4. Hooper, *Letters*, 2:623.
5. Lady Freud granted an interview to Justin Phillips on November 19, 1999. See Justin Phillips, *C. S. Lewis at the BBC* (London: HarperCollins, 2002), 175.
6. Phillips, *C. S. Lewis at the BBC*, 175–76.
7. Phillips, *C. S. Lewis at the BBC*, 176.
8. Phillips, *C. S. Lewis at the BBC*, 182.
9. Humphrey Carpenter, ed., *Letters of J. R. R. Tolkien* (London: Allen & Unwin, 1981), 71, 92.
10. Phillips, *C. S. Lewis at the BBC*, 176.
11. Phillips, *C. S. Lewis at the BBC*, 176–77.
12. C. S. Lewis, "A Tribute to E. R. Eddison," in *Of This and Other Worlds*, ed. Walter Hooper (London: Collins, 1982), 55.
13. Hooper, *Letters*, 2:535.
14. Hooper, *Letters*, 2:560.
15. Hooper, *Letters*, 2:553.
16. Humphrey Carpenter, *The Inklings* (Boston: Houghton Mifflin, 1979), 131.
17. Carpenter, *Tolkien*, 149.
18. Hooper, *Letters*, 2:183.

19. Clyde S. Kilby and Marjorie Lamp Mead, eds., *Brothers and Friends: The Diaries of Major Warren Hamilton Lewis* (New York: Harper & Row, 1982), 293.
20. Hooper, *Letters*, 2:729.
21. Owen Barfield, *Owen Barfield on C. S. Lewis*, ed. G. B. Tennyson (Middletown, CT: Wesleyan University Press, 1989), 105.
22. Hooper, *Letters*, 2:343.
23. Hooper, *Letters*, 2:350.
24. Hooper, *Letters*, 2:501.
25. Barfield, *C. S. Lewis*, 106.
26. Barfield, *C. S. Lewis*, 113–14.
27. Barfield, *C. S. Lewis*, 133.
28. Owen Barfield, "In Conversation," in *C. S. Lewis: Speaker and Teacher*, ed. Carolyn Keefe (Grand Rapids, MI: Zondervan, 1971), 105–6.
29. Barfield, "In Conversation," 127.
30. Owen Barfield, "Either: Or," in *Imagination and the Spirit: Essays in Literature and the Christian Faith Presented to Clyde S. Kilby*, ed. Charles A. Huttar (Grand Rapids, MI: Eerdmans, 1971), reprinted in Barfield, *C. S. Lewis*, 55n, 57, 65.
31. Robert E. Havard, "Philia: Jack at Ease," in *Remembering C. S. Lewis*, ed. James T. Como, 3rd ed. (San Francisco: Ignatius, 2005), 350–51. This book is the third edition of the book previously published as *C. S. Lewis at the Breakfast Table* (New York: Macmillan, 1979).
32. Havard, "Philia," 362.
33. Havard, "Philia," 352.
34. Nevill Coghill, "The Approach to English," in *Light on C. S. Lewis*, ed. Jocelyn Gibb (London: Bles, 1965), 63.
35. The recording may be ordered from the C. S. Lewis Foundation through their website at www.cslewis.org and may be found transcribed in *C. S. Lewis Remembered*, ed. Harry Lee Poe and Rebecca Whitten Poe (Grand Rapids, MI: Zondervan, 2006).
36. Poe and Poe, *C. S. Lewis Remembered*, 29.
37. Barfield, "In Conversation," reprinted in Barfield, *C. S. Lewis*, 35.
38. Hooper, *Letters*, 2:350.
39. Owen Barfield, "The Inklings Remembered," *The World & I* (April 1990), 548.
40. Poe and Poe, *C. S. Lewis Remembered*, 34.
41. Barfield made this remark in the Third Annual Marion E. Wade Lecture, delivered at Wheaton College, November 3, 1977, first printed in Barfield, *C. S. Lewis*, 100.
42. Glyer's insightful discussion of the influence of the Inklings on one another goes beyond overt suggestion or imitation to explore the many different levels at which influence occurs among friends who keep company with one another. See Diana Pavlac Glyer, *The Company They Keep* (Kent, OH: Kent State University Press, 2007).

43. Alastair Fowler, "C. S. Lewis: Supervisor," in Poe and Poe, *C. S. Lewis Remembered*, 106.
44. Lewis read *The Problem of Pain* to the Inklings as he wrote it. See Hooper, *Letters*, 2:289, 302.
45. Hooper, *Letters*, 2:283.
46. Hooper, *Letters*, 2:501.
47. Hooper, *Letters*, 2:501.
48. Hooper, *Letters*, 2:618.
49. Hooper, *Letters*, 2:656.
50. Hooper, *Letters*, 2:819.
51. Hooper, *Letters*, 2:710.
52. Hooper, *Letters*, 2:656.
53. Carpenter, *Letters of Tolkien*, 349.
54. Roma King Jr., ed., *To Michal from Serge: Letters from Charles Williams to His Wife, Florence, 1939–1945* (Kent, OH: Kent State University Press, 2002), 235–36.
55. Hooper, *Letters*, 2:557.
56. Hooper, *Letters*, 2:360.
57. Hooper, *Letters*, 2:365.
58. Humphrey Carpenter, *OUDS: A Centenary History of the Oxford University Dramatic Society, 1885–1985* (Oxford: Oxford University Press, 1985), 142–43.
59. Dacre Balsdon, "Open Letter," in *To Nevill Coghill from Friends*, ed. John Lawlor and W. H. Auden (London: Faber and Faber, 1966), 35.
60. Balsdon, "Open Letter," 35.
61. C. S. Lewis, *That Hideous Strength* (London: John Lane, The Bodley Head, 1945), 14.
62. Hooper, *Letters*, 2:398–99, 403.
63. C. S. Lewis, preface to *Essays Presented to Charles Williams*, ed. C. S. Lewis (London: Oxford University Press, 1947), viii.
64. Hooper, *Letters*, 2:302.
65. A. N. Wilson, *C. S. Lewis: A Biography* (New York: Norton, 1990), 192–93.
66. Nevill Coghill, "The Approach to English," in *Light on C. S. Lewis*, ed. Jocelyn Gibb (London: Bles, 1965), 56.
67. Hooper, *Letters*, 2:359.
68. Hooper, *Letters*, 2:289, 410.
69. Hooper, *Letters*, 2:360.
70. Hooper, *Letters*, 2:343.
71. Hooper, *Letters*, 2:405.
72. Hooper, *Letters*, 2:228, 302, 336; Carpenter, *Letters of Tolkien*, 122.
73. Hooper, *Letters*, 2:631.
74. Carpenter, *Letters of Tolkien*, 68, 73, 76, 77, 79, 81, 83, 303, 362, 366.
75. Carpenter, *Letters of Tolkien*, 71.
76. Carpenter, *Letters of Tolkien*, 342, 361.

77. Carpenter, *Letters of Tolkien*, 342.
78. Hooper, *Letters*, 2:617.
79. Hooper, *Letters*, 2:619.
80. Hooper, *Letters*, 2:635n1.
81. Hooper, *Letters*, 2:657.
82. Hooper, *Letters*, 2:648.
83. Hooper, *Letters*, 2:698.
84. Hooper, *Letters*, 2:891n91.
85. Warren H. Lewis Diaries Collection, Marion E. Wade Center, Wheaton College, Wheaton, IL, vol. 15 (1933), 117.
86. C. S. Lewis, *The Allegory of Love* (London: Oxford University Press, 1938), 115.
87. C. S. Lewis, *The Great Divorce* (London: Centenary, 1945), 57.
88. Hooper, *Letters*, 2:626.
89. Hooper, *Letters*, 2:627.
90. Hooper, *Letters*, 2:626–27.
91. Phillips C. S. *Lewis at the BBC*, 266–67.
92. Hooper, *Letters*, 2:633.
93. Kilby and Mead, *Brothers and Friends*, 180.
94. Hooper, *Letters*, 2:641, 645.
95. Hooper, *Letters*, 2:641.
96. Kilby and Mead, *Brothers and Friends*, 181.
97. Hooper, *Letters*, 2:637.
98. Hooper, *Letters*, 2:637–38.
99. Hooper, *Letters*, 2:638.
100. Hooper, *Letters*, 2:640; Walter Hooper, "A Bibliography of the Writings of C. S. Lewis," in Como, *Remembering C. S. Lewis*, 395.
101. Hooper, *Letters*, 2:207.
102. Hooper, *Letters*, 2:285.
103. David Downing has explored this mystical dimension of Lewis in *Into the Region of Awe: Mysticism in C. S. Lewis* (Downers Grove, IL: InterVarsity Press, 2005).
104. Hooper, *Letters*, 2:591.
105. Hooper, *Letters*, 2:648.
106. Hooper, *Letters*, 2:657.
107. Hooper, *Letters*, 2:657.
108. C. S. Lewis, *The Problem of Pain* (London: Centenary, 1940), 1–13.
109. C. S. Lewis, *Broadcast Talks* (London: Centenary, 1942), 24.
110. Lewis, *The Great Divorce*, 24, 35–43.
111. Lewis, *The Great Divorce*, 38.
112. Lewis, *The Great Divorce*, 38.
113. C. S. Lewis, *Miracles* (London: Centenary, 1947), 15.
114. Lewis, *Miracles*, 24.
115. Lewis, *Miracles*, 23.
116. Lewis, *Miracles*, 24–25.

117. Lewis, *Miracles*, 26.
118. Lewis, *Miracles*, 27.
119. Lewis, *Miracles*, 36–37.
120. Lewis, *The Problem of Pain*, 60.
121. Lewis, *Broadcast Talks*, 56–57.
122. Lewis, *Beyond Personality* (London: Centenary, 1944), 59.
123. Hooper, *Letters*, 2:633.
124. Richard B. Cunningham, *C. S. Lewis: Defender of the Faith* (Philadelphia: Westminster, 1967), 16–17.
125. Lewis, *Miracles*, 28–29. Lewis quoted from Haldane's *Possible Worlds*, 209.
126. Francis Darwin, ed., *The Life and Letters of Charles Darwin*, vol. 1 (1897; repr., Boston: Elibron, 2005), 285. Letter from Darwin to William Graham, July 3, 1881. Darwin died the following year. Also available online at Darwin Correspondence Project, "Letter no. 13230," accessed April 22, 2020, https://www.darwinproject.ac.uk/letter/LETT-13230.xml.
127. King, *To Michal from Serge*, 189.
128. Hooper, *Letters*, 2:649.
129. Hooper, *Letters*, 2:647–48.
130. Walter Hooper, "Oxford's Bonny Fighter," in Como, *Remembering C. S. Lewis*, 297.
131. Glyer, *The Company They Keep*, 148.
132. Lewis, preface to *Essays Presented to Charles Williams*, xiii–xiv.
133. Lewis, preface to *Essays Presented to Charles Williams*, xiv.
134. Kilby and Mead, *Brothers and Friends*, 182.
135. Carpenter, *Letters of Tolkien*, 115.
136. Lewis, preface to *Essays Presented to Charles Williams*, xiv.
137. Hooper, *Letters*, 2:651.
138. Hooper, *Letters*, 2:652.
139. Hooper, *Letters*, 2:652.
140. Hooper, *Letters*, 2:653–54.
141. Hooper, *Letters*, 2:656.
142. Hooper, *Letters*, 2:656.

Epilogue

1. C. S. Lewis, *The Pilgrim's Regress: An Allegorical Apology for Christianity, Reason and Romanticism*, 3rd ed. (London: Bles, 1943), 7.
2. When he wrote this piece in 1965, Barfield mistakenly placed Lewis's article and their exchange in 1934, when "The Personal Heresy in Criticism" was published. Owen Barfield, introduction to *Light of C. S. Lewis*, ed. Jocelyn Gibb (London: Bles, 1965), x.
3. Barfield, introduction to *Light of C. S. Lewis*, x–xi.
4. Barfield, introduction to *Light of C. S. Lewis*, x–xi.
5. Barfield, introduction to *Light of C. S. Lewis*, ix.

Index

walled garden image, 152
war, 223
Wardale, Edith Elizabeth, 65, 68, 74
Warren, Thomas Herbert, 94, 123
Watling, Edward Fairchild, 30
Watson, George, 211, 293
Webb, Miss, 275
"Weight of Glory, The" (sermon), 251
Welch, James W., 241, 288
Weldon, T. D., 109, 110, 146, 259, 282, 295
Wells, H. G., 195, 197
"What Christians Believe" (BBC broadcast talks), 273–74, 280, 329
Wheeler, Helen Tyrrell, 205–6
Whipsnade Zoo, 148, 294, 360n100
wholeness, 173
Wilbin, Miss "Smudge," 63, 64
Wilbraham, Mrs., 112–13
Wilkinson, Donald Frederick, 30
Williams, Charles, 169, 174–77, 180, 221, 306, 308, 311, 312
cockney accent, 243
death of, 331–35
on Eliot, 316–17
Festschrift for, 332

friendship with Lewis, 276, 277–78, 339
and the Inklings, 221–22, 318
lecture on *Paradise Lost*, 228–30, 255
Lewis's frustration with, 335
poetry of, 295–96, 314
writings of, 316
Wilson, A. N., 126, 207
Wilson, Frank Percy, 65, 68, 74, 93, 94
Wittgenstein, Ludwig, 110, 285
wonder, 119
Wordsworth, William, 116
worldview, 173
World War I, 209
Irish exemption from service, 209
World War II, 216–18, 222–26, 232–33, 239, 294–95, 303, 323, 325, 331, 368n8
Wrenn, Charles, 314
Wyld, Henry Cecil Kennedy, 66
Wyllie, Basil Platel, 30
Wynyard School, 31, 33, 91

Yeats, William Butler, 44–45, 101
Yorke, Henry, 114

Zeitgeistheim, 165
Zulu War (South Africa), 72

Learn More about
C. S. Lewis's Younger Years

Eastgate Hotel, Oxford.